Joe Casad

Sams **Teach Yourself**

TCP/IP

in 24 Hours

SAMS   800 East 96th Street, Indianapolis, Indiana, 46240 USA

Sams Teach Yourself TCP/IP in 24 Hours

Copyright © 2012 by Pearson Education, Inc.

ISBN-13: 978-0-672-33571-6
ISBN-10: 0-672-33571-9

Library of Congress Cataloging-in-Publication Data

Casad, Joe, 1958-
    Sams teach yourself TCP/IP in 24 hours / Joe Casad. — 5th ed.
        p. cm.
    ISBN 978-0-672-33571-6 (pbk. : alk. paper)
    1. TCP/IP (Computer network protocol) I. Title. II. Title: Teach yourself TCP/IP in 24 hours.
    TK5105.585.C37 2012
    005.7'1376—dc23
                                    2011032322
Printed in the United States of America
First Printing November 2011

Trademarks

Warning and Disclaimer

Bulk Sales

Sams Publishing offers excellent discounts on this book when ordered in quantity for bulk purchases or special sales. For more information, please contact

U.S. Corporate and Government Sales

1-800-382-3419

corpsales@pearsontechgroup.com

For sales outside of the U.S., please contact

International Sales

international@pearson.com

Editor-in-Chief
Mark Taub

Acquisitions Editor
Trina MacDonald

Development Editor
Michael Thurston

Managing Editor
Kristy Hart

Project Editor
Andy Beaster

Copy Editor
Keith Cline

Indexer
Lisa Stumpf

Proofreader
Debbie Williams

Technical Editor
Jon Snader

Publishing Coordinator
Olivia Basegio

Book Designer
Gary Adair

Compositor
Gloria Schurick

Contents at a Glance

Table of Contents

Part IV: Tools

Part V: The Internet

About the Author

Joe Casad is an engineer, author, and editor who has written widely on computer networking and system administration. He has written or cowritten 12 books on computers and networking. He currently serves as editor in chief of *Linux Pro Magazine* and *ADMIN Online*. In a past life, he was the editor of *C/C++ Users Journal* and senior editor of UnixReview.com.

Dedication

To the sound of three hands clapping.

—Joe Casad

Acknowledgments

Thanks to Trina MacDonald, Michael Thurston, Olivia Basegio, Keith Cline, Andy Beaster, and Jon Snader for their patience and good advice. I also want to acknowledge the following individuals for their contributions to previous editions of *Sams Teach Yourself TCP/IP in 24 Hours*: Bob Willsey, Sudha Putnam, Walter Glenn, Art Hammond, Jane Brownlow, Jeff Koch, Mark Renfrow, Vicki Harding, Mark Cierzniak, Marc Charney, Jenny Watson, and Betsy Harris. A special thanks to Bridget and Susan for working around the clutter at the kitchen table, and thanks with fond gratitude to the production department for bringing form and elegance to an inglorious collection of cryptic pencil sketches.

We Want to Hear from You!

As the reader of this book, *you* are our most important critic and commentator. We value your opinion and want to know what we're doing right, what we could do better, what areas you'd like to see us publish in, and any other words of wisdom you're willing to pass our way.

You can email or write me directly to let me know what you did or didn't like about this book—as well as what we can do to make our books stronger.

Please note that I cannot help you with technical problems related to the topic of this book, and that due to the high volume of mail I receive, I might not be able to reply to every message.

When you write, please be sure to include this book's title and author as well as your name and phone or email address. I will carefully review your comments and share them with the author and editors who worked on the book.

E-mail: networking@samspublishing.com

Mail: Mark Taub
          Editor-in-Chief
          Sams Publishing
          1330 Avenue of the Americas
          New York, NY 10019 USA

Reader Services

Visit our website and register this book at informit.com/register for convenient access to any updates, downloads, or errata that might be available for this book.

Introduction

Welcome to *Sams Teach Yourself TCP/IP in 24 Hours, Fifth Edition*. This book provides a clear and concise introduction to TCP/IP for newcomers, and also for users who have worked with TCP/IP but would like a little more of the inside story. Unlike other networking primers that point and click around the hard topics, *Sams Teach Yourself TCP/IP in 24 Hours* takes you down deep into the technology. You'll learn about all the important protocols of the TCP/IP suite, and you'll get a close look at how the protocols of TCP/IP build the foundation for the rich ecosystem of tools and services we know as the Internet. The fifth edition includes new material on recent developments in TCP/IP and offers a closer look at topics such as DNS security, IPv6, and cloud computing. You'll find new information about configuration, REST web services, and HTML5, as well as several new sections throughout the book on recent developments in TCP/IP.

Does Each Chapter Take an Hour?

Each chapter is organized so that you can learn the concepts within 1 hour. The chapters are designed to be short enough to read all at one sitting. In fact, you should be able to read a chapter in less than 1 hour and still have time to take notes and reread more complex sections in your 1-hour study session.

How to Use This Book

The books in the *Sams Teach Yourself* series are designed to help you learn a topic in a few easy and accessible sessions. *Sams Teach Yourself TCP/IP in 24 Hours, Fifth Edition*, is divided into six parts. Each part brings you a step closer to mastering the goal of proficiency in TCP/IP.

▶ Part I, "TCP/IP Basics," introduces you to TCP/IP and the TCP/IP protocol stack.

▶ Part II, "The TCP/IP Protocol System," takes a close look at each of TCP/IP's protocol layers: the Network Access, Internet, Transport, and Application layers. You learn about IP addressing and subnetting, as well as physical networks and application services. You also learn about the protocols that operate at each of TCP/IP's layers.

▶ Part III, "Networking with TCP/IP," describes some of the devices, services, and utilities necessary for supporting TCP/IP networks. You learn about routing and network hardware, DHCP, DNS, and IPv6.

▶ Part IV, "Tools," introduces some of the common utilities used to configure, manage, and troubleshoot TCP/IP networks. You learn about ping, Netstat, FTP, Telnet, and other network utilities, and you get a glimpse of how TCP/IP fits in with some important services, such as web servers, LDAP authentication servers, and database servers.

▶ Part V, "The Internet," describes the world's largest TCP/IP network. You learn about the structure of the Internet. You also learn about HTTP, HTML, XML, email, and Internet streaming, and you get a look at how web technologies are evolving to provide a new generation of services.

▶ Part VI, "TCP/IP at Work," provides a memorable case study showing how the components of TCP/IP interact in a real working environment.

The concepts in this book, like TCP/IP itself, are independent of any operating system and descend from the standards defined in Internet Requests for Comment (RFCs).

How This Book Is Organized

Each hour in *Sams Teach Yourself TCP/IP in 24 Hours, Fifth Edition*, begins with a quick introduction and a list of goals for the hour. You can also find the following elements.

Main Section

Each hour contains a main section that provides a clear and accessible discussion of the hour's topic. You'll find figures and tables helping to explain the concepts described in the text. Interspersed with the text are special notes labeled By the Way. These notes come with definitions, descriptions, or warnings that help you build a better understanding of the material.

> **By the Way**
>
> These boxes clarify a concept that is discussed in the text. A By the Way might add some additional information or provide an example, but they typically aren't essential for a basic understanding of the subject. If you're in a hurry, or if you want to know only the bare essentials, you can bypass these sidebars.

Q&A

Each hour ends with some questions designed to help you explore and test your understanding of the concepts described in the hour. Complete answers to the questions are also provided.

Workshops

In addition, each hour includes a Workshop—a quiz and exercises designed to help you through the details or give you practice with a particular task. Even if you don't have the necessary software and hardware to undertake some of the exercises in the Workshop, you might benefit from reading through the exercises to see how the tools work in a real network implementation.

Key Terms

Each hour includes a summary of important key terms that are introduced in the hour. The key terms are compiled into an alphabetized list at the end of each hour.

PART I

TCP/IP Basics

HOUR 1

What Is TCP/IP?

What You'll Learn in This Hour:

▶ **Networks and network protocols**

▶ **History of TCP/IP**

▶ **Important features of TCP/IP**

Transport Control Protocol/Internet Protocol (TCP/IP) is a **protocol system**—a collection of protocols that supports network communications. The answer to the question *What is a protocol?* must begin with the question *What is a network?*

This hour describes what a network is and shows why networks need protocols. You also learn what TCP/IP is, what it does, and where it began.

At the completion of this hour, you'll be able to

▶ Define the term *network*

▶ Explain what a network protocol suite is

▶ Explain what TCP/IP is

▶ Discuss the of TCP/IP

▶ List some important features of TCP/IP

▶ Identify the organizations that oversee TCP/IP and the Internet

▶ Explain what RFCs are and where to find them

Networks and Protocols

A **network** is a collection of computers or computer-like devices that can communicate across a common transmission medium. Often the transmission medium is an insulated metal wire that carries electrical pulses between the computers, but the transmission medium could also be a phone line, or even no line at all in the case of a wireless network.

Regardless of how the computers are connected, the communication process requires that data from one computer pass across the transmission medium to another computer. In Figure 1.1, computer A must be able to send a message or request to computer B. Computer B must be able to understand computer A's message and respond to it by sending a message back to computer A.

FIGURE 1.1
A typical local
network.

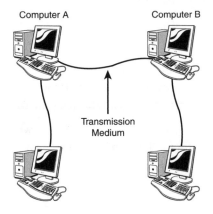

A computer interacts with the world through one or more applications that perform specific tasks and manage the communication process. On modern systems, this network communication is so effortless that the user hardly even notices it. For instance, when you surf to a website, your web browser is communicating with the web server specified in the URL. When you view a list of neighboring computers in Windows Explorer or the Mac OS Finder, the computers on your local network are communicating to announce their presence. In every case, if your computer is part of a network, an application on the computer must be capable of communicating with applications on other network computers.

A **network protocol** is a system of common rules that helps define the complex process of network communication. Protocols guide the process of sending data from an application on one computer, through the networking components of the operating system, to the network hardware, across the transmission medium, and up through the destination computer's network hardware and operating system to a receiving application (see Figure 1.2).

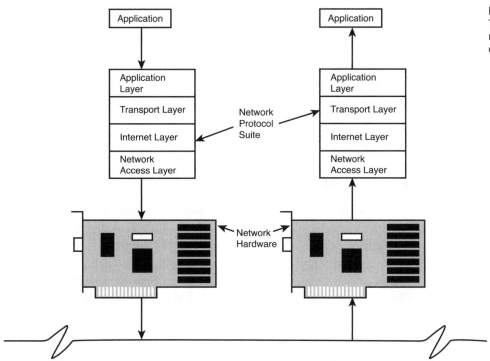

FIGURE 1.2
The role of a network proto-col suite.

The protocols of TCP/IP define the network communication process and, more importantly, define how a unit of data should look and what information it should contain so that a receiving computer can interpret the message correctly. TCP/IP and its related protocols form a complete system defining how data should be processed, transmitted, and received on a TCP/IP network. A system of related protocols, such as the TCP/IP protocols, is called a **protocol suite**.

The actual act of formatting and processing TCP/IP transmissions is performed by a software component known as the vendor's **implementation** of TCP/IP. For instance, a TCP/IP software component in Microsoft Windows enables Windows computers to process TCP/IP-formatted data and thus to participate in a TCP/IP network. As you read this book, be aware of the following distinction:

▶ A **TCP/IP standard** is a system of rules defining communication on TCP/IP networks.

▶ A **TCP/IP implementation** is a software component that performs the functions that enable a computer to participate in a TCP/IP network.

The purpose of the TCP/IP standards is to ensure the compatibility of all TCP/IP implementations regardless of version or vendor.

> **Standards and Implementations**
>
> The important distinction between the TCP/IP standards and a TCP/IP implementation is often blurred in popular discussions of TCP/IP, and this is sometimes confusing for readers. For instance, authors often talk about the layers of the TCP/IP model providing services for other layers. In fact, it is not the TCP/IP model that provides services. The TCP/IP model defines the services that *should be* provided. The vendor software implementations of TCP/IP actually provide these services.

The Development of TCP/IP

TCP/IP's design is a result of its historical role as the protocol system for what was to become the Internet. The Internet, like so many other high-tech developments, grew from research originally performed by the United States Department of Defense. In the late 1960s, Defense Department officials began to notice that the military was accumulating a large and diverse collection of computers. Some of those computers weren't networked, and others were grouped in small, closed networks with incompatible proprietary protocols.

Proprietary, in this case, means that the technology is controlled by a private entity (such as a corporation). That entity might not have any interest in divulging enough information about the protocol so that users can use it to connect to other (rival) network protocols.

Defense officials began to wonder whether it would be possible for these disparate computers to share information. These visionary soldiers created a network that became known as **ARPAnet**, named for the Defense Department's Advanced Research Projects Agency (ARPA).

As this network began to take shape, a group of computer scientists, led by Robert E. Kahn and Vinton Cerf, started to work on a versatile protocol system that would support a wide range of hardware and provide a resilient, redundant, and decentralized system for delivering data on a massive, global scale. The result of this research was the beginning of the TCP/IP protocol suite. When the National Science Foundation wanted to build a network to connect research institutions, it adopted ARPAnet's protocol system and began to build what we know as the Internet. University College of London and other European research institutes contributed to the early development of TCP/IP, and the first trans-Atlantic communications tests began around 1975. As more and more universities and research institutions became gradually connected, the Internet phenomenon began to spread around the world.

As you learn later in this book, the original decentralized vision of ARPAnet survives to this day in the design of the TCP/IP protocol system and is a big part of the success of TCP/IP and the Internet. Two important features of TCP/IP that provide for this decentralized environment are as follows:

▶ **End-node verification:** The two computers that are actually communicating—called the end nodes because they are at each end of the chain passing the message—are responsible for acknowledging and verifying the transmission. All computers basically operate as equals, and there is no central scheme for overseeing communications.

▶ **Dynamic routing:** Nodes are connected through multiple paths, and the routers choose a path for the data based on present conditions. You learn more about routing and router paths in later hours.

The Personal Computing Revolution

Around the time the Internet was catching on, most computers were multiuser systems. Several users in a single office (or campus) connected to a single computer through a text-screen interface device known as a terminal. Users worked independently, but in fact, they were all accessing the same computer, which required only one Internet connection to serve a large group of users. The proliferation of personal computers in the 1980s and 1990s began to change this scenario.

In the early days of personal computers, most users didn't even bother with networking. But as the Internet began to reach beyond its original academic roots, users with personal computers started looking for ways to connect. One solution was a dial-up connection through a modem, which offered network connectivity through a phone line.

But users also wanted to connect to other nearby computers in their own office—to share files and access peripheral devices. To address this need, another network concept, the **local area network (LAN)** began to take form.

Early LAN protocols did not provide Internet access and were designed around proprietary protocol systems. Many did not support routing of any kind. Computers in a single workgroup would talk to each other using one of these proprietary protocols, and users would either do without the Internet, or they would connect separately using a dial-up line. As the Internet service providers grew more numerous, and Internet access became more affordable, companies began to ask for a fast, permanent, always-on Internet connection. A variety of solutions began to emerge for getting LAN users connected to the TCP/IP-based Internet. Specialized **gateways** offered the protocol translation necessary for these local networks to reach the Internet. Gradually, however, the growth of the World Wide Web, and the accompanying need for end-user Internet connectivity, made TCP/IP essential, leaving little purpose for proprietary LAN protocols such as AppleTalk, NetBEUI, and Novell's IPX/SPX.

Operating system vendors such as Apple and Microsoft started to make TCP/IP the default protocol for local, as well as Internet, networking. TCP/IP grew up around UNIX, and all UNIX/Linux variants are fluent in TCP/IP. Eventually, TCP/IP became the networking protocol for the whole world—from small offices to gigantic data centers.

As you learn in Hour 3, "The Network Access Layer," the need to accommodate LANs has caused considerable innovation in the implementation of the hardware-conscious protocols that underlie TCP/IP.

TCP/IP Features

TCP/IP includes many important features that you'll learn about in this book. In particular, pay close attention to the way the TCP/IP protocol suite addresses the following problems:

▶ Logical addressing

▶ Routing

▶ Name resolution

▶ Error control and flow control

▶ Application support

These issues are at the heart of TCP/IP. The following sections introduce these important features. You learn more about these features later in this book.

Logical Addressing

A network adapter has a unique physical address. In the case of ethernet, the **physical address** (which is sometimes called a Media Access Control [MAC] address) is typically assigned to the adapter at the factory, although some contemporary devices now provide a means for changing the physical address. On a LAN, low-lying hardware-conscious protocols deliver data across the physical network using the adapter's physical address. There are many network types, and each has a different way of delivering data. On a basic ethernet network, for example, a computer sends messages directly onto the transmission medium. The network adapter of each computer listens to every transmission on the local network to determine whether a message is addressed to its own physical address.

By the Way

> **Well Not Quite So Easy**
>
> As you learn in Hour 9, "Getting Connected," today's ethernet networks are a bit more complicated than the idealized scenario of a computer sending messages directly onto the transmission line. Ethernet networks sometimes contain hardware devices such as switches to manage the signal.

On large networks, of course, every network adapter can't listen to every message. (Imagine your computer listening to *every* piece of data sent over the Internet.) As the transmission medium becomes more populated with computers, a physical addressing scheme cannot function efficiently. Network administrators often segment networks using devices such as routers to reduce network traffic. On routed networks, administrators need a way to subdivide the network into smaller subnetworks (called **subnets**) and impose a hierarchical design so that a message can travel efficiently to its destination. TCP/IP provides this subnetting capability through logical addressing. A **logical address** is an address configured through the network software. In TCP/IP, a computer's logical address is called an **IP address**. As you learn in Hour 4, "The Internet Layer," and Hour 5, "Subnetting and CIDR," an IP address can include

- A network ID number identifying a network

- A subnet ID number identifying a subnet on the network

- A host ID number identifying the computer on the subnet

The IP addressing system also lets the network administrator impose a sensible numbering scheme on the network so that the progression of addresses reflects the internal organization of the network.

By the Way

> **Internet-Ready Addresses**
>
> If your network is isolated from the Internet, you are free to use any IP addresses you want (as long as your network follows the basic rules for IP addressing). If your network will be part of the Internet, however, Internet Corporation for Assigned Names and Numbers (ICANN), which was formed in 1998, will assign a network ID to your network, and that network ID will form the first part of the IP address. (See Hours 4 and 5.) One interesting development is a system called Network Address Translation (NAT), which lets you use a private, nonroutable IP address on the local network that the router will translate into an official Internet-ready address for Internet communications. You learn more about NAT in Hour 12, "Automatic Configuration."

In TCP/IP, a logical address is resolved to and from the corresponding hardware-specific physical address using Address Resolution Protocol (ARP) and Reverse ARP (RARP), which are discussed in Hour 4.

Routing

A **router** is a special device that can read logical addressing information and direct data across the network to its destination. At the simplest level, a router divides a local subnet from the larger network (see Figure 1.3).

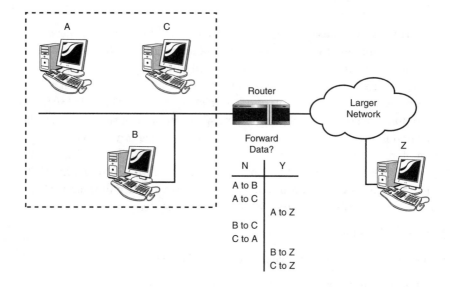

Data addressed to another computer or device on the local subnet does not cross the router and, therefore, doesn't clutter up the transmission lines of the greater network. If data is addressed to a computer outside the subnet, the router forwards the data accordingly. As previously mentioned in this hour, large networks such as the Internet include many routers and provide multiple paths from the source to the destination (see Figure 1.4).

TCP/IP includes protocols that define how the routers find a path through the network. You learn more about TCP/IP routing and routing protocols in Hour 8, "Routing."

By the Way

Other Filtering Devices

As you also learn in Hour 9, network devices such as bridges, switches, and intelligent hubs can also filter traffic and reduce network traffic. Because these devices work with physical addresses rather than logical addresses, they cannot perform the complex routing functions shown in Figure 1.4.

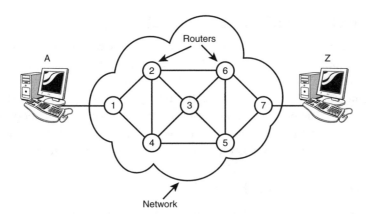

FIGURE 1.4
A routed network.

Name Resolution

Although the numeric IP address is probably more user friendly than the network adapter's prefabricated physical address, the IP address is still designed for the convenience of the computer rather than the convenience of the user. People might have trouble remembering whether a computer's address is 111.121.131.146 or 111.121.131.156. TCP/IP, therefore, provides for a parallel structure of user-oriented alphanumeric names, called **domain names** or Domain Name System (DNS) names. This mapping of domain names to an IP address is called **name resolution**. Special computers called **name servers** store tables showing how to translate these domain names to and from IP addresses.

The computer addresses commonly associated with email or the World Wide Web are expressed as DNS names (for example, www.microsoft.com, falcon.ukans.edu, and idir.net). TCP/IP's **name service** system provides for a hierarchy of name servers that supply domain name/IP address mappings for DNS-registered computers on the network. This means that the everyday user rarely has to enter or decipher an actual IP address.

DNS is the name resolution system for the Internet and is the most common name resolution method. However, other techniques also exist for resolving alphanumeric names to IP addresses. These alternative systems have gradually faded in importance in recent years, but name resolution services such as the Windows Internet Name Services (WINS), which resolves NetBIOS names to IP addresses, are still in operation around the world.

You learn more about TCP/IP name resolution in Hour 10, "Name Resolution."

Error Control and Flow Control

The TCP/IP protocol suite provides features that ensure the reliable delivery of data across the network. These features include checking data for transmission errors (to ensure that the data that arrives is exactly what was sent) and acknowledging successful receipt of a network message. TCP/IP's Transport layer (see Hour 6, "The Transport Layer") defines many of these error-control, flow-control, and acknowledgment functions through the TCP protocol. Lower-level protocols at TCP/IP's Network Access layer (see Hour 3) also play a part in the overall system of error control.

Application Support

Several network applications might be running on the same computer. The protocol software must provide some means for determining which incoming packet belongs with each application. In TCP/IP, this interface from the network to the applications is accomplished through a system of logical channels called **ports**. Each port has a number that is used to identify the port. You can think of these ports as logical pipelines within the computer through which data can flow from the application to (and from) the protocol software (see Figure 1.5).

FIGURE 1.5
Applications access the network through logical channels called ports.

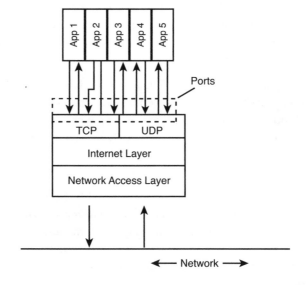

Hour 6 describes TCP and UDP ports at TCP/IP's Transport layer. You learn more about application support and TCP/IP's Application layer in Hour 7, "The Application Layer."

The TCP/IP suite also includes a number of ready-made applications designed to assist with various network tasks. Some typical TCP/IP utilities are shown in Table

TABLE 1.1 Typical TCP/IP Utilities

Utility	Purpose
ftp	File transfer
Lpr	Printing
Ping	Configuration/troubleshooting
Route	Configuration/troubleshooting
telnet	Remote terminal access
Traceroute	Configuration/troubleshooting

1.1. You learn more about these TCP/IP utilities in Hour 14, "TCP/IP Utilities."

By the Way

New Era

TCP/IP is actually entering into a new phase at the time of this writing. Technologies such as wireless networks, virtual private networks, and NAT are adding new complexities that the creators of TCP/IP wouldn't have imagined, and the next-generation IPv6 protocol will soon change the face of IP addressing. You learn more about these technologies in later hours.

Standards Organizations and RFCs

Several organizations have been instrumental in the development of TCP/IP and the Internet. Another way in which TCP/IP reveals its military roots is in the quantity and obscurity of its acronyms. Still, a few organizations in the past and present of TCP/IP deserve mention, as follows:

▶ **Internet Architecture Board (IAB):** The governing board that sets policy for the Internet and sees to the further development of TCP/IP standards.

▶ **Internet Engineering Task Force (IETF):** An organization that studies and rules on engineering issues. The IETF is divided into workgroups that study particular aspects of TCP/IP and the Internet, such as applications, routing, network management, and so forth.

▶ **Internet Research Task Force (IRTF):** The branch of the IAB that sponsors long-range research.

▶ **Internet Corporation for Assigned Names and Numbers (ICANN):** An organization established in 1998 that coordinates the assignment of Internet domain names, IP addresses, and globally unique protocol parameters such as port numbers (www.icann.com).

Because TCP/IP is a system of open standards that are not owned by any company or individual, the Internet community needs a comprehensive, independent, vendor-neutral process for proposing, discussing, and releasing additions and changes. Most of the official documentation on TCP/IP is available through a series of **Requests for Comment (RFCs)**. The library of RFCs includes Internet standards and reports from workgroups. IETF official specifications are published as RFCs. Many RFCs are intended to illuminate some aspect of TCP/IP or the Internet. You will find many references to RFCs throughout this book because most of protocols of the TCP/IP suite are defined in one or more RFCs. Although a majority of the RFCs were created by industry workgroups and research institutions, anyone can submit an RFC for review. You can either send a proposed RFC to the IETF or you can submit it directly to the RFC editor via email at rfc-editor@rfc-editor.org.

The RFCs provide essential technical background for anyone wanting a deeper understanding of TCP/IP. The list includes several technical papers on protocols, utilities, and services, as well as a few TCP/IP-related poems and Shakespeare takeoffs that, sadly, do not match the clarity and economy of TCP/IP.

You can find the RFCs at several places on the Internet. Try www.rfc-editor.org. Table 1.2 shows a few representative RFCs.

TABLE 1.2   Representative Examples of the 6,000+ Internet RFCs

Number	Title
791	Internet Protocol (IP)
792	Internet Control Message Protocol (ICMP)
793	Transmission Control Protocol
959	File Transfer Protocol
968	Twas the Night Before Start-up
1180	TCP/IP Tutorial
1188	Proposed Standard for Transmission of Datagrams over FDDI Networks
2097	The PPP NetBIOS Frames Control Protocol
4831	Network-Based Localized Mobility Management

Summary

This hour described what networks are and why networks need protocols. You learned that TCP/IP began with the U.S. Defense Department's experimental ARPAnet network and that TCP/IP was designed to provide decentralized networking in a diverse environment.

This hour also covered some important features of TCP/IP, such as logical addressing, name resolution, and application support. It described some of TCP/IP's oversight organizations and discussed RFCs (the technical papers that serve as the official documentation for TCP/IP and the Internet).

Q&A

Q. *What is the difference between a protocol standard and a protocol implementation?*

A. A protocol standard is a system of rules. A protocol implementation is a software component that applies those rules to provide networking capability to a computer.

Q. *Why was end-node verification an important feature of ARPAnet?*

A. By design, the network was not supposed to be controlled from any central point. The sending and receiving computers, therefore, had to take charge of verifying their own communication.

Q. *Why do larger networks employ name resolution?*

A. IP addresses are difficult to remember and easy to get wrong. DNS-style domain names are easier to remember because they let you associate a word or name with the IP address.

Workshop

The following workshop is composed of a series of quiz questions and practical exercises. The quiz questions are designed to test your overall understanding of the current material. The practical exercises are intended to afford you the opportunity to apply the concepts discussed during the current hour. Please take time to complete the quiz questions and exercises before continuing. Refer to Appendix A, "Answers to Quizzes and Exercises," for answers.

Quiz

1. What is a network protocol?

2. What are two features of TCP/IP that allow it to operate in a decentralized manner?

3. What system is responsible for mapping domain names to IP addresses?

4. What are RFCs?

5. What is a port?

Exercises

1. Visit www.rfc-editor.org and browse some of the RFCs.

2. Visit the IETF and explore the various active working groups at datatracker.ietf.org/wg/.

3. Visit the IRTF at www.irtf.org and explore some of the ongoing research.

4. Visit the ICANN About page at www.icann.org/en/about/ and learn about the ICANN mission.

5. Read RFC 1160 for an early history (up to 1990) of the IAB and IETF.

Key Terms

Review the following list of key terms:

▶ **ARPAnet:** An experimental network that was the birthplace of TCP/IP.

▶ **Domain name:** An alphanumeric name associated with an IP address through TCP/IP's DNS name service system.

▶ **Gateway:** A router that connects a LAN to a larger network. In the days of proprietary LAN protocols, the term *gateway* sometimes applied to a router that performed some kind of protocol conversion.

▶ **IP address:** A logical address used to locate a computer or other networked device (such as a printer) on a TCP/IP network.

▶ **Local Area Network (LAN):** A small network belonging to a single office, organization, or home, usually occupying a single geographical location.

▶ **Logical address:** A network address configured through the protocol software.

▶ **Name service:** A service that associates human-friendly alphanumeric names with network addresses. A computer that provides this service is known as a **name server**, and the act of resolving a name to an address is called **name resolution**.

▶ **Network Protocol:** A set of common rules defining a specific aspect of the communication process.

▶ **Physical address:** An address associated with the network hardware. In the case of an ethernet adapter, the physical address is typically assigned at the factory.

▶ **Port:** An internal channel or address that provides an interface between an application and TCP/IP's Transport layer.

▶ **Proprietary:** A technology controlled by a private entity, such as a corporation.

▶ **Protocol implementation:** A software component that implements the communication rules defined in a protocol standard.

▶ **Protocol system or protocol suite:** A system of interconnected standards and procedures (protocols) that enables computers to communicate over a network.

▶ **RFC (Request for Comment):** An official technical paper providing relevant information on TCP/IP or the Internet. You can find the RFCs at several places on the Internet; try www.rfc-editor.org.

▶ **Router:** A network device that forwards data by logical address and can also be used to segment large networks into smaller subnetworks.

▶ **Transport Control Protocol/Internet Protocol (TCP/IP):** A network protocol suite used on the Internet and also on many other networks around the world.

HOUR 2

How TCP/IP Works

What You'll Learn in This Hour:

▶ TCP/IP protocol system

▶ The OSI model

▶ Data packages

▶ How TCP/IP protocols interact

TCP/IP is a system (or suite) of protocols, and a protocol is a system of rules and procedures. For the most part, the hardware and software of the communicating computers carry out the rules of TCP/IP communications—the user does not have to get involved with the details. Still, a working knowledge of TCP/IP is essential if you want to navigate through the configuration and troubleshoot problems you'll face with TCP/IP networks.

This hour describes the TCP/IP protocol system and shows how the components of TCP/IP work together to send and receive data across the network.

At the completion of this hour, you will be able to

▶ Describe the layers of the TCP/IP protocol system and the purpose of each layer

▶ Describe the layers of the OSI protocol model and explain how the OSI layers relate to TCP/IP

▶ Explain TCP/IP protocol headers and how data is enclosed with header information at each layer of the protocol stack

▶ Name the data package at each layer of the TCP/IP stack

▶ Discuss the TCP, UDP, and IP protocols and how they work together to provide TCP/IP functionality

The TCP/IP Protocol System

Before looking at the elements of TCP/IP, it is best to begin with a brief review of the responsibilities of a protocol system.

A protocol system such as TCP/IP must be responsible for the following tasks:

▶ Dividing messages into manageable chunks of data that will pass efficiently through the transmission medium.

▶ Interfacing with the network adapter hardware.

▶ Addressing: The sending computer must be capable of targeting data to a receiving computer. The receiving computer must be capable of recognizing a message that it is supposed to receive.

▶ Routing data to the subnet of the destination computer, even if the source subnet and the destination subnet are dissimilar physical networks.

▶ Performing error control, flow control, and acknowledgment: For reliable communication, the sending and receiving computers must be able to identify and correct faulty transmissions and control the flow of data.

▶ Accepting data from an application and passing it to the network.

▶ Receiving data from the network and passing it to an application.

To accomplish the preceding tasks, the creators of TCP/IP settled on a modular design. The TCP/IP protocol system is divided into separate components that theoretically function independently from one another. Each component is responsible for a piece of the communication process.

The advantage of this modular design is that it lets vendors easily adapt the protocol software to specific hardware and operating systems. For instance, the Network Access layer (as you learn in Hour 3, "The Network Access Layer") includes functions relating to the specification and design of the physical network. Because of TCP/IP's modular design, a vendor such as Microsoft does not have to build a completely different software package for TCP/IP on an optical-fiber network (as opposed to TCP/IP on an ordinary ethernet network). The upper layers are not affected by the different physical architecture; only the Network Access layer must change.

The TCP/IP protocol system is subdivided into layered components, each of which performs specific duties (see Figure 2.1). This model, or **stack**, comes from the early days of TCP/IP, and it is sometimes called the TCP/IP model. The official TCP/IP protocol layers and their functions are described in the following list. Compare the functions in the list with the responsibilities listed earlier in this section, and you'll see how the responsibilities of the protocol system are distributed among the layers.

Many Models

The four-layer model shown in Figure 2.1 is a common model for describing TCP/IP networking, but it isn't the only model. The ARPAnet model, for instance, as described in RFC 871, describes three layers: the Network Interface layer, the Host-to-Host layer, and the Process-Level/Applications layer. Other descriptions of TCP/IP call for a five-layer model, with Physical and Data Link layers in place of the Network Access layer (to match OSI). Still other models might exclude either the Network Access or the Application layer, which are less uniform and harder to define than the intermediate layers.

The names of the layers also vary. The ARPAnet layer names still appear in some discussions of TCP/IP, and the Internet layer is sometimes called the Internetwork layer or the Network layer.

This book uses the four-layer model, with names shown in Figure 2.1.

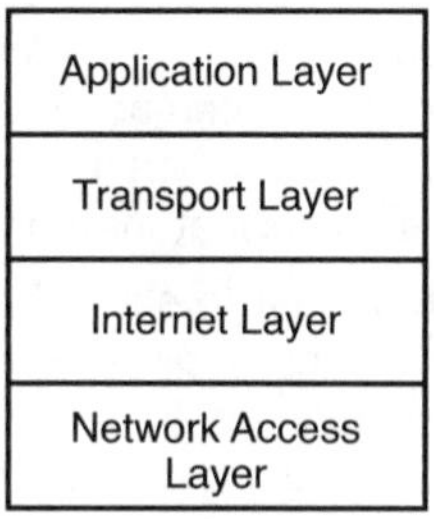

By the Way

FIGURE 2.1
The TCP/IP model's protocol layers.

▶ **Network Access layer:** Provides an interface with the physical network. Formats the data for the transmission medium and addresses data for the subnet based on physical hardware addresses. Provides error control for data delivered on the physical network.

▶ **Internet layer:** Provides logical, hardware-independent addressing so that data can pass among subnets with different physical architectures. Provides routing to reduce traffic and support delivery across the internetwork. (The term **internetwork** refers to an interconnected, greater network of local area networks (LANs), such as what you find in a large company or on the Internet.) Relates physical addresses (used at the Network Access layer) to logical addresses.

▶ **Transport layer:** Provides flow-control, error-control, and acknowledgment services for the internetwork. Serves as an interface for network applications.

▶ **Application layer:** Provides applications for network troubleshooting, file transfer, remote control, and Internet activities. Also supports the network application programming interfaces (APIs) that enable programs written for a particular operating environment to access the network.

Later hours provide more detailed descriptions of the activities at each of these TCP/IP protocol layers.

When the TCP/IP protocol software prepares a piece of data for transmission across the network, each layer on the sending machine adds a layer of information to the data that is relevant to the corresponding layer on the receiving machine. For instance, the Internet layer of the computer sending the data adds a header with some information that is significant to the Internet layer of the computer receiving the message. This process is sometimes referred to as encapsulation. At the receiving end these headers are removed as the data is passed up the protocol stack.

By the Way

Layers

The term *layer* is used throughout the computer industry for protocol component levels such as the ones shown in Figure 2.1. Header information is applied in layers to the data as it passes through the components of the protocol stack. (You'll learn more about this later in this hour.) When it comes to the components themselves, however, the term *layer* is somewhat metaphorical.

Diagrams such as Figure 2.1 are meant to show that the data passes across a series of interfaces. As long as the interfaces are maintained, the processes within one component are not affected by the processes in other components. If you turned Figure 2.1 sideways, it would look more like an assembly line, and this is also a useful analogy for the relationship of the protocol components. The data proceeds through a series of steps in the line and, as long as it arrives at each step as specified, the components can operate independently.

TCP/IP and the OSI Model

The networking industry has a standard seven-layer model for network protocol architecture called the Open Systems Interconnection (OSI) model. The OSI model represents an effort by the International Organization for Standardization (ISO), an international standards organization, to standardize the design of network protocol systems to promote interconnectivity and open access to protocol standards for software developers.

TCP/IP was already on the path of development when the OSI standard architecture appeared and, strictly speaking, TCP/IP does not conform to the OSI model. However, the two models did have similar goals, and enough interaction occurred among the designers of these standards that they emerged with a certain compatibility. The OSI model has been very influential in the growth and development of protocol implementations, and it is quite common to see the OSI terminology applied to TCP/IP.

Figure 2.2 shows the relationship between the four-layer TCP/IP standard and the seven-layer OSI model. Note that the OSI model divides the duties of the Application layer into three layers: Application, Presentation, and Session. OSI splits the activities of the Network Access layer into a Data Link layer and a Physical layer. This increased subdivision adds some complexity, but it also adds flexibility for developers by targeting the protocol layers to more specific services. In particular, the division at the lower level into the Data Link and Physical layers separates the functions related to organizing communication from the functions related to accessing the communication medium. The three upper OSI layers offer a greater variety of alternatives for an application to interface with the protocol stack.

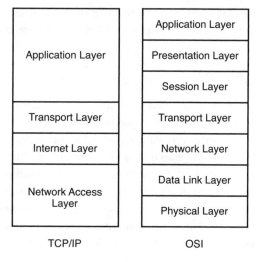

FIGURE 2.2
The seven-layer OSI model.

The seven layers of the OSI model are as follows:

- ▶ **Physical layer:** Converts the data into the stream of electric or analog pulses that will actually cross the transmission medium and oversees the transmission of the data

- ▶ **Data Link layer:** Provides an interface with the network adapter; maintains logical links for the subnet

- ▶ **Network layer:** Supports logical addressing and routing

- ▶ **Transport layer:** Provides error control and flow control for the internetwork

- ▶ **Session layer:** Establishes sessions between communicating applications on the communicating computers

▶ **Presentation layer:** Translates data to a standard format; manages encryption and data compression

▶ **Application layer:** Provides a network interface for applications; supports network applications for file transfer, communications, and so forth

It is important to remember that the TCP/IP model and the OSI model are standards, not implementations. Real-world implementations of TCP/IP do not always map cleanly to the models shown in Figures 2.1 and 2.2, and the perfect correspondence depicted in Figure 2.2 is also a matter of some discussion within the industry.

Notice that the OSI and TCP/IP models are most similar at the important Transport and Internet (called Network in OSI) layers. These layers include the most identifiable and distinguishing components of the protocol system, and it is no coincidence that protocol systems are sometimes named for their Transport and Network layer protocols. As you learn later in this book, the TCP/IP protocol suite is named for TCP, a Transport layer protocol, and IP, an Internet/Network layer protocol.

Data Packages

The important thing to remember about the TCP/IP protocol stack is that each layer plays a role in the overall communication process. Each layer invokes services that are necessary for that layer to perform its role. As an outgoing transmission passes down through the stack, each layer includes a bundle of relevant information called a **header** along with the actual data. The little data package containing the header and the data then becomes the data that is repackaged at the next lower level with the next lower layer's header. This process is shown in Figure 2.3. The reverse process occurs when data is received on the destination computer. As the data moves up through the stack, each layer unpacks the corresponding header and uses the information.

As the data moves down through the stack, the effect is a little like the nested Russian wooden dolls you might have seen; the innermost doll is enclosed in another doll, which is then enclosed in another doll, and so on. At the receiving end, the data packages are unpacked, one by one, as the data climbs back up the protocol stack. The Internet layer on the receiving machine uses the information in the Internet layer header. The Transport layer uses the information in the Transport layer header. At each layer, the package of data takes a form that provides the necessary information to the corresponding layer on the receiving machine. Because each layer is responsible for different functions, the form of the basic data package is very different at each layer.

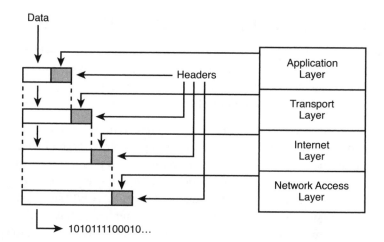

Data

Headers

Application
Layer

Transport
Layer

Internet
Layer

Network Access
Layer

1010111100010…

FIGURE 2.3
At each layer,
the data is
repackaged
with that layer's
header.

By the Way

Transporting Dolls

The networking industry has as many analogies as it has acronyms, and the Russian doll analogy, like any of the others, illustrates a point, but must not be taken too far. It is worth noting that on a physical network such as ethernet, the data is typically broken into smaller units at the Network Access layer. A more accurate analogy would call for this lowest layer to break the concentric doll system into smaller pieces, encapsulate those pieces into tinier dolls, and then grind those tiny dolls into a pattern of 1s and 0s. The 1s and 0s are received, reconstituted into tiny dolls, and rebuilt into the concentric doll system. The complexity of this scenario causes many to eschew the otherwise-promising analogy of the dolls.

The data packet looks different at each layer, and at each layer it goes by a different name. The names for the data packages created at each layer are as follows:

- ▶ The data package created at the Application layer is called a **message**.

- ▶ The data package created at the Transport layer, which encapsulates the Application layer message, is called **a segment** if it comes from the Transport layer's TCP protocol. If the data package comes from the Transport layer's **User Datagram Protocol (UDP)** protocol, it is called a **datagram**.

- ▶ The data package at the Internet layer, which encapsulates the Transport layer segment, is called a datagram.

- ▶ The data package at the Network Access layer, which encapsulates and may subdivide the datagram, is called a **frame**. This frame is then turned into a bitstream at the lowest sublayer of the Network Access layer.

You learn more about the data packages for each layer in later hours.

A Quick Look at TCP/IP Networking

The practice of describing protocol systems in terms of their layers is widespread and nearly universal. The layering system does provide insights into the protocol system, and it's impossible to describe TCP/IP without first introducing its layered architecture. However, focusing solely on protocol layers also creates some limitations.

First, talking about protocol layers rather than protocols introduces additional abstraction to a subject that is already excruciatingly abstract. Second, itemizing the various protocols as subheads within the greater topic of a protocol layer can give the false impression that all protocols are of equal importance. In fact, though every protocol has a role to play, most of the functionality of the TCP/IP suite can be described in terms of only a few of its most important protocols. It is sometimes useful to view these important protocols in the foreground, against the backdrop of the layering system described earlier in this hour.

Figure 2.4 describes the basic TCP/IP protocol networking system. Of course, there are additional protocols and services in the complete package, but Figure 2.4 shows most of what is going on.

The basic scenario is as follows:

1. Data passes from a protocol, network service, or application programming interface (API) operating at the Application layer through a TCP or UDP port to either of the two Transport layer protocols (TCP or UDP). Programs can access the network through either TCP or UDP, depending on the program's requirements:

   ▶ **TCP** is a connection-oriented protocol. As you learn in Hour 6, "The Transport Layer," connection-oriented protocols provide more sophisticated flow control and error control than connectionless protocols. TCP goes to great effort to guarantee the delivery of the data. TCP is more reliable than UDP, but the additional error checking and flow control mean that TCP is slower than UDP.

   ▶ **UDP** is a connectionless protocol. It is faster than TCP, but it is not as reliable. UDP offloads more of the error control responsibilities to the application.

2. The data segment passes to the Internet level, where the **IP** protocol provides logical-addressing information and encloses the data into a datagram.

3. The IP datagram enters the Network Access layer, where it passes to software components designed to interface with the physical network. The Network Access layer creates one or more data frames designed for entry onto the physical network. In the case of a LAN system such as ethernet, the frame may contain physical address information obtained from lookup tables maintained using the Internet layer **ARP** protocol. (ARP, Address Resolution Protocol, translates IP addresses to physical addresses.)

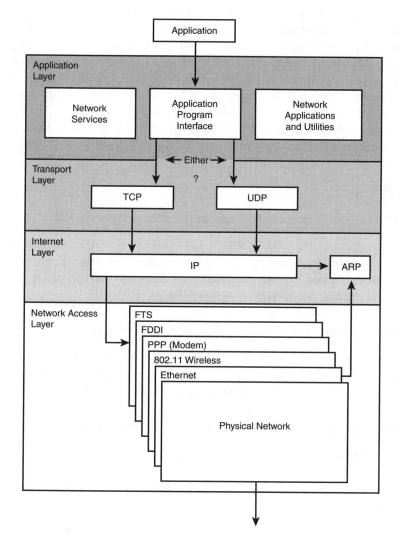

FIGURE 2.4
A quick look at the basic TCP/IP networking system.

4. The data frame is converted to a stream of bits that is transmitted over the network medium.

Of course, there are endless details describing how each protocol goes about fulfilling its assigned tasks. For instance, how does TCP provide flow control, how does ARP map physical addresses to IP addresses, and how does IP know where to send a datagram addressed to a different subnet? These questions are explored later in this book.

Summary

In this hour, you learned about the layers of the TCP/IP protocol stack and how those layers interrelate. You also learned how the classic TCP/IP model relates to the seven-layer OSI networking model. At each layer in the protocol stack, data is packaged into the form that is most useful to the corresponding layer on the receiving end. This hour discussed the process of encapsulating header information at each protocol layer and outlined the different terms used at each layer to describe the data package. Finally, you got a quick look at how the TCP/IP protocol system operates from the viewpoint of some of its most important protocols: TCP, UDP, IP, and ARP.

Q&A

Q. *What are the principal advantages of TCP/IP's modular design?*

A. Because of TCP/IP's modular design, the TCP/IP protocol stack can adapt easily to specific hardware and operating environments. Breaking the networking software into specific, well designed components also makes it easier to write programs that interact with the protocol system.

Q. *What functions are provided at the Network Access layer?*

A. The Network Access layer provides services related to the specific physical network. These services include preparing, transmitting, and receiving the frame over a particular transmission medium, such as an ethernet cable.

Q. *Which OSI layer corresponds to the TCP/IP Internet layer?*

A. TCP/IP's Internet layer corresponds to the OSI Network layer.

Q. *Why is header information enclosed at each layer of the TCP/IP protocol stack?*

A. Because each protocol layer on the receiving machine needs different information to process the incoming data, each layer on the sending machine encloses header information.

Workshop

The following workshop is composed of a series of quiz questions and practical exercises. The quiz questions are designed to test your overall understanding of the current material. The practical exercises are intended to afford you the opportunity to apply the concepts discussed during the current hour, as well as build upon the knowledge acquired in previous hours of study. Please take time to complete the quiz questions and exercises before continuing. Refer to Appendix A, "Answers to Quizzes and Exercises," for answers.

Quiz

1. What two OSI layers map into the TCP/IP Network Access layer?

2. What TCP/IP layer is responsible for routing data from one computer to another?

3. What are the advantages and disadvantages of UDP as compared to TCP?

4. Which layer deals with frames?

5. What does it mean to say that a layer encapsulates data?

Exercises

1. List the functions performed by each layer in the TCP/IP stack.

2. List the layer(s) that deal with datagrams.

3. Explain how TCP/IP would have to change to use a newly invented type of network.

4. Explain what it means to say that TCP is a reliable protocol.

Key Terms

Review the following list of key terms:

▶ **Address Resolution Protocol (ARP):** A protocol that resolves logical IP addresses to physical addresses.

▶ **Application layer:** The layer of the TCP/IP stack that supports network applications and provides an interface to the local operating environment.

▶ **Datagram:** The data package passed from the Internet layer to the Network Access layer, or a data package passed from UDP at the Transport layer to the Internet layer.

▶ **Frame:** The data package created at the Network Access layer.

▶ **Header:** A bundle of protocol information attached to the data at each layer of the protocol stack.

▶ **Internet layer:** The layer of the TCP/IP stack that provides logical addressing and routing.

▶ **IP (Internet Protocol):** The Internet layer protocol that provides logical addressing and routing capabilities.

▶ **Message:** In TCP/IP networking, a message is the data package passed from the Application layer to the Transport layer. The term is also used generically to describe a message from one entity to another on the network. The term doesn't always refer to an Application layer data package.

▶ **Network Access layer:** The layer of the TCP/IP stack that provides an interface with the physical network.

▶ **Segment:** The data package passed from TCP at the Transport layer to the Internet layer.

▶ **TCP (Transmission Control Protocol):** A reliable, connection-oriented protocol of the Transport layer.

▶ **Transport layer:** The layer of the TCP/IP stack that provides error control and acknowledgment and serves as an interface for network applications.

▶ **UDP (User Datagram Protocol):** An unreliable, connectionless protocol of the Transport layer.

PART II

The TCP/IP Protocol System

HOUR 3

The Network Access Layer

What You'll Learn in This Hour:

▶ Physical addresses
▶ Network architectures
▶ Ethernet frames

At the base of the TCP/IP protocol stack is the Network Access layer, the collection of services and specifications that provide and manage access to the network hardware. In this hour you learn about the duties of the Network Access layer and how the Network Access layer relates to the OSI model. This hour also takes a close look at the network technology known as **ethernet**.

At the completion of this hour, you'll be able to

▶ Explain the Network Access layer

▶ Discuss how TCP/IP's Network Access layer relates to the OSI networking model

▶ Describe the purpose of a network architecture

▶ List the contents of an ethernet frame

Protocols and Hardware

The Network Access layer is the most mysterious and least uniform of TCP/IP's layers. It manages all the services and functions necessary to prepare the data for the physical network. These responsibilities include

▶ Interfacing with the computer's network adapter

▶ Coordinating the data transmission with the conventions of the appropriate access method

▶ Converting the data into a format that will be transmitted into the stream of electric or analog pulses across the transmission medium

▶ Checking for errors in incoming data

▶ Adding error-checking information to outgoing data so that the receiving computer can check the data for errors

Of course, any formatting tasks performed on outgoing data must occur in reverse when the data reaches its destination and is received by the computer to which it is addressed.

The Network Access layer defines the procedures for interfacing with the network hardware and accessing the transmission medium. Below the surface of TCP/IP's Network Access layer, you'll find an intricate interplay of hardware, software, and transmission-medium specifications. Unfortunately, at least for the purposes of a concise description, there are many different types of physical networks that all have their own conventions, and any one of these physical networks can form the basis for the Network Access layer.

The good news is that the Network Access layer is almost totally invisible to the everyday user. The network adapter driver, coupled with key low-level components of the operating system and protocol software, manages most of the tasks relegated to the Network Access layer, and a few short configuration steps are usually all that is required of a user. These steps are becoming simpler with the improved plug-and-play and autoconfiguration features of desktop operating systems.

As you read through this hour, remember that the logical, IP-style addressing discussed in Hours 1, 2, 4, and 5 exists entirely in the software. The protocol system requires additional services to deliver the data across a specific local area network (LAN) system and up through the network adapter of a destination computer. These services are the purview of the Network Access layer.

> **To Be or Not to Be**
>
> It is worth mentioning that the diversity, complexity, and invisibility of the Network Access layer has caused some authors to exclude it from discussions of TCP/IP completely, asserting instead that the stack rests on LAN drivers below the Internet layer. This viewpoint has some merit, but the Network Access layer actually is part of TCP/IP, and no discussion of the network-communication process is complete without it.

By the Way

The Network Access Layer and the OSI Model

As Hour 2, "How TCP/IP Works," mentioned, TCP/IP is officially independent of the seven-layer OSI networking model, but the OSI model is often used as a general framework for understanding protocol systems. OSI terminology and concepts are particularly common in discussions of the Network Access layer because the OSI model provides additional subdivisions to the broad category of network access. These subdivisions reveal a bit more about the inner workings of this layer.

As Figure 3.1 shows, the TCP/IP Network Access layer roughly corresponds to the OSI **Physical** and **Data Link layers**. The OSI Physical layer is responsible for turning the data frame into a stream of bits suitable for the transmission medium. In other words, the OSI Physical layer manages and synchronizes the electrical or analog pulses that form the actual transmission. On the receiving end, the Physical layer reassembles these pulses into a data frame.

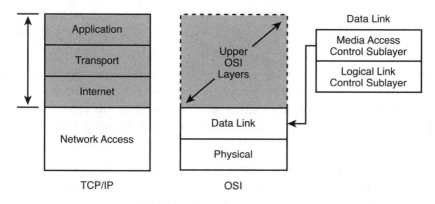

FIGURE 3.1
OSI and the Network Access layer.

The OSI Data Link layer performs two separate functions and is accordingly subdivided into the following two sublayers:

▶ **Media Access Control (MAC):** This sublayer provides an interface with the network adapter. The network adapter driver, in fact, is often called the

MAC driver, and the hardware address burned into the card at the factory is often referred to as the MAC address.

▶ **Logical Link Control (LLC):** This sublayer performs error-checking functions for frames delivered over the subnet and manages links between devices communicating on the subnet.

By the Way

> **NDIS and ODI**
>
> In real network protocol implementations, the distinction between the layers of TCP/IP and OSI systems has become further complicated by the development of the Network Driver Interface Specification (NDIS) and Open Data-Link Interface (ODI) specification. NDIS (developed by Microsoft and 3Com Corp.) and ODI (developed by Apple and Novell) are designed to let a single protocol stack (such as TCP/IP) use multiple network adapters and to let a single network adapter use multiple upper-layer protocols. This effectively enables the upper-layer protocols to float independently of the network access system, which adds great functionality to the network but also adds complexity and makes it even more difficult to provide a systematic discussion of how the software components interrelate at the lower layers.

Network Architecture

In practice, LANs are not actually thought of in terms of protocol layers but by **LAN architecture** or **network architecture**. (Sometimes a network architecture is referred to as a LAN type or a LAN topology.) A network architecture, such as ethernet, provides a bundle of specifications governing media access, physical addressing, and the interaction of the computers with the transmission medium. When you decide on a network architecture, you are in effect deciding on a design for the Network Access layer.

A network architecture is a design for the physical network and a collection of specifications defining communications on that physical network. The communication details are dependent on the physical details, so the specifications usually come together as a complete package. These specifications include considerations such as the following:

▶ **Access method:** An **access method** is a set of rules defining how the computers will share the transmission medium. To avoid data collisions, computers must follow these rules when they transmit data.

▶ **Data frame format:** The IP-level datagram from the Internet layer is encapsulated in a data frame with a predefined format. The data enclosed in the header must supply the information necessary to deliver data on the physical network. You'll learn more about data frames later in this hour.

▶ **Cabling type:** The type of cable used for a network has an effect on certain other design parameters, such as the electrical properties of the bitstream transmitted by the adapter.

▶ **Cabling rules:** The protocols, cable type, and electrical properties of the transmission have an effect on the maximum and minimum lengths for the cable and for the cable connector specifications.

Details such as cable type and connector type are not the direct responsibility of the Network Access layer, but to design the software components of the Network Access layer, developers must assume a specific set of characteristics for the physical network. Thus, the network access software must come with a specific hardware design.

The important point is that the layers above the Network Access layer *don't* have to worry about the hardware design. The TCP/IP stack is designed so that all the details of interacting with the hardware occur at the Network Access layer. This design lets TCP/IP operate over a great variety of different transmission media.

Some of the architectures inhabiting the Network Access layer are

▶ **IEEE 802.3 (ethernet):** The familiar cable-based network used in most offices and homes

▶ **IEEE 802.11 (wireless networking):** The wireless LAN networking technology found in offices, homes, and coffee houses

▶ **IEEE 802.16 (WiMAX):** A technology used for mobile wireless connectivity over long distances

▶ **Point-to-Point Protocol (PPP):** The protocol used for modem connections over a telephone line

Several other network architectures are also supported by TCP/IP. As shown in Figure 3.2, in each case, the modular nature of the protocol stack means that the hardware-conscious software components operating at this level can interface with the hardware-independent upper levels supporting services such as logical addressing.

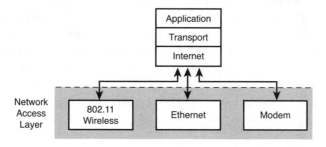

FIGURE 3.2
Because the Network Access layer encapsulates the details of the transmission medium, the upper layers of the stack can operate independently of the hardware.

Although the intricacies of protocol layer interfaces are largely invisible to the user, you can often get a glimpse of this relationship between the hardware-based layer and the logical addressing layer through the network configuration dialog for your operating system. Figure 3.3, for example, shows a Mac OS X configuration dialog that lets you associate a number of different architectures with the TCP/IP configuration, including ethernet, Bluetooth, modem, and "AirPort" wireless, which is an Apple-polished repackaging of the IEEE 802.11 wireless LAN specification.

FIGURE 3.3
Most operating systems let you associate a variety of network architectures with the TCP/IP configuration.

You learn more about modems, wireless networks, and other networking technologies in later hours.

As an example of the types of problems and solutions that occur within the Network Access layer, the following sections take a closer look at the important and ubiquitous architecture known as ethernet. Most likely, the cable connected to the back of your home or office computer is an ethernet cable, and the computers on your network are communicating using some form of ethernet networking. Even a wireless hub that connects laptops, smartphones, and other wireless devices to your home network is tethered to the wired network using ethernet cabling. As you read the rest of this hour, keep in mind that ethernet is just one example of a Network Access layer protocol system. When you learn about other hardware technologies in later hours, such as dial-up, digital subscriber line (DSL), wireless, and wide area networking methods, keep in mind that each of these technologies has its own unique requirements that are reflected in a unique design for the Network Access protocols and drivers.

Physical Addressing

As you learned in earlier hours, the Network Access layer is necessary to relate the logical IP address, which is configured through the protocol software, with the actual permanent **physical address** of the network adapter. This **physical address** is often called the MAC address because, within the OSI model, physical addressing is the responsibility of the **Media Access Control (MAC) sublayer**. Because the physical addressing system is encapsulated within the Network Access layer, the address can take on a different form depending on the network architecture specification.

In the case of ethernet, the physical address is typically burned into the networking hardware at the factory, although some modern network adapters offer a programmable physical address, A few years ago, ethernet hardware almost always consisted of a network adapter card inserted into one of the computer's expansion slots. In recent years, vendors have started building ethernet functionality into the motherboard. In either case, the hardware typically comes preconfigured with a physical address.

Data frames sent across the LAN must use this physical address to identify the source and destination adapters, but the lengthy physical address (48 bits in the case of ethernet) is so unfriendly that it is impractical for people to use. Also, encoding the physical address at higher protocol levels compromises the flexible modular architecture of TCP/IP, which requires that the upper layers remain independent of physical details. TCP/IP uses the Address Resolution Protocol (ARP) and Reverse ARP (RARP) to relate IP addresses to the physical addresses of the network adapters on the local network. ARP and RARP provide a link between the logical IP addresses seen by the user and the (effectively invisible) hardware addresses used on the LAN. You'll learn about ARP and RARP in Hour 4, "The Internet Layer."

As you read the following description of ethernet, keep in mind that the address used by the ethernet software is not the same as the logical IP address, but this address maps to an IP address at the interface with the Internet layer.

Ethernet

Ethernet is undoubtedly the most popular LAN technology in use today. The ethernet architecture has become popular because of its modest price; ethernet cable is inexpensive and easily installed. Ethernet network adapters and ethernet hardware components are also relatively inexpensive. You are probably familiar with the appearance of a typical ethernet port and cable if you have ever looked at the back of a computer. The rise of wireless networking has not diminished the importance of ethernet. An important form of wireless LAN networking is sometimes called "wireless ethernet" because it incorporates many of the principles of the original ethernet specification.

On a classic ethernet network, all computers share a common transmission medium. Ethernet uses an access method called **carrier sense multiple access with collision detect (CSMA/CD)** for determining when a computer is free to transmit data on to the access medium. Using CSMA/CD, all computers monitor the transmission medium and wait until the line is available before transmitting. If two computers try to transmit at the same time, a collision occurs. The computers then stop, wait for a random time interval, and attempt to transmit again.

CSMA/CD can be compared to the protocol followed by a room full of polite people. Someone who wants to speak first listens to determine whether anybody else is currently speaking (the carrier sense). If two people start speaking at the same moment, both people detect the problem, stop speaking, and wait before speaking again (the collision detect).

Traditional ethernet works well under light-to-moderate use but suffers from high collision rates under heavy use. On modern ethernet networks, devices such as network switches manage the traffic to reduce the incidence of collisions, thereby allowing ethernet to operate more efficiently. You learn more about hubs and switches in Hour 9, "Getting Connected."

Ethernet is capable of using a variety of media. Conventional hub-based 10BASE-T ethernet was originally intended to operate at a baseband speed of 10Mbps, but 100Mbps "fast ethernet" is now quite common. In addition, 1,000 Mbps (gigabit) ethernet systems are available. Early ethernet systems often used a continuous strand of coaxial cable as a transmission medium (Figure 3.4), but by far the most common scenario today is for the computers to attach to a single network device (Figure 3.5).

FIGURE 3.4
In an earlier form of ethernet, the computers were all attached to a single coaxial cable.

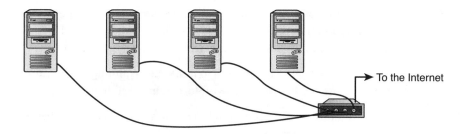

FIGURE 3.5
On modern eth-
ernet networks,
the computers
are usually
attached to a
central network
device such as
a switch.

To the Internet

Anatomy of an Ethernet Frame

The Network Access layer software accepts a datagram from the Internet layer and converts that data to a form that is consistent with the specifications of the physical network (see Figure 3.6). In the case of ethernet, the software of the Network Access layer must prepare the data for transmission through the hardware of the network adapter card.

Internet
Layer
Data

Network
Access
Layer

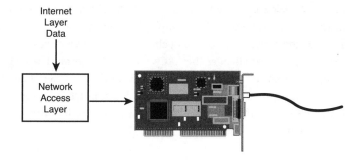

FIGURE 3.6
The Network
Access layer
formats data
for the physical
network.

When the ethernet software receives a datagram from the Internet layer, it performs the following steps:

1. Breaks Internet layer data into smaller chunks, if necessary, which are sent in the data field of the ethernet frames. The total size of the ethernet frame must be between 64 bytes and 1518 bytes, not including the preamble. (Some systems support an enlarged frame size of up to 9000 bytes. These so-called jumbo frames improve efficiency; however, they introduce some compatibility issues and are not universally supported.)

2. Packages the chunks of data into frames. Each frame includes data as well as other information that the network adapters on the ethernet need to process the frame. An IEEE 802.3 ethernet frame includes the following:

   ▶ **Preamble:** A sequence of bits used to mark the beginning of the frame (8 bytes, the last of which is the 1-byte Start Frame Delimiter).

   ▶ **Recipient address:** The 6-byte (48-bit) physical address of the network adapter that is to receive the frame.

   ▶ **Source address:** The 6-byte (48-bit) physical address of the network adapter that is sending the frame.

   ▶ **Optional VLAN tag:** This optional 16-bit field, described in the 802.1q standard, is designed to allow multiple virtual LANs to operate through the same network switch.

   ▶ **Length:** A 2-byte (16-bit) field indicating the size of the data field.

   ▶ **Data:** The data that is transmitted with the frame.

   ▶ **Frame Check Sequence (FCS):** A 4-byte (32-bit) checksum value for the frame. The **FCS** is a common means of verifying data transmissions. The sending computer calculates a **cyclical redundancy check (CRC)** value for the frame and encodes the CRC value in the frame. The receiving computer then recalculates the CRC and checks the FCS field to see whether the values match. If the values don't match, some data was lost or changed during transmission, in which case the frame is retransmitted.

3. Passes the data frame to lower-level components corresponding to OSI's Physical layer, which converts the frame into a bitstream and sends it over the transmission medium.

The other network adapters on the ethernet network receive the frame and check the destination address. If the destination address matches the address of the network adapter, the adapter software processes the incoming frame and passes the data to higher layers of the protocol stack.

Summary

This hour discussed the Network Access layer, the most diverse and arguably the most complex layer in the TCP/IP protocol stack. The Network Access layer defines the procedures for interfacing with the network hardware and accessing the transmission medium. There are many types of LAN architectures and, therefore, many different specifications for the Network Access layer. As an example of how the Network Access layer handles data transmission, this hour took a close look at ethernet.

Ethernet technology is common throughout the mechanized world, but there are many other ways to connect computers. Any networking technology must have some means of preparing data for the physical network; therefore, any TCP/IP technology must have a Network Access layer. You learn more about other physical network scenarios, such as modems, wireless LANs, mobile networking, and WAN technologies in later hours.

Q&A

Q. *What types of services are defined at the Network Access layer?*

A. The Network Access layer includes services and specifications that manage the process of accessing the physical network.

Q. *Which OSI layers correspond to the TCP/IP Network Access layer?*

A. The Network Access layer roughly corresponds with the OSI Data Link layer and Physical layer.

Q. *What is the most common LAN architecture?*

A. The most common LAN architecture is ethernet, although wireless LAN technologies are becoming increasingly popular.

Q. *What is CSMA/CD?*

A. CSMA/CD is carrier sense multiple access with collision detect, a network access method used by ethernet. Under CSMA/CD, the computers on a network wait for a moment to transmit and, if two computers attempt to transmit at once, they both stop, wait for a random interval, and transmit again.

Workshop

The following workshop is composed of a series of quiz questions and practical exercises. The quiz questions are designed to test your overall understanding of the current material. The practical exercises are intended to afford you the opportunity to apply the concepts discussed during the current hour, as well as build upon the knowledge acquired in previous hours of study. Please take time to complete the quiz questions and exercises before continuing. Refer to Appendix A, "Answers to Quizzes and Exercises," for answers.

Quiz

1. What is a CRC?

2. What is a collision detection on an ethernet network?

3. How big is an ethernet physical address?

4. What is the purpose of NDIS and ODI?

5. What does ARP do?

Exercises

1. List the two protocols that relate physical addresses with IP addresses.

2. List at least four network architectures.

3. Explain the functions performed by the OSI Media Access Control and Logical Link Control layers.

Key Terms

Review the following list of key terms:

▶ **Access method:** A procedure for regulating access to the transmission medium.

▶ **CRC (cyclical redundancy check):** A checksum calculation used to verify the contents of a data frame.

▶ **CSMA/CD (carrier sense multiple access with collision detect):** The network access method used by ethernet.

▶ **Data Link layer:** The second layer of the OSI model.

▶ **Ethernet:** A very popular LAN architecture, using the CSMA/CD network-access method.

▶ **Frame Check Sequence (FCS):** A field within an ethernet frame containing a CRC-based checksum value used to verify the data.

▶ **Logical Link Control (LLC) sublayer:** A sublayer of OSI's Data Link layer that is responsible for error checking and managing links between devices on the subnet.

▶ **Media Access Control (MAC) sublayer:** A sublayer of OSI's Data Link layer that is responsible for the interface with the network adapter.

▶ **Network architecture:** A complete specification for a physical network, including specifications for access method, data frame, and network cabling.

▶ **Physical address (or MAC address):** An address that identifies the network adapter on the physical network. In the case of ethernet, the physical address is typically assigned by the manufacturer, although some modern network adapters allow for configuration of the physical address.

▶ **Physical layer:** The first OSI layer, responsible for translating the data frame into a bitstream suitable for the transmission medium.

▶ **Preamble:** A series of bits marking the beginning of a data frame transmission.

HOUR 4

The Internet Layer

What You'll Learn in This Hour:

▶ IP addresses

▶ The IP header

▶ ARP

▶ ICMP

As you learned in the preceding hour, the computers on a single network segment such as an ethernet local area network (LAN) can communicate with each other using the physical addresses available at the Network Access layer. How, then, does an email message get from Carolina to California and arrive precisely at its destination? As you learn in this hour, the protocols at the Internet layer provide for delivery beyond the local network segment. This hour discusses the important Internet layer protocols IP, ARP, and ICMP.

The focus of this hour is on the 32-bit binary IPv4 addresses used throughout the Internet. The world is currently in transition to a new 128-bit address system known as IPv6, which offers enhanced capabilities and a much larger address space. See Hour 13, "IPv6: The Next Generation," for more on IPv6.

At the completion of this hour, you will be able to

▶ Explain the purpose of IP, ARP, and ICMP

▶ Explain what a network ID and host ID are

▶ Explain what an octet is

▶ Convert a dotted-decimal address to its binary equivalent

▶ Convert a 32-bit binary IP address into a dotted-decimal notation

▶ Describe the contents of an IP header

▶ Explain the purpose of the IP address

Addressing and Delivering

As you learned in Hour 3, "The Network Access Layer," a computer communicates with the network through a network interface device such as a network adapter card. The network interface device has a unique physical address and is designed to receive data sent to that physical address. A device such as an ethernet card does not know any of the details of the upper protocol layers. It does not know its IP address or whether an incoming frame is being sent to Telnet or FTP. It just listens to incoming frames, waits for a frame addressed to its own physical address, and passes that frame up the protocol stack.

This physical addressing scheme works well on an individual LAN segment. A network that consists of only a few computers on an uninterrupted medium can function with nothing more than physical addresses. Data can pass directly from network adapter to network adapter using the low-level protocols associated with the Network Access layer.

Unfortunately, on a routed network, it is not possible to deliver data by physical address. The discovery procedures required for delivering by physical address do not work across a router interface. Even if they did work, delivery by physical address would be cumbersome because the permanent physical address built in to a network card does not allow you to impose a logical structure on the address space.

TCP/IP therefore makes the physical address invisible and instead organizes the network around a logical, hierarchical addressing scheme. This logical addressing scheme is maintained by the **IP protocol** at the Internet layer. The logical address is called the **IP address**. Another Internet layer protocol called **Address Resolution Protocol (ARP)** assembles a table that maps IP addresses to physical addresses. This ARP table is the link between the IP address and the physical address burned into the network adapter card.

On a routed network (see Figure 4.1), the TCP/IP software uses the following strategy for sending data on the network:

1. If the destination address is on the same network segment as the source computer, the source computer sends the packet directly to the destination. The IP address is resolved to a physical address using ARP, and the data is directed to the destination network adapter.

2. If the destination address is on a different segment from the source computer, the following process begins:

    A. The datagram is directed to a gateway. A **gateway** is a device on the local network segment that is capable of forwarding a datagram to other network segments. (As you learned in Hour 1, "What Is TCP/IP?" a gateway is basically a router.) The gateway address is resolved to a physical address using ARP, and the data is sent to the gateway's network adapter.

    B. The datagram is routed through the gateway to a higher-level network segment (refer to Figure 4.1) where the process is repeated. If the destination address is on the new segment, the data is delivered to its destination. If not, the datagram is sent to another gateway.

    C. The datagram passes through the chain of gateways to the destination segment, where the destination IP address is mapped to a physical address using ARP and the data is directed to the destination network adapter.

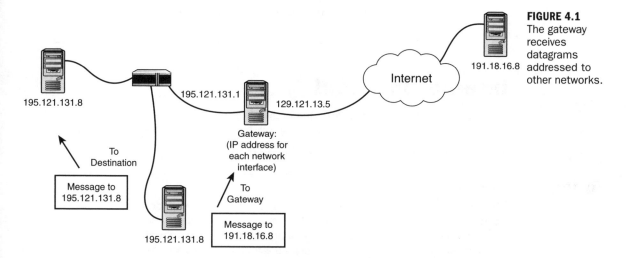

FIGURE 4.1
The gateway receives datagrams addressed to other networks.

To deliver data on a complex routed network, the Internet layer protocols must therefore be able to

- Identify any computer on the network

- Provide a means for determining when a message must be sent through the gateway

▶ Provide a hardware-independent means of identifying the destination network segment so that the datagram will pass efficiently through the routers to the correct segment

▶ Provide a means for converting the logical IP address of the destination computer to a physical address so that the data can be delivered to the network adapter of the destination computer

The most common version of IP is IPv4, although the world is theoretically in transition to a new version of IP known as IPv6. In this hour, you learn about the important IPv4 addressing system, and you learn how TCP/IP delivers datagrams on a complex network using the Internet layer's IP and ARP. You also learn about the Internet layer's ICMP protocol, which provides error detection and troubleshooting. For a discussion of the alternative IPv6 address system, which may eventually be the standard for Internet communication, see Hour 13.

Internet Layer and OSI

The Internet layer corresponds to the OSI Network layer, which is sometimes called Layer 3.

Internet Protocol

The Internet Protocol (IP) provides a hierarchical, hardware-independent addressing system and offers the services necessary for delivering data on a complex, routed network. Each network adapter on a TCP/IP network has a unique IP address.

The Host

Descriptions of TCP/IP often talk about a *computer* having an IP address. A computer is sometimes said to have an IP address because most computers have only one network adapter. However, computers with multiple network adapters are also common. A computer that is acting as a router or a proxy server, for instance, must have more than one network adapter and, therefore, has more than one IP address. The term *host* is often used for a network device associated with an IP address.

Under some operating systems, it is also possible to assign more than one IP address to a single network adapter.

IP addresses on the network are organized so that you can tell the location of the host—the network or subnet where the host resides—by looking at the address (see Figure 4.2). In other words, part of the address is a little like a ZIP code (describing a general location), and part of the address is a little like the street address (describing an exact location within that general area).

It is easy for a person to look at Figure 4.2 and say, "Every address that starts with 192.132.134 must be in Building C." A computer, though, requires a bit more hand-holding. The IP address is therefore divided into two parts:

▶ The network ID

▶ The host ID

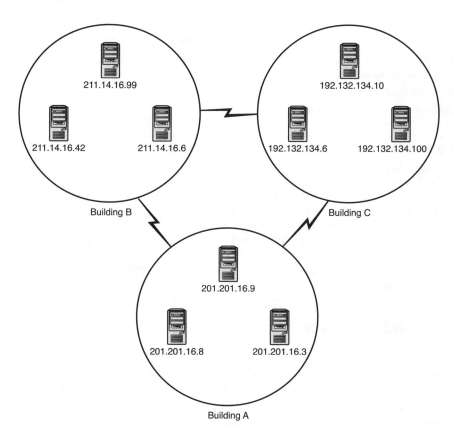

FIGURE 4.2
You can tell the network by looking at the address.

211.14.16.99

211.14.16.42   211.14.16.6

192.132.134.10

192.132.134.6   192.132.134.100

Building B   Building C

201.201.16.9

201.201.16.8   201.201.16.3

Building A

The network must provide a means for determining which part of the IP address is the **network ID** and which part is the **host ID**. Unfortunately, the variety and com-plexity of networks in the real world precludes a simple, one-size-fits-all solution to this problem. Big networks must reserve a large number of host bits for their large number of hosts. Small networks do not need many bits to give each host a unique ID; however, the vast number of small networks means that more bits of the IP address are necessary for the network ID.

As you learn later in this chapter, the original solution to this problem was to divide the IP address space into a series of address classes. Class A networks used the first 8 bits of the address for the network ID; Class B used the first 16 bits; Class C networks used the first 24 bits. This system was extended through a feature called subnetting to provide greater control at the local level for structuring the network.

A more recent technique known as classless interdomain routing (CIDR) essentially renders the address class system unnecessary. CIDR, which is now quite common on the Internet, offers a simple, flexible, and unambiguous notation for allocating blocks of IP addresses.

If you plan to make your way around TCP/IP networks, it is important to become familiar with both the class-based addressing system and CIDR addressing. You learn more about these techniques in Hour 5, "Subnetting and CIDR." For now, just keep in mind that the purpose of these notation schemes is the same: to divide the IP address into a network ID and a host ID.

> **Subnetting**
>
> Study this hour and Hour 5 together. Until you learn about subnet IDs and CIDR, you haven't really mastered the art of IP addressing. The information on IPv6 in Hour 13 is also important for building a full understanding of Internet addressing. Although the open Internet is transitioning to full support of IPv6, the widespread use of Network Address Translation (and the lack of finished applications that make use of IPv6's enhanced features) means that IPv4 will probably still be relevant for the foreseeable future. As you learn in Hour 13, IPv4 addresses map to the IPv6 address space (and thus provide some forward compatibility with the next-generation IP).

IP Header Fields

Every IP datagram begins with an IP header. The TCP/IP software on the source computer constructs the IP header. The TCP/IP software at the destination uses the information enclosed in the IP header to process the datagram. The IP header contains a great deal of information, including the IP addresses of the source and destination computers, the length of the datagram, the IP version number, and special instructions to routers.

> **More on Headers**
>
> For additional information about IP headers, see RFC 791.

The minimum size for an IP header is 20 bytes. Figure 4.3 shows the contents on the IP header.

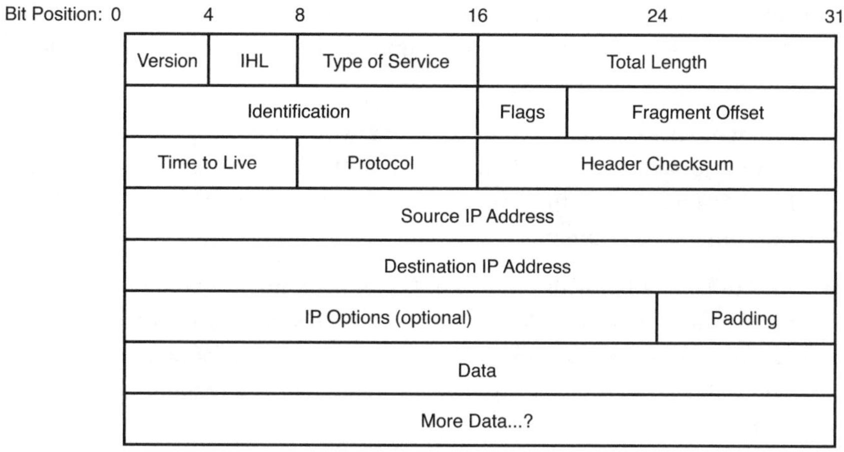

FIGURE 4.3
IP header field.

The header fields in Figure 4.3 are as follows:

▶ **Version:** This 4-bit field indicates which version of IP is being used. The current version of IP is 4. The binary pattern for 4 is 0100.

▶ **IHL (Internet Header Length):** This 4-bit field gives the length of the IP header in 32-bit words. The minimum header length is five 32-bit words. The binary pattern for 5 is 0101.

▶ **Type of Service:** The source IP can designate special routing information. Some routers ignore the Type of Service field, although this field recently has received more attention with the emergence of quality of service (QoS) technologies. The primary purpose of this 8-bit field is to provide a means of prioritizing datagrams that are waiting to pass through a router. Most implementations of IP today simply put all 0s in this field.

▶ **Total Length:** This 16-bit field identifies the length, in octets, of the IP datagram. This length includes the IP header and the data payload.

▶ **Identification:** This 16-bit field is an incrementing sequence number assigned to messages sent by the source IP. When a message is sent to the IP layer and it is too large to fit in one datagram, IP fragments the message into multiple datagrams, giving all datagrams the same identification number. This number is used on the receiving end to reassemble the original message.

▶ **Flags:** The Flags field indicates fragmentation possibilities. The first bit is unused and should always have a value of 0. The next bit is called the DF (Don't Fragment) flag. The DF flag signifies whether fragmentation is allowed (value = 0) or not (value = 1). The next bit is the MF (More

Fragments) flag, which tells the receiver that more fragments are on the way. When MF is set to 0, no more fragments need to be sent or the datagram never was fragmented.

- ▶ **Fragment Offset:** This 13-bit field is a numeric value assigned to each successive fragment. IP at the destination uses the fragment offset to reassemble the fragments into the proper order. The offset value found here expresses the offset as a number of 8-byte units.

- ▶ **Time To Live (TTL):** This bit field indicates the amount of time in seconds or router hops that the datagram can survive before being discarded. Every router examines and decrements this field by at least 1, or by the number of seconds the datagram is delayed inside the router. The datagram is discarded when this field reaches 0.

    A **hop** represents the number of routers a datagram must cross on the way to its destination. If a datagram passes through five routers before arriving at its destination, the destination is said to be five hops, or five router hops, away.

- ▶ **Protocol:** The 8-bit Protocol field indicates the protocol that will receive the data payload. A datagram with the protocol identifier 6 (binary 00000110) is passed up the stack to the TCP module, for example. The following are some common protocol values:

Protocol Name	Protocol Identifier
ICMP	1
TCP	6
UDP	17

- ▶ **Header Checksum:** This field holds a 16-bit calculated value to verify the validity of the header only. This field is recomputed in every router as the TTL field decrements.

- ▶ **Source IP Address:** This 32-bit field holds the address of the source of the datagram.

- ▶ **Destination IP Address:** This 32-bit field holds the destination address of the datagram and is used by the destination IP to verify correct delivery.

- ▶ **IP Options:** This field supports a number of optional header settings primarily used for testing, debugging, and security. Options include Strict Source Route (a specific path router path that the datagram should follow),

Internet Timestamp (a record of timestamps at each router), and security restrictions.

▶ **Padding:** The IP Options field may vary in length. The Padding field provides additional 0 bits so that the total header length is an exact multiple of 32 bits. (The header must end after a 32-bit word because the IHL field measures the header length in 32-bit words.)

▶ **IP Data Payload:** This field typically contains data destined for delivery to TCP or UDP (in the Transport layer), ICMP, or IGMP. The amount of data is variable but could include thousands of bytes.

IP Addressing

An IP address is a 32-bit binary address. This 32-bit address is subdivided into four 8-bit segments called **octets**. Humans do not work well with 32-bit binary addresses or even 8-bit binary octets, so the IP address is almost always expressed in what is called **dotted-decimal** format. In dotted-decimal format, each octet is given as an equivalent decimal number. The four decimal values (4 x 8 = 32 bits) are then separated with periods. Eight binary bits can represent any whole number from 0 to 255, so the segments of a dotted-decimal address are decimal numbers from 0 to 255. You have probably seen examples of dotted-decimal IP addresses on your computer, in this book, or in other TCP/IP documents. A dotted-decimal IP address looks like this: 209.121.131.14.

Part of the IP address is used for the network ID, and part of the address is used for the host ID. As you learned earlier in this hour, the original scheme for specifying the network and host ID is through a system of **address classes**. Although the more recent CIDR classless addressing has reduced the importance of the class system, address classes are still important enough to describe here as a starting point for understanding addressing in TCP/IP. See Hour 5 for more on IP addressing techniques.

The address class system divides the IP address space into address classes. Most IP addresses fall into the following classes:

▶ **Class A addresses:** The first 8 bits of the IP address are used for the network ID. The final 24 bits are used for the host ID.

▶ **Class B addresses:** The first 16 bits of the IP address are used for the network ID. The final 16 bits are used for the host ID.

▶ **Class C addresses:** The first 24 bits of the IP address are used for the network ID. The final 8 bits are used for the host ID.

More bits lead to more bit combinations. As you might guess, the Class A format provides a small number of possible network IDs and a huge number of possible host IDs for each network. A Class A network can support approximately 2^{24}, or 16,777,216 hosts. A Class C network, on the other hand, can provide host IDs for only a small number of hosts (254, which is 2^8, or 256, minus the unusable all 0s and all 1s addresses), but many more combinations of network IDs are available in the Class C format.

You might be wondering how a computer or router knows whether to interpret an IP address as a Class A, Class B, or Class C address. The designers of TCP/IP wrote the address rules such that the class of an address is obvious from the address itself. The first few bits of the binary address specify whether the address should be interpreted as a Class A, Class B, or Class C address (see Table 4.1). The rules for interpreting addresses are as follows:

▶ If the 32-bit binary address starts with a 0 bit, the address is a Class A address.

▶ If the 32-bit binary address starts with the bits 10, the address is a Class B address.

▶ If the 32-bit binary address starts with the bits 110, the address is a Class C address.

This scheme (thankfully) is easy to convert to dotted-decimal notation because these rules have the effect of limiting the range of values for the first term in the dotted-decimal address. For instance, because a Class A address must have a 0 bit in the leftmost place of the first octet, the first term in a Class A dotted-decimal address cannot be higher than 127. You learn more about converting binary numbers to decimal later in this hour. For purposes of this discussion, Table 4.1 shows the address ranges for Class A, B, and C networks. Note that some address ranges are listed as excluded addresses. Certain IP address ranges are not assigned to networks because they are reserved for special uses. You learn more about special IP addresses later in this hour.

TABLE 4.1 Address Ranges for Class A, B, and C Networks

Address Class	Binary Address Must Begin With	First Term of Dotted-Decimal Address Must Be	Excluded Addresses
A	0	0 to 127	10.0.0.0 to 10.255.255.255
			127.0.0.0 to 127.255.255.255
B	10	128 to 191	172.16.0.0 to 172.31.255.255
C	110	192 to 223	192.168.0.0 to 192.168.255.255

By the
Way

Classes D and E

The Internet specifications also define special-purpose Class D and Class E addresses. Class D addresses are used for multicasting. A **multicast** is a single message sent to a subset of the network, as opposed to a broadcast, which is processed by all nodes on the local net. The four leftmost bits of a Class D network address always start with the binary pattern 1110, which corresponds to decimal numbers 224 through 239. Class E networks are considered experimental and are not normally used in production environments. The five leftmost bits of a Class E network always start with the binary pattern 11110, which corresponds to decimal numbers 240 through 247.

The owner of a network can divide the network into smaller subnetworks called **subnets**. Subnetting essentially borrows some of the bits of the host ID to create additional networks within the network. As you can probably guess, Class A and B networks, with their large host ID address spaces, make extensive use of subnetting. Subnetting is also used on Class C networks. You learn more about subnetting in Hour 5.

By the
Way

Unique or Not

Theoretically, every computer on the Internet must have a unique IP address. In practice, the use of proxy server software and Network Address Translation (NAT) devices makes it possible for unregistered and nonunique addresses to operate on the Internet. You learn more about NAT devices in Hour 12, "Configuration."

Converting a 32-Bit Binary Address to Dotted-Decimal Format

Binary (base 2) numbers are similar to decimal (base 10) numbers except that the place values are multiples of 2 instead of multiples of 10. As Figure 4.4 shows, a decimal whole number begins with the ones place on the right, and each successive value to the left is a higher multiple of 10. A value of a decimal number is just the sum of the values for each decimal place. For instance, (as shown) the value of the decimal number 126,325 is determined as follows: (1 x 100,000) + (2 x 10,000) + (6 x 1000) + (3 x 100) + (2 x 10) + (5 x 1) = 126,325.

A binary whole number also starts with the ones place on the right. Each successive value to the left is a higher multiple of 2 (see Figure 4.5).

FIGURE 4.4
The base 10
number system.

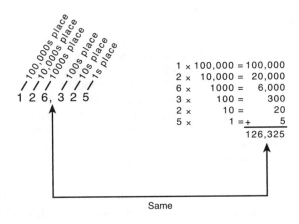

FIGURE 4.5
The binary
(base 2) num-
ber system.

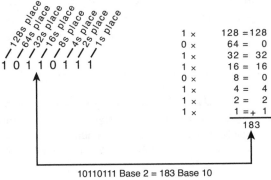

10110111 Base 2 = 183 Base 10

> **By the Way**
>
> **Zeroes and Ones**
>
> Computers work in binary because a bit pattern of 0s and 1s corresponds easily
> to the discrete on and off states used within digital circuitry.

To determine the decimal equivalent of a binary value, add the place values of any
bit that holds a 1. Remember that the IP address is comprised of four octets that
must each be converted separately to decimal format. Following is an example
showing how to convert a 32-bit binary IP address to dotted-decimal format.

To convert the binary address 01011001000111011100110000011000, follow these
steps:

1. First break the address into 8-bit octets:

   Octet 1: 01011001
   Octet 2: 00011101
   Octet 3: 11001100
   Octet 4: 00011000

2. Convert each octet to a decimal number. This process is illustrated in
   Table 4.2.

TABLE 4.2 Converting a Binary Address to Dotted-Decimal Format

Octet	Binary Value	Calculation	Decimal Value
1	01011001	1 + 8 + 16 + 64	89
2	00011101	1 + 4 + 8 + 16	29
3	11001100	4 + 8 + 64 + 128	204
4	00011000	8 + 16	24

3. Write out the decimal equivalent values in order from left to right. Separate the values with periods:

   The address is 89.29.204.24.

If you need more practice converting a binary address to dotted-decimal format, check the "Workshop" section at the end of this hour.

Converting a Decimal Number to a Binary Octet

The process of converting a decimal number to binary is a matter of going backward through the process shown in Figure 4.5. If you need to convert a dotted-decimal address to a 32-bit binary address, convert each period-separated number in the address to a binary octet and then concatenate the octets. The following procedure shows how to convert the decimal number 207 to a binary octet.

More Places

This procedure assumes you started with a decimal number representing an IP address octet. If the number you are converting is higher than 255, you need to extend the binary place value diagram shown in Figure 4.5 and adapt the procedure accordingly.

By the Way

To convert the decimal number 207 to a binary octet, follow these steps:

1. Compare the decimal number you want to convert (in this case 207) to the number 128. If the decimal number is greater than or equal to 128, subtract 128 and write down a 1. If the decimal number is less than 128, subtract 0 and write down a 0.

   207 > 128
   207 − 128 = 79
   Write down 1 for the 128's place
   Answer so far: 1

2. Take the result from step 1 (79 in this case) and compare it to the number 64. If the decimal number is greater than or equal to 64, subtract 64 and write down a 1. If the decimal number is less than 64, subtract 0 and write down a 0.

   79 > 64

79 – 64 = 15
Write down a 1 for the 64's place
Answer so far: 11

3. Take the result from step 2 (15 in this case) and compare it to the number 32. If the decimal number is greater than or equal to 32, subtract 32 and write down a 1. If the decimal number is less than 32, subtract 0 and write down a 0.

    15 < 32
    15 – 0 = 15
    Write down a 0 in the 32's place
    Answer so far: 110

4. Compare the result from step 3 to the number 16. If the number is greater than or equal to 16, subtract 16 and write down a 1. If the number is less than 16, subtract 0 and write down a 0.

    15 < 16
    15 – 0 = 15
    Write down a 0 in the 16's place
    Answer so far: 1,100

5. Compare the result of step 4 to the number 8. If the decimal number is greater than or equal to 8, subtract 8 and write down a 1. If the decimal number is less than 8, subtract 0 and write down a 0.

    15 > 8
    15 – 8 = 7
    Write down a 1 in the 8's place
    Answer so far: 11001

6. Compare the result of step 5 to the number 4. If the decimal number is greater than or equal to 4, subtract 4 and write down a 1. If the decimal number is less than 4, subtract 0 and write down a 0.

    7 > 4
    7 – 4 = 3
    Write down a 1 in the 4's place
    Answer so far: 110011

7. Compare the result of step 6 to the number 2. If the decimal number is greater than or equal to 2, subtract 2 and write down a 1. If the decimal number is less than 2, subtract 0 and write down a 0.

    3 > 2
    3 – 2 = 1
    Write down a 1 in the 2's place
    Answer so far: 1100111

8. If the result of step 7 is a 1, write down a 1. If the result of step 7 is a 0, write down a 0.

    1 = 1
    Write down a 1 in the 1's place
    Final answer: 11001111

You have now converted the decimal number 207 to its binary equivalent 11001111.

Special IP Addresses

A few IP addresses have special meanings and are not assigned to specific hosts. An all-0 host ID refers to the network itself. For instance, the IP address 129.152.0.0 refers to the Class B network with the network ID 129.152.

An all-1s host ID signifies a broadcast. A broadcast is a message sent to all hosts on the network. The IP address 129.152.255.255 is the broadcast address for the Class B network with the network ID 129.152. (Note that the dotted-decimal term 255 corresponds to the all-ones binary octet 11111111.)

The address 255.255.255.255 can also be used for broadcast on the network.

Addresses beginning with the decimal number 127 are loopback addresses. A message addressed to a loopback address is sent by the local TCP/IP software to itself. The loopback address is used to verify that the TCP/IP software is functioning. See the discussion of the ping utility in Hour 14, "TCP/IP Utilities." The loopback address 127.0.0.1 is commonly used.

RFC 1597 (which was later updated with RFC 1918) reserves some IP address ranges for private networks. The assumption is that these private address ranges are not connected to the Internet, so the addresses don't have to be unique. In today's world, these private address ranges are often used for the protected network behind Network Address Translation (NAT) devices, which you learn about in Hour 12.

- ▶ 10.0.0.0 to 10.255.255.255

- ▶ 172.16.0.0 to 172.31.255.255

- ▶ 192.168.0.0 to 192.168.255.255

Because the private address ranges don't have to be synchronized with the rest of the world, the complete address range is available for any network. A network administrator using these private addresses has more room for subnetting, and many more assignable addresses.

The address range 169.254.0.0 to 169.255.255.255 is reserved for autoconfiguration. You learn more about the Zeroconf system and other autoconfiguration protocols in Hour 12.

Address Resolution Protocol

As you learned earlier in this hour, the computers on a local network use an Internet layer protocol called **Address Resolution Protocol (ARP)** to map IP addresses to physical addresses. A host must know the physical address of the destination network adapter to send any data to it. For this reason, ARP is an important protocol. However, TCP/IP is implemented in such a way that ARP and all the details of physical address translation are almost totally invisible to the user. As far as the user is concerned, a network adapter is identified by its IP address. Behind the scenes, though, the IP address must be mapped to a physical address for a message to reach its destination (see Hour 3).

Each host on a network segment maintains a table in memory called the ARP table or ARP cache. The ARP cache associates the IP addresses of other hosts on the network segment with physical addresses (see Figure 4.6). When a host needs to send data to another host on the segment, the host checks the ARP cache to determine the physical address of the recipient. The ARP cache is assembled dynamically. If the address that is to receive the data is not currently listed in the ARP cache, the host sends a broadcast called an ARP request frame.

FIGURE 4.6
ARP maps IP addresses to physical addresses.

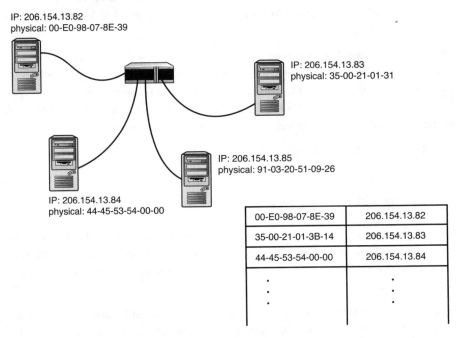

The ARP request frame contains the unresolved IP address. The ARP request frame also contains the IP address and physical address of the host that sent the request. The other hosts on the network segment receive the ARP request, and the host that owns the unresolved IP address responds by sending its physical address to the host that sent the request. The newly resolved IP address-to-physical address mapping is then added to the ARP cache of the requesting host.

Typically, the entries in the ARP cache expire after a predetermined period. When the lifetime of an ARP entry expires, the entry is removed from the table. The resolution process begins again the next time the host needs to send data to the IP address of the expired entry.

Reverse ARP

RARP stands for Reverse ARP. RARP is the opposite of ARP. ARP is used when the IP address is known but the physical address is not known. RARP is used when the physical address is known but the IP address is not known. RARP is often used in conjunction with the **BOOTP** protocol to boot diskless workstations.

BOOTP (Boot PROM)

Many network adapters contain an empty socket for insertion of an integrated circuit known as a boot PROM. The boot PROM firmware starts as soon as the computer is powered on. It loads an operating system into the computer by reading it from a network server instead of a local disk drive. The operating system downloaded to the BOOTP device is preconfigured for a specific IP address.

By the Way

Internet Control Message Protocol

Data sent to a remote computer often travels through one or more routers; these routers can encounter a number of problems in sending the message to its ultimate destination. Routers use **Internet Control Message Protocol (ICMP)** messages to notify the source IP of these problems. ICMP is also used for other diagnosis and troubleshooting functions.

The most common ICMP messages are listed here. Quite a few other conditions generate ICMP messages, but their frequency of occurrence is quite low.

▶ **Echo Request and Echo Reply:** ICMP is often used during testing. A technician who uses the ping command to check connectivity with another host is using ICMP. The ping command sends a datagram to an IP address and requests the destination computer to return the data sent in a response datagram. The commands actually used by ping are the ICMP Echo Request and Echo Reply.

▶ **Source Quench:** If a fast computer is sending large amounts of data to a remote computer, the volume can overwhelm the router. The router might use ICMP to send a Source Quench message to the source IP to ask it to slow down the rate at which it is shipping data. If necessary, additional source quenches can be sent to the source IP.

▶ **Destination Unreachable:** If a router receives a datagram that cannot be delivered, ICMP returns a `Destination Unreachable` message to the source IP. One reason that a router cannot deliver a message is a network that is down because of equipment failure or maintenance.

▶ **Time Exceeded:** ICMP sends this message to the source IP if a datagram is discarded because TTL reaches 0. This indicates that the destination is too many router hops away to reach with the current TTL value, or it indicates router table problems that cause the datagram to loop through the same routers continuously.

A **routing loop** occurs when a datagram circulates endlessly and never reaches its destination. Suppose three routers are located in Los Angeles, San Francisco, and Denver. The Los Angeles router sends datagrams to San Francisco, which sends them to Denver, which sends them back to Los Angeles again. The datagram becomes trapped and will circulate continuously through these three routers until the TTL reaches 0. A routing loop should not occur, but occasionally it does. Routing loops sometimes occur when a network administrator places static routing entries in a routing table.

▶ **Fragmentation Needed:** ICMP sends this message if it receives a datagram with the `Don't Fragment` bit set and if the router needs to fragment the datagram to forward it to the next router or the destination.

Other Internet Layer Protocols

A number of other protocols also inhabit the Internet layer. Some of these other protocols, such as Border Gateway Protocol (BGP) and Routing Information Protocol (RIP), facilitate the routing process. See Hour 8, "Routing," for more on routing in TCP/IP.

The IPsec protocols, which are optional in IPv4 but are an integral part of IPv6, operate at the Internet layer to provide secure encrypted communication (see Hour 11, "TCP/IP Security"). Other Internet layer protocols assist with tasks such as multicasting. As mentioned earlier, the Internet protocol layer is known in OSI shorthand as Layer 3. Any protocol referred to as a Layer 3 protocol is operating at the Internet layer.

Summary

In this hour, you learned about the Internet layer protocols IP, ARP, RARP, and ICMP. IP provides a hardware-independent addressing system for delivering data over the network. You learned about binary and dotted-decimal IP address formats and about the IP address classes A, B, C, D, and E. You also learned about ARP, a protocol that resolves IP addresses to physical addresses. RARP is the opposite of ARP, a protocol that lets a diskless computer query a server for its own IP address. ICMP is a protocol used for diagnosis and testing.

Q&A

Q. *What common address notation is used to simplify a 32-bit binary address?*

A. Dotted-decimal notation.

Q. *ARP returns what type of information when given an IP address?*

A. The corresponding physical (or MAC) address.

Q. *If a router is unable to keep up with the volume of traffic, what type of ICMP message is sent to the source IP?*

A. A Source Quench message.

Q. *What class does an IP address belong to that starts with the binary pattern 110 as the 3 leftmost bits?*

A. A Class C network.

Workshop

The following workshop is composed of a series of quiz questions and practical exercises. The quiz questions are designed to test your overall understanding of the current material. The practical exercises are intended to afford you the opportunity to apply the concepts discussed during the current hour, as well as build upon the knowledge acquired in previous hours of study. Please take time to complete the quiz questions and exercises before continuing. Refer to Appendix A, "Answers to Quizzes and Exercises," for answers.

Quiz

1. What is the purpose of the TTL field in the IP header?

2. How big are the network and host ID fields for a Class A address?

3. What is an octet?

4. What is the IP address an address of?

5. What is the difference between ARP and RARP?

Exercises

1. Convert the following binary octets to their decimal number equivalents:

00101011	Answer = 43
01010010	Answer = 82
11010110	Answer = 214
10110111	Answer = 183
01001010	Answer = 74
01011101	Answer = 93
10001101	Answer = 141
11011110	Answer = 222

2. Convert the following decimal numbers to their binary-octet equivalents:

13	Answer = 00001101
184	Answer = 10111000
238	Answer = 11101110
37	Answer = 00100101
98	Answer = 01100010
161	Answer = 10100001
243	Answer = 11110011
189	Answer = 10111101

3. Convert the following 32-bit IP addresses into dotted-decimal notation:

11001111 00001110 00100001 01011100	Answer = 207.14.33.92
00001010 00001101 01011001 01001101	Answer = 10.13.89.77
10111101 10010011 01010101 01100001	Answer = 189.147.85.97

Key Terms

Review the following list of key terms:

- **Address Class:** A classification system for IP addresses. The network class determines how the address is subdivided into a network ID and host ID.

- **Address Resolution Protocol (ARP):** A key Internet layer protocol used to obtain the physical address associated with an IP address. ARP maintains a cache of recently resolved physical address-to-IP address pairs.

- **BOOTP:** A protocol used to boot a computer or other network device from a remote location.

- **Dotted Decimal:** Base 10 representation of a binary IP address using 4 numerals representing the 4 octets of the original address, separated by periods (209.121.131.14).

- **Host ID:** A portion of the IP address that refers to a node on the network. Each node within a network should have an IP address that contains a unique host ID.

- **Internet Control Message Protocol (ICMP):** A key Internet layer protocol used by routers to send messages that inform the source IP of routing problems. ICMP is also used by the ping command to determine the status of other hosts on the network.

- **Internet Protocol (IP):** A key Internet layer protocol used for addressing, delivering, and routing datagrams.

- **Multicast:** A technique that allows datagrams to be delivered to a group of hosts simultaneously.

- **Network ID:** A portion of the IP address that identifies the network.

- **Octet:** An eight-digit binary number.

- **Reverse Address Resolution Protocol (RARP):** A TCP/IP protocol that returns an IP address if given a physical address. This protocol is typically used by a diskless workstation that has a remote boot PROM installed in its network adapter.

- **Subnet:** A logical division of a TCP/IP address space.

HOUR 5

Subnetting and CIDR

What You'll Learn in This Hour:

▶ Subnetting
▶ Subnet masks
▶ CIDR notation

Subnetting evolved as a means for using IP addressing to break up a physical network into smaller logical entities called subnets. Later developments, such as classless interdomain routing (CIDR, discussed at the end of this hour) and IPv6 (see Hour 13, "IPv6: The Next Generation"), have reduced the need for the classical approach to subnetting, but these later techniques borrow from the basic subnetting principles, and no discussion of TCP/IP is complete without a description of subnetting. This hour addresses the needs and benefits of subnetting and describes the steps and procedures you should follow to generate a subnet mask.

At the completion of this hour, you will be able to

▶ Explain how subnets are used

▶ Explain the benefits of subnetting

▶ Develop a subnet mask that meets business needs

▶ Describe supernetting and CIDR notation

Subnets

An IP address must identify both the host and the network where that host resides. As you learned in Hour 4, "The Internet Layer," the IP address class system gives a clue for how to distinguish the network and host portion of the address. But the address class system is too inflexible to do the job alone. In the real world, networks come in all sizes, and many networks are divided into smaller units. Furthermore, the world is running out of class-level networks. Internet service providers (ISPs) and network admins need a flexible way to subdivide a class-level network so that datagrams arrive at routers serving a smaller address space.

Subnetting lets you break the network into smaller units called **subnets.** The concept of a subnet originally evolved around the address class system, and subnetting is best explained in the context of Class A, B, and C networks. However, hardware vendors and the Internet community have settled on a new system for interpreting addresses called **classless interdomain routing (CIDR)** that doesn't require an emphasis on address class. This chapter starts with a look at subnetting in the address class system and then takes on the topic of CIDR notation.

Dividing the Network

The address class system described in Hour 4 enables all hosts to identify the network ID in an IP address and send a datagram to the correct network. However, identifying a network segment by its Class A, B, or C network ID presents some limitations. The principal limitation of the address class system is that it doesn't provide any logical subdivision of the address space beneath the network level.

Figure 5.1 shows a Class A network. As described in Hour 4, datagrams arrive efficiently at the gateway and pass into the 99.0.0.0 address space. However, the picture gets more complicated when you consider how to deliver the datagram after it passes into the 99.0.0.0 address space. A Class A network has room for over 16 million host IDs. This network could include millions of hosts, many more than would be possible on a single subnet.

FIGURE 5.1
Delivering data
to a Class A
network.

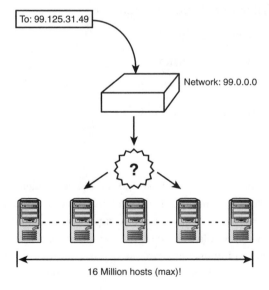

To: 99.125.31.49

Network: 99.0.0.0

?

16 Million hosts (max)!

To provide for more efficient delivery on a large network, the address space can be subdivided into smaller network segments (see Figure 5.2). Segmenting into separate physical networks increases the overall capacity of the network and, therefore, enables the network to use a greater portion of the address space. In this common scenario, the routers that separate the segments within the address space need some indication of where to deliver the data. They can't use the network ID because every datagram sent to the network has the same network ID (99.0.0.0). Though it might be possible to organize the address space by host ID, such a solution would be very cumbersome, inflexible, and totally impractical on a network with 16 million hosts. The only practical solution is to create some subdivision of the address space beneath the network ID so that the hosts and routers can tell from the IP address which network segment should receive the delivery.

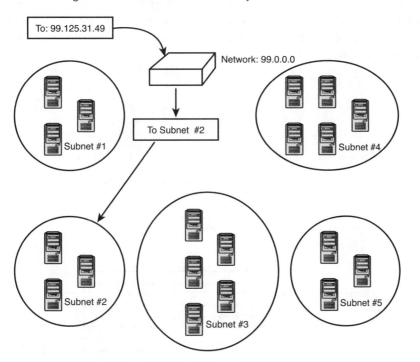

FIGURE 5.2
Organizing the network for efficient delivery.

Subnetting provides that second tier of logical organization beneath the network ID. The routers can deliver a datagram to a subnet address within the network (generally corresponding to a network segment), and when the datagram reaches the subnet, it can be resolved to a physical address using ARP (see Hour 4).

You are probably wondering where this subnet address comes from, because all 32 bits of the IP address are used for the network ID and the host ID. The answer is that the designers of TCP/IP provided a means to borrow some of the bits from the host ID to designate a subnet address. A parameter called the **subnet mask** tells how much of the address should be used for the subnet ID and how much is left for the actual host ID.

Like an IP address, a subnet mask is a 32-bit binary number. The bits of the subnet mask are arranged in a pattern that reveals the subnet ID of the IP address to which the mask is associated. Figure 5.3 shows an IP address/subnet mask pair. Each bit position in the subnet mask represents a bit position in the IP address. The subnet mask uses a 1 for every bit in the IP address that is part of the network ID or subnet ID. The subnet mask uses a 0 to designate any bit in the IP address that is part of the host ID. You can think of the subnet mask as a map used for reading the IP address. Figure 5.4 shows the allocation of address bits in a subnetted network versus a nonsubnetted network.

FIGURE 5.3
An IP address/
subnet mask
pair.

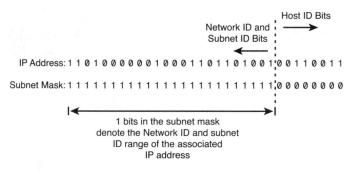

FIGURE 5.4
Allocation of
address bits in
a subnetted
network versus
a nonsubnetted
network.

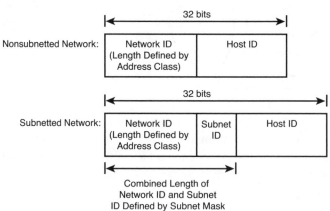

The routing tables used by routers and hosts on a subnetted network include information on the subnet mask associated with each IP address. (You learn more about routing in Hour 8, "Routing.") As Figure 5.5 shows, an incoming datagram is routed to the network using the network ID field, which is determined by the address class (see Hour 4). When the datagram reaches the network, it is routed to the proper segment using the subnet ID. After it reaches the segment, the host ID is used to deliver the datagram to the correct computer.

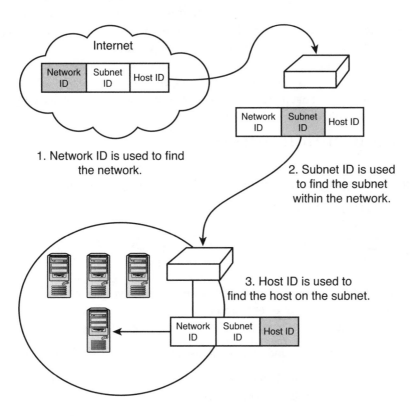

FIGURE 5.5
Incoming datagrams on a subnetted network.

Converting a Subnet Mask to Dotted-Decimal Notation

The network administrator typically assigns a subnet mask to each host as part of the TCP/IP configuration. If the host receives an IP address through DHCP (see Hour 12, "Automatic Configuration"), the DHCP server can assign a subnet mask along with the IP address.

Subnet masks must be carefully calculated and must reflect the internal organization of the network. All the hosts within a subnet should have the same subnet ID and subnet mask. For the benefit of people, the subnet mask is usually expressed in dotted-decimal notation similar to the notation used for an IP address.

As you'll recall from the preceding section, the subnet mask is a 32-bit binary number. You can convert the binary subnet mask to a dotted-decimal address using the address conversion techniques described in Hour 4. A subnet mask is usually much easier to convert to dotted-decimal format than an IP address. The subnet mask bits representing the IP address's network ID and the subnet ID are 1 bits. The bits representing the IP address's host ID are 0 bits. This means that (with a few rare and bewildering exceptions) the 1 bits are all on the left and the 0 bits are all on the right. Any full octet of 1s in the subnet mask appears as 255 (binary 11111111) in the dotted-decimal subnet mask. Any full octet of 0s appears as 0 (binary 00000000) in the subnet mask. Hence, the common subnet mask

> 11111111111111111111111100000000

is expressed in dotted-decimal notation as 255.255.255.0. Likewise, the subnet mask

> 11111111111111110000000000000000

is expressed in dotted-decimal notation as 255.255.0.0.

As you can see, it is easy to determine the dotted-decimal equivalent of a subnet mask that divides the address at an octet boundary. However, some subnet masks do not divide the address at an octet boundary. In that case, you must simply determine the decimal equivalent of the mixed octet (the octet containing both 1s and 0s).

To convert a binary subnet mask to dotted-decimal notation, follow these steps:

1. Divide the subnet mask into octets by writing the 32-bit binary subnet mask with periods inserted at the octet boundaries:

   11111111.11111111.11110000.00000000

2. For every all-1s octet, write down **255**. For every all-0s octet, write down **0**.

3. Convert the mixed octet to decimal using the binary conversion techniques discussed in Hour 4. To summarize, add up the bit position values for all 1 bits (refer to Figure 4.5).

4. Write down the final dotted-decimal address:

255.255.240.0

In most cases, this dotted-decimal subnet mask is the value you will enter as part of a computer's TCP/IP configuration.

Working with Subnets

The subnet mask defines how many bits after the network ID are used for the subnet ID. The subnet ID can vary in length, depending on the value you select for the subnet mask. As the subnet ID grows larger, fewer bits are left for the host ID. In other words, if your network has many subnets, you are limited to fewer hosts on each subnet. If you have only a few subnets and require only a few bits for the subnet ID, you can place more hosts on a subnet.

Class and Mask

Note that the address class also defines how many bits will be available for the subnet ID. The mask

11111111111111111110000000000000

specifies 19 bits for the network ID and subnet ID together. If this mask is used with a Class B address (which has a 16-bit network ID), only 3 bits are available for subnetting. The same mask is used with a Class A address (which has an 8-bit network ID); 11 bits are available for subnetting.

By the Way

The assignment of subnet IDs (and hence the assignment of a subnet mask) depends on your network configuration. The best solution is to plan your network first and determine the number and location of all network segments; then assign each segment a subnet ID. You'll need enough subnet bits to assign a unique subnet ID to each subnet. Save room, if possible, for additional subnet IDs in case your network expands.

A simple example of subnetting is a Class B network in which the third octet (the third term in the dotted-decimal IP address) is reserved for the subnet number. In Figure 5.6, the network 129.100.0.0 is divided into four subnets. The IP addresses on the network are given the subnet mask 255.255.255.0, signifying that the network ID and subnet mask span three octets of the IP address. Because the address is a Class B address (see Hour 4), the first two octets in the address form the network ID. Subnet A in Figure 5.6, therefore, has the following parameters:

▶ **Network ID:** 129.100.0.0

▶ **Subnet ID:** 0.0.128.0

Network/subnet and host IDs of either all 1s or all 0s cannot be assigned. The configuration shown in Figure 5.6, therefore, supports a possible 254 subnets and 254 addresses per subnet. This is a very sensible solution so long as you don't have more than 254 addresses on a subnet and as long as you have access to a Class B network address (which is getting harder to find).

FIGURE 5.6
A subnetted
Class B network.

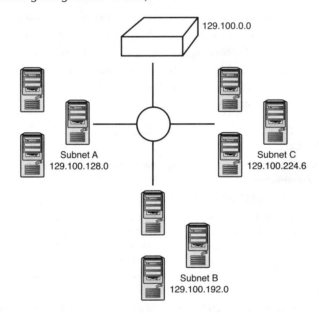

129.100.0.0

Subnet A
129.100.128.0

Subnet C
129.100.224.6

Subnet B
129.100.192.0

It often isn't possible to assign a full octet to the subnet ID. On a Class C network, for instance, if you assigned a full octet to the subnet ID, you wouldn't have any bits left for the host ID. Even on a Class B network, you might not be able to use a full octet for the subnet ID, because you might need to make room for more than 254 hosts on a subnet. The subnetting rules do not require you to place the subnet ID at an octet boundary. The concept of a subnet ID that doesn't fall on an octet boundary is easy to visualize in binary form but becomes a bit more confusing when you return to dotted-decimal format.

By the Way

Zeroes and Ones

Although use of the all zero subnet and all ones subnet is officially discouraged, some router manufacturers are unwilling to give up this valuable address space and support them anyway.

Consider a Class C network that must be divided into five small subnets. The class addressing rules provide 8 bits after the network ID to use for the subnet ID and the host ID in a Class C network. You could designate three of those bits for the subnet ID using this subnet mask:

11111111111111111111111111100000

The remaining 5 bits are then available for the host ID. The 3 bits of the subnet ID provide eight possible bit patterns. As mentioned earlier, the official subnetting rules exclude the all-1s pattern and the all-0s pattern from the pool of subnet IDs (although many routers actually support the assignment of the all-1s or all-0s subnet ID). In any case, this configuration is sufficient for six small subnets. The 5 bit places of the host ID offer 32 possible bit combinations. Excluding the all-0s pattern and the all-1s pattern, the subnets could each hold 30 hosts.

To express this subnet mask in dotted-decimal notation, follow the procedure described in the preceding section:

1. Add periods to mark the octet boundaries:

    11111111.11111111.11111111.11100000

2. Write down **255** for each all-1s octet. Convert the mixed octet to decimal:

    128 + 64 + 32 = 224

3. The dotted-decimal version of this subnet mask is 255.255.255.224.

Suppose you start placing hosts on this subnetted network (see Figure 5.7). Because this network is a Class C network, the first three octets are the same for all hosts. To obtain the fourth octet of the IP address, simply write down the binary subnet ID and host ID in their respective bit positions. In Figure 5.7, for instance, the subnet ID field for Subnet C has the bit pattern 011. Because this pattern is on the left end of the octet, the bit positions of the subnet ID actually represent the pattern 01100000, which means that the subnet number is 96. If the host ID is 17 (binary 10001), the fourth octet is 01110001, which converts to 113. The IP address of this host is, therefore, 212.114.32.113.

Naming Subnets

Many admins would still call the subnet in this example subnet 3 (for 011 binary) and would simply say that subnet 3 is represented by the number 96 (01100000 or 96) in these kinds of conversion calculations.

By the Way

FIGURE 5.7
A subnetted
Class C net-
work.

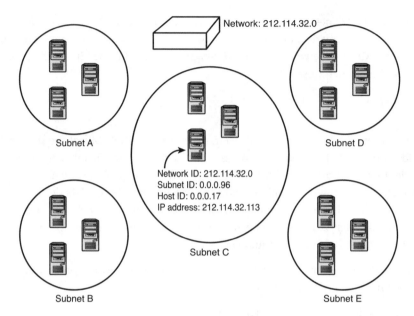

Network: 212.114.32.0

Subnet A

Network ID: 212.114.32.0
Subnet ID: 0.0.0.96
Host ID: 0.0.0.17
IP address: 212.114.32.113

Subnet D

Subnet C

Subnet B

Subnet E

Table 5.1 shows the binary pattern equivalents of the dotted-notation subnet masks. This table shows all valid subnet mask patterns. The Description column in Table 5.1 tells how many additional 1 bits are present beyond the 1 bits present in the default mask provided by the class designation. These mask bits are available for the subnet ID. For example, the default Class A mask has eight 1 bits; the row that displays 2 mask bits means there are 8 plus 2 (or a total of 10) 1 bits present in the subnet mask.

TABLE 5.1   Subnet Mask Dotted Notation to Binary Pattern

Description	Dotted Notation	Binary Pattern
Class A		
Default Mask	255.0.0.0	11111111 00000000 00000000 00000000
1 subnet bit	255.128.0.0	11111111 10000000 00000000 00000000
2 subnet bits	255.192.0.0	11111111 11000000 00000000 00000000
3 subnet bits	255.224.0.0	11111111 11100000 00000000 00000000
4 subnet bits	255.240.0.0	11111111 11110000 00000000 00000000
5 subnet bits	255.248.0.0	11111111 11111000 00000000 00000000
6 subnet bits	255.252.0.0	11111111 11111100 00000000 00000000
7 subnet bits	255.254.0.0	11111111 11111110 00000000 00000000
8 subnet bits	255.255.0.0	11111111 11111111 00000000 00000000

TABLE 5.1   Subnet Mask Dotted Notation to Binary Pattern

Description	Dotted Notation	Binary Pattern
9 subnet bits	255.255.128.0	11111111 11111111 10000000 00000000
10 subnet bits	255.255.192.0	11111111 11111111 11000000 00000000
11 subnet bits	255.255.224.0	11111111 11111111 11100000 00000000
12 subnet bits	255.255.240.0	11111111 11111111 11110000 00000000
13 subnet bits	255.255.248 0	11111111 11111111 11111000 00000000
14 subnet bits	255.255.252.0	11111111 11111111 11111100 00000000
15 subnet bits	255.255.254.0	11111111 11111111 11111110 00000000
16 subnet bits	255.255.255.0	11111111 11111111 11111111 00000000
17 subnet bits	255.255.255.128	11111111 11111111 11111111 10000000
18 subnet bits	255.255.255.192	11111111 11111111 11111111 11000000
19 subnet bits	255.255.255.224	11111111 11111111 11111111 11100000
20 subnet bits	255.255.255.240	11111111 11111111 11111111 11110000
21 subnet bits	255.255.255.248	11111111 11111111 11111111 11111000
22 subnet bits	255.255.255.252	11111111 11111111 11111111 11111100
Class B		
Default Mask	255.255.0.0	11111111 11111111 00000000 00000000
1 subnet bit	255.255.128.0	11111111 11111111 10000000 00000000
2 subnet bits	255.255.192.0	11111111 11111111 11000000 00000000
3 subnet bits	255.255.224.0	11111111 11111111 11100000 00000000
4 subnet bits	255.255.240.0	11111111 11111111 11110000 00000000
5 subnet bits	255.255.248.0	11111111 11111111 11111000 00000000
6 subnet bits	255.255.252.0	11111111 11111111 11111100 00000000
7 subnet bits	255.255.254.0	11111111 11111111 11111110 00000000
8 subnet bits	255.255.255.0	11111111 11111111 11111111 00000000
9 subnet bits	255.255.255.128	11111111 11111111 11111111 10000000
10 subnet bits	255.255.255.192	11111111 11111111 11111111 11000000
11 subnet bits	255.255.255.224	11111111 11111111 11111111 11100000
12 subnet bits	255.255.255.240	11111111 11111111 11111111 11110000
13 subnet bits	255.255.255.248	11111111 11111111 11111111 11111000
14 subnet bits	255.255.255.252	11111111 11111111 11111111 11111100

TABLE 5.1 Subnet Mask Dotted Notation to Binary Pattern

Description	Dotted Notation	Binary Pattern
Class C		
Default Mask	255.255.255.0	11111111 11111111 11111111 00000000
1 subnet bit	255.255.255.128	11111111 11111111 11111111 10000000
2 subnet bits	255.255.255.192	11111111 11111111 11111111 11000000
3 subnet bits	255.255.255.224	11111111 11111111 11111111 11100000
4 subnet bits	255.255.255.240	11111111 11111111 11111111 11110000
5 subnet bits	255.255.255.248	11111111 11111111 11111111 11111000
6 subnet bits	255.255.255.252	11111111 11111111 11111111 11111100

By the Way

Impractical Mask

Some of the patterns in Table 5.1 are not practical and are included for illustration purposes only. For instance, a Class C network with 6 subnet bits has only 2 bits left for assigning host IDs. Of those 2 bits, the all-1s address (11) is reserved for broadcast, and the all-0s address (00) is typically not used. This subnet, therefore, only has room for two hosts.

Classless Interdomain Routing

In February 2011, Internet Corporation for Assigned Names and Numbers (ICANN) announced that it was officially out of IPv4 addresses. As you learned in Hour 4 (and learn more about in Hour 13), the long-term solution to the problem of IP address depletion is the new IPv6 address system, which provides many more available addresses. However, just because ICANN is out of unassigned addresses doesn't mean the world has stopped using them. ISPs buy, sell, trade, and assign classic IPv4 addresses all the time. This high-volume trade in IP addresses, and the need to limit the proliferation of address entries in routing tables, has led to another form of routing notation that provides a more uniform means for aggregating and subdividing the IP address space.

Class A addresses are long gone, and the world is quickly running out of Class B addresses. Class C addresses are still available, but the small address space of a Class C network (254 hosts maximum) is a severe limitation in the high-volume game of ISPs. It is possible to assign a range of Class C networks to a network owner who needs more than 254 addresses. However, treating multiple Class C networks as separate entities when they are all going to the same place only clutters up routing tables unnecessarily.

As you learned earlier in this hour, the address class system is relatively inflexible and requires a subnetting system for more granular control. Classless interdomain routing (CIDR) is a more fluid and flexible technique for defining blocks of addresses in routing tables. The CIDR system does not depend on a predefined network ID of 8, 16, or 24 bits. Instead, a single number called the CIDR prefix specifies the number of bits within the address that serve as the network ID. This prefix is sometimes called a variable-length subnet mask (VLSM). The prefix can fall anywhere within the address space, giving admins a flexible means for defining subnets and a simple, convenient notation for specifying the boundary between the network and the host portion of the address. CIDR notation uses a slash (/) separator followed by a base 10 numeral to specify the number of bits in the network portion of the address. For example, in the CIDR address 205.123.196.183 /25, the /25 specifies that 25 bits of the address refer to the network, which corresponds to a subnet mask of 255.255.255.128.

The CIDR prefix essentially defines the number of leading bits in the IP address that are shared for all hosts within the network. One powerful feature of CIDR is that it doesn't just support subdividing of the network but also allows an ISP or admin to *aggregate* or combine multiple consecutive Class C networks into a single entity. This feature of CIDR has prolonged the life of the IPv4 Internet by greatly simplifying Internet routing tables. An ISP that leases a series of consecutive Class C networks needs only one entry to define them all. In this case, the CIDR prefix acts as what is called a **supernet mask**. For example, an ISP might be assigned all Class C addresses in the range 204.21.128.0 (11001100000101011000000000000000) to 204.21.255.255 (11001100000101011111111111111111).

The network addresses are identical up to the seventeenth bit counting from the left. The supernet mask would, therefore, be 11111111111111110000000000000000, which is equivalent to the dotted-decimal mask 255.255.128.0.

The address block is specified using the lowest address in the range followed by the supernet mask. Hence, the CIDR-enabled routing tables around the Internet can refer to this entire range of addresses with the single CIDR entry 204.21.128.0/17. This entry applies to all addresses that match the first 17 bits of the address 204.21.128.0.

Summary

This hour described how to divide a TCP/IP address space through subnetting. Subnetting adds an intermediate tier to the IP addressing structure, providing a means for grouping IP addresses in the address space below the network ID. Subnetting is a common feature on networks that include multiple physical segments separated by routers.

A more recent technique known as classless interdomain routing (CIDR) offers a flexible means for dividing the address space without the need for the address class system discussed in Hour 4.

Q&A

Q. *How large is the subnet ID field on a Class B network with the mask 255.255.0.0?*

A. Zero bits (no subnet ID field). The mask 255.255.0.0 is the default condition for a Class B network. All 16 mask bits are used for the network ID, and no bits are available for subnetting.

Q. *A network admin calculates that he needs 21 mask bits for his network. What subnet mask should he use?*

A. 21 mask bits: 111111111111111111111100000000000 is equivalent to two full octets plus an additional 5 bits. Each full octet is expressed in the mask as 255. The five bits in the third octet are equivalent to 128 + 64 + 32 + 16 + 8 = 248. The mask is 255.255.248.0.

Q. *You have a Class C network address. You also have employees at 10 locations, and each location has no more than 12 people. What subnet mask or masks would enable you to install a workstation for each user?*

A. The subnet mask 255.255.255.240 assigns 4 bits to the host ID, which is enough for each user to have a separate address.

Q. *Billy wants to use three subnet bits for subnetting on a Class A network. What should he use for a subnet mask?*

A. A Class A network means that the first octet will be devoted to the network ID. The first octet of the mask is equivalent to 255. The 3 subnet bits in the second octet are equivalent to 128 + 64 + 32 = 224. The subnet mask is 255.224.0.0.

Q. *What IP addresses are assigned in the CIDR range 212.100.192.0/20?*

A. The /20 supernet parameter specifies that 20 bits of the IP address will be constant and the rest will vary. The binary version of the initial address is

11010100.01100100.11000000.00000000

The first 20 bits of the highest address must be the same as the initial address, and the rest of the address bits can vary. Show the varying bits as the opposite end of the range (all 1s instead of all 0s):

11010100.01100100.11001111.11111111

The address range is 212.100.192.0 to 212.100.207.255.

Workshop

The following workshop is composed of a series of quiz questions and practical exercises. The quiz questions are designed to test your overall understanding of the current material. The practical exercises are intended to afford you the opportunity to apply the concepts discussed during the current hour, as well as build upon the knowledge acquired in previous hours of study. Please take time to complete the quiz questions and exercises before continuing. Refer to Appendix A, "Answers to Quizzes and Exercises," for answers.

Quiz

1. Where do the bits for the subnet ID come from?

2. Why isn't subnetting as important now as it was in the past?

3. What does classless in classless interdomain routing refer to?

4. How many hosts can there be on a /26 network?

5. What is combining several smaller networks into a single larger network range called?

Exercises

1. Calculate the CIDR network address you get if you combine the network addresses 180.4.0.0 through 180.7.255.255 into a single network?

2. Determine how many hosts are possible on the subnet 192.100.50.192 if the subnet mask is 255.255.255.224.

3. In Exercise 2, calculate how many subnets are possible with the given subnet mask?

4. Determine the lowest IP address representing a host in the network 195.50.100.0/23.

5. In Exercise 4, find the highest IP address representing a host.

Key Terms

Review the following list of key terms:

▶ **CIDR:** Classless interdomain routing. A technique that allows a block of network IDs to be treated as a single entity.

▶ **Subnet:** A logical subdivision of the address space defined by a TCP/IP network ID.

▶ **Subnet mask:** A 32-bit binary value used to assign some of the bits of an IP address to a subnet ID.

▶ **Supernet mask:** A 32-bit value used to aggregate multiple consecutive network IDs into a single entity.

HOUR 6

The Transport Layer

What You'll Learn in This Hour:

▶ Connections-oriented and connectionless protocols
▶ Ports and sockets
▶ TCP
▶ UDP

The Transport layer provides an interface for network applications and offers optional error checking, flow control, and verification for network transmissions. This hour describes some important Transport layer concepts and introduces the TCP and UDP protocols.

At the completion of this hour, you will be able to

▶ Describe the basic duties of the Transport layer

▶ Explain the difference between a connection-oriented protocol and a connectionless protocol

▶ Explain how Transport layer protocols provide an interface to network applications through ports and sockets

▶ Describe the differences between TCP and UDP

▶ Identify the fields that make up the TCP header

▶ Describe how TCP opens and closes a connection

▶ Describe how TCP sequences and acknowledges data transmissions

▶ Identify the four fields that comprise the UDP header

Introducing the Transport Layer

The TCP/IP Internet layer, as you learned in Hour 4, "The Internet Layer," and Hour 5, "Subnetting and CIDR," is full of useful protocols that are effective at providing the necessary addressing information so that data can make its journey across the network. Addressing and routing, however, are only part of the picture. The developers of TCP/IP knew they needed another layer above the Internet layer that would cooperate with IP by providing additional necessary features. Specifically, they wanted the Transport layer protocols to provide the following:

▶ **An interface for network applications:** That is, a way for applications to access the network. The designers wanted to be able to target data not just to a destination computer, but to a particular application running on the destination computer.

▶ **A mechanism for multiplexing/demultiplexing:** Multiplexing, in this case, means accepting data from different applications and computers and directing that data to the intended recipient application on the receiving computer. In other words, the Transport layer must be capable of simultaneously supporting several network applications and managing the flow of data to the Internet layer. On the receiving end, the Transport layer must accept the data from the Internet layer and direct it to multiple applications. This feature, known as **demultiplexing**, allows one computer to simultaneously support multiple network applications, such as a web browser, an email client, and a file-sharing application. Another aspect of multiplexing/demultiplexing is that a single application can simultaneously maintain connections with more than one computer.

▶ **Error checking, flow control, and verification:** The protocol system needs an overall scheme that ensures delivery of data between the sending and receiving machines.

The last item (error checking, flow control, and verification) is the most open ended. Questions of quality assurance always balance on questions of benefit and cost. An elaborate quality assurance system can increase your certainty that a delivery was successful, but you pay for it with increased network traffic and slower processing time. For many applications, this additional assurance simply isn't worth it. The Transport layer, therefore, provides two pathways to the network, each with the interfacing and multiplexing/demultiplexing features necessary for supporting applications, but each with a very different approach to quality assurance, as follows:

▶ **Transport Control Protocol (TCP):** TCP provides extensive error control and flow control to ensure the successful delivery of data. TCP is a connection-oriented protocol.

▶ **User Datagram Protocol (UDP):** UDP provides extremely rudimentary error checking and is designed for situations when TCP's extensive control features are not necessary. UDP is a connectionless protocol.

You learn more about connection-oriented and connectionless protocols and about the TCP and UDP protocols later in this hour.

Transport in OSI

The TCP/IP Transport layer corresponds to the Open Systems Interconnection (OSI) model's Transport layer. OSI's Transport layer is also called Layer 4.

By the Way

Transport Layer Concepts

Before moving to a more detailed discussion of TCP and UDP, it is worth pausing for a moment to focus on a few of the important concepts:

▶ Connection-oriented and connectionless protocols

▶ Ports and sockets

▶ Multiplexing/demultiplexing

These important concepts are essential to understanding the design of the Transport layer. You learn about these concepts in the following sections.

Connection-Oriented and Connectionless Protocols

To provide the appropriate level of quality assurance for any given situation, developers have come up with two alternative protocol archetypes:

▶ A **connection-oriented protocol** establishes and maintains a connection between communicating computers and monitors the state of that connection over the course of the transmission. In other words, each package of data sent across the network receives an acknowledgment, and the sending machine records status information to ensure that each package is received without errors, retransmitting the data if necessary. At the end of the transmission, the sending and receiving computers gracefully close the connection.

▶ A **connectionless protocol** sends a one-way datagram to the destination and doesn't worry about officially notifying the destination machine that data is on the way. The destination machine receives the data and doesn't worry about returning status information to the source computer.

Figure 6.1 shows two people demonstrating connection-oriented communication. Of course, they are not intended to show the true complexity of digital communications but simply to illustrate the concept of a connection-oriented protocol.

FIGURE 6.1
Connection-
oriented
communication.

Figure 6.2 shows how the same data would be sent using a connectionless protocol.

FIGURE 6.2
Connectionless
communication.

Ports and Sockets

The Transport layer serves as an interface between network applications and the network and provides a method for addressing network data to particular applications. In the TCP/IP system, applications can address data through either the TCP or UDP protocol module using port numbers. A **port** is a predefined internal address that serves as a pathway from the application to the Transport layer or from the Transport layer to the application (see Figure 6.3). For instance, a client computer typically contacts a server's FTP application through TCP port 21.

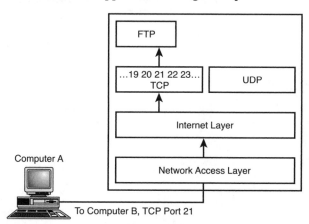

FIGURE 6.3
A port address targets data to a particular application.

A closer look at the Transport layer's application-specific addressing scheme reveals that TCP and UDP data is actually addressed to a socket. A **socket** is an address formed by concatenating the IP address and the port number. For instance, the socket number 111.121.131.141:21 refers to port 21 on the computer with the IP address 111.121.131.141.

Figure 6.4 shows how computers using TCP exchange socket information when they form a connection.

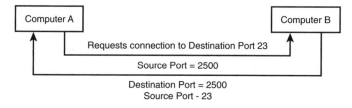

FIGURE 6.4
Exchanging the source and destination socket numbers.

The following is an example of how a computer accesses an application on a destination machine through a socket:

1. Computer A initiates a connection to an application on Computer B through a well-known port. A **well-known port** is a port number that is assigned to a specific application by the Internet Assigned Numbers

Authority (IANA). See Tables 6.1 and 6.2 for lists of some well-known TCP and UDP ports. Combined with the IP address, the well-known port becomes the destination socket address for Computer A. The request includes a data field telling Computer B which socket number to use when sending back information to Computer A. This is Computer A's source socket address.

TABLE 6.1   Well-Known TCP Ports

Service	TCP Port Number	Brief Description
tcpmux	1	TCP port service multiplexor
compressnet	2	Management utility
compressnet	3	Compression utility
echo	7	Echo
discard	9	Discard or null
systat	11	Users
daytime	13	Daytime
netstat	15	Network status
qotd	17	Quote of the day
chargen	19	Character generator
ftp-data	20	File Transfer Protocol data
ftp	21	File Transfer Protocol control
ssh	22	Secure Shell
telnet	23	Terminal network connection
smtp	25	Simple Mail Transport Protocol
nsw-fe	27	NSW user system
time	37	Time server
name	42	Hostname server
domain	53	Domain Name Server (DNS)
gopher	70	Gopher service
finger	79	Finger
http	80	WWW service
link	87	TTY link
supdup	95	SUPDUP Protocol
pop2	109	Post Office Protocol 2

TABLE 6.1 Well-Known TCP Ports

Service	TCP Port Number	Brief Description
pop3	110	Post Office Protocol 3
auth	113	Authentication service
uucp-path	117	UUCP path service
nntp	119	Usenet Network News Transfer Protocol
Netbios-ssnn	139	NetBIOS session service

TABLE 6.2 Well-Known UDP Ports

Service	UDP Port Number	Description
echo	7	Echo
discard	9	Discard or null
systat	11	Users
daytime	13	Daytime
qotd	17	Quote of the day
chargen	19	Character generator
time	37	Time server
domain	53	Domain Name Server (DNS)
bootps	67	Bootstrap protocol service/DHCP
bootpc	68	Bootstrap protocol client/DHCP
tftp	69	Trivial File Transfer Protocol
ntp	123	Network Time Protocol
netbios-ns	137	NetBIOS name
snmp	161	Simple Network Management Protocol
snmptrap	162	Simple Network Management Protocol trap

2. Computer B receives the request from Computer A through the well-known port and directs a response to the socket listed as Computer A's source address. This socket becomes the destination address for messages sent from the application on Computer B to the application on Computer A.

You learn more about how to initiate a TCP connection later in this hour.

Multiplexing/Demultiplexing

The socket addressing system enables TCP and UDP to perform another important Transport layer task: multiplexing and demultiplexing. As described earlier, multiplexing is the act of braiding input from several sources into a single output, and demultiplexing is the act of receiving input from a single source and delivering it to multiple outputs (see Figure 6.5).

Multiplexing/demultiplexing enables the lower levels of the TCP/IP stack to process data without regard to which application initiated that data. All associations with the originating application are settled at the Transport layer, and data passes to and from the Internet layer in a single, application-independent pipeline.

The key to multiplexing and demultiplexing is the socket address. Because the socket address combines the IP number with the port number, it provides a unique identifier for a specific application on a specific machine. See the FTP server depicted in Figure 6.6. All client machines use the well-known port address TCP 21 to contact the FTP server, but the destination socket for each of the connecting PCs is unique. Likewise, all network applications running on the FTP server use the server's IP address, but only the FTP service uses the socket address, consisting of the server's IP address plus TCP port 21.

FIGURE 6.5
Multiplexing and demultiplexing.

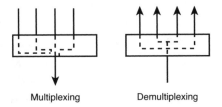

Multiplexing   Demultiplexing

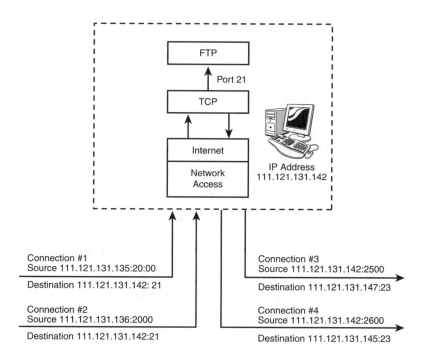

FIGURE 6.6
The socket address unique-ly identifies an application on a particular server.

Connection #1
Source 111.121.131.135:20:00
Destination 111.121.131.142: 21

Connection #2
Source 111.121.131.136:2000
Destination 111.121.131.142:21

Connection #3
Source 111.121.131.142:2500
Destination 111.121.131.147:23

Connection #4
Source 111.121.131.142:2600
Destination 111.121.131.145:23

Understanding TCP and UDP

As this hour has already mentioned, TCP is a connection-oriented protocol that pro-vides extensive error control and flow control. UDP is a connectionless protocol with much less sophisticated error control. You might say that TCP is built for reliability, and UDP is built for speed. Applications that must support interactive sessions, such as Telnet and FTP, tend to use TCP. Applications that do their own error checking or that don't need much error checking tend to use UDP.

A software developer designing a network application can choose whether to use TCP or UDP as a transport protocol. UDP's simpler control mechanisms should not necessarily be considered limiting. First, less quality assurance does not necessarily mean lower quality. The extra checks and controls provided by TCP are entirely unnecessary for many applications. In cases where error control and flow control are necessary, some developers prefer to provide those control features within the appli-cation itself, where they can be customized for the specific need, and to use the lean-er UDP transport for network access. The Application layer's Remote Procedure Call (RPC) protocol, for instance, can support sophisticated applications, but RPC devel-opers sometimes opt to use UDP at the Transport layer and provide error and flow control through the application rather than slowing down the connection with TCP.

TCP: The Connection-Oriented Transport Protocol

This hour has already described TCP's connection-oriented approach to communication. TCP has a few other important features that warrant mentioning:

- **Stream-oriented processing:** TCP processes data in a stream. This stream-oriented processing means that TCP can accept data a byte at a time rather than as a preformatted block. TCP formats the data into variable-length segments, which it will pass to the Internet layer.

- **Resequencing:** If data arrives at the destination out of order, the TCP module is capable of resequencing the data to restore the original order.

- **Flow control:** TCP's flow-control feature ensures that the data transmission won't outrun or overrun the destination machine's capability to receive the data. This is especially critical in a diverse environment in which there may be considerable variation of processor speeds and buffer sizes.

- **Precedence and security:** The Department of Defense specifications for TCP call for optional security and priority levels that can be set for TCP connections. Many TCP implementations, however, do not provide these security and priority features.

- **Graceful close:** TCP is as careful about closing a connection as it is about opening a connection. The graceful close feature ensures that all segments have been sent and received before a connection is closed.

A close look at TCP reveals a complex system of announcements and acknowledgments supporting TCP's connection-oriented structure. The following sections take a closer look at TCP data format, TCP data transmission, and TCP connections. The technical nature of this discussion should reveal how complex TCP really is. This discussion of TCP also underscores the fact that a protocol is more than just a data format: It is a whole system of interacting processes and procedures designed to accomplish a set of well-defined objectives.

As you learned in Hour 2, "How TCP/IP Works," layered protocol systems such as TCP/IP operate through an information exchange between a given layer on the sending machine and the corresponding layer on the receiving machine. In other words, the Network Access layer on the sending machine communicates with the Network Access layer on the computer that will read the frame. The Internet layer on the sending machine communicates with the Internet layer of the next computer on the delivery path, and so forth.

The TCP software communicates with the TCP software on the machine to which it has established (or wants to establish) a connection. In any discussion of TCP, if you hear the phrase "Computer A establishes a connection with Computer B," what that really means is that the TCP software of Computer A has established a connection with the TCP software of Computer B, both of which are acting on behalf of a local application. The subtle distinction yields an interesting observation concerning the concept of end-node verification that was introduced in Hour 1, "What Is TCP/IP?"

Recall that end nodes are responsible for verifying communications on a TCP/IP network. (The end nodes are the nodes that are actually attempting to communicate—as opposed to the intermediate nodes, which forward the message.) In a typical internetworking situation (see Figure 6.7), the data is passed from the source subnet to the destination subnet by routers. These routers typically operate at the Internet layer, the layer below the Transport layer. (You learn more about routers in Hour 8, "Routing.") The important point is that the routers are not concerned with the information at the Transport level. They simply pass on the Transport layer data as cargo for the IP datagram. The control and verification information encoded in a TCP segment is intended solely for the TCP software of the destination machine. This speeds up routing over TCP/IP internetworks (because routers do not have to participate actively in TCP's elaborate quality assurance ritual) and at the same time enables TCP to fulfill the Department of Defense's objective of providing a network with end-node verification.

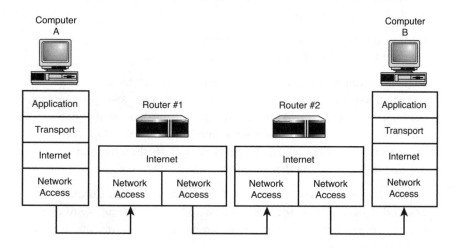

FIGURE 6.7
Routers forward but do not process Transport layer data.

TCP Data Format

The TCP data format is shown in Figure 6.8. The complexity of this structure reveals the complexity of TCP and the many facets of its functionality.

FIGURE 6.8
TCP data format.

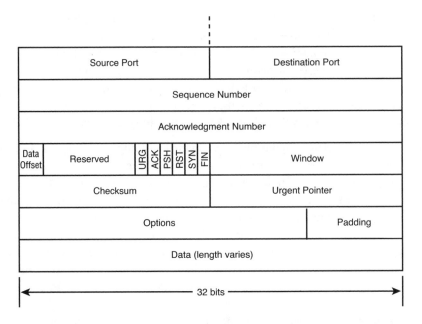

The fields are as follows. You'll have a better idea of how these data fields are used after reading the next section, which discusses TCP connections:

▶ **Source Port (16-bit):** The **source port** number is the port assigned to the application on the source machine.

▶ **Destination Port (16-bit):** The **destination port** number is the port assigned to the application on the destination machine.

▶ **Sequence Number (32-bit):** The **sequence number** of the first byte in this particular segment, unless the SYN flag is set to 1. If the SYN flag is set to 1, the Sequence Number field provides the initial sequence number (ISN), which is used to synchronize sequence numbers. If the SYN flag is set to 1, the sequence number of the first octet is one greater than the number that appears in this field (in other words, ISN + 1).

▶ **Acknowledgment Number (32-bit):** The **acknowledgment number** acknowledges a received segment. The value is the *next* sequence number the receiving computer is expecting to receive, in other words, the sequence number of the last byte received + 1.

▶ **Data offset (4 bits):** A field that tells the receiving TCP software how long the header is and, therefore, where the data begins. The data offset is expressed as an integer number of 32-bit words.

▶ **Reserved (6 bits):** Reserved for future use. The Reserved field provides room to accommodate future developments of TCP and must be all 0s.

▶ **Control flags (1 bit each):** The **control flags** communicate special information about the segment.

▶ **URG:** A value of 1 announces that the segment is urgent and the Urgent Pointer field is significant.

▶ **ACK:** An **ACK** value of 1 announces that the Acknowledgment Number field is significant.

▶ **PSH:** A value of 1 tells the TCP software to push all the data sent so far through the pipeline to the receiving application.

▶ **RST:** A value of 1 resets the connection.

▶ **SYN:** A **SYN** value of 1 announces that sequence numbers will be synchronized, marking the beginning of a connection. See the discussion of the three-way handshake, later in this hour.

▶ **FIN:** A value of 1 signifies that the sending computer has no more data to transmit. This flag is used to close a connection.

▶ **Window (16-bit):** A parameter used for flow control. The window defines the range of sequence numbers beyond the last acknowledged sequence number that the sending machine is free to transmit without further acknowledgment.

▶ **Checksum (16-bit):** A field used to check the integrity of the segment. A receiving computer performs a checksum calculation based on the segment and compares the value to the value stored in this field. TCP and UDP include a pseudo-header with IP addressing information in the checksum calculation. See the discussion of the UDP pseudo-header later in this hour.

▶ **Urgent Pointer (16-bit):** An offset pointer pointing to the sequence number that marks the beginning of any urgent information.

▶ **Options:** Specifies one of a small set of optional settings.

▶ **Padding:** Extra 0 or more bits (as needed) to ensure that the data begins on a 32-bit boundary.

▶ **Data:** The data being transmitted with the segment.

TCP needs all these data fields to successfully manage, acknowledge, and verify network transmissions. The next section shows how the TCP software uses some of these fields to manage the tasks of sending and receiving data.

TCP Connections

Everything in TCP happens in the context of a connection. TCP sends and receives data through a connection, which must be requested, opened, and closed according to the rules of TCP.

As you learned earlier in this hour, one of the reasons for TCP is to provide an interface so that applications can have access to the network. That interface is provided through the TCP ports and, to provide a connection through the ports, the TCP interface to the application must be open. TCP supports two open states:

▶ **Passive open:** A given application process notifies TCP that it is prepared to receive incoming connections through a TCP port. Thus, the pathway from TCP to the application is opened in anticipation of an incoming connection request.

▶ **Active open:** An application requests that TCP initiates a connection with another computer that is in the passive open state. (Actually, TCP can also initiate a connection to a computer that is in the active open state, in case both computers are attempting to open a connection at once.)

In a typical situation, an application wanting to receive connections, such as an FTP server, places itself and its TCP port status in a passive open state. On the client computer, the FTP client's TCP state is most likely closed until a user initiates a connection from the FTP client to the FTP server, at which time the state for the client becomes active open. The TCP software of the computer that switches to active open (that is, the client) then initiates the exchange of messages that leads to a connection. That exchange of information, the so-called three-way handshake, is discussed later in this hour.

A client is a computer requesting or receiving services from another computer on the network.

A server is a computer offering services to other computers on the network.

TCP sends segments of variable length; within a segment, each byte of data is assigned a sequence number. The receiving machine must send an acknowledgment for every byte it receives. TCP communication is thus a system of transmissions and acknowledgments. The Sequence Number and Acknowledgment Number fields of the TCP header (described in the preceding section) provide the communicating TCP software with regular updates on the status of the transmission.

A separate sequence number is not encoded with each individual byte. Instead, the Sequence Number field in the header gives the sequence number of the first byte of data in a segment.

There is one exception to this rule. If the segment occurs at the beginning of a connection (see the description of the three-way handshake later in this section), the Sequence Number field contains the **ISN**, which is actually one less than the sequence number of the first byte in the segment. (The first byte is ISN + 1.)

If the segment is received successfully, the receiving computer uses the Acknowledgment Number field to tell the sending computer which bytes it has received. The Acknowledgment Number field in the acknowledgment message will be set to the last received sequence number + 1. In other words, the Acknowledgment Number field defines which sequence number the computer is prepared to receive next.

If an acknowledgment is not received within the specified time period, the sending machine retransmits the data beginning with the byte after the last acknowledged byte.

Establishing a Connection

For the sequence/acknowledgment system to work, the computers must synchronize their sequence numbers. In other words, Computer B must know what initial sequence number (ISN) Computer A used to start the sequence. Computer A must know what ISN Computer B will use to start the sequence for any data Computer B will transmit.

This synchronization of sequence numbers is called a **three-way handshake**. The three-way handshake always occurs at the beginning of a TCP connection. The three steps of a three-way handshake are as follows:

1. Computer A sends a segment with

   SYN = 1

   ACK = 0

   Sequence Number = X (where X is Computer A's ISN)

   The active open computer (Computer A) sends a segment with the SYN flag set to 1 and the ACK flag set to 0. SYN is short for synchronize. This flag, as described earlier, announces an attempt to open a connection. This first segment header also contains the initial sequence number (ISN), which marks the beginning of the sequence numbers for data that Computer A will transmit. The first byte transmitted to Computer B will have the sequence number ISN + 1.

2. Computer B receives Computer A's segment and returns a segment with

   SYN = 1 (still in synchronization phase)

   ACK = 1 (the Acknowledgment Number field will contain a value)

   Sequence number = Y, where Y is Computer B's ISN

   Acknowledgment number = M + 1, where M is the last sequence number received from Computer A

3. Computer A sends a segment to Computer B that acknowledges receipt of Computer B's ISN:

   SYN = 0

   ACK = 1

   Sequence number = Next sequence number in series (M + 1)

   Acknowledgment number = N + 1 (where N is the last sequence number received from Computer B)

After the three-way handshake, the connection is open, and the TCP modules transmit and receive data using the sequence and acknowledgment scheme described earlier in this section.

TCP Flow Control

The Window field in the TCP header provides a flow control mechanism for the connection. The purpose of the Window field is to ensure that the sending computer doesn't send too much data too quickly, which could lead to a situation in which data is lost because the receiving computer can't process incoming segments as quickly as the sending computer can transmit them. The flow control method used by TCP is called the **sliding window** method. The receiving computer uses the Window field (also known as the **buffer size** field) to define a window of sequence numbers beyond the last acknowledged sequence number that the sending computer is authorized to transmit. The sending computer cannot transmit beyond that window until it receives the next acknowledgment.

Closing a Connection

When it is time to close the connection, the computer initiating the close, Computer A, places a segment in the queue with the FIN flag set to 1. The application then enters the **fin-wait state**. In the fin-wait state, Computer A's TCP software continues to receive segments and processes the segments already in the queue, but no additional data is accepted from the application. When Computer B receives the FIN segment, it returns an acknowledgment to the FIN, sends any remaining segments, and notifies the local application that a FIN was received. Computer B sends a FIN segment to Computer A, which Computer A acknowledges, and the connection is closed.

UDP: The Connectionless Transport Protocol

UDP is much simpler than TCP, and it doesn't perform any of the functions listed in the preceding section. However, there are a few observations about UDP that this hour should mention.

First, although UDP is sometimes described as having no error-checking capabilities, in fact, it is capable of performing rudimentary error checking. It is best to characterize UDP as having the capability for limited error checking. The UDP datagram includes a checksum value that the receiving machine can use to test the integrity of the data. (Often, this checksum test is optional and can be disabled on the receiving machine to speed up processing of incoming data.) The UDP datagram includes a pseudo-header that encompasses the destination address for the datagram, thus providing a means of checking for misdirected datagrams. Also, if the receiving UDP module receives a datagram directed to an inactive or undefined UDP port, it returns an Internet Control Message Protocol (ICMP) message notifying the source machine that the port is unreachable.

Second, UDP does not offer the **resequencing** of data provided by TCP. Resequencing is most significant on a large network, such as the Internet, where the segments of data might take different paths and experience significant delays in router buffers. On local networks, the lack of a resequencing feature in UDP typically does not lead to unreliable reception.

UDP and Broadcasts

UDP's lean, connectionless design makes it the protocol of choice for network broadcast situations. A broadcast **is** a single message that will be received and processed by all computers on the subnet. Understandably, if the source computer had to simultaneously open a TCP-style connection with every computer on the subnet to send a single broadcast, the result could be a significant erosion of network performance.

By the
Way

The primary purpose of the UDP protocol is to expose datagrams to the Application layer. The UDP protocol does little and, therefore, employs a simple header structure. The RFC that describes this protocol, RFC 768, is only three pages in length. As mentioned earlier, UDP does not retransmit missing or corrupted datagrams, sequence datagrams received out of order, eliminate duplicated datagrams, acknowledge the receipt of datagrams, or establish or terminate connections. UDP is primarily a mechanism for application programs to send and receive datagrams without the overhead of a TCP connection. The application can provide for any or all of these functions, if they are necessary for the application's purpose.

The UDP header consists of four 16-bit fields. Figure 6.9 shows the layout of the UDP datagram header.

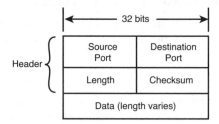

The following list describes these fields:

- ▶ **Source Port:** This field occupies the first 16 bits of the UDP header. This field typically holds the UDP port number of the application sending this datagram. The value entered in the Source Port field is used by the receiving application as a return address when it is ready to send a response. This field is considered optional, and it is not required that the sending application include its port number. If the sending application does not include its port number, the application is expected to place 16 0 bits into the field. Obviously, if there is no valid source port address, the receiving application will be unable to send a response. However, this might be the desired functionality, as in the case of a unidirectional message where no response is expected.

- ▶ **Destination Port:** This 16-bit field holds the port address to which the UDP software on the receiving machine will deliver this datagram.

- ▶ **Length:** This 16-bit field identifies the length in octets of the UDP datagram. The length includes the UDP header as well as the UDP data payload. Because the UDP header is eight octets in length, the value will always be at least 8.

- ▶ **Checksum:** This 16-bit field is used to determine whether the datagram was corrupted during transmission. The checksum is the result of a special calculation performed on a string of binary data. In the case of UDP, the checksum is calculated based on a pseudo-header, the UDP header, the UDP data, and possibly the filler 0 octets to build an even octet length checksum input. The checksums generated at the source and verified at the destination allow the client application to determine if the datagram has been corrupted.

Because the actual UDP header does not include the source or destination IP address, it is possible for the datagram to be delivered to the wrong computer or service. Part of the data used for the checksum calculation is a string of values extracted from the

IP header known as the **pseudo-header**. The pseudo-header provides destination IP addressing information so that the receiving computer can determine whether a UDP datagram has been misdelivered.

Other Transport Layer Protocols

A number of other protocols also operate from the Transport layer. Datagram Congestion Control Protocol (DCCP) and Stream Control Transmission Protocol (SCTP) provide some enhanced features not available with conventional TCP and UDP. The Real-time Transport Protocol (RTP) offers a structure for transmitting real-time audio and video.

Firewalls and Ports

A **firewall** is a system that protects a local network from attack by unauthorized users attempting to access the LAN from the Internet. The word *firewall* has entered the lexicon of Internet jargon, and it is one of many computer terms that can fall within a wide range of definitions. Firewalls perform a number of functions. However, one of the most basic features of a firewall is something that is pertinent to this hour.

That important feature is the capability of a firewall to block off access to specific TCP and UDP ports. The word *firewall*, in fact, is sometimes used as a verb, meaning to close off access to a port.

For example, to initiate a Secure Shell (SSH) session with the server, a client machine must send a request to SSH's well-known port address, TCP port 22. (You learn more about SSH in Hour 15, "Monitoring and Remote Access.") If you are worried about outside intruders accessing your server through SSH, you could configure the server to stop using port 22; for that matter, the server can simply stop using SSH altogether, but that extreme solution would prohibit authorized users on the LAN from using SSH for authorized activities. (Why have it if you're not going to use it?) An alternative is to install a firewall, as shown in Figure 6.10, and configure that firewall to block access to TCP port 22. The result is that users on the LAN, from inside the firewall, have free access to TCP port 22 on the server. Users from the Internet, outside the LAN, do not have access to the server's TCP port 22 and, therefore, cannot access the server through SSH. In fact, users from the Internet cannot use SSH at all to access any computer on the LAN.

This scenario uses SSH and TCP port 22 as an example. Firewalls typically block access to any or all ports that might pose a security threat. Network administrators often block access to all ports except those that are absolutely necessary, such as a port that handles incoming email. You often find devices that provide the company's Internet presence, such as a web server, placed outside the firewall so that access to the Internet device will not result in unauthorized access to the LAN.

FIGURE 6.10
A typical firewall
scenario.

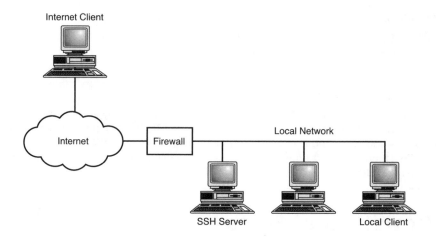

Summary

This hour covered some key features of TCP/IP's Transport layer. You learned about connection-oriented and connectionless protocols, multiplexing and demultiplexing, and ports and sockets. This hour also introduced TCP/IP's Transport layer protocols, TCP and UDP, and described some important TCP and UDP features. You learned how TCP fulfills the TCP/IP objective of providing end-node verification. You also learned about TCP data format, flow control, and error recovery, and the three-way handshake TCP uses to open a connection. This hour also described the format of a UDP header.

By the
Way

> **Both Ways**
>
> Just as a firewall can keep outside users from accessing services within the net-work, it can keep inside users from accessing services outside the network.

Q&A

Q. Why are multiplexing and demultiplexing necessary?

A. If TCP/IP did not provide multiplexing and demultiplexing, only one applica-tion could use the network software at a time, and only one computer could connect to a given application at a time.

Q. Why would a software developer use UDP for a transport protocol when TCP offers better quality assurance?

A. TCP's quality assurance comes at the price of slower performance. If the extra error control and flow control of TCP are not necessary, UDP is a better choice because it is faster.

Q. *Why do applications that support interactive sessions, such as Telnet and FTP, tend to use TCP rather than UDP?*

A. TCP's control and recovery features provide the reliable connection necessary for an interactive session.

Q. *Why would a network administrator want to use a firewall to intentionally close off Internet access to a TCP or UDP port?*

A. Internet firewalls close off access to specific ports to deny external users access to the applications that use those ports. Firewalls can also close off access to the Internet so that users on the internal LAN cannot make use of certain services available on the Internet.

Q. *Why don't routers send TCP connection acknowledgments to the computer initiating a connection?*

A. Routers operate at the Internet layer (below the Transport layer) and, therefore, do not process TCP information.

Q. *Would a functioning FTP server most likely be in a passive open, active open, or closed state?*

A. A working FTP server would most likely be in a passive open state, ready to accept an incoming connection.

Q. *Why is the third step in the three-way handshake necessary?*

A. After the first two steps, the two computers have exchanged ISN numbers, so theoretically they have enough information to synchronize the connection. However, the computer that sent its ISN in step 2 of the handshake still hasn't received an acknowledgment. The third step acknowledges the ISN received in the second step.

Q. *Which field is optional in the UDP header and why?*

A. The Source Port field. Because UDP is a connectionless protocol, the UDP software on the receiving machine does not have to know the source port. The source port is provided as an option in case the application receiving the data needs the source port for error checking or verification.

Q. *What happens if the source port is equal to 16 0 bits?*

A. The application on the destination machine will be unable to send a response.

Workshop

The following workshop is composed of a series of quiz questions and practical exercises. The quiz questions are designed to test your overall understanding of the current material. The practical exercises are intended to afford you the opportunity to apply the concepts discussed during the current hour, as well as build upon the knowledge acquired in previous hours of study. Please take time to complete the quiz questions and exercises before continuing. Refer to Appendix A, "Answers to Quizzes and Exercises," for answers.

Quiz

1. What service runs on TCP port 25?

2. What service runs on UDP port 53?

3. What is the largest record size that you can send with TCP?

4. What is the difference between a TCP active open and a TCP passive open?

5. What is the minimum number of steps to open a TCP connection?

Exercises

Imagine you were creating your own network service for one of the following purposes:

▶ To communicate with a remote user through a specialized hardware interface to provide real-time instruction for brain surgery procedures.

▶ To efficiently pass occasion statistical information from computers participating in a high-performance cluster.

▶ To let a primitive field device pass environmental data to a home network.

In each of these cases, think about whether you would design the service around the TCP or UDP transport protocol. In your analysis, consider the following factors:

▶ Performance

▶ Reliability

▶ Programming time

Keep in mind that the TCP and UDP protocols offer a collection of pre-defined functions, but they are only the starting point for a programmer who is implementing a complete application. TCP is more reliable than UDP, but that reliability comes at the cost of performance. It is possible to custom-code some of the reliability features associated through TCP, but that requires additional programming time.

Key Terms

Review the following list of key terms:

▶ **ACK:** A control flag specifying that the Acknowledgment Number field in the TCP header is significant.

▶ **Acknowledgment Number field:** A field in the TCP header specifying the next sequence number the computer is expecting to receive. The acknowledgment number, in effect, acknowledges the receipt of all sequenced bytes prior to the byte specified in the acknowledgment number.

▶ **Active open:** A state in which TCP is attempting to initiate a connection.

▶ **Connection-oriented protocol:** A protocol that manages communication by establishing a connection between the communicating computers.

▶ **Connectionless protocol:** A protocol that transmits data without establishing a connection with the remote computer.

▶ **Control flag:** A 1-bit flag with special information about a TCP segment.

▶ **Demultiplexing:** Directing a single input to several outputs.

▶ **Destination port:** The TCP or UDP port number of the application on the destination machine that will be the recipient of the data in a TCP segment or UDP datagram.

▶ **FIN:** A control flag used in the process of closing a TCP connection.

▶ **Firewall:** A device that protects a network from unauthorized Internet access.

▶ **Initial sequence number (ISN):** A number that marks the beginning of the range of numbers a computer will use for sequencing bytes transmitted through TCP.

▶ **Multiplexing:** Combining several inputs into a single output.

▶ **Passive open:** A state in which the TCP port (usually a server application) is ready to receive incoming connections.

▶ **Port:** An internal address that provides an interface from an application to a Transport layer protocol.

▶ **Pseudo-header:** A structure derived from fields from the IP header that is used to calculate the TCP or UDP checksum and to verify that the datagram has not been delivered to the wrong destination due to alteration of information in the IP header.

▶ **Resequencing:** Assembling incoming TCP segments so that they are in the order in which they were actually sent.

▶ **Sequence number:** A unique number associated with a byte transmitted through TCP.

▶ **Sliding window:** A window of sequence numbers that the receiving computer has authorized the sending computer to send. The sliding window flow control method is the method used by TCP.

▶ **Socket:** The network address for a particular application on a particular computer, consisting of the computer's IP address followed by the port number of the application.

▶ **Source port:** The TCP or UDP port number of the application sending a TCP segment or UDP datagram.

▶ **Stream-oriented processing:** Continuous (byte-by-byte) input, rather than input in predefined blocks of data.

▶ **SYN:** A control flag signifying that sequence number synchronization is taking place. The **SYN** flag is used at the beginning of a TCP connection as part of the three-way handshake.

▶ **TCP:** A reliable connection-oriented Transport protocol in the TCP/IP suite.

▶ **Three-way handshake:** A three-step procedure that synchronizes sequence numbers and begins a TCP connection.

▶ **UDP:** A nonreliable connectionless transport protocol in the TCP/IP suite.

▶ **Well-known port:** Predefined standard port numbers for common applications. Well-known ports are specified by the Internet Assigned Numbers Authority (IANA).

HOUR 7

The Application Layer

What You'll Learn in This Hour:

- ▶ Network services
- ▶ APIs
- ▶ TCP/IP utilities

At the top of TCP/IP's stack is the Application layer, a loose collection of networking components perched above the Transport layer. This hour describes some of the kinds of Application layer components and shows how those components help bring the user to the network. Specifically, this hour examines Application layer services, operating environments, and network applications.

At the completion of this hour, you'll be able to

- ▶ Describe the Application layer

- ▶ Describe some of the Application layer's network services

- ▶ List some of TCP/IP's important utilities

What Is the Application Layer?

The Application layer is the top layer in TCP/IP's protocol suite. In the Application layer, you find network applications and services that communicate with lower layers through the TCP and UDP ports discussed in Hour 6, "The Transport Layer." You might ask why the Application layer is considered part of the stack at all, as the TCP and UDP ports form such a well-defined interface to the network. But it is important to remember that, in a layered architecture such as TCP/IP, *every* layer is an interface to the network. The Application layer must be as aware of TCP and UDP ports as the Transport layer is and must channel data accordingly.

TCP/IP's Application layer is an assortment of network-aware software components sending information to and receiving information from the TCP and UDP ports. These Application layer components are not parallel in the sense of being logically similar or equivalent. Some of the components at the Application layer are simple utilities that collect information about the network configuration. Other Application layer components might be a user interface system (such as the X Window System interface) or an **application programming interface (API)** that supports a desktop operating environment. Some Application layer components provide services for the network, such as file and print services or name resolution services. (You learn more about name resolution in Hour 10, "Name Resolution.") This hour shows you some of the kinds of services and applications that are usually found in the Application layer. The actual implementation of these components hinges on details of programming and software design.

But first this hour begins with a quick comparison of TCP/IP's Application layer with the corresponding layers defined through TCP/IP's counterpart, the Open Systems Interconnection (OSI) model.

The TCP/IP Application Layer and OSI

As mentioned in Hour 2, "How TCP/IP Works," TCP/IP does not officially conform to the seven-layer OSI networking model. The OSI model, however, has been influential in the development of networking systems, and the trend toward multiprotocol networking has increased reliance on OSI terminology and concepts. The Application layer can draw from a vast range of operating and networking environments, and in many of those environments, the OSI model is an important tool for defining and describing network systems. A look at the OSI model will help you understand the processes that take place at the TCP/IP Application layer.

The TCP/IP Application layer corresponds with the OSI Application, Presentation, and Session layers (see Figure 7.1). The extra subdivisions of the OSI model (three layers instead of one) provide some additional organization of features that TCP/IP theorists have traditionally grouped into the heading of *Application-level* (sometimes called *Process/Application-level*) services.

Descriptions of the OSI layers corresponding to TCP/IP's Application layer are as follows:

▶ **Application layer:** OSI's Application layer (not to be confused with TCP/IP's Application layer) has components that provide services for user applications and support network access.

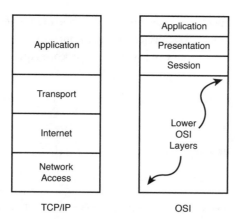

FIGURE 7.1
The Application layer corresponds to OSI's Application, Presentation, and Session layers.

▶ **Presentation layer:** The Presentation layer translates data into a platform-neutral format and handles encryption and data compression.

▶ **Session layer:** The Session layer manages communication between applications on networked computers. This layer provides some functions related to the connections that aren't available through the Transport layer, such as name recognition and security.

All of these services are not necessary for all applications and implementations. In the TCP/IP model, implementations are not required to follow the layering of these OSI subdivisions, but overall, the duties defined for OSI's Application, Presentation, and Session layers fall within the range of the TCP/IP Application layer's responsibility.

Network Services

Many Application layer components are network services. In earlier hours, you might have read that a layer of the protocol system provides services for other layers of the system. In many cases, these services are a well-defined, integral part of the protocol system. In the case of the Application layer, the services are not all required for the operation of the protocol software and are more likely provided for the direct benefit of a user or to link the network with the local operating system.

It is fair to say that the lower layers of the protocol stack relate to the mechanics of the communication process and are not especially relevant to the everyday user. The Application layer, on the other hand, hosts the great variety of network services that support the user experience: file services, remote-access services, email, and the HTTP web service protocol. In fact, a large portion of this book is dedicated to describing the network services that fall within the scope of the Application layer.

Table 7.1 describes some of the most important Application layer protocols and services. You learn more about these services in later hours, but in the meantime, the following sections highlight a few of the more significant Application layer activities, including

▶ File and print services

▶ Name resolution services

▶ Remote-access services

▶ Web services

Other important network services, such as mail services and network management services, are discussed in other hours.

TABLE 7.1   Some Application Layer Protocols

Protocol	Description
BitTorrent	A peer-to-peer file sharing protocol often used for fast download of large files on the Internet
Common Internet File System (CIFS)	Enhanced version of the SMB file service protocol
Domain Name System (DNS)	A hierarchical system for mapping Internet names to IP addresses
Dynamic Host Configuration Protocol (DHCP)	A protocol used for automatically assigning IP addresses and other network configuration parameters
File Transfer Protocol (FTP)	A popular protocol for uploading and downloading files
Finger	A protocol used for viewing and requesting user information
Hypertext Transfer Protocol (HTTP)	The communication protocol of the World Wide Web
Internet Message Access Protocol (IMAP)	A common protocol for accessing email messages
Lightweight Directory Access Protocol (LDAP)	A protocol used for implementing and managing information directory services
Network File System (NFS)	A protocol that provides a remote user with access to file resources
Network Time Protocol (NTP)	A protocol used for synchronizing clocks and other time sources over a TCP/IP network

TABLE 7.1   Some Application Layer Protocols

Protocol	Description
Post Office Protocol (POP)	A protocol used for downloading email from a mail server
Remote Procedure Call (RCP)	A protocol that lets a program on one computer call a subroutine or procedure on another computer
Server Message Block (SMB)	File and print service protocol
Simple Network Management Protocol (SNMP)	A protocol for managing network devices

File and Print Services

As you learned in earlier hours, a **server** is a computer that provides services for other computers. Two common services provided by network servers are **file service** and **print service**.

A print server operates a printer and fulfills requests to print documents on that printer. A file server operates a data storage device, such as a hard drive, and fulfills requests to read or write data to that device.

Because file service and print service are such common networking activities, they are often thought of together. Often the same computer (or sometimes even the same service) provides both file and print service capabilities. Whether they're together, the theory is the same. Figure 7.2 shows a typical file service scenario. A request for a file comes across the network and up through the Protocol layers to the Transport layer, where it is routed through the appropriate port to the file server service.

By the Way

Short Version

Figure 7.2 shows only the basic components as they relate to TCP/IP. In a real protocol and operating system implementation, additional layers or components might assist with forwarding the data to the file server service.

File service systems such as the UNIX/Linux Network File System (NFS), and Microsoft's Common Internet File System (CIFS) and Server Message Block (SMB) operate at the Application layer, as do the classic file transfer utilities File Transfer Protocol (FTP) and Trivial File Transfer Protocol (TFTP).

FIGURE 7.2
File service.

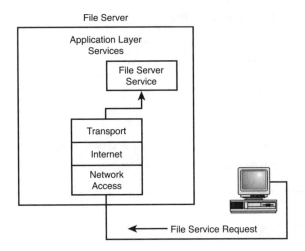

Name Resolution Services

As you learned in Hour 1, "What Is TCP/IP?" **name resolution** is the process of mapping predefined, user-friendly alphanumeric names to IP addresses. The Domain Name System (DNS) service provides name resolution for the Internet and can also provide name resolution for isolated TCP/IP networks. DNS uses **name servers** to resolve DNS name queries. A name server service runs at the Application layer of the name server computer and communicates with other name servers to exchange name resolution information. Other name resolution systems exist, such as Network Information Service (NIS), NetBIOS name resolution, and a number of name service variants associated with the Light Directory Access Protocol (LDAP).

Remote Access

The Application layer is home to a collection of technologies that let users initiate interactive connections from one computer to another. For instance, as you learn in Hour 15, "Monitoring and Remote Access," tools such as Telnet and Secure Shell (SSH) let the user log in to a remote system and send commands across the network. Modern screen-sharing tools offer a similar effect for desktop graphical user interface (GUI) systems.

To integrate the local environment with the network, some network operating systems use a service called a **redirector**. A redirector is sometimes called a requester.

A redirector intercepts service requests in the local computer and checks to see whether the request should be fulfilled locally or forwarded to another computer on the network. If the request is addressed to a service on another machine, the redirector redirects the request to the network (see Figure 7.3).

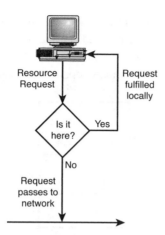

FIGURE 7.3
A redirector.

A redirector provides a general solution for the user to access network resources as if they were part of the local environment. For instance, a remote disk drive could appear as a local disk drive on the client machine.

Web Services

Hypertext Transfer Protocol (HTTP) is an Application layer protocol that is at the heart of the ecosystem we know as the World Wide Web. HTTP was originally intended for transmitting text and graphic images, but the evolution of the web service model has given rise to a collection of web-related protocols and components for building custom tools that operate within a web browser. You learn more about the web service paradigm in Hour 20, "Web Services."

APIs and the Application Layer

An application programming interface (API) is a predefined collection of programming components that an application can use to access other parts of the operating environment. Programs use API functions to communicate with the operating system. A network protocol stack is a classic application of the API concept. As shown in Figure 7.4, a network API provides an interface from the application to the protocol stack. The application program uses functions from the API to open and close connections and write or read data to the network.

The Sockets API was originally developed for Berkeley Software Distribution (BSD) UNIX as an interface for applications to access the TCP/IP protocol stack. Sockets is now used widely on other systems as a program interface for TCP/IP. Several years ago, Microsoft created a version of the Sockets interface called WinSock. In Windows 3.1 and earlier, the user had to install and configure an implementation of WinSock to set up TCP/IP networking. Starting with Windows 95, Microsoft built a TCP/IP program interface directly in to the Windows operating system.

FIGURE 7.4
A network API enables an application to access the network through TCP/IP.

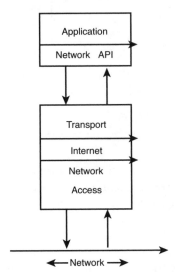

Network APIs such as the Sockets API receive data through a socket (see Hour 6) and pass that data to the application. These APIs therefore are operating at the Application layer.

TCP/IP Utilities

Other residents of the Application layer are TCP/IP's utilities (shown in Table 7.2). The TCP/IP utilities originally were developed around the Internet and early UNIX networks. These utilities are now used to configure, manage, and troubleshoot TCP/IP networks throughout the world, and versions of these utilities are available with Windows and other network operating systems.

TABLE 7.2 TCP/IP Utilities

Utility	Description
Connectivity Utilities	
IPConfig	A Windows utility that displays TCP/IP configuration settings. (The UNIX utility ifconfig is similar.)
Ping	A utility that tests for network connectivity.
Arp	A utility that lets you view (and possibly modify) the Address Resolution Protocol (ARP) cache of a local or remote computer. The ARP cache contains the physical address to IP address mappings (see Hour 4, "The Internet Layer").
Traceroute	A utility that traces the path of a datagram through the internetwork.
Route	A utility that lets you view, add, or edit entries in a routing table (see Hour 8, "Routing").
Netstat	A utility that displays IP, UDP, TCP, and ICMP statistics.
NBTstat	A utility that displays statistics on NetBIOS and NBT.
Hostname	A utility that returns the hostname of the local host.
File Transfer Utilities	
Ftp	A basic file transfer utility that uses TCP.
Tftp	A basic file transfer utility that uses UDP. Tftp is used for tasks such as downloading code to network devices.
Rcp	A simple remote file transfer utility.
Remote Utilities	
Telnet	A remote terminal utility.
Rexec	A utility that runs commands on a remote computer through the rexecd daemon.
Rsh	A utility that invokes the shell on a remote computer to execute a command.
Finger	A utility that displays user information.
Internet Utilities	
Browsers	Utilities that provide access to World Wide Web HTML content.
Newsreaders	Utilities that connect with Internet newsgroups.

TABLE 7.2   TCP/IP Utilities

Utility	Description
Email readers	Utilities that provide a means of sending and receiving email.
Archie	A once-popular Internet utility that provides access to indexes of anonymous FTP sites. The World Wide Web and its search engines have reduced the importance of Archie.
Gopher	A menu-based Internet information utility. Like Archie, Gopher looks old-fashioned next to the World Wide Web and is no longer popular.
Whois	A utility that provides access to directories with personal contact information, similar to Internet white pages.

Summary

This hour introduced TCP/IP's Application layer and described some of the applications and services the Application layer supports. You also learned about some of TCP/IP's native utilities.

Q&A

Q. *A computer that is acting as a file server is running and is connected to the network, but the users can't access files. What could be wrong?*

A. Any number of things could be wrong, and a closer look at the particular operating system and configuration will yield a more detailed analysis. For purposes of understanding this hour, the first step is to check to see whether the computer's file server service is running. A file server is not just a computer; it is a service running on that computer that fulfills file requests.

Q. *Why does the OSI model divide the functions of the Application layer into three separate layers (Session, Presentation, and Application)?*

A. The Application layer provides a broad range of services, and the additional subdivisions defined in the OSI model offer a modular structure that helps software developers organize the components. The additional layers also offer additional options for application developers to interface their programs with the protocol stack.

Workshop

The following workshop is composed of a series of quiz questions and practical exercises. The quiz questions are designed to test your overall understanding of the current material. The practical exercises are intended to afford you the opportunity to apply the concepts discussed during the current hour, as well as build upon the knowledge acquired in previous hours of study. Please take time to complete the quiz questions and exercises before continuing. Refer to Appendix A, "Answers to Quizzes and Exercises," for answers.

Quiz

1. What network utility enables you to check connectivity?

2. What Application layer protocol is used to load web pages?

3. What two Application layer protocols are used to retrieve mail?

4. What protocol maps host names to IP addresses?

5. What protocol is used to synchronize computer clocks?

Exercise

Most of the topics introduced in this hour are described in greater detail later in this book. The standard TCP/IP configuration utilities that reside at the Application layer are for configuration and network troubleshooting. To get a first glimpse at the TCP/IP utilities at work, go to the terminal window and type `ipconfig` for Windows systems, or `ifconfig` for Mac OS, Unix, and Linux systems. The `ifconfig` (or `ipconfig`) utility provides information about lower protocol levels, but the fact that you can work with it interactively and access it through a terminal window means the command is acting through the application level. The terminal will display network configuration information for your computer.

Key Terms

Review the following list of key terms:

▶ **Application Programming Interface (API):** A predefined collection of programming components that an application can use to access other parts of the operating environment.

▶ **File service:** A service that fulfills network requests to write or read files to or from storage.

▶ **Print service:** A service that fulfills network requests to print documents.

▶ **Redirector:** A service that checks local resource requests and forwards them to the network if necessary.

▶ **Sockets API:** A network API originally developed for BSD UNIX that provides applications with access to TCP/IP.

PART III

Networking with TCP/IP

HOUR 8

Routing

What You'll Learn in This Hour:

- ▶ IP forwarding
- ▶ Direct and indirect routing
- ▶ Routing protocols

The infrastructure that supports global networks such as the Internet could not function without routers. TCP/IP was designed to operate through routers, and no discussion of TCP/IP is complete without a discussion of what the routers are doing. As you learn in this hour, a router participates in a complex process of communication with other routers on the network to determine the best path to each destination. In this hour, you learn about routers, routing tables, and routing protocols.

At the end of this hour, you will be able to

- ▶ Describe IP forwarding and how it works

- ▶ Distinguish between distance-vector routing and link-state routing

- ▶ Discuss the roles of core, interior, and exterior routers

- ▶ Describe the common interior routing protocols RIP and OSPF

Routing in TCP/IP

In its most basic form, a **router** is a device that filters traffic by logical address. A classic network router operates at the Internet layer (Open Systems Interconnection [OSI] model's Network layer) using IP addressing information in the Internet layer header. In OSI shorthand, the Network layer is also known as Layer 3, and a router is sometimes called a Layer 3 device. In recent years, hardware vendors have developed routers that operate at higher layers of the OSI stack. You learn about Layer 4–7 routers later in this hour, but for now, think of a router as a device that is operating at the Internet layer or OSI Layer 3 (the same level as IP addressing).

Routers are an essential part of any large TCP/IP network. Without routers the Internet could not function. In fact, the Internet never would have grown to what it is today without the development of network routers and TCP/IP routing protocols.

A large network such as the Internet contains many routers that provide redundant pathways from the source to the destination nodes. The routers must work independently, but the effect of the system must be that data is routed accurately and efficiently through the internetwork.

Routers replace Network Access layer header information as they pass data from one network to the next, so a router can connect dissimilar network types. Many routers also maintain detailed information describing the best path based on considerations of distance, bandwidth, and time. (You learn more about route-discovery protocols later in this hour.)

Routing in TCP/IP is a subject that has filled 241 Requests for Comment [RFCs] (as of the latest edition of this book) and could easily fill a dozen books. What is truly remarkable about TCP/IP routing is that it works so well. An average homeowner can call up an Internet browser and connect with a computer in China or Finland without a passing thought to the many devices forwarding the request around the world. Even on smaller networks, routers play a vital role in controlling traffic and keeping the network fast.

What Is a Router?

The best way to describe a router is to describe how it looks. In its simplest form (or, at least, in its most fundamental form) a router looks like a computer with two network adapters. The earlier routers were actually computers with two or more network adapters (called multihomed computers). Figure 8.1 shows a multihomed computer acting as a router.

The first step to understanding routing is to remember that the IP address belongs to the adapter and not to the computer. The computer in Figure 8.1 has two IP addresses, one for each adapter. In fact, it is possible for the two adapters to be on completely different IP subnets corresponding to completely different physical networks (as shown in Figure 8.1). In Figure 8.1, the protocol software on the multihomed computer can receive the data from Segment A, check the IP address information to see whether the data belongs on Segment B, replace the Network Access layer header with a header that provides physical address information for Segment B (if the

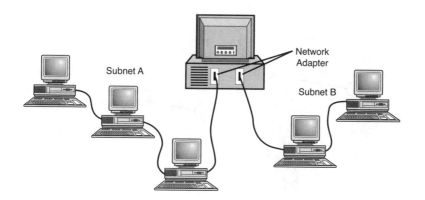

FIGURE 8.1
A multihomed computer acting as a router.

data is addressed to Segment B), and transmit the data onto Segment B. In this simple scenario, the multihomed computer acts as a router.

If you want to understand the scope of what the world's networks are doing, imagine the scenario in the preceding paragraph with the following complications:

▶ The router could possibly have more than two ports (adapters) and can, therefore, interconnect more than two networks. The decision of where to forward the data then becomes more complicated, and the possibility for redundant paths increases. (In fact, the routers encountered by end users on most LANs are designed for connecting two network segments, but more complex scenarios can occur within the structure of the Internet.)

▶ The networks that the router interconnects are each interconnected with other networks. In other words, the router sees network addresses for networks to which it is not directly connected. The router must have a strategy for forwarding data addressed to networks to which it is not directly attached.

▶ The network of routers provides redundant paths, and each router must have a way of deciding which path to use.

The simple configuration in Figure 8.1, combined with the preceding three complications, offers a more detailed view of the router's role (see Figure 8.2).

On today's networks, most routers are not multihomed computers. It is more cost-effective to assign routing responsibilities to a specialized device. The routing device is specifically designed to perform routing functions efficiently, and the device does not include all the extra features found in a complete computer.

FIGURE 8.2
Routing on a
complex net-
work.

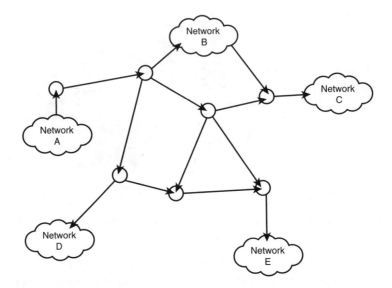

The Routing Process

Building on the discussion of the simple router described in the preceding section, a more general description of the router's role is as follows:

1. The router receives data from one of its attached networks.

2. The router passes the data up the protocol stack to the Internet layer. In other words, the router discards the Network Access layer header information and reassembles (if necessary) the IP datagram.

3. The router checks the destination address in the IP header.

4. If the data is destined for a different network, the router consults a routing table to determine where to forward the data.

5. After the router determines which of its adapters will receive the data, it passes the data down through the appropriate Network Access layer software for transmission through the adapter.

The routing process is shown in Figure 8.3. It might occur to you that the routing table described in step 4 is a rather crucial element. In fact, the routing table and the protocol that builds the routing table are distinguishing characteristics of the router. Most of the discussion of routers is about how routers build routing tables and how the route protocols that assemble routing table information cause the collection of routers to serve as a unified system.

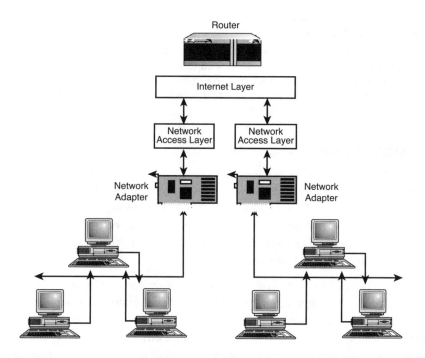

FIGURE 8.3
The routing
process.

The two primary types of routing are named for where they get their routing table information:

▶ **Static routing:** Requires the network administrator to enter route information manually.

▶ **Dynamic routing:** Builds the routing table dynamically based on routing information obtained using routing protocols.

Static routing can be useful in some contexts, but as you might guess, a system that requires the network administrator to enter routing information manually has some severe limitations. First, static routing does not adapt well to large networks with hundreds of possible routes. Second, on all but the simplest networks, static routing requires a disproportionate investment of time from the network administrator, who must not only create but also continually update the routing table information. Also, a static router cannot adapt as quickly to changes in the network, such as a downed router.

Preconfigured Routes

Most dynamic routers give the administrator the option of overriding dynamic route selection and configuring a static path to a specific address. Preconfigured static routes are sometimes used for network troubleshooting. In other cases, the administrator might provide a static path to take advantage of a fast network connection or to balance network traffic.

Routing Table Concepts

The role of the routing table and other Internet layer routing elements is to deliver the data to the proper local network. After the data reaches the local network, network access protocols will see to its delivery. The routing table, therefore, does not need to store complete IP addresses and can simply list addresses by network ID. (See Hour 4, "The Internet Layer" and Hour 5, "Subnetting and CIDR," for a discussion of the host ID and network ID portions of the IP address.)

The contents of an extremely basic routing table are shown in Figure 8.4. A routing table essentially maps destination network IDs to the IP address of the next hop—the next stop the datagram makes on its path to the destination network. Note that the routing table makes a distinction between networks directly connected to the router itself and networks connected indirectly through other routers. The next hop can be either the destination network (if it is directly connected) or the next downstream router on the way to the destination network. The Router Port Interface in Figure 8.4 refers to the router port through which the router forwards the data.

FIGURE 8.4
The routing table.

Destination	Next Hop	Router Port Interface
129.14.0.0	Direct Connection	1
150.27.0.0	131.100.18.6	3
155.111.0.0	Direct Connection	2
165.48.0.0	129.14.16.1	1

The next-hop entry in the routing table is the key to understanding dynamic routing. On a complex network, several paths to the destination might exist, and the router must decide which of these paths the next hop will follow. A dynamic router makes this decision based on information obtained through routing protocols.

Routing Table

A host computer, like a router, can have a routing table; because the host does not have to perform routing functions, its routing table usually isn't as complicated. Hosts often make use of a *default router* or *default gateway*. The default gateway is the router that receives the datagram if it can't be delivered on the local network or to another router.

A Look at IP Forwarding

Both hosts and routers have routing tables. A host's routing table can be much simpler than a router's routing table. The routing table for a single computer might contain only two lines: an entry for the local network and a default route for packets that can't be delivered on the local segment. This rudimentary routing information is enough to point a datagram toward its destination. You learn later in this hour that a router's role is a bit more complex.

As you learned in Hour 4, the TCP/IP software uses ARP to resolve an IP address to a physical address on the local segment. But what if the IP address isn't on the local segment? As Hour 4 explains, if the IP address isn't on the local segment, the host sends the datagram to a router. You might have noticed by now that the situation is actually a bit more complicated. The IP header (refer to Figure 4.3) lists only the IP address of the source and destination. The header doesn't have room to list the address of every intermediate router that passes the datagram toward its destination. As you read this hour, it is important to remember that the IP forwarding process does not actually place the router's address in the IP header. Instead, the host passes the datagram and the router's IP address down to the Network Access layer, where the protocol software uses a separate lookup process to enclose the datagram in a frame for local delivery to the router. In other words, the IP address of a forwarded datagram refers to the host that will eventually receive the data. The physical address of the frame that relays the datagram to a router on the local network is the address of the local adapter on the router.

A brief description of this process is as follows (see Figure 8.5):

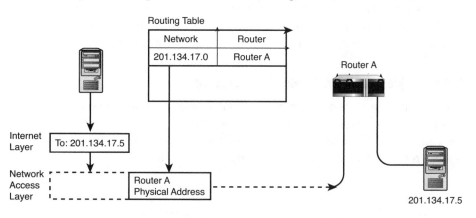

FIGURE 8.5
The IP forwarding process.

1. A host wants to send an IP datagram. The host checks its routing table.

2. If the datagram cannot be delivered on the local network, the host extracts from the routing table the IP address of the router associated with the destination address. (In the case of a host on a local segment, this router IP

address will most likely be the address of the default gateway.) The router's IP address is then resolved to a physical address using ARP.

3. The datagram (addressed to the remote host) is passed to the Network Access layer along with the physical address of the router that will receive the datagram.

4. The network adapter of the router receives the frame because the destination physical address of the frame matches the router's physical address.

5. The router unpacks the frame and passes the datagram up to the Internet layer.

6. The router checks the IP address of the datagram. If the IP address matches the router's own IP address, the data is intended for the router itself. If the IP address does not match the router's IP address, the router attempts to forward the datagram by checking its own routing table to find a route associated with the datagram's destination address.

7. If the datagram cannot be delivered on any of the segments connected to the router, the router sends the datagram to another router, and the process repeats (go to step 1) until the last router is able to deliver the datagram directly to the destination host.

The IP forwarding process described in step 6 of the preceding procedure is an important characteristic of a router. It is important to remember that a device will not act like a router just because it has two network cards. Unless the device has the necessary software to support IP forwarding, data will not pass from one interface to another. When a computer that is not configured for IP routing receives a datagram addressed to a different computer, the datagram is simply ignored.

Direct Versus Indirect Routing

If a router just connects two subnets, that router's routing table can be simple. The router in Figure 8.6 will never see an IP address that isn't associated with one of its ports, and the router is directly attached to all subnets. In other words, the router in Figure 8.6 can deliver any datagram through direct routing.

FIGURE 8.6
A router connecting two segments can reach each segment directly.

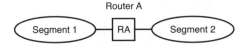

Consider the slightly more complex network shown in Figure 8.7. In this case, Router A is not attached to Segment 3 and does not have a way of finding out about Segment 3 without some help. This situation is called **indirect routing**. Most routed networks depend to some degree on indirect routing. Large corporate networks might have dozens of routers, with no more than one or two connected directly to each network segment. You learn more about these larger networks later in this hour. For now, the important questions to ask about Figure 8.7 are the following: How does Router A find out about Segment 3? How does Router A know that datagrams addressed to Segment 3 should be sent to Router B and not to Router C?

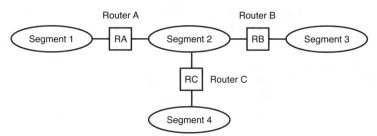

FIGURE 8.7
A router must perform indirect routing if it forwards datagrams to a network to which it isn't directly attached.

There are two ways that routers learn about indirect routes: from a system administrator or from other routers.

These two options correspond (respectively) to the static routing and dynamic routing methods. A system administrator can enter network routes directly into the routing table (static routing), or Router B can tell Router A about Segment 3 (dynamic routing). Dynamic routing offers several advantages. First, it does not require human intervention. Second, it is responsive to changes in the network. If a new network segment is attached to Router B, Router B can inform Router A about the change.

As it turns out, static routing is sometimes an effective approach for small, simple, and permanent networks. Static routing would probably be acceptable on the simple network shown in Figure 8.7, but as the number of routers increases, static routing becomes inadequate. The number of possible routes multiplies as you add segments to the network, creating additional work for the administrator. More important, the interaction of static routes on a large network can lead to inefficiencies and to quirky behavior, such as routing loops, in which a datagram cycles endlessly through the chain of routers until its TTL expires and it is dropped.

Most modern routers use some form of dynamic routing. The routers communicate with each other to share information on network segments and network paths, and each router builds its routing table using the information obtained through this communication process. The following sections describe how dynamic routing works.

Static and Dynamic

Routers sometimes use a combination of static and dynamic routing. A system administrator might configure a few static paths and let others be assigned dynamically. Static routes are sometimes used to force traffic over a specific path. For example, a system administrator might want to configure the routers so that traffic is funneled to a high-bandwidth link.

Dynamic Routing Algorithms

The routers in a router group exchange enough information about the network so that each router can build a table that describes which way to send datagrams addressed to any particular segment. What exactly do the routers communicate? How does a router build its routing table? As you have probably figured out by now, the behavior of a router depends entirely upon the routing table. Several routing protocols are currently in use. Many of those routing protocols are designed around one of two routing methods: distance-vector routing and link-state routing.

These methods are best understood as different approaches to the task of communicating and collecting routing information. The following sections discuss distance-vector and link-state routing. Later in this hour, you take a closer look at a pair of routing protocols that use these methods: Routing Information Protocol (RIP, a distance-vector routing protocol) and Open Shortest Path First (OSPF, a link-state routing protocol).

Protocols and Implementations

Distance-vector and link-state are *classes* of routing protocols. The implementations of actual protocols include additional features and details. Also, many routers support startup scripts, static routing entries, and other features that complicate any idealized description of distance-vector or link-state routing.

Distance-Vector Routing

Distance-vector routing (also called Bellman-Ford routing) is an efficient and simple routing method employed by many routing protocols. Distance-vector routing once dominated the routing industry, and it is still quite common, although recently more sophisticated routing methods (such as link-state routing) have been gaining popularity.

Distance-vector routing is designed to minimize the required communication among routers and to minimize the amount of data that must reside in the routing table. The underlying philosophy of distance-vector routing is that a router does not have to know the complete pathway to every network segment—it only has to know in which direction to send a datagram addressed to the segment (hence the term *vector*). The distance between network segments is measured in the number of routers a datagram must cross to travel from one segment to the other. Routers using a distance-vector algorithm attempt to optimize the pathway by minimizing the number of routers that a datagram must cross. This distance parameter is referred to as the *hop count*.

Distance-vector routing works as follows:

1. When Router A initializes, it senses the segments to which it is directly attached and places those segments in its routing table. The hop count to each of those directly attached segments is 0 (zero), because a datagram does not have to pass through any routers to travel from this router to the segment.

2. At some periodic interval, the router receives a report from each neighboring router. The report lists any network segments the neighboring router knows about and the hop count to each of those segments.

3. When Router A receives the report from the neighboring router, it integrates the new routing information into its own routing table as follows:

   ▶ If Router B knows about a network segment that Router A doesn't currently have in its routing table, Router A adds the segment to its routing table. The route for the new segment is Router B, meaning that if Router A receives a datagram addressed to the new segment, it forwards that datagram to Router B. The hop count for the new segment is whatever Router B listed as the hop count plus 1, because Router A is one hop farther away from the segment than Router B was.

   ▶ If Router B lists a segment that is already in Router A's routing table, Router A adds 1 to the hop count received from B and compares the revised hop count to the value stored in its own routing table. If the path through B is more efficient (fewer hops) than the path Router A already knows about, Router A revises its routing table to list Router B as the route for datagrams addressed to this segment.

   ▶ If the revised hop count for the path to the segment through Router B (the hop count received from B plus 1) is greater than the hop count currently listed in Router A's routing table, the route through B is not used. Router A continues to use the route already stored in its routing table.

With each round of routing table updates, the routers receive a more complete picture of the network. Information about routes slowly disseminates across the network. Assuming nothing changes on the network, the routers will eventually learn the most efficient path to every segment.

An example of a distance-vector routing update is shown in Figure 8.8. Note that at this point, other updates have already taken place because both Router A and Router B know about the network to which they are not directly attached. In this case, Router B has a more efficient path to Network 14, so Router A updates its routing table to send data addressed to Network 14 to Router B. Router A already has a better way to reach Network 7, so the routing table is not changed.

FIGURE 8.8
A distance-vector routing update.

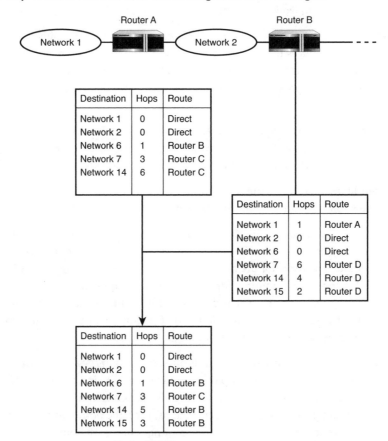

Destination	Hops	Route
Network 1	0	Direct
Network 2	0	Direct
Network 6	1	Router B
Network 7	3	Router C
Network 14	6	Router C

Destination	Hops	Route
Network 1	1	Router A
Network 2	0	Direct
Network 6	0	Direct
Network 7	6	Router D
Network 14	4	Router D
Network 15	2	Router D

Destination	Hops	Route
Network 1	0	Direct
Network 2	0	Direct
Network 6	1	Router B
Network 7	3	Router C
Network 14	5	Router B
Network 15	3	Router B

Router A Table

Link-State Routing

Distance-vector routing is a worthy approach if you assume that the efficiency of a path coincides with the number of routers a datagram must cross. This assumption is a good starting point, but in some cases it is an oversimplification. (A route through a slow link takes longer than a route through a high-speed link, even if the number of hops is the same.) Also, distance-vector routing does not scale well to large groups of routers. Each router must maintain a routing table entry for every destination, and the table entries are merely vector and hop-count values. The router cannot economize its efforts through some greater knowledge of the network's structure. Furthermore, complete tables of distance and hop-count values must pass among routers even if most of the information isn't necessary. Computer scientists began to ask whether they could do better, and link-state routing evolved from this discussion. Link-state routing is now the primary alternative to distance-vector routing.

The philosophy behind link-state routing is that every router attempts to build its own internal map of the network topology. Each router periodically sends status messages to the network. These status messages list the network's other routers to which the router is directly connected and also the status of the link (whether the link is currently operational). The routers use the status messages received from other routers to build a map of the network topology. When a router has to forward a datagram, it chooses the best path to the destination based on the existing conditions.

Link-state protocols require more processing time on each router, but the consumption of bandwidth is reduced because every router is not required to propagate a complete routing table. Also, it is easier to trace problems through the network because the status message from a given router propagates unchanged through the network. (The distance-vector method, on the other hand, increments the hop count each time the routing information passes to a different router.)

Routing on Complex Networks

So far this hour has focused on a single router or single group of routers. In fact, some large networks might contain hundreds of routers. The Internet contains thousands of routers. On large networks such as the Internet, it is not feasible for all routers to share all the information necessary to support the routing methods described in previous sections. If every router had to compile and process routing information for every other router on the Internet, the volume of router protocol traffic and the size of the routing tables would soon overwhelm the infrastructure. But it isn't necessary for every router on the Internet to know about every other router. A router in a dentist's office in Istanbul could operate for years without ever having to learn about another router in an office pool at a paint factory in Lima, Peru. If the network is organized efficiently, most routers need to exchange routing protocol information only with other nearby routers.

In the ARPAnet system that led to the Internet, a small group of core routers served as a central backbone for the internetwork, linking individual networks that were configured and managed autonomously. The core routers knew about every network, though they did not have to know about every subnet. As long as any datagram could find a path to a core router, it could reach any point in the system. The routers in the tributary networks beneath the core didn't have to know about every network in the world, they just had to know how to send data among themselves and how to reach the core routers.

This system evolved into the complex modern Internet you'll learn more about in Hour 17, "The Internet: A Closer Look."

The Internet is made up of independently managed networks called **autonomous systems**. An autonomous system might represent a corporate network or, more commonly in recent times, a network associated with an Internet service provider (ISP). The owner of the autonomous system manages the details of configuring individual routers. Most routers fall within the following general categories. Although it is possible to use a router in more than one role, the hardware, and perhaps more importantly, the protocols used by the router, are tailored to its role on the network:

- ▶ **Exterior routers:** Exterior routers communicate routing information between autonomous networks. They maintain routing information about their own and neighboring autonomous networks. Exterior routers traditionally have used a protocol called Exterior Gateway Protocol (EGP). The actual EGP protocol is now outdated, but newer routing protocols that serve exterior routers are commonly referred to as EGPs. A popular EGP now in use is Border Gateway Protocol (BGP). Often an exterior router is also participating as an interior router within its autonomous system.

- ▶ **Interior routers:** Routers within an autonomous region that share routing information are called **interior gateways**. These routers use a class of routing protocols called Interior Gateway Protocols (IGPs). Examples of interior routing protocols include RIP and OSPF. You learn more about RIP and OSPF later in this hour.

- ▶ **Core routers:** Although the original ARPAnet backbone network no longer exists at the center of the Internet itself, large autonomous systems sometimes build their own backbone structures to subdivide and isolate traffic. Core router supports a backbone system. Examples of core router routing protocols include Gateway-to-Gateway Protocol (GGP) and a more recent routing protocol called SPREAD.

It is important to note that the routers within one of the autonomous networks might also have a hierarchical configuration. A large autonomous system might consist of multiple groups of interior routers with exterior routers passing routing information between the interior groups. Managers of the autonomous network are free to design a router configuration that works for the network and to choose routing protocols accordingly.

Examining Interior Routers

As you learned earlier in this hour, interior routers operate within an autonomous network. An interior router should have complete knowledge of any network segments attached to other routers within its group, but it does not need complete knowledge of networks beyond the autonomous system.

Several interior routing protocols are available. A network administrator must choose an interior routing protocol appropriate for the conditions of the network and compatible with the network hardware. The following sections discuss the important interior routing protocols: RIP and OSPF.

RIP is a distance-vector protocol, and OSPF is a link-state protocol. In each case, the real protocol must address details and problems that weren't discussed in the broad methodologies described earlier.

Multi-Protocol

Most routers available today support multiple routing protocols.

By the Way

Routing Information Protocol

RIP is a distance-vector protocol, which means that it determines the optimum route to a destination by hop count. (See the section "Distance-Vector Routing" earlier in this hour.) RIP was developed at the University of California, Berkeley, and originally gained popularity through the distribution of the Berkeley Systems Design (BSD) versions of UNIX. RIP became an extremely popular routing protocol, and it is still used widely, although it is now considered somewhat outdated. The appearance of the RIP II standard cleared up some of the problems associated with RIP I. Many routers now support RIP I and RIP II. An extension of RIP II designed for IPv6 networks is known as RIPng.

> **routed**
>
> RIP is implemented on UNIX and Linux systems through the `routed` daemon.

As described earlier in this hour, RIP (as a distance-vector protocol) requires routers to listen for and integrate route and hop count messages from other routers. RIP participants are classified as either active or passive. An active RIP node is typically a router participating in the normal distance-vector data exchange process. The active RIP participant sends its routing table to other routers and listens for updates from other routers. A passive RIP participant listens for updates but does not propagate its own routing table. A passive RIP node is typically a host computer. (Recall that a host needs a routing table also.)

When you read the earlier discussion of distance-vector routing, you might have wondered what happens when a hop count received and incremented is exactly equal to the hop count already present in the routing table. That is the kind of detail that is left to the individual protocol. In the case of RIP, if two alternative paths to the same destination have the same hop count, the route that is already present in the routing table is retained. This prevents the superfluous route oscillation that would occur if a router continually changed a routing table entry whenever there was a tie in the hop count.

A RIP router broadcasts an update message every 30 seconds. It also can request an immediate update. Like other distance-vector protocols, RIP works best when the network is in equilibrium. If the number of routers becomes too large, problems can occur because of the slow convergence of the routing tables. For this reason, RIP sets a limit on the maximum number of router hops from the first router to the destination. The hop count limit in RIP is 15. This threshold limits the size of a router group, but if the routers are arranged hierarchically, it is possible to encompass a large group in 15 hops.

Although the distance-vector method does not specifically provide for considerations of line speed and physical network type, RIP lets the network administrator influence route selection by manually entering artificially large hop counts for inefficient pathways.

The venerable RIP protocol is gradually being replaced by newer routing protocols, such as OSPF, which you learn about in the next section.

Open Shortest Path First

OSPF is a more recent interior routing protocol that is gradually replacing RIP on many networks. OSPF is a link-state routing protocol. OSPF first appeared in 1989 with RFC 1131. Several updates have occurred since then. RFC 2328 covers OSPF version 2, and some later RFCs add additional extensions and alternatives for the OSPF protocol. OSPF version 3, which supports IPv6 networks, was defined in RFC 2740, which was later updated with RFC 5340.

Each router in an OSPF router group is assigned a router ID. The router ID is typically the numerically highest IP address associated with the router. (If the router uses a loopback interface, the router ID is the highest loopback address. See Hour 4 for more on loopback addresses.)

As you learned earlier in this hour, link-state routers build an internal map of the network topology. Other routers use the router ID to identify a router within the topology. Each router organizes the network into a tree format with itself at the root. This network tree is known as the **shortest path tree (SPT)**. Pathways through the network correspond to branching pathways through the SPT. The router computes the cost for each route. The cost metric can include parameters for the number of router hops and other considerations, such as the speed and reliability of a link.

Exterior Routers: BGP

You learn more about the structure of the Internet in Hour 17, but for now, suffice it to say that the Internet is full of redundant pathways through, between, and around autonomous systems.

As you learned earlier in this hour, external routers play an important role in passing traffic through the web of autonomous systems. The most common protocol for exterior routers on the Internet today is the Border Gateway Protocol (BGP). BGP has gone through several revisions. The current version, which is known as BGP 4, is described in RFP 4271.

Actually, the versatile BGP is also used as an interior protocol within autonomous systems to help subdivide networks into smaller regions. The version of BGP used on the edge of an autonomous system to pass messages to other autonomous systems is known as External Border Gateway Protocol (eBGP). The flavor of BGP used inside of an autonomous system is called Internal Border Gateway Protocol (iBGP).

BGP is extremely robust and scalable. As you learned earlier in this hour, BGP replaces earlier external protocols and is designed to serve the needs of today's Internet. Actually, today's Internet couldn't exist without BGP. Reports on the full size of the core BGP routing table vary, but it has been growing exponentially in recent years and is now over 300,000 entries.

The IANA assigns a unique number to each autonomous system called an AS number or ASN. BGP uses these ASN numbers to build a map of the Internet and associate CIDR-based, classless IP addresses with routes through autonomous systems. The ASN number provides a means for identifying a network that is independent of a particular IP address or address range. This approach provides for redundant pathways to an autonomous system (as opposed to a single path through the IP address space). But because the ASN numbers are nonhierarchical, the BGP router must know about, or have the potential to learn about, all the other BGP routers on the network.

> **Public and Private ASNs**
>
> When iBGP is used internally to route traffic within an autonomous system, it does not require public ASNs assigned by the IANA. An interior BGP router instead uses private ASNs that are not forwarded beyond the autonomous system.

BGP routers communicate through reliable TCP-based connections, passing information about address ranges and building chains of ASNs describing paths through the network. The BGP protocol includes a variety of provisions for path discovery, and well as techniques for choosing the most efficient path among several options.

Unless you work for an ISP or serve in the IT department for an enterprise company, you might not ever have to deal directly with BGP, but some background knowledge of BGP is useful for understanding the structure of the Internet.

Classless Routing

As you learned in Hours 4 and 5, the TCP/IP routing system is designed around the concept of a network ID, which was originally dependent on the address class. As you also learned in Hour 5, the address class system has some limitations and is sometimes an inefficient method for assigning blocks of addresses to a single provider. Classless interdomain routing (CIDR) offers an alternative method for assigning addresses and determining routes. (See the section titled "Classless Interdomain Routing" in Hour 5.) The CIDR system specifies a host through an address/mask pair, such as 204.21.128.0/17. The mask number represents the number of address bits associated with the network ID.

The CIDR system offers more efficient routing if the routing protocols support it. CIDR reduces the necessary information that must pass between routers because it lets the routers treat multiple class networks as a single entity. Recent protocols, such as OSPF and BGP4, support classless addressing. The original RIP protocol did not support CIDR, but the later RIP II update supports CIDR.

Higher in the Stack

Hardware and software have gradually become much more sophisticated since the appearance of the first routers. Several years ago, hardware vendors began to notice the benefits of forwarding and filtering at higher levels of the protocol stack.

As you learned in Hours 2 through 7, each layer of the stack offers different services and encodes different information in its header. A router with access to higher layers of the stack has additional information on which to base its decisions. For instance, a router that sees the Transport layer could form inferences on the nature of the data based on knowledge of the source and destination port. A router that sees the Application layer would have even more complete knowledge of the application that sent the data and the protocols used by that application.

Routers that access higher layers have several advantages. Greater knowledge of the connection and the source application can lead to better security. Another important reason for this technology is a concept called quality of service (QoS). Some types of data, such as a packet from an Internet telephony client, are much more time sensitive than other types, such as an email message. Once the connection is established, the packets must arrive in a reasonable time frame or the phone call will sound choppy. A router that operates at the Application layer can prioritize packets based on quality of service criteria.

As you will learn in Hour 13, "IPv6: The Next Generation," the new IPv6 Internet protocol system provides other methods for handling QoS considerations. For purposes of understanding this hour, just keep in mind that many sophisticated modern routers are not limited to just IP forwarding but also perform many additional services based on information at higher layers of the stack.

These routers are typically classified in terms of the OSI reference model. As you learned in Hour 2, "How TCP/IP Works," the OSI model comes in seven layers. A classic router performing the classic task of forwarding IP datagrams is operating at the third layer (counting from the bottom) of the OSI stack, so in OSI terminology, a basic router is called a Layer 3 or L3 router. An L4 router operates at the Transport layer. An L7 router functions at the highest layer of the OSI stack and, thus, has the maximum knowledge of the applications participating in the connection.

Summary

This hour took a close look at routing. You learned about the distance-vector and link-state routing methods. You also learned about IP forwarding, core routers, interior routers, and exterior routers. Finally, this hour described a pair of common interior routing protocols, RIP and OSPF, and introduced the concept of routing at higher protocol layers.

Q&A

Q. *Why must a computer be configured for IP forwarding to act as a router?*

A. A router receives datagrams that have addresses other than its own. Typically, the TCP/IP software ignores a datagram if it is addressed to a different host. IP forwarding provides a means for accepting and processing datagrams that must be forwarded to other networks.

Q. *Why is link-state routing better for larger networks?*

A. Distance-vector routing is not efficient for large numbers of routers. Each router must maintain a complete table of destinations. Network data is altered at each step in the propagation path. Also, entire routing tables must be sent with each update even though most of the data might be unnecessary.

Q. *What is the purpose of the exterior router?*

A. The exterior router is designated to exchange routing information about the autonomous system with other autonomous systems. Assigning this role to a specific router protects the other routers in the system from having to get involved with determining routes to other networks.

Q. *Why does RIP set a maximum hop count of 15?*

A. If the number of routers becomes too large, problems can result from the slow convergence of the routers to an equilibrium state.

Workshop

The following workshop is composed of a series of quiz questions and practical exercises. The quiz questions are designed to test your overall understanding of the current material. The practical exercises are intended to afford you the opportunity to apply the concepts discussed during the current hour, as well as build upon the knowledge acquired in previous hours of study. Please take time to complete the quiz questions and exercises before continuing. Refer to Appendix A, "Answers to Quizzes and Exercises," for answers.

Quiz

1. What are two types of dynamic routing?

2. Why must a router be multihomed?

3. What is the most common router protocol for exterior routers?

4. Why can classless routing be more efficient?

5. OSPF is an example of what type of routing?

Exercises

1. List three routing protocols in current use.

2. Explain how OSPF offers a more flexible method of choosing best routes than RIP does.

3. List some advantages and disadvantages of static routing.

Key Terms

Review the following list of key terms:

- ▶ **Autonomous system:** A network participating in a larger network that is maintained by an autonomous entity.

- ▶ **Border Gateway Protocol (BGP):** A protocol used to route traffic between autonomous networks. BGP is also used as an internal protocol inside an autonomous system.

- ▶ **Dynamic routing:** A router technique in which the router builds a routing table based on information obtained through routing protocols.

- ▶ **Exterior router:** A router in an autonomous system that passes routing information to other autonomous systems.

- ▶ **Indirect routing:** Routing between two networks that are not directly attached.

- ▶ **Interior router:** A router within an autonomous system that exchanges routing information with other computers in the autonomous system.

- ▶ **IP forwarding:** The process of passing an IP datagram from one network interface to another network interface of the same device.

▶ **OSPF (Open Shortest Path First):** A common link-state interior routing protocol.

▶ **RIP (Routing Information Protocol):** A common distance-vector interior routing protocol.

▶ **Routing protocol:** Any of several protocols used by routers to assemble route information.

▶ **SPT (shortest path tree):** A tree-like map of the network assembled by an OSPF router.

▶ **Static routing:** A routing technique that requires the network administrator to enter route information dynamically.

HOUR 9

Getting Connected

What You'll Learn in This Hour:

- ▶ Dial-up networking
- ▶ Broadband technologies like cable and DSL
- ▶ Wide area networks
- ▶ Wireless networking
- ▶ Connectivity devices

As you learned in previous hours, the Network Access layer manages the interface with the physical network. But what exactly is the physical network? After all the conceptual sketches of bits, bytes, ports, and protocol layers, sooner or later, an Internet connection requires some form of device connecting a computer or local network segment to the larger network beyond. This hour examines some of the devices and processes supporting access to TCP/IP networks.

At the completion of this hour, you will be able to

- ▶ Describe how computers communicate over phone lines with dial-up networking

- ▶ Understand the basics of cable broadband

- ▶ Discuss defining features of DSL

- ▶ Describe the topologies of wireless networks and the elements and the function of wireless security schemes such as WEP and WPA2

This hour also introduces connectivity devices commonly found on TCP/IP networks, such as switches, hubs, and bridges.

As you read through this hour, keep in mind that these hardware-based technologies inhabit the lowest level of the TCP/IP protocol stack (Layers 1 and 2 of the Open Systems Interconnection [OSI] stack) and are largely invisible to protocols and applications operating at higher levels. A web browser is still a web browser, regardless of whether it is connected to a switch, cable modem, digital subscriber line (DSL), or wireless access point.

Dial-Up Networking

In the recent past, one of the most common methods for connecting to a TCP/IP network such as the Internet was through a phone line. Over the past few years, broadband techniques such as cable modems and DSL have reduced the importance of dial-up networking, but many computers still support dial-up connections, and the telephone modem is still an important connectivity tool in many areas.

A **modem** provides network access through a phone line. The term is short for MOdulator/DEModulator. Engineers created modems because the industry saw the enormous benefit of providing a way for computers to communicate over the world's most accessible transmission medium: the global telephone system. Telephone lines have grown more sophisticated in recent years. Some lines are now capable of transmitting digitized data; other lines are not. In any case, even digital telephone systems are not designed to automatically handle a network protocol like TCP/IP. The purpose of a modem is to transform the digital protocol transmissions from a computer into an analog signal that can pass through the interface with the phone system and to transform incoming analog signals from the phone line into a digital signal that the receiving computer understands.

Point-to-Point Connections

As you learned in Hour 3, "The Network Access Layer," local networks such as ethernet employ elaborate access strategies for enabling the computers to share the network medium. By contrast, the two computers at either end of a phone line do not have to compete for the transmission medium with other computers; they have to share it only with each other. This type of connection is called a **point-to-point** connection (see Figure 9.1).

FIGURE 9.1
A point-to-point connection.

A point-to-point connection is simpler than a local area network (LAN)-based configuration because it doesn't have to provide a means for multiple computers to share the transmission medium. At the same time, a connection through a phone line has some limitations. One of the biggest limitations is that transmission rates over a phone connection are much slower than rates over a LAN-based network such as ethernet. This reduced transmission speed lends itself to a protocol that minimizes the data overhead of the protocol itself—less is better. As you learn in this hour, as modems have become faster, modem protocols have taken on additional responsibilities.

Another challenge of dial-up protocols is the great diversity of hardware and software configurations they must support. On a local network, a system administrator oversees and controls the configuration of each computer, and the protocol system depends on a high degree of uniformity among the communicating devices. A dial-up connection, on the other hand, can occur from almost anywhere in the world. Dial-up protocols must contend with a wider and more varied range of possibilities regarding the hardware and software of the communicating machines.

Modem Protocols

You might wonder why this point-to-point connection, with its two computers, even needs the complication of the TCP/IP stack to make a connection. The simple answer is that it doesn't.

Early modem protocols were merely a method for passing information across the phone line, and in that situation, the logical addressing and internetwork error control of TCP/IP were not necessary or even desirable. Later, with the arrival of local networks and the Internet, engineers began to think about using a dial-up connection as a means of providing network access. The first implementations of this remote network access concept were an extension of earlier modem protocols. In these first *host dial-up* schemes, the computer attached to the network assumed all responsibility for preparing the data for the network. Either explicitly or implicitly, the remote computer acted more like a terminal (see Figure 9.2), directing the networked host to perform networking tasks and sending and receiving data across the modem line through an entirely separate process.

However, these early host dial-up schemes had some limitations. They reflected an earlier, centralized model of computing that placed huge demands on the computer providing the network access. (Imagine the configuration in Figure 9.2 with several computers simultaneously connected to the dial-up server.) They also made inefficient use of the processing power of the remote computer.

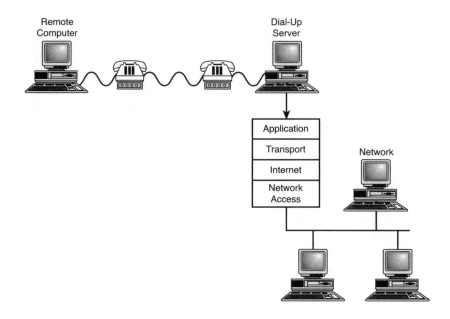

As TCP/IP and other routable protocols began to emerge, designers began to imagine another solution in which the remote computer would take more responsibility
for networking tasks, and the dial-up server would act more like a router. This solution (shown in Figure 9.3) was more consistent with the newer, less-centralized paradigm of computer networks and also closer to the true nature of TCP/IP. In this
arrangement, the remote computer operates its own protocol stack, with the modem
protocols acting at the Network Access layer. The dial-up server accepts the data and
routes it to the greater network.

Dial-up protocols, therefore, began to work directly with TCP/IP and became an
integral part of the stack. The two most common TCP/IP modem protocols are

▶ **Serial Line Internet Protocol (SLIP):** An early TCP/IP-based modem protocol, SLIP was simple and therefore had some limitations.

▶ **Point-to-Point Protocol (PPP):** Currently the most popular protocol for
modem connections, PPP began as a refinement of SLIP. It offers many
important features that weren't available with its predecessor.

PPP has replaced SLIP as the method of choice for dial-up Internet connections. The
following sections take a closer look at PPP.

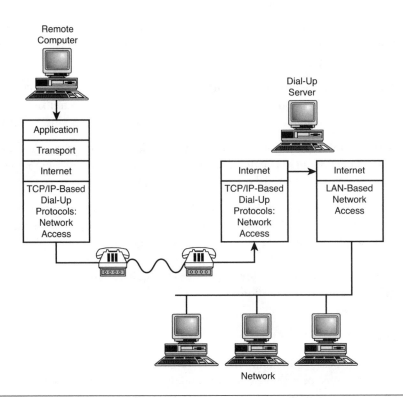

FIGURE 9.3
A true TCP/IP dial-up connection.

Down Low

Both SLIP and PPP are built on lower-level serial communication protocols that see to the details of actually modulating and demodulating the signal. These serial communication protocols provide what would be considered OSI Physical layer functions.

By the Way

Point-to-Point Protocol

When industry experts began to design the PPP standard, they had a much better idea of what features would be useful for the emerging Internet. They also knew that modems and phone lines were getting faster and could support a greater amount of protocol overhead. PPP was an effort to address some of the shortcomings of SLIP.

The designers of PPP also wanted PPP to be capable of dynamically negotiating configuration settings at the beginning of a connection and to be capable of managing the link between the communicating computers throughout the session.

PPP is actually a collection of protocols that interact to supply a full complement of modem-based networking features. The design of PPP evolved through a series of

Request for Comment [RFCs]. The current PPP standard is RFC 1661; subsequent documents have clarified and extended PPP components. RFC 1661 divides the components of PPP into three general categories:

▶ **A method for encapsulating multiprotocol datagrams:** SLIP and PPP both accept datagrams and prepare them for the Internet. But PPP, unlike SLIP, must be prepared to accept datagrams from more than one protocol system.

▶ **A Link Control Protocol (LCP) for establishing, configuring, and testing the connection:** PPP negotiates configuration settings and thus eliminates compatibility problems encountered with SLIP connections.

▶ **A family of network control protocols (NCPs) supporting upper-layer protocol systems:** PPP can include separate sublayers that provide separate interfaces to TCP/IP and to alternative network protocols.

Much of PPP's power and versatility comes from the LCP functions that establish, manage, and terminate connections.

PPP Data

The primary purpose of PPP (and also SLIP) is to forward datagrams. One challenge of PPP is that it must be capable of forwarding more than one type of datagram. In other words, the datagram could be an IP datagram, or it could be some OSI Network layer datagram.

> **Packets**
>
> The PPP RFCs use the term *packet* to describe a bundle of data transmitted in a PPP frame. A packet can consist of an IP (or other upper-layer protocol) datagram, or it can consist of data formatted for one of the other protocols operating through PPP. The word *packet* is an often-imprecise term used throughout the networking industry for a package of data transmitted across the network. For the most part, this book has attempted to use a more precise term, such as *datagram*. Not all PPP data packages, however, are datagrams, so in keeping with the RFCs, this hour uses the term *packet* for data transmitted through PPP.

PPP must also forward data with information relating to its own protocols: the protocols that establish and manage the modem connection. Communicating devices exchange several types of messages and requests over the course of a PPP connection. The communicating computers must exchange LCP packets, used to establish, manage, and close the connection; authentication packets, which support PPP's optional authentication protocols; and NCP packets, which interface PPP with various protocol suites. The LCP data exchanged at the beginning of the connection configures the connection parameters that are common to all protocols. NCP protocols then configure suite-specific parameters relating to the individual protocol suites supported by the PPP connection.

The data format for a PPP frame is shown in Figure 9.4. The fields are as follows:

▶ **Protocol:** A 1- or 2-byte field providing an identification number for the protocol type of the enclosed packet. Possible types include an LCP packet, an NCP packet, an IP packet, or an OSI Network layer protocol packet. Internet Corporation for Assigned Names and Numbers (ICANN) maintains a list of standard identification numbers for the various protocol types.

▶ **Enclosed data (zero or more bytes):** The control packet or upper-layer datagram being transmitted with the frame.

▶ **Padding (optional and variable length):** Additional bytes as required by the protocol designated in the protocol field. Each protocol is responsible for determining how it will distinguish padding from the enclosed datagram.

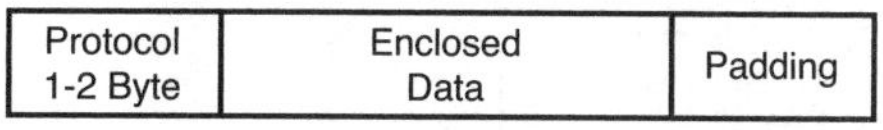

Protocol 1-2 Byte	Enclosed Data	Padding

FIGURE 9.4
The PPP data format.

PPP Connections

The life cycle of a PPP connection is as follows:

1. The connection is established using the LCP negotiation process.

2. If the negotiation process in step 1 specifies a configuration option for authentication, the communicating computers enter an authentication phase. RFC 1661 offers the authentication options Password Authentication Protocol (PAP) and Challenge Handshake Authentication Protocol (CHAP). Additional authentication protocols are also supported.

3. PPP uses NCP packets to specify protocol-specific configuration information for each supported protocol.

4. PPP transmits datagrams received from upper-layer protocols. If the negotiation phase in step 1 includes a configuration option for link quality monitoring, then monitoring protocols will transmit monitoring information. NCP might transmit information regarding specific protocols.

5. PPP closes the connection through the exchange of LCP termination packets.

Cable Broadband

Demand for Internet services, and the ever-increasing capacity of computer systems, caused the industry to look for alternatives to the conventional technique of connecting to the Internet through a slow and finicky phone modem. Rather than undertaking the huge expense of providing a whole new cabling infrastructure for every home that wanted access, service vendors looked for ways to provide Internet services over existing wires.

One form of residential cabling that has proved quite capable of supporting Internet services is the cable television network. Cable-based broadband is now common in many parts of the world. A typical cable modem connection is shown in Figure 9.5.

FIGURE 9.5
A typical cable modem configuration.

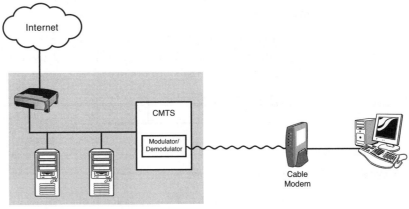

The cable modem connects directly to a coaxial cable that is connected to the cable TV service network. The modem typically has a single ethernet port, which is connected either to a single PC or to a switch or router attached to a small local network.

As you learned earlier in this hour, the term *modem* is short for modulate/demodulate. A cable modem, like a phone modem, modulates digital network transmissions to and from analog form to pass the data efficiently along the cable connection.

Another device called a **cable modem termination system (CMTS)** receives the signal from the cable modem and converts it back to digital form at the interface with the cable provider's network. The provider, in turn, leases bandwidth from an upstream Internet service provider (ISP), and a router on the provider's network connects the user with the rest of the Internet. The provider might also offer other support services, such as a Dynamic Host Configuration Protocol (DHCP) server to assign dynamic IP addresses to users on the network.

Although the cable modem does serve as an interface between two different transmission media, it is not actually a router but is, instead, more like a network bridge (which you learn about later in this hour). The cable modem filters traffic by the physical (Media Access Control [MAC]) address at the Network Access layer. In recent years, however, some manufacturers have begun building a cable modem into some residential router devices, so you might come across a combination device that serves as both a router and a cable modem.

Early cable modem vendors each had their own proprietary standards for managing communication over the cable medium. In the late 1990s, several cable companies developed the **Data Over Cable Service Interface Specification (DOCSIS)** standard for cable modem networks. As long as the CMTS and the cable modem are both DOCSIS compliant, the connection can occur without any special effort from the user, although, as a precaution against stolen services, cable companies typically require the user to preregister the MAC address of the cable modem to participate in the network.

Digital Subscriber Line

The other promising candidate for a home broadband transmission medium is the telephone network. Of course, the conventional telephone modem already uses the phone network, but telephone companies thought they could get better performance if they used a different approach. The result of this effort is a communications form known as **digital subscriber line (DSL)**.

In fact, the twisted-pair cabling used in telephone networks has much more capacity than is typically used for voice communication. The DSL transceiver, which acts as an interface from the local network to the telephone network, operates in a frequency range that doesn't interfere with voice communication over the line. Consequently, DSL can operate continually without tying up the line or interfering with phone service.

Like a cable network, a DSL network requires a device at the other end of the line that receives the signal and interfaces with the Internet through the provider's network. A device known as a **digital subscriber line access multiplexer (DSLAM)** serves as the other endpoint for the DSL connection (see Figure 9.6). Unlike on a cable network, where the medium is essentially shared by users on the segment, each DSL customer has a dedicated line from the transceiver to the DSLAM, which means that performance is less susceptible to degradation with increased traffic. You might say that, whereas a cable network is similar to a LAN, a DSL line is more like a point-to-point telephone connection.

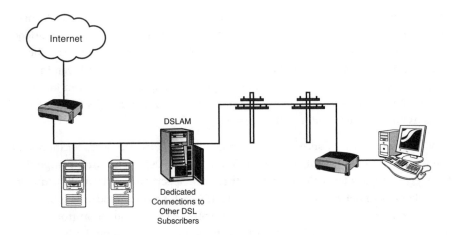

DSL comes in several forms, including ADSL (asynchronous DSL, the most popular variant for small office and homes), HDSL (high bit-rate DSL), VDSL (very high bit-rate DSL), SDSL (symmetric DSL, in which the upstream and downstream bandwidths are equal), and IDSL (ISDN over DSL). The view of DSL from the protocol level varies depending on the equipment and implementation. Some DSL devices are integrated with switches or routers. Other devices act as bridges (similar to a cable modem), filtering traffic at the Network Access layer by physical (MAC) address. DSL devices often encapsulate data in a point-to-point protocol such as PPP. The so-called PPP over Ethernet protocol (PPPoE), for instance, is a popular option for DSL.

Wide Area Networks

Companies and large organizations with lots of computers require access options that aren't available through small-scale technologies such as dial-up and DSL. One crucial question is how to connect branch offices in different locations through an exclusive link that approximates a local network in privacy and provides adequate performance at high usage levels. This question gave rise to the development of the wide area network (**WAN**).

WAN technologies offer fast, high-bandwidth networking over large distances. Although WAN performance is not as fast as the performance of a LAN, it is typically much faster (and more secure) than using standard networking techniques to connect to a remote location over the open Internet. WAN-style connections often provide a means for providing Internet access to high volume corporate networks, and, in some cases, WAN technologies form the mysterious, high-bandwidth heart of the cloud we know as the Internet itself.

A few of the many WAN options are

- ▶ Frame Relay

- ▶ Integrated Services Digital Network (ISDN)

- ▶ High-Level Data Link Control (HDLC)

- ▶ Asynchronous Transfer Mode (ATM)

Although these technologies might seem vastly complex and intimidating (and they are), they are also just another form of physical network specification managed through protocols operating at the TCP/IP Network Access layer. (WAN protocols are almost always centered on the OSI model, so keep in mind that the Network Access layer is equivalent to OSI's Physical and Data Link layers, also known as Layers 1 and 2.)

A typical WAN scenario is shown in Figure 9.7. A service provider operates a WAN with access to the Internet and access to the customer's branch office. A local loop connects the provider's office with a point called the demarcation point, which is the point at which the customer connects to the network. The customer provides the router or other specialized equipment necessary to connect the local network to the WAN.

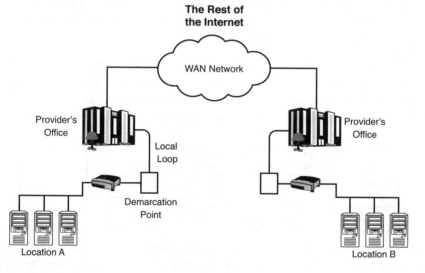

FIGURE 9.7
A typical WAN scenario.

The provider guarantees a specified bandwidth and level of service starting from the demarcation point. Service arrangements vary. WAN service can consist of a dedicated leased line or a pay-for-what-you-use arrangement based on circuit or packet switching.

Wireless Networking

Technology has now reached the point where vendors and users are both wondering whether the continual task of running cables and connecting computers through ethernet ports is even worth the effort. A number of standards are designed to integrate wireless networking with TCP/IP. The following sections describe some of those technologies, including the following:

▶ 802.11 networks

▶ Mobile IP

▶ Bluetooth

Many of the details for how these technologies are incorporated into products and services depend on the vendor. The following sections introduce you to some of the concepts.

802.11 Networks

As you learned in Hour 3, the details of the physical network reside at the Network Access layer of the TCP/IP protocol stack. The easiest way to imagine a wireless TCP/IP network is simply as an ordinary network with a wireless architecture at the Network Access layer. The popular **IEEE 802.11** specifications provide a model for wireless networking at the Network Access layer.

The 802.11 protocol stack is shown in Figure 9.8. The wireless components at the Network Access layers are equivalent to the other network architectures you learned about in previous hours. In fact, the 802.11 standard is often called wireless ethernet because of its similarity and compatibility with the IEEE 802.3 ethernet standard.

FIGURE 9.8
The 802.11 protocols reside at the TCP/IP Network Access layer.

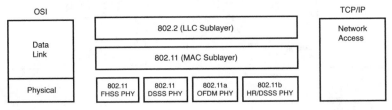

In Figure 9.8, note that the 802.11 specification occupies the MAC sublayer of the OSI reference model. The MAC sublayer is part of the OSI Data Link layer. Recall from Hour 2, "How TCP/IP Works," that the OSI Data Link and Physical layers correspond to the TCP/IP Network Access layer. The various options for the Physical layer represent different wireless broadcast formats, including frequency-hopping spread spectrum (FHSS), direct-sequence spread spectrum (DSSS), orthogonal frequency-division multiplexing (OFDM), and high-rate direct-sequence multiplexing (HR/DSSS).

One quality that distinguishes wireless networks from their wired counterparts is that the nodes are mobile. In other words, the network must be capable of responding to changes in the locations of the participating devices. As you learned in earlier hours, the original delivery system for TCP/IP networks is built around the assumption that each device is in some fixed location. Indeed, if a computer is moved to a different network segment, it must be configured with a different address or it won't even work. By contrast, devices on a wireless network move about constantly. And, although many of the conventions of ethernet are preserved in this environment, the situation is certainly more complicated and calls for some new and different strategies.

802.11 Family

802.11 is actually the collective name for a series of standards. The original (1997) 802.11 standard provided transmission speeds of up to 2Mbps in the 2.4GHz frequency range. The 802.11a standard offers speeds of up to 54Mbps in the 5GHz range. The 802.11b standard provides transmissions at 5.5Mbps and 11Mbps in the 2.4GHz range. Later standards include 802.11g (adopted in 2003) and 902.11n (2008).

By the Way

Independent and Infrastructure Networks

The simplest form of wireless network consists of two or more devices with wireless network cards communicating with each other directly (see Figure 9.9). This type of network, which is officially called an **independent basic service set (independent BSS, or IBSS)**, is more commonly known as an ad hoc network. An independent BSS is often adequate for small collections of computers in a compact space. A classic example of an independent BSS is a laptop computer that networks temporarily with a home PC when the owner returns from a road trip and transfers files through a wireless connection. Independent BSS networks sometimes occur spontaneously at workshops or sales meetings when participants around a table link through a wireless network to share information. The independent BSS network is somewhat limited, because it depends on the proximity of the participating computers, provides no infrastructure for managing connections, and offers no means of linking with bigger networks such as the local LAN or the Internet.

Another form of wireless network, called an **infrastructure basic service set (infrastructure BSS)**, is more common on corporate networks and other institutional settings—and it is now quite popular as an option for the home and coffee shop due to a new generation of inexpensive wireless routing devices. An infrastructure BSS depends on a fixed device called an **access point** to facilitate communication among the wireless devices (see Figure 9.10). An access point communicates with the wireless network through wireless broadcasts and is wired to an ordinary ethernet network through a conventional connection. Wireless devices communicate through the access point. If a wireless device wants to communicate with other wireless devices in the same zone, it sends a frame to the access point and lets the access point deliver the message to its destination. For communication to or from the conventional network, the access point acts as a bridge. The access point forwards any frames addressed to the devices on the conventional network and keeps all frames addressed to the wireless network on the wireless side.

FIGURE 9.9
An independent BSS (ad hoc network).

FIGURE 9.10
An infrastructure BSS contains one or more access points.

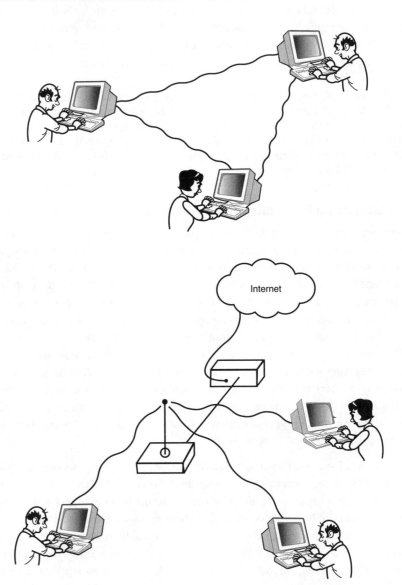

The network shown in Figure 9.10 lets the computers function much as they would with an ordinary wired ethernet network. The infrastructure BSS configuration also offers benefits if you consider a larger area served by a collection of access points connected by conventional ethernet (see Figure 9.11).

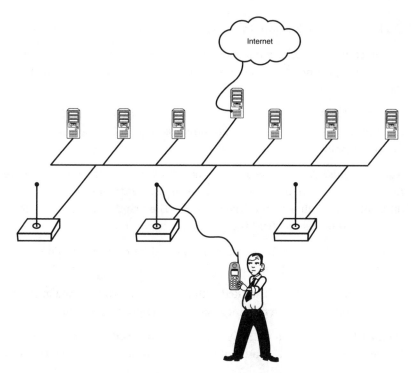

FIGURE 9.11
An infrastruc-
ture BSS with
multiple access
points.

802.11 was devised to address situations like the network depicted in Figure 9.11. The idea is for the roving device to remain connected as it travels anywhere within the area served by the network. The first thing to notice is that, if the device is to receive any network transmissions, the network must know which access point to use to reach the device. This concern is, of course, compounded by the fact that the device is possibly moving, and the appropriate access point might change without warning. Another thing to notice is that the classic concepts of a source address and destina-tion address are not always sufficient for delivering data on a wireless network. In fact, the 802.11 frame makes provision for four addresses:

▶ **Destination address:** The devices to which the frame is addressed.

▶ **Source address:** The device that sent the frame.

▶ **Receiver address:** The wireless device that should process the 802.11 frame. If the frame is addressed to a wireless device, the receiver address is the same as the destination address. If the frame is addressed to a device beyond the wireless network, the receiver address is the address of the access point that will receive the frame and forward it to the ethernet distribution network.

▶ **Transmitter address:** The address of the device that forwarded the frame onto the wireless network.

The 802.11 frame format is shown in Figure 9.12. Some important fields are as follows:

▶ **Frame control:** A collection of smaller fields describing the protocol version, the frame type, and other values necessary for interpreting the contents of the frame.

▶ **Duration/ID:** A field that provides an estimate of approximately how long the transmission will last. This field may also request buffered frames from the access point.

▶ **Address fields:** 48-bit physical address fields. As noted earlier, 802.11 sometimes requires up to four different addresses. The addresses fields are used differently depending on the type of frame. The first field is typically the receiver and the second field is typically the transmitter.

▶ **Sequence control:** The fragment number (used for defragmentation) and a sequence number for the frame.

▶ **Frame body:** The data transmitted with the frame. As you learned in Hour 2, the data transmitted with a frame also contains upper-layer protocol headers.

▶ **Frame Check Sequence (FCS):** A cyclic redundancy check, used to check for transmission errors and verify that the frame has not been altered in transit.

FIGURE 9.12
802.11 frame
format.

Frame CTL (2 Bytes)	Duration ID (2 Bytes)	Address 1 (6 Bytes)	Address 2 (6 Bytes)	Address 3 (6 Bytes)	Seq Control (2 Bytes)	Address 4 (6 Bytes)	Frame Body (0-2304 Bytes)	Frame Check Seq (4 Bytes)

Note that because 802.11 is a Network Access layer protocol set, the addresses used in 802.11 frames are the 48-bit physical addresses you learned about in Hour 3, not IP addresses. As the device moves across the wireless network, it registers itself with the nearest available access point. (Technically, it registers itself with the access point that has the strongest signal and least interference.) This registration process is known as **association**. When the device roams closer to another access point, it reassociates with the new access point. This association process lets the network determine which access point to use to reach each device.

Wi-Fi Alliance

To ensure the compatibility of 802.11 devices, a group called the Wireless Ethernet Compatibility Alliance (WECA) formed in 1999 to provide a certification program for wireless products. The group later changed its name to the Wi-Fi Alliance. To earn Wi-Fi (Wireless Fidelity) certification, a product must be tested for interoperability with other wireless devices. To learn more about the Wi-Fi Alliance, visit www.wi-fi.org.

802.11 Security

As you can probably guess, an unprotected wireless network is extremely unsecure. To eavesdrop on a conventional network, you must at least be somehow connected to the transmission medium. A wireless network, on the other hand, is vulnerable from anywhere within broadcast distance. Not only can an intruder listen in, but an enterprising attacker can also simply show up with a wireless device and start participating in the network if the network has no protections to prevent such activities.

To address these concerns, IEEE developed an optional security protocol standard to accompany 802.11. The **Wired Equivalent Privacy (WEP)** standard was designed to provide a level of privacy approximately equivalent to the privacy provided by a conventional wired network. The goal of WEP was to address the following concerns:

▶ **Confidentiality:** Protection from eavesdropping

▶ **Integrity:** Assurance that the data is unaltered

▶ **Authentication:** Assurance that the communicating parties are who they say they are, and that they have the necessary authorization to operate on the network

WEP handles the confidentiality and integrity goals through encryption using the RC4 algorithm. The sending device generates an Integrity Check Value (ICV). The ICV is a value that results from a standard calculation based on the contents of the frame. The ICV is then encrypted using the RC4 algorithm and transmitted to the receiver. The receiving device decrypts the frame and calculates the ICV. If the calculated ICV value matches the value transmitted with the frame, the frame has not been altered.

WEP, unfortunately, has met with objections from security experts. Most experts now regard WEP as ineffective. Some of the objections to WEP are actually objections to the implementation of the RC4 encryption algorithm. WEP theoretically uses a 64-bit key, but 24 bits of the key are used for initialization. Only 40 bits of the key are used as a shared secret. This 40-bit secret is too short, according to the experts, and WEP is therefore insufficient for effective protection. Experts also point to problems with the key management system and with the 24-bit initialization vector used to begin the encryption.

An update to WEP known as WEP2 increased the initialization vector to 128 bits and added Kerberos authentication to organize the use and distribution of secret keys. However, WEP2 didn't solve all the problems of WEP. Several other protocols, such as Extensible Authentication Protocol (EAP), have appeared to address the concerns about WEP.

The 802.11i draft standard for a better wireless security protocol appeared in 2004 and was incorporated into the 802.11 standard in 2007. This new approach, which is known as **Wi-Fi Protected Access II (WPA2)**, uses an AES block cipher for encryption rather than RC4 and also comes with more secure procedures for authentication and key distribution. WPA2 appears to be a big advance in wireless security and has largely replaced WEP as the preferred security method for wireless networking.

Many wireless devices also support other security measures. For instance, many wireless routers let you enter the MAC addresses of computers that are authorized to operate on the network. These kinds of measures are often effective for stopping your next door neighbor from embezzling your bandwidth, but be aware that experienced intruders have ways to get around these kinds of controls.

Mobile IP

You might have noticed that devices moving around the world pose a significant problem for delivering responses to Internet requests: The Internet addressing system is organized hierarchically with the assumption that the target device is located on the network segment defined through the IP address. Because a mobile device can be anywhere, the rules for communicating with the device become much more complicated. To maintain a TCP connection, the device must have a constant IP address, which means that a roaming device cannot simply use an address assigned by the nearest transmitter. Significantly, because this problem relates to Internet addressing, it can't be solved strictly at the Network Access layer and requires an extension to the Internet layer's IP protocol. The **Mobile IP** extension was described in RFC 3220, which has since been updated. The latest IPv4 mobile standard is RFC 5944.

Mobile IP solves the addressing problem by associating a second (in care of) address with the permanent IP address. The Mobile IP environment is depicted in Figure 9.13. The device retains a permanent address for the home network. A specialized router known as the Home Agent, located on the home network, maintains a table that binds the device's current location to its permanent address. When the device enters a new network, the device registers with a Foreign Agent process operating on the network. The Foreign agent adds the mobile device to the Visitor list and sends information on the devices current location to the Home Agent. The Home Agent then updates the mobility binding table with the current location of the device. When a datagram address to the device arrives on the home network, the datagram is encapsulated in a packet addressed to the foreign network, where it is delivered to the device.

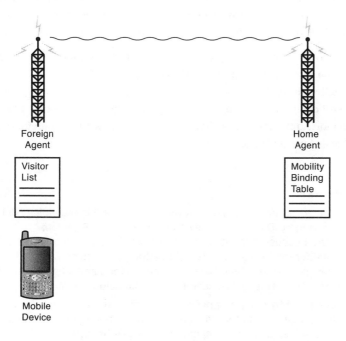

Foreign
Agent

Visitor
List

Mobile
Device

Home
Agent

Mobility
Binding
Table

FIGURE 9.13
Mobile IP pro-
vides a means
for delivering
datagrams to a
roaming device.

Bluetooth

The **Bluetooth** protocol architecture is another specification for wireless devices that is gaining popularity throughout the networking industry. Bluetooth was originally developed by Ericsson and later developed by a group of other companies, including Intel and IBM. Like 802.11, the Bluetooth standard defines the OSI Data Link and Physical layers (equivalent to the TCP/IP Network Access layer). The Bluetooth trademark is controlled by an association known as the Bluetooth Special Interest Group (SIG).

Although the Bluetooth standard is often used for peripheral devices such as headsets and wireless keyboards, Bluetooth is also used in place of 802.11 in some cases, and Bluetooth backers are always eager to state that some of the security problems related to 802.11 do not apply to Bluetooth. However, Bluetooth and 802.11 are considered "complementary technologies." Whereas 802.11 is designed to provide an equivalent to ethernet for wireless networks, Bluetooth focuses on providing a reliable and high-performing environment for wireless devices operating in a short range (10 meters). Bluetooth is designed to facilitate communication among a group of interacting wireless devices in a small work area defined within the Bluetooth specification as a personal area network (PAN).

Like other wireless forms, Bluetooth uses an access point to connect the wireless network to a conventional network. (The access point is known as a network access point, or NAP, in Bluetooth terminology.) The Bluetooth Encapsulation Protocol encapsulates TCP/IP packets for distribution for delivery over the Bluetooth network.

Of course, if a Bluetooth device is to be accessible through the Internet, it must be accessible through TCP/IP. Vendors envision a class of Internet-ready Bluetooth devices accessible through a Bluetooth-enabled Internet bridge (see Figure 9.14). A Bluetooth NAP device acts as a network bridge, receiving incoming TCP/IP transmissions and replacing the incoming Network Access layer with the Bluetooth network access protocols for delivery to a waiting device.

By the Way

Why Bluetooth?

Authors and linguists are delighted that the creators of this technology did not use an acronym for it. But why did they choose the name *Bluetooth*? Because it crunches data? Because it takes bytes? Forget about finding a metaphor. Bluetooth is named for the Viking King Harald Bluetooth, who ruled Denmark and Norway in the eleventh century. King Harald is famous for converting to Christianity after watching a German priest succeed with a miraculous dare.

Bluetooth was loved by many, but his rule was often arbitrary. He seems to be the model for the bad guy in the William Tell legend, having once commanded that one of his subjects shoot an apple off his son's head. The marksman made the shot, but then announced that, if he'd missed, he had three more arrows to shoot into Bluetooth's heart. As we enter the wireless Valhalla, we will hope the devices ruled by the new Bluetooth do not exhibit this same propensity for spontaneous vengeance.

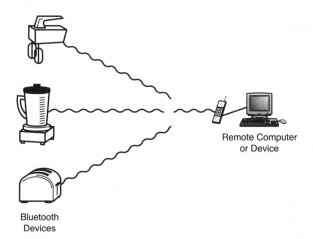

FIGURE 9.14
A Bluetooth-
enabled
Internet bridge.

Remote Computer
or Device

Bluetooth
Devices

Connectivity Devices

The previous hour dealt extensively with the important topic of routers on TCP/IP
networks. Although routers are an extremely important and fundamental concept,
they are just one of many connectivity devices you'll find on a TCP/IP network.

Many types of connectivity devices exist, and they all play a role in managing traffic
on TCP/IP networks. The following sections discuss bridges, hubs, and switches.

Bridges

A **bridge** is a connectivity device that filters and forwards packets by physical
address. Bridges operate at the OSI Data Link layer (which, as described in Hour 3,
falls within the TCP/IP Network Access layer). In recent years, bridges have become
much less common as networks move to more versatile devices, such as switches.
However, the simplicity of the bridges makes it a good starting point for this discussion of connectivity devices.

Although a bridge is not a router, a bridge still uses a routing table as a source for
delivery information. This physical address–based routing table is considerably different from and less sophisticated than the routing tables described later in this hour.

A bridge listens to each segment of the network it is connected to and builds a table
showing which physical address is on which segment. When data is transmitted on
one of the network segments, the bridge checks the destination address of the data
and consults the routing table. If the destination address is on the segment from
which the data was received, the bridge ignores the data. If the destination address is
on a different segment, the bridge forwards the data to the appropriate segment. If
the destination address isn't in the routing table, the bridge forwards the data to all
segments except the segment from which it received the transmission.

> **Physical Versus Logical**
>
> It is important to remember that the hardware-based physical addresses used by a bridge are different from the logical IP addresses. See Hours 1–4 for more on the difference between physical and logical addresses.

Bridges were once common on LANs as an inexpensive means of filtering traffic, and therefore increasing the number of computers that can participate in the network. As you learned earlier in this hour, the bridge concept is now embodied in certain network access devices such as cable modems and some DSL devices. Because bridges use only Network Access layer physical addresses and do not examine logical addressing information available in the IP datagram header, bridges are not useful for connecting dissimilar networks. Bridges also cannot assist with the IP routing and delivery schemes used to forward data on large networks such as the Internet.

Hubs

In the early years of ethernet, most networks used a scheme that connected the computers with a single, continuous coaxial cable. In later years, however, engineers started to see the advantage of using a central device to which the computers on the network connect (see Figure 9.15).

FIGURE 9.15
A hub-based ethernet network.

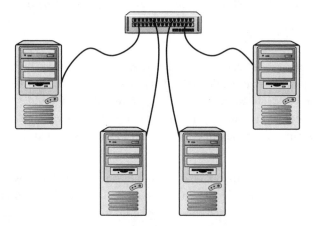

As you'll recall from Hour 3, the classic ethernet concept calls for all computers to share the transmission medium. Each transmission is heard by all network adapters. An ethernet **hub** evolved as a network device that receives a transmission from one of its ports and echoes that transmission to all of its other ports (refer to Figure 9.15). In other words, the network behaves as if all computers were connected using a single continuous line. The hub does not filter or route any data. Instead, the hub just receives and retransmits signals.

One of the principal reasons for the rise of hub-based ethernet is that in most cases a hub simplifies the task of wiring the network. Each computer is connected to the hub through a single line. A computer can easily be detached and reconnected. In an office setting where computers are commonly grouped together in a small area, a single hub can serve a close group of computers and can be connected to other hubs in other parts of the network. With all cables connected to a single device, vendors soon began to realize the opportunities for innovation. More sophisticated hubs, called **intelligent hubs**, began to appear. Intelligent hubs provided additional features, such as the capability to detect a line problem and block off a port. The hub has now largely been replaced by the switch, which you learn about in the next section.

Switches

A hub-based ethernet network still faces the principal liability of the ethernet: Performance degrades as traffic increases. No computer can transmit unless the line is free. Furthermore, each network adapter must receive and process every frame placed on the ethernet. A smarter version of a hub, called a **switch**, was developed to address these problems with ethernet. In its most fundamental form, a switch looks similar to the hub shown in Figure 9.15. Each computer is attached to the switch through a single line. However, the switch is smarter about where it sends the data received through one of its ports. Most switches associate each port with the physical address of the adapter connected to that port (see Figure 9.16). When one of the computers attached to the port transmits a frame, the switch checks the destination address of the frame and sends the frame to the port associated with that destination address. In other words, the switch sends the frame only to the adapter that is supposed to receive it. Every adapter does not have to examine every frame transmitted on the network. The switch reduces superfluous transmissions and therefore improves the performance of the network.

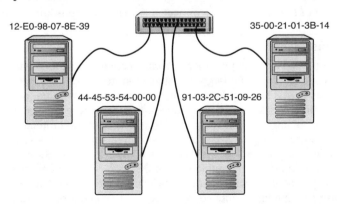

12-E0-98-07-8E-39   35-00-21-01-3B-14

44-45-53-54-00-00   91-03-2C-51-09-26

FIGURE 9.16
A switch associates each port with a physical address.

Note that the type of switch I just described operates with physical addresses (see Hour 3) and not IP addresses. The switch is not a router. Actually, a switch is more like a bridge—or, more accurately, like several bridges in one. The switch isolates each of its network connections so that only data coming from or going to the computer on the end of the connection enters the line (see Figure 9.17).

FIGURE 9.17
A switch isolates each computer to reduce traffic.

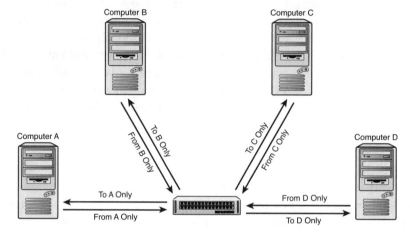

Several types of switches are now available. Two of the most common switching methods are

▶ **Cut-through:** The switch starts forwarding the frame as soon as it obtains the destination address.

▶ **Store and forward:** The switch receives the entire frame before retransmitting. This method slows down the retransmission process, but it can sometimes improve overall performance because the switch filters out fragments and other invalid frames.

Switches have become increasingly popular in recent years. Corporate LANs often use a collection of layered and interconnected switches for optimum performance.

Switches and Layers

Some vendors now view the fundamental switch concept described earlier in this section as a special case of a larger category of switching devices. More sophisticated switches operate at higher protocol layers and can, therefore, base forwarding decisions on a greater variety of parameters. In this more general approach to switching, devices are classified according to the highest OSI protocol layer at which they operate. Thus, the basic switch described earlier in this section, which operates at OSI's Data Link layer, is known as a *Layer 2* switch. Switches that forward based on IP address information at the OSI Network layer are called *Layer 3* switches. (As you might guess, a Layer 3 switch is essentially a type of router.) If no such layer designation is applied to the switch, assume it operates at Layer 2 and filters by physical (MAC) address, as described in this section.

Summary

This hour discussed some different technologies for connecting to the Internet or other large networks. You learned about modems, point-to-point connections, and host dial-up access. You also learned about some popular broadband technologies, such as cable networking and DSL, as well as WAN techniques. This hour also toured some important wireless network protocols and described some popular connectivity devices found on TCP/IP networks.

Q&A

Q. Why don't SLIP and PPP require a complete physical addressing system such as the system used with ethernet?

A. A point-to-point connection doesn't require an elaborate physical addressing system such as ethernet's because only the two computers participating in the connection are attached to the line. However, SLIP and PPP do provide full support for logical addressing using IP or other Network layer protocols.

Q. My cable modem connection slows down at about the same time every day. What's the problem? What can I do about it?

A. A cable modem shares the transmission medium with other devices, so performance can decline at high usage levels. Unless you can connect to a different network segment (which is unlikely), you'll have to live with this effect if you use cable broadband. You might try switching your service to DSL, which provides a more consistent level of service. You might find, however, that DSL is not faster overall than cable—it depends on the details of the service, the local traffic levels, and the providers in your area.

Q. Why does a mobile device associate (register) with an access point?

A. Incoming frames from the conventional network are relayed to the mobile device by the access point to which the device is associated. By associating with an access point, the device tells the network that the access point should receive any frames addressed to the device.

Workshop

The following workshop is composed of a series of quiz questions and practical exercises. The quiz questions are designed to test your overall understanding of the current material. The practical exercises are intended to afford you the opportunity to apply the concepts discussed during the current hour, as well as build upon the knowledge acquired in previous hours of study. Please take time to complete the quiz questions and exercises before continuing. Refer to Appendix A, "Answers to Quizzes and Exercises," for answers.

Quiz

1. What is the predominate protocol used to transmit IP datagrams over a phone line?

2. Name two land-line based broadband technologies available for home use.

3. Name four wide area network technologies.

4. What is another name for an independent basic service set wireless network?

5. What is the difference between a hub and a switch?

Exercises

1. List some of the disadvantages of a dial-up connection.

2. If you can get access to DSL and cable modem networks, try them both. Determine whether there is a performance difference.

3. If your computer is Wi-Fi enabled, try to find out which 802.11 protocol it's using.

4. If you are connected to a Wi-Fi network, determine how the performance compares to a wired network such as ethernet.

5. Investigate the prices of switches and hubs. Based on the results of your investigation and what you learned this hour, determine what you would use for a small home network.

Key Terms

Review the following list of key terms:

▶ **802.11:** A set of protocols for wireless communication. The 802.11 protocols occupy the Network Access layer of the TCP/IP stack, which is equivalent to the OSI Data Link and Physical layers.

▶ **Access point:** A device that serves as a connecting point from a wireless network to a conventional network. An access point typically acts as a network bridge, forwarding frames to and from a wireless network to a conventional ethernet network.

▶ **Association:** A procedure in which a wireless device registers its affiliation with a nearby access point.

▶ **Bluetooth:** A protocol architecture for wireless appliances and devices in close proximity.

▶ **Bridge:** A connectivity device that forwards data based on physical address.

▶ **Cable modem termination system (CMTS):** A device that serves as an interface from a cable modem connection to the provider network.

▶ **Cut-through switching:** A switching method that causes the switch to start forwarding the frame as soon as it obtains the destination address.

▶ **Data Over Cable Service Interface Specification (DOCSIS):** A specification for cable modem networks.

▶ **Digital subscriber line (DSL):** A form of broadband connection over a telephone line.

▶ **Digital subscriber line access multiplexer (DSLAM):** A device that serves as an interface from a DSL connection to the provider network.

▶ **Hub:** A connectivity device to which network cables are attached to form a network segment. Hubs typically do not filter data and instead retransmit incoming frames to all ports. The once-common hub has now been replaced by the switch, but hubs are still important for understanding the evolution of LAN networking devices.

▶ **Independent basic service set (Independent BSS or IBSS):** A wireless network consisting of two or more devices communicating with each other directly (also known as an ad hoc network).

▶ **Infrastructure basic service set (Infrastructure BSS):** A wireless network in which the wireless devices communicate through one or more access points connected to a conventional network.

▶ **Intelligent hub:** A hub capable of performing additional tasks such as blocking off a port when a line problem is detected.

▶ **Link Control Protocol (LCP):** A protocol used by PPP to establish, manage, and terminate dial-up connections.

▶ **Mobile IP:** An IP addressing technique designed to support roaming mobile devices.

▶ **Modem:** A device that translates a digital signal to or from an analog signal.

▶ **Network control protocol (NCP):** One of a family of protocols designed to interface PPP with specific protocol suites.

▶ **Point-to-point connection:** A connection consisting of exactly two communicating devices sharing a transmission line.

▶ **Point-to-Point Protocol (PPP):** A dial-up protocol. PPP supports TCP/IP and also other network protocol suites. PPP is newer and more powerful than SLIP.

▶ **Serial Line Internet Protocol (SLIP):** An early TCP/IP-based dial-up protocol.

▶ **Store-and-forward switching:** A switching method that causes the switch to receive the entire frame before retransmitting.

▶ **Switch:** A connectivity device. A switch is aware of the address associated with each of its ports and forwards each incoming frame to the correct port. Switches can base forwarding decisions on a variety of parameters encapsulated in the headers of the protocol stack.

▶ **Wide area network (WAN):** A collection of technologies designed to provide relatively fast and high-bandwidth connections over large distances.

▶ **Wi-Fi Protected Access II (WPA2):** An advanced wireless security standard that has largely replaced WEP. WPA2 uses an AES block cipher for encryption.

▶ **Wired Equivalent Privacy (WEP):** A standard for security on 802.11 wireless networks. WEP is now considered obsolete.

HOUR 10

Name Resolution

What You'll Learn in This Hour:

- ▶ Hostname resolution
- ▶ DNS
- ▶ DNSSEC
- ▶ Dynamic DNS
- ▶ NetBIOS

In Hour 2, "How TCP/IP Works," you learned about name resolution, a powerful technique that associates an alphanumeric name with the 32-bit IP address. The name resolution process accepts a name for a computer and attempts to resolve the name to the corresponding address. In this hour, you learn about hostnames, domain names, and fully qualified domain names (FQDNs). You also learn about the alternative NetBIOS name resolution system commonly used on Microsoft networks.

At the completion of this hour, you will be able to

- ▶ Explain how name resolution works
- ▶ Explain the differences between hostnames, domain names, and FQDNs
- ▶ Describe hostname resolution
- ▶ Describe DNS name resolution
- ▶ Describe NetBIOS name resolution

What Is Name Resolution?

When the early TCP/IP networks went online, users quickly realized that it was not healthy or efficient to attempt to remember the IP address of every computer on the network. The people at the research center were much too busy to have to remember whether Computer A in Building 6 had the address 100.12.8.14 or 100.12.8.18. Programmers began to wonder whether it would be possible to assign each computer a descriptive, human-friendly name and then let the computers on the network take care of associating the name with an address.

The hostname system is a simple name resolution technique developed early in the history of TCP/IP. In this system, each computer is assigned an alphanumeric name called a **hostname**. If the operating system encounters an alphanumeric name where it is expecting an IP address, the operating system consults a **hosts file** (see Figure 10.1). The hosts file contains a list of hostname-to-IP-address associations. If the alphanumeric name is on the list of hostnames, the computer reads the IP address associated with the name. The computer then replaces the hostname in the command with the corresponding IP address and executes the command.

FIGURE 10.1
Hostname resolution.

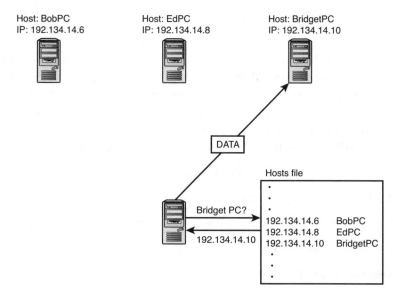

The hosts file system worked well (and still does) on small local networks. However, this system becomes inefficient on larger networks. The host-to-address associations have to reside in a single file, and the search efficiency of that file diminishes as the file expands. In the ARPAnet days, a single master file called hosts.txt maintained a list of name-to-address associations, and local administrators had to continually update hosts.txt to stay current. Furthermore, the hosts name space was essentially flat. All nodes were equal, and the name resolution system could not make use of the efficient, hierarchical structure of the IP address space.

Even if the ARPAnet engineers could have solved these problems, the hosts file system could never work with a huge network with millions of nodes like the Internet. The engineers knew they needed a hierarchical name resolution system that would

▶ Distribute the responsibility for name resolution among a group of special name resolution servers. The name resolution servers maintain the tables that define name-to-address associations.

▶ Grant authority for local name resolution to a local administrator. In other words, instead of maintaining a centralized, master copy of all name-to-address pairs, let an administrator on Network A be responsible for name resolution on Network A, and let an admin of Network B manage name resolution for Network B. That way, the individuals responsible for any changes on a network are also responsible for making sure those changes are reflected in the name resolution infrastructure.

These priorities led to the development of the **Domain Name System (DNS)**. DNS is the name resolution method used on the Internet and is the source of common Internet names such as www.unixreview.com and www.slashdot.org. As you will learn later in this hour, DNS divides the namespace into hierarchical entities called **domains**. The **domain name** can be included with the hostname in what is called a **fully qualified domain name (FQDN)**. For instance, a computer with the hostname maybe in the domain whitehouse.gov would have the FQDN maybe.whitehouse.gov.

Through the years, the DNS system continued to evolve, and DNS now offers options for better security, dynamic address mapping, and autodiscovery. This hour describes hostname resolution and DNS name resolution. You also learn about NetBIOS, a name resolution system used on some Microsoft networks.

Name Resolution Using Hosts Files

As you learned earlier in this hour, a hosts file is a file containing a table that associates hostnames to IP addresses. Hostname resolution was developed before the more sophisticated DNS name resolution, and newer, more sophisticated name resolution methods make the hosts file a bit anachronistic in contemporary environments. However, this legacy hostname resolution technique is still a good starting point for a discussion of name resolution.

Configuring hostname resolution on a small network is usually simple. Operating systems that support TCP/IP recognize the hosts file and use it for name resolution with little or no intervention from the user. The details for configuring hostname resolution vary, depending on the implementation. The steps are roughly as follows:

1. Assign an IP address and hostname to each computer.

2. Create a hosts file that maps the IP address to the hostname of each computer. The hosts file is often named hosts, although some implementations use the filename hosts.txt.

3. Place the hosts file in the designated location on each computer. The location varies, depending on the operating system.

The hosts file contains entries for hosts that a computer needs to communicate with, allowing you to enter an IP address with a corresponding hostname, an FQDN, or other aliases statically. Also, the file usually contains an entry for the loopback address, 127.0.0.1. The loopback address is used for TCP/IP diagnostics and represents "this computer."

The following example shows what a hosts file might look like (the IP address of the system is on the left, followed by the hostname and an optional comment about the entry):

```
127.0.0.1        localhost           #this machine

198.1.14.2       bobscomputer        #Bob's workstation

198.1.14.128     r4downtown          #gateway
```

When an application on a computer needs to resolve a name to an IP address, the system first compares its own name to the name being requested. If there is no match, the system then looks in the hosts file (if one is present) to see whether the computer name is listed.

If a match is found, the IP address is returned to the local computer and, as you learned in earlier hours, is used with the Address Resolution Protocol (ARP) to obtain the hardware address of the other system. Now communication between the two computers can take place.

If you're using hosts files for name resolution, a change to the network forces you to edit or replace the hosts file on every computer. You can use a number of text editors to edit the hosts file. On a UNIX or Linux system, use a text editor such as vi, Pico, or Emacs; on Windows, use Notepad. Some systems also provide TCP/IP configuration tools that act as a user interface for configuring the hosts file.

When you create or edit the hosts file, be sure to keep the following points in mind:

▶ The IP address must be left-justified and separated from the hostname by one or more spaces.

▶ Names must be separated by at least one space.

▶ Additional names on a single line become aliases for the first name.

▶ The file is parsed (that is, read by the computer) from top to bottom. The IP address associated with the first match is used. When the match is made, parsing stops.

▶ Because it is parsed from top to bottom, you should put the most commonly used names at the top of the list. This can help speed up the process.

▶ Comments might be placed to the right of a # symbol.

▶ Remember that the hosts file is static; you must manually change it when an IP address changes.

▶ Although FQDNs are allowed and work in hosts files, their use in hosts files is discouraged and can lead to problems that are difficult for an administrator to diagnose. The local administrator who controls the hosts file does not have any control over the allocation of IP addresses and hostnames on a remote network. Therefore, if a server on the remote network is assigned a new IP address, and the FQDN in the local hosts file is not updated, the hosts file continues to point to the old IP address.

A hosts file is an efficient and simple way to provide name resolution for a small, isolated TCP/IP network. Of course, isolated networks aren't as common as they once were. Also, Windows, Mac OS, and other operating systems offer more automated techniques for name resolution on a small scale, thus rendering the hosts file unnecessary in most situations. Larger networks depend on DNS for name resolution.

DNS Name Resolution

The designers of DNS wanted to avoid having to keep an up-to-date name resolution file on each computer. DNS instead places name resolution data on one or more special servers. The DNS servers provide name resolution services for the network (see Figure 10.2). If a computer on the network encounters a hostname where it is expecting an IP address, it sends a query to the server asking for the IP address associated with the hostname. If the DNS server has the address, it sends the address back to the requesting computer. The computer then invisibly substitutes the IP address for the hostname and executes the command. When a change occurs on the network (such as a new computer or a change to a hostname), the network administrator has to change only the DNS configuration once (on the DNS server). The new information is then available to any computer that initiates a DNS query to the server. Also, the DNS server can be optimized for search speed and can support a larger database than would be possible with each computer searching separately through the cumbersome hosts file.

FIGURE 10.2
A DNS server provides name resolution services for the network.

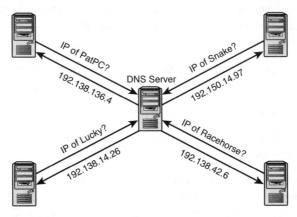

The DNS server shown in Figure 10.2 provides several advantages over hosts file-name resolution. It offers a single DNS configuration point for a local network and provides more efficient use of network resources. However, the configuration shown in Figure 10.2 still does not solve the problem of providing decentralized management of a vast network infrastructure. Like the hosts file, the configuration in Figure 10.2 would not scale well to a huge network like the Internet. The name server in Figure 10.2 could not operate efficiently with a database that included a record for every host on the Internet. Even if it could, the logistics of maintaining an all-Internet database would be prohibitive. Whoever configured the server would have to know about every change to any Internet host anywhere in the world.

A better solution, reasoned the designers, was to let every office or institution configure a local name server to operate, as shown in Figure 10.2, and then to provide a means for all the name servers to talk to each other (see Figure 10.3). In this scenario, when a DNS client sends a name resolution request to a name server, the name server does one of the following:

▶ If the name server can find the requested address in its own address database, it immediately sends the address to the client.

▶ If the name server cannot find the address in its own records, it queries other name servers to find the address and then sends the address to the client.

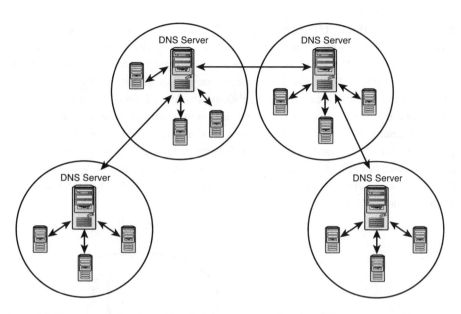

FIGURE 10.3
On large networks, DNS servers communicate with each other to provide name resolution services.

You might be wondering how the first name server knows which name server to contact when it begins the query process that will lead to the address. Actually, this query process is closely associated with the design of the DNS namespace. Keep in mind that DNS is not working strictly with a hostname. As described earlier in this hour, DNS works with FQDNs. An FQDN consists of both a hostname and a name specifying the domain.

The DNS namespace is a multitiered arrangement of domains (see Figure 10.4). A domain is a collection of computers under a single authority sharing a common portion of the namespace (that is, bearing the same domain name). At the top of the DNS tree is a single node known as root. Root is sometimes shown as a period (.), although the actual symbol for root is a null character. Beneath root is a group of domains known as top level domains (TLDs). Figure 10.4 shows some of the TLDs for the world's most famous DNS namespace: the Internet. TLDs include the familiar .com, .org, and .edu domains, as well as domains for national governments, such as .us (United States), .uk (United Kingdom), .fr (France), and .jp (Japan).

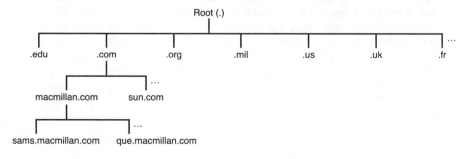

FIGURE 10.4
The DNS namespace.

Beneath each of these TLDs is another tier of domains that (in the case of the Internet) are operated by companies, institutions, or organizations. The institutional name is prefixed to the TLD name. For instance, in Figure 10.5, DeSade College has the domain name DeSade.edu. The organization with authority over a domain can create one or more additional tiers of subdomains. At each level, the name of the local domain is prefixed to the parent domain name. For example, the department of recreational pyrotechnics at DeSade has the domain name flames.DeSade.edu (refer to Figure 10.5), and the department's popular lounge (which the students affectionately call "the dungeon") has the name dungeon.flames.DeSade.edu. In all, the DNS system supports up to 127 levels of domains, although a name of that length would evoke agony.

FIGURE 10.5
An appropriate
DNS scenario.

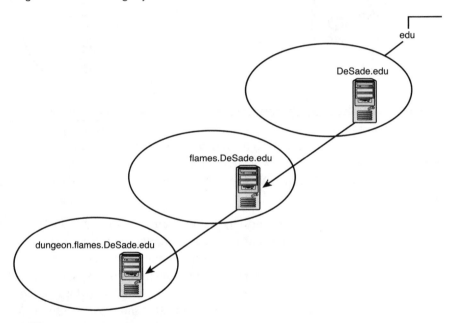

By the
Way

Those Tiers Again
If you've worked much with the Internet, you have probably noticed that extended domain names with several levels (such as the scenario shown in Figure 10.5) are relatively uncommon. Websites, especially in the crowded .com TLD, are typically referenced as the institutional domain name with the www prefix: www.ibm.com. However, keep in mind that a website might be served from a single server or group of servers at a single location. Multitiered domain names are encountered more commonly by network admins accessing resources on a large corporate network that spans several locations. TLDs in the public sector (such as .gov) tend to make more use of multitiered names.

The domain name shows the chain of domains from the top of the tree. The name server in the domain sams.com holds name resolution information for hosts located in sams.com. The authoritative name server for a domain can delegate name resolution for a subdomain to another server. For instance, the authoritative name server in sams.com can delegate authority for the subdomain edit.sams.com to another name server. The name resolution records for the subdomain edit.sams.com are then located on the name server that has been delegated authority for the subdomain. Authority for name resolution is thus delegated throughout the tree, and the administrators for a given domain can have control of name-to-address mappings for the hosts in that domain.

When a host on the network needs an IP address, it usually sends a recursive query to a nearby name server. This query tells the name server, "either give me the IP address associated with this name or else tell me that you can't find it." If the name server cannot find the requested address among its own records, it initiates a process of querying other name servers to obtain the address. This process is shown in Figure 10.6. Name server A is using what is called an iterative query to find the address. An iterative query tells the next name server "either send me the IP address or give me a clue to where I might find it." To summarize this process, the client sends a single recursive query to the name server. The name server then issues a series of iterative queries to other name servers to resolve the name. When the name server gets the address associated with the name, it replies to the client's query with the address.

The process for DNS name resolution is as follows (refer to Figure 10.6):

1. Host1 sends a query to name server A asking for the IP address associated with the domain name trog.DogInStarlight.marines.mil.

2. Name server A checks its own records to see if it has the requested address. If server A has the address, it returns the address to Host1.

3. If name server A does not have the address, it initiates the process of finding the address. Name server A sends an iterative request for the address to name server B, a top-level name server for the .mil domain, asking for the address associated with the name trog.DogInStarlight.marines.mil.

4. Name server B is not able to supply the address, but it is able to send name server A the address of name server C, the name server for marines.mil.

5. Name server A sends a request for the address to name server C. Name server C is not able to supply the address, but it is able to send the address of name server D, the name server for DogInStarlight.marines.com.

FIGURE 10.6
The name reso-
lution process.

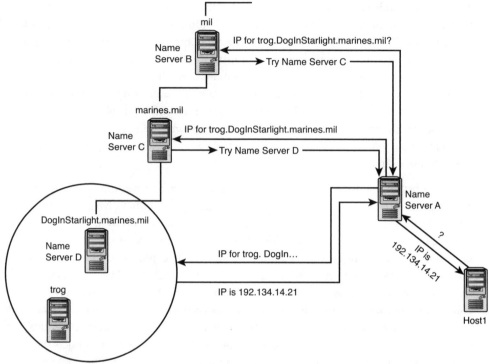

6. Name server A sends a request for the IP address to name server D. Name
   server D looks up the address for the host trog.DogInStarlight.marines.mil
   and sends the address to name server A. Name server A then sends the
   address to Host1.

7. Host1 initiates a connection to the host trog.DogInStarlight.marines.mil.

This process occurs thousands (if not millions) of times a day on the Internet. This
tidy scenario is complicated somewhat by some additional features of the modern
network, including address caching, Dynamic Host Configuration Protocol (DHCP),
and **dynamic DNS**. However, the functionality of most TCP/IP networks depends on
this form of DNS name resolution.

It is also important to note that the network is not required to have a separate name
server for each node on the domain tree. A single name server can handle multiple
domains. It is also common for multiple name servers to serve a single domain.

Registering a Domain

The Internet is only one example of a DNS namespace. You do not have to be connected to the Internet to use DNS. If you are not connected to the Internet, you do not have to worry about registering your domain names. However, organizations that want to use their own domain names on the Internet (such as BuddysCars.com) must register that name with the proper registration authority.

Internet Corporation for Assigned Names and Numbers (ICANN) oversees the task of domain name registration but delegates registration for particular TLDs to other groups. Registration services for a number of commonly used TLDs are listed here:

- **.com, .org, and .net:** A number of companies (known as registrars) are authorized to provide domain name resolution services for the popular .com, .org, and .net TLDs, as well as for lesser-known domains such as .info, .museum, .name, and .pro. See the official list of ICANN-accredited registrars at http://www.internic.net/regist.html.

- **.gov:** The .gov domain is reserved for the U.S. federal government. State and local government names branch from the U.S. TLD. Registration services for the .gov domain are located at https://www.dotgov.gov/portal/web/dotgov/ welcome.

For other domains, including the domains associated with countries, registration procedures may vary.

By the Way

Registration Game

The game of name registration has grown more competitive in recent years. Some companies have made a science out of registering domain names on speculation of perceived value. You might have even had the experience of typing a name incorrectly in your web browser and suddenly seeing a page that asks if you want to register the name you just typed. If you do have a name you want to register, work directly with an official registrar. Experts advise against "checking" to see whether the name is registered by typing it directly into a web browser. Some users have reported seeing the name they wanted mysteriously registered to a speculator after they type the address, although major Internet companies deny involvement with such tactics.

Name Server Types

When implementing DNS on your network, you need to choose at least one server to be responsible for maintaining your domain. This is referred to as your primary name server, and it gets all the information about the zones it is responsible for from local files. Any changes you make to your domain are made on this server.

Many networks also have at least one more server as a backup, or secondary name server. If something happens to your primary server, this machine can continue to service requests. The secondary server gets its information from the primary server's **zone file**. When this exchange of information takes place, it is referred to as a zone transfer.

A third type of server is called a caching-only server. A cache is part of a computer's memory that keeps frequently requested data ready to be accessed. As a caching-only server, it responds to queries from clients on the local network for name resolution requests. It queries other DNS servers for information about domains and computers that offer services such as Web and FTP. When it receives information from other DNS servers, it stores that information in its cache in case a request for that information is made again.

Caching-only servers are used by client computers on the local network to resolve names. Other DNS servers on the Internet will not know about them and, therefore, will not query them. This is desirable if you want to distribute the load your servers are put under. A caching-only server is also simple to maintain.

DNS Implementations
DNS must be implemented as a service or daemon running on the DNS server machine. Windows servers have a native DNS service, though some Microsoft admins prefer to use third-party DNS implementations. The UNIX/Linux world has a number of DNS implementation options, but the most popular choice is Berkeley Internet Name Domain (BIND).

Domains and Zones

A group of DNS hosts in a collective configuration with a common set of DNS servers is called a **zone**. On simple networks, a zone might represent a complete DNS domain. For instance, the domain punyisp.com might be treated as a single zone for purposes of DNS configuration. On more complex networks, the DNS configuration for a subdomain is sometimes delegated to another zone that serves the subdomain. Zone delegation lets administrators with more immediate knowledge of a subnetwork manage the DNS configuration for that subnetwork. For instance, the DNS administrators for the domain cocacola.com might delegate the DNS configuration of the subdomain dallas.cocacola.com to a zone controlled by the DNS administrators in the Dallas office, who have a closer watch on hosts in dallas.cocacola.com.

You might ask, "What's the difference between a zone and a domain?" It is important to note that, aside from the subtle semantic difference (a domain is a subdivision of the namespace and a zone is a collection of hosts), the concepts of a zone and a domain are not exactly parallel. As you read this section, keep the following facts in mind:

▶ Membership in a subdomain implies membership in the parent domain. For instance, a host in dallas.cocacola.com is also part of cocacola.com. By contrast, if the zone for dallas.cocacola.com is delegated, a host in dallas.cocacola.com *is not* part of the cocacola.com zone.

▶ If a subdomain is not specifically delegated, it does not require a separate zone and is simply included with the zone file for the parent domain.

The details of how to delegate a DNS zone depend on the DNS server application. For now, the important thing to remember is that a zone represents a collective configuration for a group of DNS servers and hosts, and DNS administrators can optionally delegate portions of the namespace to other zones for administrative efficiency.

Zone Files

As the previous section stated, a DNS zone is an administrative unit representing a collection of computers inhabiting a portion of the DNS namespace. The DNS configuration for a zone is stored in a zone file. DNS servers refer to the information in the zone file when responding to queries and initiating requests. A zone file is a text file with a standardized structure. The contents of the zone file consist of multiple **resource records**. A resource record is a one-line statement providing a chunk of useful information about the DNS configuration. Some common types of resource records include the following:

▶ **SOA:** SOA stands for Start of Authority. The SOA record designates the authoritative name server for the zone.

▶ **NS:** NS stands for Name Server. The NS record designates a name server for the zone. A zone may have several name servers (and, hence, several NS records) but only one SOA record for the authoritative name server.

▶ **A:** An A record maps a DNS name to an IPv4 address.

▶ **AAAA:** An AAAA record maps a DNS name to an IPv6 address.

▶ **PTR:** A PTR record maps an IP address to a DNS name.

▶ **CNAME:** CNAME is short for canonical name. A CNAME record maps an alias to the actual hostname represented by an A record.

Thus, the zone file tells the DNS server the following:

▶ The authoritative DNS server for the zone

▶ The DNS servers (authoritative and nonauthoritative) in the zone

▶ The DNS-name-to-IP-address mappings for hosts within aliases (alternative names) for hosts within the zone

Other resource record types provide information on topics such as mail servers (MX records), IP-to-DNS-name mappings (PTR records), and well-known services (WKS records). A sample zone file looks something like this:

```
@ IN    SOA     boris.cocacola.com.    hostmaster.cocacola.com. (
        201.9       ; serial number incremented with each
                    ; file update
                    ;
        3600        ; refresh time (in seconds)
        1800        ; retry time (in seconds)
        4000000     ; expiration time (in weeks)
        3600)       ; minimum TTL

IN    NS    horace.cocacola.com.
IN    NS    boris.cocacola.com.
;
; Host to IP address mappings
;
localhost    IN    A    127.0.0.1
chuck        IN    A    181.21.23.4
amy          IN    A    181.21.23.5
darrah       IN    A    181.21.23.6
joe          IN    A    181.21.23.7
bill         IN    A    181.21.23.8
;
; Aliases
;
ap              IN CNAME    amy
db              IN CNAME    darrah
bu              IN CNAME    bill
```

Note that the SOA record includes several parameters governing the process of updating the secondary DNS servers with the master copy of the zone data on the primary DNS server. In addition to a serial number representing the version number of the zone file itself, there are parameters that represent the following:

▶ **Refresh time:** The time interval at which secondary DNS servers should query the primary server for an update of zone information

▶ **Retry time:** The time to wait before trying again if a zone update is unsuccessful

▶ **Expiration time:** The upper limit for how long the secondary name servers should retain a record without a refresh

▶ **Minimum Time to Live (TTL):** The default TTL for exported zone records

The rightmost term of the SOA record is actually the email address for the person with responsibility for the zone. Replace the first period with an @ sign to form the email address.

The preceding example is, of course, the simplest of zone files. Larger files might include hundreds of address records and other less common record types representing other aspects of the configuration. The name of the zone file, and in some cases the format, can vary depending on the DNS server software. This example is based on the popular BIND (Berkeley Internet Name Domain), the most common name server on the Internet.

It is worth remembering, also, that the honored practice of configuring services by manipulating text files is fading from favor. Many DNS server applications provide a user interface that hides the details of the zone file from the reader. Dynamic DNS (described later in this chapter) provides yet another layer of separation from the details of the configuration.

The Reverse Lookup Zone File

Another type of zone file necessary for DNS name resolution is the reverse lookup file. This file is used when a client provides an IP address and requests the corresponding hostname. In IP addresses, the leftmost portion is general, and the rightmost portion is specific. However, in domain names the opposite is true: The left portion is specific, and the right portion, such as com or edu, is general. To create a reverse lookup zone file, you must reverse the order of the network address so the general and specific portions follow the same pattern used within domain names. For example, the zone for the 192.59.66.0 network would have the name 66.59.192.in-addr.arpa.

The in-addr portion stands for *inverse address*, and the arpa portion is another TLD and is a holdover from the original ARPAnet that preceded the Internet.

The file starts out as an ordinary zone file (see the previous example), with an SOA record and NS records defining name servers for the zone, but instead of A records mapping the domain name to an address, the reverse lookup zone file contains PTR records mapping addresses to names. Only the host portion of the address is included in the address mapping—the network portion is obtained from the filename:

```
; zone file for 23.21.181.in-addr.arpa
@ IN   SOA    boris.cocacola.com.   hostmaster.cocacola.com. (
       201.9      ; serial number incremented with each
                  ; file update
                  ;
       3600       ; refresh time (in seconds)
       1800       ; retry time (in seconds)
       4000000    ; expiration time (in weeks)
       3600)      ; minimum TTL

IN   NS    horace.cocacola.com.
IN   NS    boris.cocacola.com.
;
; IP address to host mappings
;
4    IN    PTR    chuck
5    IN    PTR    amy
```

As you will learn in Hour 13, "IPv6: The Next Generation," the next-generation
Internet Protocol (IPv6) includes a massive 128-bit address space. The reverse lookup
zone file still plays the same role on IPv6 subnets, but the name of the file changes
and the entries get longer.

The original plan was for the IPv6 reverse lookup zone file to end in ip6.int, but the
Internet is currently transitioning to the ending ip6.arpa. You might encounter either
form. As with IPv4, the network portion of the address is reflected in the filename (in
reverse order); the host ID is given as an entry in the file (also in reverse order) and
mapped to a host name. See Hour 13 for more on IPv6.

DNS Security Extensions (DNSSEC)

The DNS system has served the Internet community for more than a generation.
Users are accustomed to receiving fast, efficient answers to name service queries, and
in truth, the Internet as a worldwide end-user enterprise would not function very well
at all without DNS. However, experts have known for some time that the DNS system
as it was originally envisioned is inherently unsecure.

DNS data is intended to be public, so in this case, secure does not mean private. But
clients still need a means for ensuring that the reply to a DNS query came from the
real DNS server that is supposed to be overseeing the zone.

Attackers have developed several techniques for sending fake responses to DNS
queries. An attacker who intercepts a DNS query can send a false response, redirect-
ing the client to a clandestine DNS server that will serve as a means for launching
an attack. As long as the false reply arrives before the real reply, the DNS client is
none the wiser.

The solution to this problem is to provide a means of validating the source for the DNS data returned. The **DNS Security Extensions (DNSSEC)** provides this system for validating DNS data. Many operating systems today offer an option for DNSSEC, although it still hasn't been implemented on a massive scale. But several high-profile domains have rolled out support for DNSSEC, which could reduce the barriers for more universal acceptance.

The original DNS security system appeared with RFC 2535 in 1999. This original system, however, proved difficult to implement, and it did not scale well to the Internet, so it was rarely used. A new initiative to secure DNS picked up steam in 2005 with the appearance of RFCs 4033, 4034, and 4035. This new DNSSEC system has been adopted by several important TLDs, such as .com, .org, and some national domains. The signing of the root domain in 2010 will ease the way to universal acceptance.

DNSSEC works through a system of encryption keys and digital signatures. You learn more about signatures and encryption in Hour 11, "TCP/IP Security." Refer to Hour 11 for background information on the digital signature process.

DNSSEC requires support for the Extension Mechanisms for DNS (EDNS), which is defined in RFC 2671. The EDNS DO header bit signals a DNSSEC query.

DNSSEC adds a validation process to ensure that the results of the DNS lookup are authentic. Like the basic DNS name resolution process, DNSSEC works down through a series of parent and child steps to reach the zone associated with the name given in the query. However, DNSSEC adds a chain-of-trust style of validation. The idea is to start with a trusted source and then pass the request down through a series of known and verified steps to reach the server that holds a signature validating the source of the DNS data.

To accomplish this goal, DNSSEC adds four new DNS resource record types:

▶ **DNSKEY:** Public key used to sign and authenticate DNS resource record set

▶ **DS:** Resource record pointing to (and validating) the DNSKEY of a child zone

▶ **RRSIG:** Digital signature associated with zone data

▶ **NSEC:** The next owner name containing authoritative data

The servers holding the secure DNS data form a chain of trust. The resolver must have independent access to the public key associated with a DNSKEY record for the top-level zone. This key is obtained separately. The public key authenticates the data stored on the trust anchor, including a DS record, which validates and authenticates the DNSKEY associated with the child zone at the next step of the lookup process.

The resolver traverses the chain of trust, stepping through lower-level subzones using a DS key on the parent to validate the DNSKEY on the child. At the final step, the DNSKEY decrypts the digital signature stored in the RRSIG resource record and compares it to the signature returned with the normal DNS lookup process. If this process completes successfully, the source for the DNS query is verified, and the data is considered authentic.

The DNSSEC process is depicted in Figure 10.7. A preconfigured key to the trust anchor unlocks the chain of trust. (Ideally, the TLD serves as a trust anchor, but other options are also possible.)

FIGURE 10.7
The DNSSEC
process.

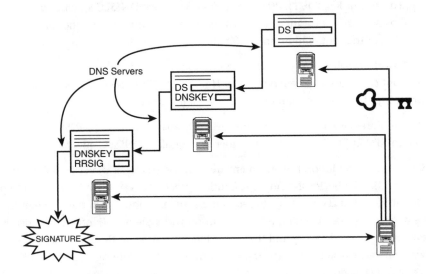

The DNS data stored at the initial entry point includes DS records for any child zones. For example, the authoritative server for the .com zone includes a DS record for famousIT.com. The DS record identifies and authenticates the DNSKEY for the child zone.

If the name includes a series of additional subzones, the resolver proceeds through the chain of trust, obtaining DS records to authenticate lower-level DNSKEYs, leading to other DS records.

When the process reaches the lowest-level child zone, the DNSKEY decrypts the signature for the zone data stored in the RRSIG record. This signature validates the DNS data returned in response to the original query.

As you can see, DNSSEC depends on a chain of interaction between DNSKEY and DS resource records. The DNSKEY and DS resource records are closely related, and both are based on similar information. According to RFC 4034, "A DS RR refers to a DNSKEY RR by storing the key tag, algorithm number, and a digest of the DNSKEY

RR. The DS RR and its corresponding DNSKEY RR have the same owner name, but they are stored in different locations. The DS RR appears only on the upper (parental) side of a delegation, and is authoritative data in the parental zone. For example, the DS RR for example.com is stored in the .com zone rather than in the example.com zone."

The parent zone might include DS records for multiple child zones, and each DS record provides the necessary information to verify that the corresponding DNSKEY record in the child zone is correct and represents a server within the chain of trust.

Another essential ingredient is the RRSIG record containing the signature for the zone data. According to RFC 4035, "To sign a zone, the zone's administrator generates one or more public/private key pairs and uses the private key(s) to sign authoritative RRsets in the zone. For each private key used to create RRSIG records in a zone, the zone should include a zone DNSKEY containing the corresponding public key."

The RRSIG record contains information such as the owner name, a class value, a TTL value, the name of the zone containing the data, and other data identifying the record.

The NSEC record is used in cases of a name error or when an exact match for the lookup name is not available.

DNS Utilities

You can use any network utility that supports name resolution to test whether your network is resolving names properly. A web browser, an FTP client, a Telnet client, or the ping utility can tell you whether your computer is succeeding with name resolution. If you can connect to a resource using its IP address but you cannot connect to the resource using a hostname or FQDN, there is a good chance the problem is a name resolution problem.

If your computer uses a hosts file and also uses DNS, keep in mind that you need to disable or rename the hosts file temporarily when you test DNS. Otherwise it will not be easy to determine whether the name was resolved through the hosts file or DNS. The following section describes how to use ping to test DNS. A later section describes the NSLookup utility, which provides a number of DNS configuration and troubleshooting features.

Checking Name Resolution with Ping

The simple and useful ping utility is a good candidate for testing your DNS configuration. Ping sends a signal to another computer and waits for a reply. If a reply

arrives, you know that the two computers are connected. If you know the IP address
of a remote computer, you can ping the computer by IP address:

```
ping 198.1.14.2
```

If this command succeeds, you know your computer can connect to the remote computer by IP address.

Now try to ping the remote computer by DNS name:

```
ping williepc.remotenet.com
```

If you can ping the remote computer by IP address but not by DNS name, you might
have a name resolution problem. If you can ping by DNS name, name resolution is
working properly.

You learn more about ping in Hour 14, "TCP/IP Utilities."

Checking Name Resolution with NSLookup

The NSLookup utility enables you to query DNS servers and view information such
as their resource records, and it is useful when troubleshooting DNS problems. The
NSLookup utility operates in two modes:

▶ **Batch mode:** In Batch mode, you start NSLookup and provide input
parameters. NSLookup performs the functions requested by the input
parameters, displays the results, and then terminates.

▶ **Interactive mode:** In Interactive mode, you start NSLookup without supplying input parameters. NSLookup then prompts you for parameters. When
you enter the parameters, NSLookup performs the requested actions, displays the results, returns to a prompt, and waits for the next set of parameters. Most administrators use Interactive mode because it is more convenient when performing a series of actions.

NSLookup has an extensive list of options. A few basic options covered here give you
a feel for how NSLookup works.

To run NSLookup in Interactive mode, enter the name nslookup from a command
prompt.

As shown in Figure 10.8, each NSLookup response starts with the name and IP
address of the DNS server that NSLookup is currently using, as follows:

```
Default Server:    dnsserver.Lastingimpressions.com
Address:    192.59.66.200
>
```

The chevron character (>) is NSLookup's prompt.

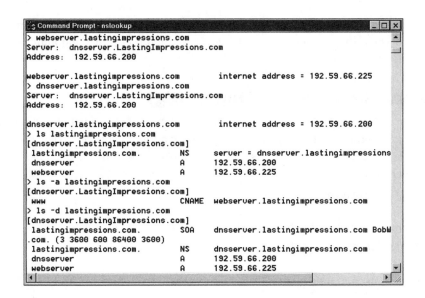

FIGURE 10.8
NSLookup
responses.

NSLookup has about 15 settings that you can change to affect how it operates. A few of the most commonly used settings are listed here:

▶ **?; and help:** These commands are used to view a list of all NSLookup commands.

▶ **server:** This command specifies which DNS server to query.

▶ **ls:** This command is used to list the names in a domain, as shown near the middle of Figure 10.8.

▶ **ls -a:** This command lists canonical names and aliases in a domain, as shown in Figure 10.8.

▶ **ls -d:** This command lists all resource records, as shown near the bottom of Figure 10.8.

▶ **set all:** This command displays the current value of all settings.

NSLookup is not restricted to viewing information from your DNS server; you can view information from virtually any DNS server. If you have an Internet service provider (ISP), you should have IP addresses for at least two DNS servers. NSLookup can use either IP addresses or domain names. You can switch NSLookup to another DNS server by entering the `server` command followed by either the IP address or the FQDN. For instance, to connect NSLookup to the E root server, you can enter `server 192.203.230.10`. Then you can enter almost any domain name, such as `samspublishing.com`, and see the IP addresses registered for that domain name.

Be aware that most commercial DNS servers and root servers will refuse ls commands because they can generate a tremendous amount of traffic and might pose a security leak.

Domain Information Groper (Dig)

Another DNS command utility that is popular on Linux (which is popular in server rooms) is Domain Information Groper (dig). Many admins consider dig easier and more flexible than NSLookup. In its most basic form, dig returns the IP address if you enter the hostname:

```
dig host.domain.com
```

Put @server in front of the host to specify the DNS server to query:

```
dig @14.13.18.20 host.domain.com
```

The preceding command queries the DNS server with the address 14.13.18.20.

To query for a specific resource record type, add the name of the resource type:

```
dig host.domain.com NS
```

The preceding command displays NS records associated with the domain name. To find mail servers, try the following:

```
dig host.domain.com MX
```

The -x option performs a reverse lookup when you specify the IP address. The -4 option limits the query to IPv4. Use -6 for IPv6 results.

Dynamic DNS

DNS, as it has been described so far, is designed for situations in which there is a permanent (or at least semipermanent) association of a hostname with an IP address. In today's networks (as you learn in the next hour), IP addresses are often assigned dynamically. In other words, a new IP address is assigned to a computer through Dynamic Host Configuration Protocol (DHCP) each time the computer starts. This means that if the computer is to be registered with DNS and accessible by its hostname, the DNS server must have some way to learn the IP address the computer is using.

The recent popularity of dynamic IP addressing has forced DNS vendors to adapt. Some IP implementations (including BIND) now offer dynamic update of DNS records. In a typical scenario (see Figure 10.9), the host obtains an IP address from the DHCP server and then updates the DNS server with the new address. You learn more about DHCP in Hour 12, "Configuration."

Enterprise directory systems such as Microsoft's Active Directory use dynamic DNS to manage DHCP client systems within the directory structure. Dynamic DNS services are also popular on the Internet. Several online services offer a means for registering a permanent DNS name for computers with dynamic addresses. Users can access these services to remotely connect to a home network using the DNS name or to operate a personal website without a static address.

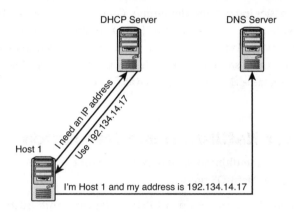

DHCP Server   DNS Server

Host 1

I need an IP address

Use 192.134.14.17

I'm Host 1 and my address is 192.134.14.17

FIGURE 10.9
Dynamic DNS
update.

DNS Service Discovery

Another recent innovation in DNS is DNS service discovery. See Hour 12 for more on DNS service discovery and other zero configuration techniques.

By the Way

NetBIOS Name Resolution

NetBIOS is an application programming interface (API) and name resolution system originally developed by IBM that is common on Microsoft Windows networks. The NetBIOS name is the computer name you assign to your Windows computer. The NetBIOS computer name is used to identify the computer in Explorer and My Computer. NetBIOS was developed for networks that don't use TCP/IP. The NetBIOS name system is actually a little redundant on TCP/IP networks because the NetBIOS name serves a role that is similar to the role of the hostname. Microsoft deemphasized NetBIOS in Windows 2000/XP, and Windows Vista and Windows 7 continue the trend. The official line from Microsoft is that best practices favor using DNS instead of NetBIOS name resolution; however, recent Windows versions fully support NetBIOS name resolution techniques, and the huge install base of NetBIOS-enabled computers means that no discussion of name resolution would be complete without some attention to NetBIOS. Furthermore, NetBIOS isn't just all Windows anymore. The popular open source Samba file service and other independent tools also support NetBIOS name resolution.

From the user's point of view, the distinction between NetBIOS and DNS name resolution has blurred in recent Windows versions. Windows essentially maintains the two systems in parallel. Depending on your configuration, the familiar Windows computer name can serve as either or both a DNS-style hostname and a NetBIOS name.

Because NetBIOS operates through broadcasts, a user on a small network doesn't have to do anything to configure NetBIOS name resolution (other than setting up networking and assigning a computer name). On a larger network, though, NetBIOS is more complex. Large networks can use NetBIOS name servers called **Windows Internet Name Service (WINS)** servers for resolving NetBIOS names to IP addresses. You can also configure a static **LMHosts** file (similar to the hosts file under DNS) for name resolution lookups. The following sections take a closer look at NetBIOS name resolution.

Methods for NetBIOS Name Resolution

On TCP/IP networks, the ultimate goal of NetBIOS name resolution is to provide an IP address for a given NetBIOS name.

NetBIOS names are single names up to 15 characters in length, such as Workstation1, HRServer, and CorpServer. NetBIOS does not allow for duplicate computer names on a network.

> **NetBIOS Names**
>
> Technically, a NetBIOS name contains 16 characters. However, the 16th character is used by the underlying application and in general is not directly configurable by the user. These characters are discussed later in this hour.

NetBIOS names, like hostnames, are said to be in a flat namespace, because there is no hierarchy or capability to qualify the names. In the following sections, you examine several ways to resolve NetBIOS names to their corresponding IP addresses:

- ▶ Broadcast-based name resolution
- ▶ LMHosts filename resolution
- ▶ WINS name resolution

Broadcast-Based Name Resolution

One way for NetBIOS name resolution to take place is through broadcasts. A **broadcast** occurs when a computer announces to all the other machines on its network segment that it needs the address of a particular computer. All the computers on the segment hear the broadcast, but only the machine specified in the broadcast responds to the request.

This method of name resolution, also known as **B-Node name resolution**, works well in a LAN environment but does not work in networks that extend beyond the LAN, because routers block broadcasts by design.

The broadcast name resolution process is simple and requires no extra configuration to set up or use. Simply installing a network card and TCP/IP networking software onto a Windows operating system enables these systems to use broadcasts to locate other computers through NetBIOS name resolution.

LMHosts Files Name Resolution

Windows systems can also resolve NetBIOS names to IP addresses using the LMHosts file. The LMHosts file is similar to the hosts file (described earlier in this hour). An LMHosts file associates NetBIOS names to IP addresses. The IP address is listed in the left column of the file with the corresponding computer name to the right separated by at least one space; comments can be put in the file by placing them after a # character. LMHosts requires a static mapping of IP addresses to NetBIOS names. A separate LMHosts file resides on each computer. You have to manually configure the LMHosts file. If a new computer is added to the network, the other computer will not be able to find it through LMHosts until an entry for that computer is manually added to each LMHosts file.

On a network consisting of a single segment, an LMHosts file is usually not necessary, because computers on the network can resolve NetBIOS names through broadcast. On larger networks consisting of more than one segment, broadcast cannot be used to resolve names beyond the router. In that case, computers must perform NetBIOS name resolution using either LMHosts or a WINS server (described in the next section). In some cases, LMHosts is useful for pointing the way to a domain controller on a different network segment. (A domain controller is necessary for authentication in a domain-based Windows environment.)

By the Way

LAN Man

The LM in LMHosts is a holdover from Microsoft's LAN Manager, a networking product that predates Windows NT.

The following is an example of what a basic LMHosts file looks like:

```
192.59.66.205    marketserv      #file server for marketing department
192.59.66.206    marketapp       #application server for marketing
192.59.66.207    bobscomputer    #bob's workstation
```

Recently resolved NetBIOS names are stored in the NetBIOS name cache. Whenever a user attempts to locate a specific computer, the system always consults the NetBIOS name cache before searching the LMHosts file. If no match is found, the entries within the LMHosts file can then be scanned for the requested name. This can be a time-consuming process if there are many entries in the LMHosts file, so to speed up the process, you can designate certain high-use entries to be preloaded into the NetBIOS name cache by including the #PRE keyword (see Figure 10.10). The LMHosts file is scanned once in its entirety when networking starts, so for efficiency the lines that include #PRE keywords are usually placed toward the bottom of the LMHosts file. These lines need to be read only once, and placing them later in the file lessens the chance that they will be reread.

By the Way

Viewing the Cache

You can use the NBTStat utility to view and manipulate the NetBIOS name cache. To view the contents of the cache, enter nbtstat –c at the command prompt.

Maintaining static files such as hosts and LMHosts is difficult because these files are located on each individual computer and, therefore, are not centralized. You can address that problem in the LMHosts file by using the keyword #INCLUDE followed by an entry for the path to the LMHosts files on other machines. With this keyword, the local LMHosts file can include the location of a server-based LMHosts file for use by the local machine. This enables edits to be performed on the server-based LMHosts file, but the changes are accessible from the user's computer.

If there is more than one #INCLUDE entry, they need to be placed between the keywords #BEGIN ALTERNATE and #END ALTERNATE, as shown in Figure 10.10.

FIGURE 10.10
Contents of an LMHosts file.

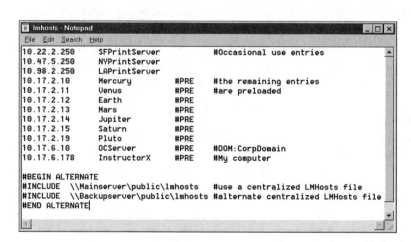

```
lmhosts - Notepad
File  Edit  Search  Help
10.22.2.250       SFPrintServer              #Occasional use entries
10.47.5.250       NYPrintServer
10.98.2.250       LAPrintServer
10.17.2.10        Mercury          #PRE      #the remaining entries
10.17.2.11        Venus            #PRE      #are preloaded
10.17.2.12        Earth            #PRE
10.17.2.13        Mars             #PRE
10.17.2.14        Jupiter          #PRE
10.17.2.15        Saturn           #PRE
10.17.2.19        Pluto            #PRE
10.17.6.10        OCServer         #PRE      #DOM:CorpDomain
10.17.6.178       InstructorX      #PRE      #My computer

#BEGIN ALTERNATE
#INCLUDE  \\Mainserver\public\lmhosts    #use a centralized LMHosts file
#INCLUDE  \\Backupserver\public\lmhosts  #alternate centralized LMHosts file
#END ALTERNATE
```

As mentioned previously, LMHosts can be used to locate a Windows domain controller on a different network segment. The #DOM keyword identifies an LMHosts entry that represents a domain controller.

On Windows 7 systems, you'll find a sample LMHosts file called lmhosts.sam in the Windows/System32/drivers/etc directory. To implement an LMHosts file, modify this sample file and save it to lmhosts (without the .sam) in the same directory.

WINS Name Resolution

Windows Internet Name Service (WINS) was created to address the same types of shortcomings in LMHosts that DNS was created to address regarding hosts files. When a client needs to get the IP address for a computer, it can query the WINS server for the information. WINS used to be an important feature of Microsoft networks; however, with the new emphasis on DNS and Active Directory, the need for a separate WINS server has diminished considerably. WINS servers still play a role on some segmented networks, in which NetBIOS name resolution is blocked by routers.

WINS maintains a database of registered NetBIOS names for a variety of objects, including users, computers, services running on those computers, and workgroups. However, instead of the entries in this database coming from manually edited text files, as in most DNS implementations, a client computer registers its name and IP address with the WINS server dynamically when it starts up.

The WINS server receives and responds to NetBIOS name resolution requests (see Figure 10.11). If the WINS server in Figure 10.11 looks similar to the DNS server in Figure 10.2, that's because it is. A WINS server does for NetBIOS name resolution what the DNS server does for domain name resolution. However, the flat NetBIOS namespace provides no equivalent to the hierarchical name resolution techniques available through DNS.

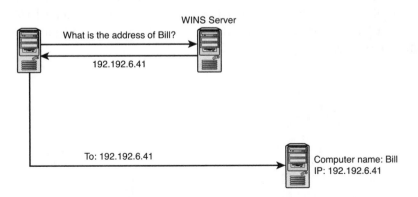

FIGURE 10.11
WINS NetBIOS name resolution.

What is WINS Really?

WINS is the name assigned to Microsoft's implementation of what is generically known as a NetBIOS name server or NBNS.

Windows offers a number of methods for configuring a client system to use WINS. If the computer receives a dynamic TCP/IP configuration through DHCP (see Hour 12), the WINS configuration can be delivered to the client automatically through DHCP. You can also manually enter WINS server addresses and manage other settings related to NetBIOS name resolution through the TCP/IP configuration dialog box.

The precise steps for configuring WINS vary depending on the Windows version. In Windows 7, you can manage the WINS configuration through the WINS tab of the Advanced TCP/IP Settings dialog box (see Figure 10.12). Follow these steps to access the Advanced TCP/IP Settings dialog box:

1. Select Network in the Start menu.

2. Go to the Network Sharing Center.

3. Select Manage Network Connections.

4. Right-click the network connection you want to configure and select Properties. (You'll need the authorization of an administrator account.)

5. Select Internet Protocol Version 4 (TCP/IPv4) and click Properties.

6. In the TCP/IPv4 Properties dialog box, click the Advanced button.

7. Select the WINS tab.

As shown in Figure 10.12, the WINS tab lets you manually add the addresses of WINS servers. You can also enable LMHosts lookup and import an existing LMHosts file. Note that, by default, the system receives a NetBIOS setting from the DHCP server, but you can also elect to override the DHCP setting by enabling or disabling NetBIOS over TCP/IP.

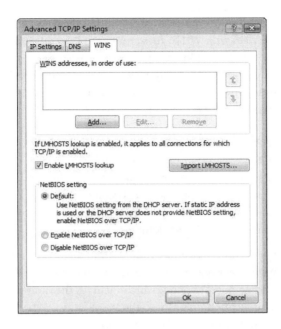

FIGURE 10.12
Configuring
WINS in
Windows 7.

When a WINS client computer boots after being configured to use WINS, the following process occurs:

1. **Service startup:** As the computer boots, various services are started, some of which need to be made known to other computers.

2. **Registration request:** To be known to other computers on the network, the service must register. A WINS client computer packages the NetBIOS name and the computer's IP address inside a name registration request, and the registration request is sent to the WINS server. On receiving the registration request, WINS checks its database to see whether the name is already registered.

   If the name does not exist, WINS adds the NetBIOS name and IP address pair to its database and sends a name registration response indicating the name was successfully registered. If the requested NetBIOS name already exists in the WINS database, WINS challenges the computer currently registered by sending a message to the registered IP address. If the currently registered computer responds, a negative acknowledgment is sent to the computer attempting to register the name. If the computer being challenged doesn't respond, WINS allows the registration to occur and overwrites the previous registration.

3. **Lease:** Assuming the computer is successful in registering its NetBIOS names and services with WINS, these names are considered leased. In essence, the computer is allowed to use the NetBIOS name for a specified period of time (for instance, 6 days), but the client can renew the lease before it expires. The client typically renews the lease at 50% of the total lease time or in this case every 3 days.

Earlier I noted that the 16th character of a NetBIOS name is not configurable by the user. During the WINS registration process, the 16th character is appended to the name by the WINS server based on what type of service the computer is trying to register before it is placed in the database. Between computer names, workgroup names, and a number of services, it is not unusual for a single computer to have 5 to 10 registration entries in the WINS database.

As another example of the WINS name resolution process, suppose a user on a computer uses a utility such as Network Neighborhood to connect to another computer on the network. A name query request, which includes the desired NetBIOS name, is constructed by the application and sent to the WINS server. When WINS receives the request, it queries its database for a matching registration. If the requested name is found, WINS returns the corresponding IP address in the response packet. After the client computer has the IP address for the requested computer, the client can then communicate directly.

Testing NetBIOS Name Resolution

You can test NetBIOS name resolution using NetBIOS-based utilities. One typical test of name resolution on a Windows system is using the `net view` command, which enables you to view the names of shares on a server. (Remember that a **share** is a directory that is made available for network access.) To perform this test, choose a computer that has one or more shares. At a command prompt, enter the following, where `computername` is the name of the computer you selected:

```
net view \\computername
```

If `net view` is capable of resolving the computer name to an IP address, you should see the names of shares listed in the first command and response.

You can also use the ubiquitous ping utility to test NetBIOS name resolution. On most Windows systems, if NetBIOS name resolution is working properly, you should be able to ping a computer by its NetBIOS computer name. For instance, if a computer has the computer name Shirley, you should be able to enter the following and receive a response:

```
ping Shirley
```

Summary

Name resolution enables the use of meaningful, easy-to-remember names for computers instead of the IP address assigned to a computer. This hour described name resolution by hostname and also through DNS. You learned about DNS configuration files and the name resolution process. You also studied some more recent innovations such as dynamic DNS and DNSSEC. This hour closed with a look at the NetBIOS name resolution system still sometimes used with Windows and other SMB-based networks.

Q&A

Q. *What is a domain name?*

A. A domain name is a name used to identify a network. The domain name is administered by a central authority to ensure the name's uniqueness.

Q. *What is a hostname?*

A. A hostname is a single name that is assigned to a particular host and mapped to an IP address.

Q. *What is an FQDN?*

A. A combination of a hostname concatenated to a domain name by the addition of a dot character. For example, a hostname bigserver and a domain name mycompany.com when combined become the FQDN bigserver.mycompany.com.

Q. *What are DNS resource records?*

A. Resource records are the entries contained in a DNS zone file. Different resource records are used to identify different types of computers or services.

Workshop

The following workshop is composed of a series of quiz questions and practical exercises. The quiz questions are designed to test your overall understanding of the current material. The practical exercises are intended to afford you the opportunity to apply the concepts discussed during the current hour, as well as build on the knowledge acquired in previous hours of study. Please take time to complete the quiz questions and exercises before continuing. Refer to Appendix A, "Answers to Quizzes and Exercises," for answers.

Quiz

1. What type of resource record is used for an alias?

2. Why are the DS resource record and the DNSKEY resource record stored on different servers?

3. How do you centrally administer entries in an LMHosts file?

4. How can you create static NetBIOS entries in the NetBIOS name cache?

Exercises

1. At the command line of your computer, enter the command `ping localhost` and write down the IP address that you see.

2. At the command line of your computer, enter the command hostname and write down the hostname that is returned.

3. Enter a `ping` command followed by the hostname for your computer.

4. If your computer has a domain name, ping your FQDN.

5. Determine whether IP is configured to use a DNS server. If so, try the following pings:

   ```
   ping www.internic.net
   ping www.whitehouse.gov
   ```

6. Use NSLookup to connect to one of your ISP's DNS servers.

Key Terms

Review the following list of key terms:

▶ **DNSSEC (DNS Security Extensions):** A system for verifying the authenticity of DNS query responses.

▶ **Domain:** A hierarchical division of the DNS namespace.

▶ **Domain name:** A name assigned to a hierarchical partition of the DNS namespace.

▶ **Domain Name System (DNS):** A system for naming resources on TCP/IP networks.

▶ **Dynamic DNS:** A technique for associating a static DNS name with a dynamic IP address.

▶ **Fully qualified domain name (FQDN):** The name generated by concatenating a hostname with a domain name.

▶ **Hostname:** A single name used to identify a computer (host).

▶ **Hosts file:** A file that associates IP addresses to host names.

▶ **LMHosts:** A file that associates IP addresses to NetBIOS names.

▶ **NetBIOS:** An API and name resolution system originally developed by IBM and used on many Microsoft networks. The NetBIOS name system has been deemphasized in recent years, but it is still used on many Windows networks and on some non-Windows SMB/CIFS networks.

▶ **Resource record:** An entry added to zone files. There are a number of resource record types, and each type has a specific purpose.

▶ **WINS (Windows Internet Naming Service):** A WINS server is a Microsoft implementation of a NetBIOS name server.

▶ **Zone file:** The configuration files used by DNS servers. These text files are used to configure DNS servers.

HOUR 11

TCP/IP Security

What You'll Learn in This Hour:

▶ Firewalls and proxy service

▶ Network intrusion techniques

▶ Network security best practices

▶ Encryption

▶ Digital signatures

▶ VPNs

▶ Kerberos

Today's users are well aware of the dangers lurking on the Internet. You don't really know who might be out there trying to steal information or get access to your system. Some intruders are in it for the money; others are just on a joyride. In either case, you need to be wary and take precautions to ensure that your network is secure.

In this hour, you learn about some tools and technologies for protecting TCP/IP networks, and you explore some techniques the intruders use to slip past Internet defenses. The first section begins with a look at one of the most important components of any security system, the network firewall.

What Is a Firewall?

The term **firewall** has taken on many meanings through the years, and the device we know now as a firewall is the result of a long evolution (keeping in mind that 28 years is a long time in cyberspace).

A firewall is a device that is placed in the network pathway in such a way that it can examine, accept, or reject inbound packets headed for the network. This might sound like a router; in fact, a firewall doesn't have to be a router, but firewall functionality is often built in to routers. The important distinction is that a conventional router forwards packets when it can—a firewall forwards packets when it wants to. Forwarding decisions are not based solely on addressing but are instead based on rules configured by the network owner regarding what type of traffic is permissible on the network.

The value of a firewall is evident when you look at even a simple sketch of a firewall environment (see Figure 11.1). As you can see, the firewall is in a position to stop any or all outside traffic from reaching the network, but the firewall doesn't interfere at all with communication on the internal network.

FIGURE 11.1
A firewall can stop any or all inbound traffic from reaching the local network.

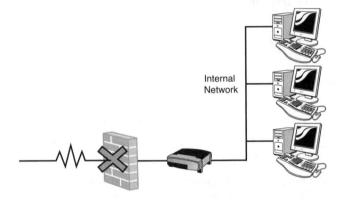

The earliest firewalls were **packet filters**. They examined packets for clues about the intended purpose. As you learned in Hour 6, "The Transport Layer," many packet filtering firewalls watch the well-known Transport Control Protocol (TCP) and User Datagram Protocol (UDP) port numbers encoded in the Transport layer header. Because most Internet services are associated with a port number, you can determine the purpose of a packet by examining the port number to which it is addressed. This form of packet filtering allowed admins to say, "Outside clients cannot access Telnet services on the internal network"—at least as long as the Telnet service is using the well-known port assigned to Telnet.

This type of control was a big advance over what had come before, and to this day it does manage to ward off many kinds of attacks; however, packet filtering is still not a complete solution. For one thing, an intruder who gets inside can secretly reconfigure the port numbers used by network services. For instance, if the firewall is configured to look for Telnet sessions on TCP port 23, and the intruder sets up a secret Telnet service running on a different port number, the simple act of watching well-known ports won't catch the problem.

Another development in the evolution of the firewall was the arrival of so-called stateful firewalls. A **stateful firewall** does not simply examine each packet in isolation but is aware of where the packet fits within the sequence of a communication session. This sensitivity to state helps the stateful firewall watch for tricks such as invalid packets, session hijacking attempts, and certain denial-of-service attacks.

The latest generation of Application layer firewalls is designed to operate at TCP/IP's Application layer, where it can obtain a much more complete understanding of the protocols and services associated with the packet.

Modern firewalls often perform a combination of packet filtering, state watching, and Application layer filtering. Some firewalls also work as DHCP servers and network address translation tools. Firewalls can be hardware or software tools—simple or sophisticated—but whether you administer a thousand-node network or just hack around on a single PC you'll do better with a basic understanding of firewalls if you plan to go anywhere near the Internet.

Firewall Options

Although firewalls were once tools for IT professionals, the rising hobby of network intrusion and the appearance of automated port scanners randomly searching for open ports on the Internet have necessitated the development of personal firewalls for single-user systems. Many contemporary Windows, Mac OS, and Linux systems have personal desktop firewall applications designed to prevent access to specific ports and services on the system. Of course, an end-user client system typically doesn't have the need to run a lot of network services, which makes the firewall seem redundant. (Why close off ports to services that aren't running in the first place?) But the fact is, modern computer systems are so complex that the owner of the system sometimes isn't even sure what is running and what isn't. Even ordinary file and print sharing theoretically opens up a conduit for attack. Also computer exploits are sometimes subtle, and it often isn't easy to be certain that your system is truly safe. Personal firewalls are therefore a good idea, especially for systems that won't be operating behind some other form of firewall system.

At the next level of sophistication are the firewall/router devices available for small office/home office (SOHO) networks. These tools typically provide Dynamic Host Configuration Protocol (DHCP) service and Network Address Translation. They are designed to operate much like the classic firewall scenario depicted in Figure 11.1, allowing internal clients to access services on the internal network but preventing outside access attempts.

One problem with SOHO firewalls (as well as personal firewalls) is that they are designed to be operated by nonspecialists, so they offer few configuration options, and often it isn't clear what techniques they are using to filter protocol traffic. Security experts don't consider these devices totally safe, although they are certainly better than having no firewall at all.

Another option is to configure a network firewall using a computer as a firewall/router device. UNIX/Linux systems come with sophisticated firewall capabilities. Firewalls are also available for certain versions of Windows systems. Note that a computer acting as a network firewall is not the same as the personal firewall discussed earlier in this section. In this case, the computer isn't just filtering traffic addressed to itself; it is actually acting as a firewall for the network. For this to work, the system must be fitted with two or more network cards and actually configured for port forwarding—the system is actually functioning as a router. If you have a spare computer, this solution provides a much more sophisticated range of firewall functions than a typical SOHO firewall. Of course, you have to know what you are doing.

If you are administering a firewall in any kind of professional capacity, you are probably using some form of commercial firewall device. Professional-grade firewall/routers are considerably more advanced than the SOHO models. Internally, these devices are actually much more like the computer-based firewall, although they look different on the outside. Most industrial firewall devices are embedded computer systems. As you learn later in this hour, commercial firewalls and firewall-computers let you configure a custom set of filtering rules defining the traffic you want to allow or deny. These tools are much more powerful and versatile than the check box style configuration of your SOHO or personal firewall tool, although they require deeper knowledge and much more attention to configure correctly.

The DMZ

The firewall provides a protected space for the internal network that is difficult to access from the outside. This concept works well for workgroups of web clients with a few scattered file servers filling internal requests. In many cases, however, an organization might not want to protect all its resources from outside access. A public web server, for instance, needs to be accessible from the outside. Many organizations also maintain File Transfer Protocol (FTP) servers, email servers, and other systems that need to be accessible from the Internet. Although it is theoretically possible to open a port on the firewall to allow outside clients to access a specific service on a specific system, thus allowing the server to operate from inside the firewall, inviting traffic onto the internal network poses a series of traffic and security concerns that many network administrators would prefer to avoid.

One easy solution is to place Internet-accessible services outside the firewall (see Figure 11.2). The idea is that the server (for instance, a web server) undergoes some additional scrutiny to ensure that it truly is secure, and then it is simply placed on the open Internet—in front of the firewall—to isolate it from internal clients and enable it to receive Internet requests. In theory, a properly configured server should be capable of defending itself from Internet attack. Only essential ports are opened, and only essential services are running. The security system is ideally configured so that, even if an attacker gains access to the system, the attacker's privileges are limited. Of course, such precautions are no guarantee the system won't get hacked, but the idea is, even if the system is hacked, an intruder who gains access to the web server still has to get through the firewall before reaching the internal network.

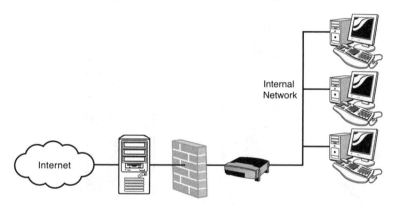

Internal Network

Internet

FIGURE 11.2
Web servers and other Internet-facing computers are often placed outside of the firewall.

This technique of placing local resources behind the firewall and Internet-accessible resources in front is a common practice on many small networks; however, larger networks with professional-level IT management and security often prefer a more refined approach. Another alternative to the option shown in Figure 11.2 is to use two firewalls—one in front of the Internet servers and one behind them. The front firewall provides a first tier of security that is, obviously, porous enough to permit the connections to the servers, and the back-end firewall provides the usual tight protection for resources on the local net. The space between the firewalls is commonly known as the **DMZ** (for a Vietnam-era military term *demilitarized zone*). The DMZ provides an intermediate level of security that is safer than the open Internet but not as secure as the internal network.

It might occur to you that the scenario depicted in Figure 11.3 can also be approximated using a single firewall with connections to multiple network segments. As shown in Figure 11.4, if the firewall/router has three or more interfaces, it can connect to both the internal network and the DMZ through separate interfaces, with a different set of filtering rules for each interface.

FIGURE 11.3
A DMZ sitting
between two
firewalls.

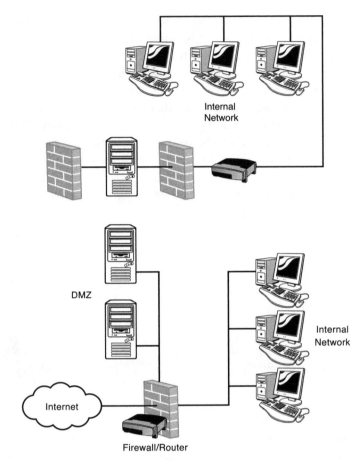

FIGURE 11.4
A single firewall
with at least
three interfaces
can provide the
equivalent of a
DMZ if you con-
figure different
firewall rules for
each internal
segment.

Firewall Rules

Personal firewalls and other small-scale, GUI-based firewall tools usually let you
define the firewall's filtering characteristics by checking boxes (Figure 11.5). But full,
industrial-strength firewall tools let you create a configuration file with the firewall
configuration expressed in a series of commands or rules defining the firewall's
behavior. These commands or rules are known as firewall rules. Different tools use
different commands and syntax, but firewall rules typically let the network administrator create associations consisting of

▶ A source address or address range

▶ A destination address range

▶ A service

▶ An action

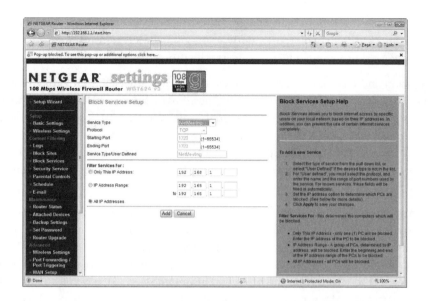

FIGURE 11.5
Most SOHO
firewalls let you
block services
by name or port
number.

These parameters provide a vast range of options. You can shut off all traffic from or to specific address ranges. You can shut out a specific service, such as Telnet or FTP, coming from a specific address. You can shut out that service coming from all addresses. The action could be "accept, "deny," or any number of other options. Sometimes the rule can even refer to a specific extension or script, or it might be an alert that pages or emails the firewall administrator in case of trouble.

The combination of these parameters allows much more flexibility than simply turning on or off services by port number.

Proxy Service

A firewall is at the center of a whole collection of technologies designed to protect and simplify the internal network and confine the unpredictable and potentially unsecure Internet activity to the perimeter. Another related technology is known as proxy service. A **proxy server** intercepts requests for Internet resources and forwards the requests on behalf of the client, acting as an intermediary between the client and the server that is the target of the request (see Figure 11.6). Although a proxy

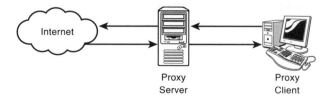

Proxy
Server

Proxy
Client

FIGURE 11.6
A proxy server
requests servic-
es on behalf of
the client.

server is not necessarily sufficient to protect the network by itself, it is often used in conjunction with a firewall (particularly in the context of a Network Address Translation environment, which you learn about in Hour 12, "Configuration").

By placing and receiving Internet requests on behalf of the client, the proxy server protects the client from direct contact with possibly malicious web resources. Some proxies perform a kind of content filtering to watch for blacklisted servers or potentially dangerous content. Proxy servers are also used to limit the range of browsing options for clients on the internal network. For instance, a school network might use a proxy server to prevent students from surfing to exhilarating sites that are intended for the category of adult education.

In many situations, the primary purpose of a proxy server is performance rather than security. Proxy servers often perform a service known as content caching. A content-caching proxy server stores a copy of the web pages it accesses. Future requests for the page can thus be served locally with a much faster response than if the request were served from the Internet. This might seem like a lot of trouble just to help a user visit the same site twice, but if you consider the browsing habits of a typical user, it is quite common to click around several times at a website and visit a page more than once—or to leave the page and come back after only a short interval. The proxy server is usually configured to hold the page only for a specific time interval before releasing the cache and requesting a new version of the page.

Reverse Proxy

The conventional proxy server (described in the preceding section) acts as a proxy for outgoing Internet requests. Another form of proxy server known as a **reverse proxy** receives requests from external sources and forwards them to the internal network. A reverse proxy offers the same caching and content filtering features provided by a conventional proxy server. Because reverse proxies are primarily used with computers offering services on the Internet, the security concerns are particularly important.

A reverse proxy system hides the details of the computer that is actually fulfilling the client's request. The reverse proxy can also improve performance by caching large files or frequently accessed pages. Reverse proxies are also sometimes used as a form of load balancing. For instance, a reverse proxy could receive requests under a single web address and then distribute the workload to servers upstream.

Attack Techniques

The growth of the Internet has created unlimited opportunity for intruders to steal secrets, tinker with websites, abscond with credit card information, or just generally make mischief. Internet intruders have also spawned a whole new mythology. They are celebrated for their skill and daring. Some ascribe lofty artistic and political motives to these bandwidth banditos. But the professionals who install and maintain computer networks are not impressed with the activities of network intruders.

Just because you have a firewall doesn't mean your network is safe. The following sections explore some of the techniques attackers use to gain control of computer systems. As you study these techniques, you'll notice that many of the concepts are built around fundamental properties of TCP/IP that you learned about in earlier hours. The Internet literature is full of vague psycho-profiles of who these intruders are and how they think. Much of this information is based on anecdotes and speculation. However, there is general agreement that computer attackers tend to fall within the following broad categories:

▶ **Adolescent amateurs:** These are kids who are just playing around. The so-called **script kiddies** often have only a rudimentary knowledge of computer systems and primarily just apply intrusion scripts and techniques available on the Internet.

▶ **Recreational intruders:** This category of "adult" attackers encompasses a broad range of motivations. Most are in it purely for the intellectual challenge. Some want to make a statement against a particular industry or organization, and others are disgruntled former employees. At about this same level is a new class of very sloppy, low-end quasi-professional ne'er-do-wells who break into systems to steal banking passwords or credit card numbers, or to trade the access to a higher end pro for a per-break-in bounty.

▶ **Professionals:** This dangerous group consists of experienced experts who know a lot about computers. They are hard to trace because they know all the tricks. In fact, they invented some of the tricks. These intruders are in the game strictly for the financial reward, but they wouldn't have gotten where they are if they didn't love what they do. Many of these professionals concentrate on activities such as credit card fraud and identity theft. A recent trend has been the rise of attacks on home computers to co-opt systems for the purpose of sending spam email.

It is impossible to describe all the various scams and tricks used by intruders to gain access to computer systems. As you read through the techniques described in the following sections, remember the most important rule of computer security: If you think you've secured your network, think again. Someone out there is spending a lot of time and effort trying to find a new way in.

What Do Intruders Want?

As the preceding section mentioned, network attackers approach their craft from a number of motivations. Their goals might differ, but they all have the goal of gaining power and control of a computer system or network. Many of their intermediate steps are therefore the same.

The computer attack and infiltration process is organized around the following steps:

1. Get access to the system.

2. Get privileges.

3. Get comfortable.

4. Get ready for the next attack.

It is also worth noting that for coordinated and well-organized attacks on computer networks a separate reconnaissance phase often precedes these steps.

Attackers have several methods for gaining entry and getting comfortable, and although it isn't possible to describe them all, it is possible to classify these techniques into three basic categories:

▶ **Credential attacks:** These attacks focus on getting credentials to log in to the system normally. In essence, the attack takes place before the intruder even infiltrates the security system. A variation of this technique is privilege escalation, in which the attacker gains low-level access and then works to attain higher privilege levels.

▶ **Network-level attacks:** The attacker slips in by finding an open port, unsecured service, or gap in the firewall. Other network-level attack techniques exploit nuances of the TCP/IP protocol system to gain information or reroute connections.

▶ **Application-level attacks:** The attacker exploits known flaws in the program code of an application running on the system, such as a web server, tricking the application into executing arbitrary commands or otherwise behaving in a way the programmer never intended.

A full-scale network intrusion often uses a combination of these attack techniques. In a typical scenario, an attacker might use an application-level attack for the initial breach, then escalate privileges to administrator-level status, and then open a hidden back door for unlimited access through the system.

A **back door** is a means for the intruder to log in to the system undetected. Intruders use many different kinds of back doors. As you learn later in this hour, the intruder often attempts to install a *rootkit* to gain a foothold on the system and then cover up the intrusion. But system access isn't the only goal of the intruder. Another powerful attack technique that doesn't result in system access but is, nevertheless, damaging and disruptive is the so-called denial-of-service attack, in which the attacker causes a crash or system overload, so the system can't function normally. You learn more about denial-of-service attacks later in this hour.

A full-scale attack on a corporate network begins with a broad sweep to determine as much information as possible about the company. This process is sometimes called footprinting. Some of this information can be collected over the Web: company locations, email addresses, and affiliations, and links to other websites. The intruder attempts to obtain any and all domain names used by the company. The domain names are then used to query domain name system (DNS) servers for company IP addresses.

Network security scanners such as Nmap scan the perimeter of the network, looking for open ports or other potential attack vectors. (One of the great ironies of the security business is that IT pros and network intruders use the same tools. Admins often scan their own networks with Nmap just to find any problems before the intruders find them.)

On modern networks, the first step is often to find a service running on an open port, such as a web server, and to exploit a flaw in the service through an application-level attack. A good intruder, however, varies the attack based on the situation. The following sections study some of the tools in the attacker's toolbox.

Credential Attacks

The classic way to gain access to a computer system is to find out the password and log in. An intruder who gains interactive entry to a system can employ other techniques to build system privileges. Therefore, finding a password—any password—is often the first step in cracking a network. Methods for getting passwords range from high tech (password-cracking dictionary scripts and deencryption programs) to extremely low tech (digging around in trash cans and peeking in users' desk drawers). Some common password attack methods include

▶ Looking outside the box

▶ Trojan horses

▶ Guessing

▶ Intercepting

The following sections discuss these methods for clandestinely obtaining user passwords.

Looking Outside the Box

No matter how secure your system is, your network won't be safe unless users protect their passwords. A major source of password compromise is the inattentiveness of users. The earliest intruders often obtained passwords by looking for clues in discarded computer printouts. Since that time, operating system vendors thankfully have become more sophisticated about protecting password information. However, a significant percentage of password-compromise cases still result from offline detection. Users tell their passwords to other users or write down their passwords in some easily accessible place. The physical security of a workplace often is far less rigid than network security. Janitorial staff, disgruntled co-workers, or even unauthorized outsiders are often free to slip into the office unsupervised and look for password clues. When a worker quits or is dismissed, the worker's account is deactivated, but what about other user accounts belonging to users who have shared their passwords with the former employee?

Some experienced intruders are skilled at getting users to reveal their passwords or getting network admins to tell them passwords. They'll call the help desk, act a little lost, and say, "Uh, I forgot my password." This sounds silly, but it saves the intruder a lot of effort, and it is often the first thing he tries. Every organization should clearly instruct computer professionals not to reveal password information to any user without taking precautions to ensure that the request is legitimate.

As you learn later in this hour, the ultimate goal of the intruder is to achieve administrative-level privileges. Every password should be protected, because any access can often lead to administrative access, but it is especially important to protect administrative accounts from compromise. The administrative username is another line of defense against intrusion that should also be protected. Most computer systems come with a well-documented and well-known default administrative account. An intruder who is familiar with the operating system has a head start in gaining administrative privileges with knowledge of the username of the administrative account. Experts therefore recommend changing the username of the administrative account.

Trojan Horses

A common tool of computer intruders is the so-called **Trojan horse**. In general, a Trojan horse is a computer program that purports to do one thing but actually takes other unseen and malicious actions behind the scenes. One early form of the Trojan horse was a fake login screen. The screen looks just like the login screen used for the system, but when the user attempts to log in, the username and password are captured and stored in some secret location accessible to the intruder (see Figure 11.7).

FIGURE 11.7
Stealing passwords with a Trojan horse login program.

As you might guess, this technique for stealing passwords is designed for a public setting such as a computer lab in which multiple users might use a common set of terminals or workstations. In recent years, operating systems have become more proficient at preventing or detecting this form of password capture.

So Many Trojans

Not all Trojan horses capture passwords, and not all password Trojans are as blatant as the example described in this section. Many other types of Trojan horse programs are available on the Internet. Some take the form of games or false system utilities. Many of these Trojan horse programs are distributed as freeware or shareware over the Internet. The best defense against this kind of attack is to be careful what you download. Before you download and install a free utility, read the project documentation and search the Internet for any security warnings. Or to paraphrase an earlier warning about a particularly virulent Trojan that showed up around 800 B.C., "Beware of geeks bearing gifts."

By the Way

Guessing

Some passwords are so simple or poorly formed that they can easily be guessed by the intruder. You would be surprised how many users use a password that is the same as their username. Some users use a street name, a maiden name, or the name of a child for a password, and some use easily guessable character combinations, such as 123456, abcde, or zzzzzz.

An intruder who knows a little about the user can often guess bad passwords the user might choose. In fact, the intruder doesn't even have to guess anymore, because tools now exist that automate the process of guessing passwords. The attack tools guess through a list of obvious character combinations. Some tools even use a dictionary to guess every possible word or name in the language. This might require thousands of attempts, but computers can guess quickly.

Intercepting

Packet sniffers and other tools that monitor network traffic can easily capture passwords transmitted over the network in clear text (unencrypted) form. Many classic TCP/IP utilities such as Telnet and the r* utilities or SNMP (see Hour 15, "Monitoring and Remote Access") were designed to transmit passwords in clear text form. Some later versions of these utilities offer password encryption or operate through secure channels. In their basic form, however, the clear text password security of these applications makes them hopelessly ill-suited for an open and hostile environment such as the Internet.

By the Way

No Safe Networks

Even in a closed environment such as a corporate network, clear text passwords are not really safe. Some experts estimate that one corporate employee in a hundred is actively engaged in trying to thwart network security. Although 1% is a small fraction, when you consider a network with 1,000 users that 1% amounts to 10 users who would love to get their hands on someone else's clear text password.

Several methods exist for encrypting passwords. These password-encryption methods are much better than the clear text option, but password encryption still has some limitations. Tools such as the LC5 and John the Ripper can decrypt encrypted passwords using dictionary and brute-force techniques.

Attackers operating on the Internet can intercept packets that contain encrypted passwords and uncover the passwords using these password-recovery utilities. Recent developments in encrypted channel technologies, such as Secure Sockets Layer (SSL) and IP Security (IPsec) raise the bar considerably higher for intruders who want to eavesdrop on TCP/IP to obtain sensitive information such as passwords.

An attacker who has gained initial access to the system has a variety of options for intercepting or discovering other system passwords (including administrative passwords). Some tools allow the intruder to capture and log the keystrokes of a user typing a password at the keyboard. The attacker also might obtain access to an encrypted system file with password information and analyze the file offline using standard password attack techniques to uncover passwords.

What to Do About Credential Attacks

The best defense against credential attacks is eternal vigilance. Networks have employed a number of strategies for reducing the incidence of password compromise. A few of the more obvious guidelines are as follows:

1. Provide a good, clear password policy for the users in your organization. Warn them about the danger of telling their password to other users, writing their password down on a sticky note by their desk, or even storing their password in a file.

2. Configure all computer systems to support mandatory password policies. Set a minimum length for passwords (usually 6 to 8 characters). Don't let a user use the name of a dog or the name of a child as a password. In fact, passwords should not consist of any standard word, phrase, or name. All passwords should contain a combination of letters and numbers and at least one nonalphanumeric character that is not the first or last character. To prevent password-guessing attacks, make sure the computer is configured to disable the account after a predefined number of failed logon attempts.

3. Make sure that passwords are never transmitted over public lines in clear text form. If possible, it is better not to transmit clear text passwords on your internal network either, especially on large networks.

Some systems have methods for controlling the number of passwords that each user must remember. Microsoft networks feature a passwords cache and a unified network logon through the domain security system. UNIX systems offer systems such as Kerberos authentication. These methods are useful for controlling password proliferation in some environments. The downside of these unified logon methods is that an intruder who gets one password has unlocked access to all the user's resources.

Network-Level Attacks

As you learned in Hour 6, access to network applications is managed through logical channels known as ports operating at the Transport layer of the TCP/IP stack. Attackers often gain access to a system by finding an open port that leads to a network service listening for network connections. In some cases, the service might be running by default without the owner of the system even knowing it. Other times, the service might be misconfigured, or it might allow access through a default or anonymous user account.

Scanning tools such as Nmap and Nessus automate the process of looking for open ports. These scanners are used by both intruders (looking for gaps so that they can gain access) and IT professionals (looking for gaps so that they can plug them and prevent access). Other more-specialized tools search out gaps in specific network protocols and services. In many cases, the mere existence of an open port isn't enough to get the intruder in, but it provides an opportunity for the attacker to launch an application-level attack to exploit a known vulnerability of the service listening on the port.

Scanners are literally running constantly on the Internet, continually traversing the full range of IP addresses in search of open ports and unprotected services. As you learned earlier in this hour, an important function of a firewall is to lock down access to prevent network scanners from learning information about services operating on the network.

Other network-level attack strategies operate on the open Internet to intercept and subvert TCP/IP traffic. **Session hijacking**, for instance, is an advanced technique that exploits a vulnerability in the TCP protocol. As you learned in Hour 6, the TCP protocol establishes a session between network hosts. Session hijacking calls for the intruder to eavesdrop on a TCP session and insert packets into the stream that appear to be part of the TCP session. The intruder can use this technique to slip commands into the security context of the original session. One common use of session hijacking is to get the system to reveal or change a password.

Of course, an attacker does not manually compose spoofed TCP segments on-the-fly. Session hijacking requires special tools. One famous tool used for session hijacking is a freeware application called Juggernaut. Juggernaut listens on a local network, maintaining a database of TCP connections. An intruder can monitor TCP traffic to play back the connection history or hijack an active session by injecting arbitrary commands. The best defense against session hijacking and other protocol-based techniques is to secure the session using a virtual private network (VPN) or some other form of encryption communication.

Application-Level Attacks

You might expect that if the software is configured properly and you can keep the passwords out of enemy hands you won't have any problem with Internet intruders. Unfortunately, the real situation is a bit more complicated. Many programs running on the Internet today were written years ago, before the art of intrusion had even evolved, and they contain some program code that is intrinsically unsecure. Even programs written today are too often written in way too much of a hurry—by programmers with vastly varying reserves of training and expertise. Intruders have developed a number of techniques for exploiting unsecure program code to breach system security.

One popular example of an application-level attack technique is **buffer overflow**. When a computer receives data over a network connection (or for that matter, even when it receives data from a keyboard), the computer must reserve enough memory space to receive the complete data set. This reception space is called a buffer. If user input overflows the buffer, strange things happen. If the input is not properly managed, the data that overflows the buffer can become resident in the CPU's execution area, which means that commands sent to the computer through a buffer overflow can actually be executed (see Figure11.8). The commands execute with the privileges of the application that received the data. Other buffer-overflow attacks capitalize on the fact that some applications run in an elevated security context that can remain active when the application terminates unexpectedly.

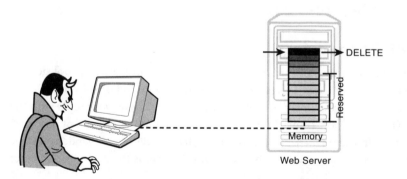

DELETE

Reserved

Memory

Web Server

FIGURE 11.8
A buffer-overflow attack overflows the memory space reserved for program input, causing the program to crash, behave strangely, or execute arbitrary code.

To avoid buffer-overflow problems, applications must provide a means for receiving and checking the size of the data before inserting the data into an application buffer. The solutions are largely a matter of good programming practice. Poorly designed applications are especially susceptible to buffer-overflow attacks.

Some popular and famous network applications have buffer-overflow vulnerabilities. Many of these exploits are well known around the Internet, so intruders know exactly how and where to launch an attack. The UNIX-based email server Sendmail is a common target for buffer-overflow attacks. Microsoft's Internet Information Server (IIS) and other Microsoft products have also been victim to buffer-overflow attacks in recent years. When a vendor discovers a possible buffer-overflow vulnerability, the vendor often releases a patch that fixes the problem. Because of the huge public relations problems caused by public notice of a buffer-overflow vulnerability, vendors have become vigilant about quickly repairing their software when an exploit is discovered. It is not surprising for a vendor to publish a patch within days or even hours of when a security problem is discovered. And good system administrators pay close attention to security alerts from organizations such as the Common Vulnerabilities and Exposures project (http://cve.mitre.org) so that they'll know when and where to obtain the latest patches for their systems. Organizations such as SANS (http://www.sans.org) also provide email newsletters with information on recent security threats.

Part of the solution to problems like buffer overflow is good programming, not just in vendor-based software but also in the homegrown scripts created by web developers and IT staff. Another part of the solution is to keep your system up to date by installing all patches and updates. Some operating systems let you limit the scope of privileges available to the remote user who is attempting to exploit a buffer overflow. If possible, don't let network applications run with root or administrative privileges. (In some cases, you might not have a choice.) For applications that require a high privilege level to function, *jail* or *sandbox* tools such as the UNIX/Linux tool chroot can create a limited security environment that prevents the intruder from gaining access to the rest of the system.

Root Access

The holy grail of the network intruder is always administrative or **root access** to the system. A user with root access can execute any command or view any file. When you have root access, you can essentially do whatever you want to do with the system. The term "root" comes from the UNIX world, but the concept of a powerful account with the privileges to control the system applies to all vendors and platforms. On Windows networks, this account is known as the Administrator account.

After the intruder is inside, often one of the first tasks is to upload a **rootkit**. A rootkit is a set of tools used for establishing a more permanent foothold on the system. Some of the tools are used to compromise new systems and new accounts. Other tools are designed to hide the attacker's presence on the systems. These obfuscation tools might include doctored versions of standard network utilities such as netstat, or applications that remove the trail of the intruder from system log files. Other tools in the rootkit might help the intruder explore the network or intercept more passwords. Some rootkits might actually enable the intruder to alter the operating system itself.

Modern rootkits provide additional features. *Key loggers* capture and log keyboard entries, waiting for the user to type a password. So-called kernel rootkits run at the highest security level of the operating system itself and are almost impossible to detect using conventional detection techniques.

The intruder sets out to establish one or more back doors to the system—secret ways of getting in to the system that are difficult for a network administrator to detect. The point of a back door is to enable the intruder to avoid the logging and monitoring processes that surround everyday interactive access. A back door might consist of a hidden account or hidden privileges associated with an account that should have only limited access. In some cases, the back door path might include services such as Telnet mapped to unusual port numbers where the local administrator would not expect to find them.

After the intruder has uploaded the necessary tools and has made provisions to cover the tracks and come back later, the next step is to go about any dastardly business the attacker might have in mind for the network, such as stealing files and credit information or configuring the system as a spambot. Another goal is to start getting ready for the next attack. A careful intruder never likes to leave a trail to home. The preferred method is to launch an attack from a system that has already been compromised. Some attackers operate through a chain of several remote systems. This strategy makes it almost impossible to determine the actual location of the intruder.

Going Phishing

The widespread use of firewalls, encryption techniques, and other security measures has made it more difficult for intruders to simply waltz right onto the network uninvited. The attackers have responded with their own new generation of techniques for foiling these security measures. One important new strategy is to entice the unsuspecting user into launching the attack by offering a fraudulent link, email message, or web page as bait. This type of attack falls under the category of **phishing**. A phishing attack might consist of an email message that asks the user to log in to an online banking site and update account information but actually leads to a faked web page managed by the attacker.

Phishing attacks often exploit the fact that the text shown with a link is independent of the actual URL. As you learn in Hour 18, "HTTP, HTML, and the World Wide Web," a web developer can specify a hypertext link using syntax such as the following:

```
<a href="http://www.MyBank.com/">MyBank</a>
```

In this case, the words *MyBank* would appear with a link that would lead to a home page at http://www.MyBank.com/. However, what if a morally challenged web developer encoded a link like the following:

```
<a href="http://www.NOT_MyBank_$$&%%??!!!.biz/">MyBank</a>
```

In that case, the link still appears with the label MyBank, but it leads to a different website. If you look carefully, you will sometimes see one of these phishing URLs in the address bar of your web browser or in flyover balloon text when you hover the mouse cursor over the link.

The best strategy is not to click links in unsolicited email messages, and never give up any financial information online unless you initiated the activity yourself and you are pretty sure you know where you are going.

Other more advanced phishing techniques are more difficult to trace and detect. One strategy known as cross-site scripting bypasses browser security using code injection to initiate a nefarious script that isn't easily traceable to the page the user is viewing.

This technique of inviting the user to initiate the attack has implications beyond the simple trick of linking to fake websites. Devices such as firewalls are primarily intended to stop attacks originating from the outside. By getting the user to initiate the connection, the attacker circumvents many of the protections built into the network security infrastructure (see Figure 11.9). The browser and the firewall have no easy way of knowing this connection is different from any other connection to an external website. When the connection is established, the attacker can employ a number of strategies for compromising security that wouldn't have been possible if the attack were launched from beyond the firewall. This kind of attack is even immune from Network Address Translation (NAT) (see Hour 12), which assigns the user's system a presumably nonroutable IP address. The firewall device simply translates the session traffic as it would for any other HTTP connection.

FIGURE 11.9
A home firewall that blocks connection attempts from the outside is often ineffective if the user initiates the connection to a fraudulent web server.

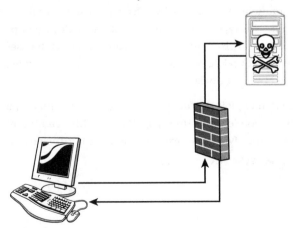

Better Firewalls

The possibility of this kind of user-initiated attack is one reason why security experts don't place a lot of faith in home style off-the-shelf firewall devices. The experts prefer more sophisticated firewall tools that provider a greater variety of syntax rules and filtering mechanisms.

Denial-of-Service Attacks

A recent craze in Internet intrusion is the **denial-of-service (DoS)** attack. A DoS attack is almost impossible to stop once it starts because it does not require the attacker to have any particular privileges on the system. The point of a DoS attack is to tie up the system with so many requests that system resources are all consumed and performance degrades. High-profile DoS attacks have been launched against websites of the U.S. government and those associated with major Internet search engines.

The most dangerous DoS attack is the distributed DoS (DDoS) attack. In a distributed DoS attack, the attacker uses several remote computers to direct other remote computers into launching a coordinated attack. Sometimes hundreds or even thousands of computers can participate on an attack against a single IP address.

DoS attacks often use standard TCP/IP connectivity utilities. The famous Smurf attack, for instance, uses the ping utility (see Hour 14, "TCP/IP Utilities") to unleash a flood of ping responses on the victim (see Figure 11.10). The attacker sends a ping request to an entire network through directed broadcast. The source address of the ping is doctored to make it appear that the request is coming from the victim's IP address. All the computers on the network then simultaneously respond to the ping. The effect of the Smurf attack is that the original ping from the attacker is multiplied into many pings on the amplification network. If the attacker initiates the process on several networks at once, the result is a huge flood of ping responses tying up the victim's system.

FIGURE 11.10
A DoS attack.

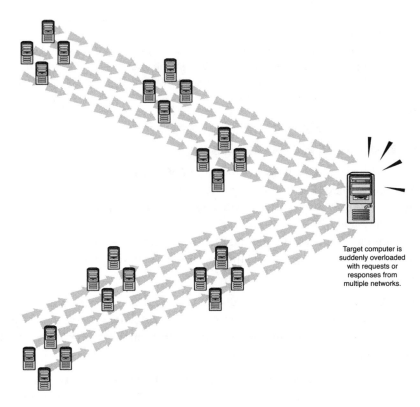

FIGURE 11.10
A DoS attack.

Target computer is suddenly overloaded with requests or responses from multiple networks.

What to Do

Professional security experts spend their whole lives figuring out what to do to prevent network attacks. Of course, they work on complex networks with hundreds of nodes and large amounts of Internet exposure. On a smaller scale, a few best practices can increase your chances of defeating many of the techniques discussed in this hour:

▶ Use a properly configured firewall.

▶ Use safe passwords. Strategies differ, but most experts recommend a minimum length of six to eight characters, with a combination of letters, numbers, and punctuation marks ($%^!,).

▶ Don't share passwords. Don't write down passwords and leave them in obvious places.

▶ Don't click suspicious links.

▶ Operate with minimal privileges.

▶ If you run Windows, be sure to have some form of virus protection.

▶ Turn off all services you don't need.

- ▶ If you must allow access to your internal network, set up a VPN for encrypted communication.

- ▶ Use a firewall. Close all ports, and turn off all network services unless you really need them.

- ▶ Run network services in a sandbox environment so that intrusion won't lead to privilege escalation.

- ▶ Use encryption for wireless networks.

- ▶ Install security updates often.

You still have to keep watching, but these time-honored techniques are a minimum for any conscientious Internet user.

Encryption and Secrecy

It is easy to intercept and read an unprotected packet of data traveling over a public network. In some cases, that data might contain user or password information. In other cases, the data might contain other sensitive information you don't want anyone else to see, such as credit card numbers or company secrets. The fact is that even if the data isn't particularly secret, many users are justifiably uncomfortable with the prospect of eavesdroppers listening in on their electronic communication.

The following sections discuss some security methods designed to make the network more secret. Many of these methods use a concept known as **encryption**. Encryption is the process of systematically altering data to make it unreadable to unauthorized users. Data is encrypted by the sender. The data then travels over the network in coded, unreadable form. The receiving computer then decrypts the data to read it.

In fact, encryption does not require a computer at all. Encryption methods have been around for centuries. As long as people have written secret messages, they have looked for codes or tricks to keep those messages secret. In the computer age, however, encryption has gotten much more sophisticated because of the ease with which computers can manipulate huge, messy numbers. Most computer encryption algorithms result from the manipulation of large prime numbers. The algorithms themselves are intensely mathematical, and I do not exaggerate to say that most of the experts who create and deploy encryption algorithms have graduate degrees in computer science or mathematics.

Encryption is an important foundation of almost all TCP/IP security. The following sections discuss some important encryption concepts. As you read the rest of this hour, it is important to keep in mind that the security infrastructure actually has multiple goals, and security methods must address multiple needs. The beginning of this section discussed the goal of confidentiality (keeping data secret). The security system must also address such needs as

▶ **Authentication:** Making sure that the data comes from the source to which it is attributed

▶ **Integrity:** Making sure that data has not been tampered with in transit

Encryption techniques are used to help ensure authentication and integrity as well as confidentiality.

The rest of this hour concentrates on securing the TCP/IP protocols from eavesdropping, interception, and manipulation.

Algorithms and Keys

As you learned in the previous section, encryption is a process for rendering data unreadable to everything and everyone who doesn't have the secret for unlocking the encryption code. For encryption to work, the two communicating entities must have the following:

▶ A process for making the data unreadable (encryption)

▶ A process for restoring the unreadable data to its original, readable form (decryption)

When programmers first began to write encryption software, they realized they must contend with the following problems:

▶ If every computer used the exact same process for encrypting and decrypting data, the program would not be acceptably secure because any eavesdropper could just obtain a copy of the program and start decrypting messages.

▶ If every computer used a totally different and unrelated process for encrypting and decrypting data, every computer would need a totally different and unrelated program. Each pair of computers that wanted to communicate would need separate software. This would be highly expensive and impossible to manage on large, diverse networks.

Intractable as these problems might seem, the large minds who develop encryption techniques quickly saw a solution. The solution is that the process for encrypting or decrypting the data must be divided into a standard, reproducible part (which is always the same) and a unique part (which forces a secret relationship between the communicating parties).

The standard part of the encryption process is called the encryption algorithm. The encryption algorithm is essentially a set of mathematical steps used to transform the data into its unreadable form. The unique and secret part of the process is called the **encryption key**. The science of encryption is extremely complex, but for purposes of discussion, you can think of the key as a large number that is used within the algorithm as a variable. The result of the encryption process depends on the value of the key. Therefore, as long as the value of the key is kept secret, unauthorized users will not be able to read the data even if they have the necessary decryption software.

The strangeness and obscurity of good encryption algorithms cannot be overstated. However, the following example illustrates the key and algorithm concepts.

A man does not want his mother to know how much he pays for furniture. He knows his mother is mathematically inclined, and he does not want to risk using a simple factor or multiplier to obscure the true value for fear that she will uncover the pattern. He has arranged with his lover that, if his mother is visiting and asks the cost, he will divide the real cost by a new, spontaneous number, multiply the result by 2, and then add $10. In other words, the man arranges to use the following algorithm:

```
(real cost) / n × 2 + $10 = reported cost
```

The new, spontaneous number (n) is the key. This same algorithm can be used every time the mother visits. The mother will have no way of determining a pattern for obscuring the real cost of the item so long as she does not know the key used in the calculation.

If the man comes home with a chair or table and sees his mother in the yard, he secretly signals a number to his lover (see Figure 11.11). When his mother asks the cost of the piece, he processes the algorithm and uses the number he signaled to his lover as the key. For instance, if the key is 3 and the chair cost is $600, he would report the following:

```
($600)/3 × 2 + $10 = $410
```

The lover, who is aware of the shared secret, knows that she must process the algorithm in reverse to obtain the true cost:

```
($410 -$10)/2 × 3 = $600
```

This simple example, which is intended only as an illustration of the difference between an algorithm and a key, does not reveal the real complexity of computer encryption methods. It is also important to remember that the goal of changing a value is not exactly the same as the goal of making data unreadable. However, in the binary world of computers, this distinction is less pronounced than it might seem.

FIGURE 11.11
An extremely primitive algorithm for disguising communication.

To a computer, all data takes the form of binary data bits representing 1s and 0s and is, therefore, subject to mathematical manipulation. Any process that transforms the string of data bits into a different string of data bits conceals the nature of the information. The important thing is that the recipient must have some means of working backward through the encrypted data to uncover the original information, and the encryption process must accommodate some form of shared secret value (a key) without which the decryption becomes impossible.

Encryption is at the heart of almost all secure networking techniques. Secure systems encrypt passwords, login procedures, and sometimes entire communication sessions. The encryption process is typically invisible to the user, although the applications and components that manage encryption are often invoked intentionally by the developer or network administrator.

Symmetric (Conventional) Encryption

Symmetric encryption is sometimes called conventional encryption because it preceded the development of newer, asymmetric techniques. Symmetric encryption is still the most common form, although public key asymmetric encryption (discussed later in this hour) has recently received considerable attention.

Symmetric encryption is called symmetric because the encryption and decryption processes use the same key, or at least, keys that are related in some predictable way. Figure 11.12 shows a symmetric encryption/decryption process. The steps are as follows:

1. A secret key is made known to both the sending and receiving computers.

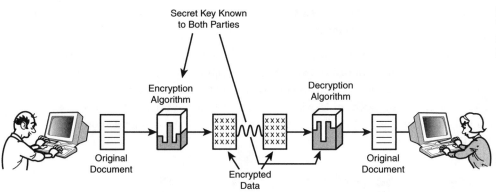

FIGURE 11.12
The symmetric encryption process.

2. The sending computer encrypts the data using a prearranged encryption algorithm and the secret key.

3. The encrypted (unreadable) text is delivered to the destination computer.

4. The receiving computer uses a corresponding decryption algorithm (along with the secret key) to decrypt the data.

The furniture man and his lover (see the example in the preceding section) use a symmetric algorithm to hide the true value of the chair.

Symmetric encryption can be extremely secure if it is performed carefully. The most important considerations for the security of any encryption scheme (symmetric or asymmetric) are as follows:

▶ The strength of the encryption algorithm

▶ The strength of the keys

▶ The secrecy of the keys

Breaking through an encryption algorithm that uses a 128-bit key might seem completely impossible, but it can happen. Key-cracking utilities are freely available on the Internet, and some 128-bit encryption algorithms that were once considered unbreakable are now considered unsecure. Another way to steal encrypted data is to steal the key. The software must provide some secure means for delivering the key to the receiving computer. Various key delivery systems exist, and you learn about some of these systems later in this hour. In the case of symmetric encryption, the secret key is the whole secret. If you capture the key, you have everything. Most systems, therefore, call for a periodic renewal of the key. The unique key used by a pair of communicating computers might be re-created with every session or after a given time interval. Key renewal increases the number of keys crossing the network, which compounds the need for effective key protection.

Several common encryption algorithms make use of symmetric encryption. The **Data Encryption Standard (DES)** was once a popular option, but its 56-bit key is now considered too short. Modern encryption techniques often allow for a variable key length. A descendent of DES known as the **Advanced Encryption Standard (AES)** supports keys of 128, 192, or 256 bits. The **Blowfish** symmetric algorithm provides a key length of up to 448 bits.

Asymmetric (Public Key) Encryption

An alternative encryption method that has emerged over the past 30 years provides an answer to some of the key distribution problems implicit with symmetric encryption. **Asymmetric encryption** is called asymmetric because the key used to encrypt the data is different from the key used to decrypt the data.

Asymmetric encryption is commonly associated with an encryption method known as public key encryption. In public key encryption, one of the two keys (called the **private key**) is held securely on a single computer. The other key (the **public key**) is made available to computers that want to send data to the holder of the private key. The steps are as follows:

1. Computer A attempts to establish a connection with Computer B.

2. The encryption software on Computer B generates a private key and a public key. The private key is shared with no one. The public key is made available to Computer A.

3. Computer A encrypts the data with the public key received from Computer B and transmits the data. The public key from Computer B is stored on Computer A for future reference.

4. Computer B receives the data and decrypts it using the private key.

Confidentiality and Authenticity

It can be argued that although an eavesdropper who intercepts the public key cannot read data sent from Computer A, the eavesdropper can still pretend to be Computer A by encrypting new data and sending it on to Computer B. Therefore, although public key encryption provides confidentiality, it does not necessarily provide authenticity. However, several methods exist for enclosing authentication information within the encrypted data so that when the data is decrypted, Computer B will have some assurance that the data actually came from Computer A. See the sections "Digital Signatures" and "Digital Certificates," later in this hour.

An important aspect of public key methods is that the encryption performed through the public key is a one-way function. The public key can be used to encrypt the data, but only the private key can decrypt the data after it is encrypted. An eavesdropper who intercepts the public key will still not be able to read messages encrypted using the public key.

Public key encryption is often used for establishing a secure connection. The data transmitted through public key encryption often includes a symmetric session key that is then used to encrypt the data transmitted within the session.

Public key encryption methods are commonly used for protected Internet transactions. You learn later in this hour about public key certificates, which are used for TCP/IP security protocols such as SSL and IPsec.

Digital Signatures

It is sometimes important to ensure the authenticity of a message even if you don't care whether the content of the message is confidential. For instance, a stockbroker might receive an email message that says

```
Sell 20 shares of my Microsoft stock.
-Bennie
```

Selling 20 shares might be an entirely routine event for this investor. The investor and the broker might not care if the transaction is totally immune from eavesdropping. However, they might consider it extremely important to ensure that this sell notice came from Bennie and not from someone pretending to be Bennie.

A **digital signature** is a method for ensuring that the data came from the source to which it is attributed and that the data has not been altered along its delivery path.

A digital signature is a block of encrypted data included with a message. The block of encrypted data is sometimes called an authenticator. A digital signature typically uses the public key encryption process in reverse (see Figure 11.13):

1. Computer B wants to send a document to Computer A that bears a digital signature. Computer B creates a small segment of data with information necessary to verify the contents of the document. In other words, some mathematical calculation is performed on the bits in the document to derive a value. The authenticator might also contain other information useful for verifying the authenticity of the message, such as a time-stamp value or other parameters that associate the authenticator with the message to which it is attached.

FIGURE 11.13
The digital sig-
nature process.

Receiving computer
checks authentication
data with document.

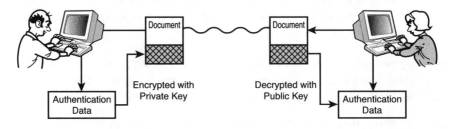

2. Computer B encrypts the authenticator using a private key. (Note that this is backward from the public key encryption process described in the preceding section. In the preceding section, the private key decrypts the data.) The authenticator is then affixed to the document, and the document is sent to Computer A.

3. Computer A receives the data and decrypts the authenticator using Computer B's public key. The information inside the authenticator lets Computer A verify that the data has not been altered in transit. The fact that the data could be decrypted using Computer B's public key proves that the data was encrypted using Computer B's private key, which ensures that the data came from Computer B.

The digital signature thus ensures that the data was not altered and that it came from its presumptive source. As a rudimentary security measure, the entire message could be encrypted with Computer B's private key rather than just the authenticator. However, encrypting with a private key and decrypting with a public key does not really offer confidentiality, as the public key, which is used for decryption, is sent over the Internet and, therefore, might not be secret. An eavesdropper who has the public key can decrypt the encrypted authenticator. However, the eavesdropper cannot encrypt a new authenticator and, therefore, cannot pretend to be Computer B.

Digital Certificates

The grand design of making the public key available to anyone who requests it is an interesting solution, but it still has some limitations. The fact is, an attacker can still make mischief with the public key. The attacker might be able to decrypt digital signatures (see the preceding section) or even read passwords encrypted with the user's private key. It is safer to provide some kind of security system for ensuring who gets access to a public key.

One answer to this problem is what is called a **digital certificate**. A digital certificate is essentially an encrypted copy of the public key. The certificate process is shown in Figure 11.14. This process requires a third-party certificate server that has a secure relationship with both the parties that want to communicate. The certificate server is also called a **certificate authority (CA)**.

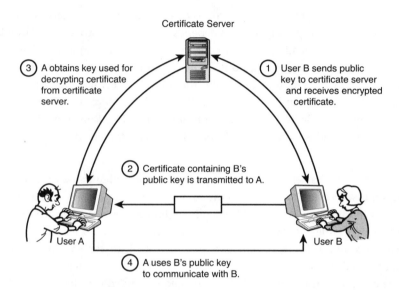

FIGURE 11.14
Authentication using digital certificates.

Several companies provide certificate services for the Internet. One major certificate authority is VeriSign Corp. Some large organizations provide their own certificate services. The certificate process varies among the various vendors. A rough schematic description of the process is as follows:

1. User B sends a copy of his public key to the certificate server through a secure communication.

2. The certificate server encrypts User B's public key (along with other user parameters) using a different key. This newly encrypted package is called the certificate. Included with the certificate is the digital signature of the certificate server.

3. The certificate server returns the certificate to User B.

4. User A needs to obtain User B's public key. Computer A asks Computer B for a copy of User B's certificate.

5. Computer A obtains a copy of the key used to encrypt the certificate through a secure communication with the certificate server.

6. Computer A decrypts the certificate using the key obtained from the certificate server and extracts User B's public key. Computer A also checks the digital signature of the certificate server (see step 2) to ensure that the certificate is authentic.

The best-known standard for the certification process is the **X.509** standard, which is described in several RFCs. X.509 version 3 is described in RFC 2459 and later RFCs. The latest version is RFC 5280.

The digital certificate process is designed to serve a community of users. As you might guess, the security of the process depends on the safe distribution of any keys necessary for communicating with the certificate server. This might seem like simply transferring the problem. (You guarantee safe communication with the remote host by presupposing safe communication with the certificate server.) However, the fact that the protected communication channel is limited to a single certificate server (as opposed to any possible host within the community) makes it much more feasible to impose the overhead of additional safeguards necessary for ensuring a secure exchange.

The certificate process described earlier in this hour conveniently assumes the certificate server assigned to Computer A is the same server that provides certificates for User B. The certificate process might actually require a number of certificate servers spread across a large network. In that case, the process might require a series of communications and certificate exchanges with other certificate servers to reach the server that provided the User B certificate. As RFC 2459 states, "In general, a chain of multiple certificates might be needed, comprising a certificate of the public key owner (the end entity) signed by one CA, and zero or more additional certificates of CAs signed by other CAs. Such chains, called certification paths, are required because a public key user is only initialized with a limited number of assured CA public keys." Luckily, like most of the details related to encryption, this process is built into the software and doesn't require direct oversight from the user.

The X.509 certificate process is used in some of the TCP/IP security protocols discussed later in this hour, such as SSL and IPsec.

Securing TCP/IP

In recent years, vendors have been busy extending and expanding their TCP/IP implementations to incorporate the security and encryption techniques discussed earlier in this hour. The following sections describe how encryption techniques are integrated into two Internet security protocol systems: SSL/TLS and IPsec.

Other public security protocols are also in development, and some security software vendors have developed their own systems. The following sections are intended to give you an idea of the kind of solutions necessary to incorporate the promise of encryption into the business of a real network.

SSL and TLS

Secure Sockets Layer (SSL) is a collection of TCP/IP security protocols introduced by Netscape for securing web communication. The purpose of SSL is to provide a layer of security between the sockets at the Transport layer (see Hour 6) and the application accessing the network through the sockets. Figure 11.15 shows the position of SSL in the TCP/IP protocol stack. The idea is that, when SSL is active, network services such as FTP and HTTP are protected from attack by the secure SSL protocols. Transport Layer Security (TLS) is a protocol standard originally described in RFC 2246 and last updated with RFC 5246. **TLS,** which is based on SSL 3.0, is a successor to SSL, and it is the industry standard at this point. However, references to SSL persist in product names as well as in actual software. Following is a brief description of SSL; the TLS protocol is similar.

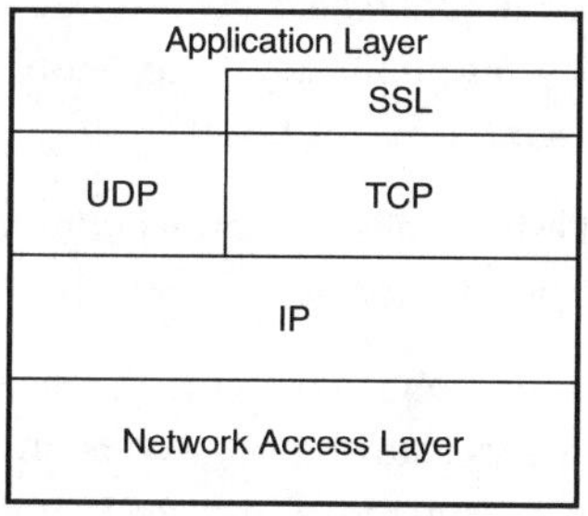

	Application Layer	
		SSL
UDP	TCP	
IP		
Network Access Layer		

FIGURE 11.15
The TCP/IP stack with SSL.

A closer look at the SSL layer reveals two sublayers (see Figure 11.16). The SSL Record Protocol is a standard base for accessing TCP. Above the Record Protocol is a group of SSL-related protocols that perform specific services:

▶ **SSL Handshake Protocol:** The base protocol used to access TCP

▶ **SSL Change Cipher Spec Protocol:** Supports changes to encryption suite settings

▶ **SSL Alert Protocol:** Sends alerts

FIGURE 11.16
SSL sublayers.

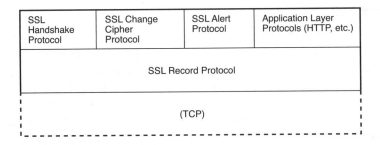

SSL Handshake Protocol	SSL Change Cipher Protocol	SSL Alert Protocol	Application Layer Protocols (HTTP, etc.)
SSL Record Protocol			
(TCP)			

SSL-enabled services operate directly through the SSL Record Protocol. After the connection is established, the SSL Record Protocol provides the encryption and verification necessary to ensure the confidentiality and integrity of the session.

As with other protocol security techniques, the trick is to verify the identity of the participants and securely exchange the keys that will be used for encrypting and decrypting transmissions. SSL uses public key encryption and provides support for digital certificates (described earlier in this hour).

The SSL Handshake Protocol establishes the connection and negotiates any connection settings (including encryption settings).

SSL is used on many websites to establish a secure connection for the exchange of financial information and other sensitive data. A version of the HTTP web protocol with SSL encryption is known as Hypertext Transfer Protocol Secure (HTTPS). Most mainstream browsers are capable of establishing SSL connections with little or no input from the user. One problem with SSL is that because SSL operates above the Transport layer, the applications using the connection must be SSL aware (unless they operate through some kind of compatibility software that is SSL aware). The next section describes an alternative TCP/IP security system (IPsec) that operates at a lower layer and, therefore, hides the details of the security system from the application.

> SSL and TLS are designed to operate with connection-oriented, TCP connections. Another protocol known as Datagram Transport Protocol Security (DTLS) provides TLS-like security in a way that also supports connectionless communication with UDP. See RFC 4347 for more on DTLS.

IPsec

IP Security (IPsec) is an alternative security protocol system used on TCP/IP networks. IPsec operates inside the TCP/IP protocol stack, beneath the Transport layer. Because the security system is implemented beneath the Transport layer, the applications operating above the Transport layer do not need knowledge of the security system. IPsec is designed to provide support for confidentiality, access control, authentication, and data integrity. IPsec also protects against replay attacks, in which a packet is extracted from the data stream and reused later by the attacker.

IPsec, which is essentially a set of extensions to the IP protocol, is described in several RFCs, starting with RFC 2401 and including RFCs 4301, 4302, and 4303. The RFCs describe IP security extensions for both IPv4 and IPv6. IPsec is built in to the structure of IPv6 protocol system. In IPv4, IPsec is considered an extension, but IPsec support is nevertheless built in to many IPv4 implementations.

IPsec provides the benefit of encryption-based security to any network application, regardless of whether the application is security-aware. However, the protocol stacks of both computers must support IPsec. Because the security is invisible to high-level applications, IPsec is ideal for providing security for network devices such as routers and firewalls. IPsec can operate in either of two modes:

▶ Transport mode provides encryption for the payload of an IP packet. The payload is then enclosed in a normal IP packet for delivery.

▶ Tunnel mode encrypts an entire IP packet. The encrypted packet is then included as the payload in another outer packet.

Tunnel mode is used to build a secure communication tunnel in which all details of the network are hidden. An eavesdropper cannot even read the header to obtain the source IP address. IPsec tunnel mode is often used for VPN products, which are intended to create a totally private communication tunnel across a public network.

IPsec uses a number of encryption algorithms and key distribution techniques. Data is encrypted using conventional encryption algorithms such as AES, RC5, or Blowfish. Authentication and key distribution might employ public key techniques.

VPNs

The problem of remote access has appeared many times in this book. This problem has actually been an important issue throughout the evolution of TCP/IP. How do you connect computers that are not close enough for a LAN-style cable connection? System administrators have always relied on two important methods for remote connections:

▶ **Dial-up:** A remote user connects through a modem to a dial-up server, which acts as a gateway to the network.

▶ **Wide area network (WAN):** Two networks are connected through a dedicated leased-line connection through a phone company or Internet provider.

Both these methods also have disadvantages. Dial-up connections are notoriously slow, and they depend on the quality of the phone connection. A WAN connection is also sometimes slow, but more significantly, a WAN is expensive to build and maintain and is not mobile. A WAN connection is not an option for a remote user of uncertain location traveling with a laptop.

One answer to these problems is to connect directly to the remote network over the open Internet. This solution is fast and convenient, but the Internet is so hostile and unsecure that such an option simply is infeasible without providing some way of preventing eavesdropping. Experts began to wonder if there were some way to use the tools of encryption to create a private channel through a public network. The solution to this problem emerged in what we know now as a virtual private network (VPN). A VPN establishes a point-to-point "tunnel" across the network through which ordinary TCP/IP traffic can pass securely.

> **VPN Protocols**
>
> Whereas IPsec (described earlier in this hour) is a protocol that supports secure network connections, a VPN is the connection itself. A VPN application is a program that creates and sustains these private remote connections. Some VPN tools use IPsec for encryption, and others rely on other SSL or other encryption techniques. Microsoft systems used to provide VPN tunneling through the Point-to-Point Tunneling Protocol (which is derived from the PPP modem protocol). More recent Microsoft systems use the Layer 2 Tunneling Protocol (L2TP) for VPN sessions.

The encryption techniques described earlier in this hour do not work well if every router in the delivery chain needs knowledge of the encryption key. Encryption is intended for point-to-point connections. The idea is that the VPN client software on the remote server establishes a connection with a VPN server that is acting as a gateway to the network (see Figure 11.17). The VPN client and server exchange plain, routable TCP/IP datagrams that pass normally through the Internet. However, the payload (the data) sent through the VPN connection is actually an encrypted datagram. The encrypted datagrams (which are unreadable on the open Internet) are enclosed in the plain, readable datagrams forwarded to the VPN server. The VPN server software then extracts the encrypted datagram, decrypts the datagram using the encryption key, and forwards the enclosed data to its destination address on the protected network.

Although it is possible for an eavesdropping cyber thief to intercept a nonencrypted packet sent between the VPN client and server, the useful information is all within the encrypted payload, which the listener cannot unencrypt without the necessary key.

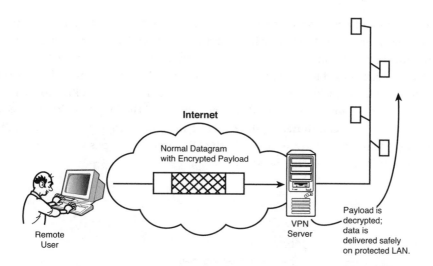

FIGURE 11.17
A VPN provides a private tunnel through a public network.

With the arrival of VPNs, it is now common for users to establish secure LAN-like connections with remote networks over the Internet. On most systems, the details of establishing and maintaining a VPN connection are handled within the software. The user just has to start the VPN application and enter authentication information. After the connection is established, the user interacts with the network as if connected locally.

Kerberos

Kerberos is a network-based authentication and access control system designed to support secure access over hostile networks. Kerberos was developed at MIT as part of the Athena project. The Kerberos system was originally intended for UNIX-based systems, but it has since been ported to other environments. Microsoft provides a version of Kerberos for Windows networks.

As you have probably figured out by now, the short answer to the question of secure communication on hostile networks is encryption. The long answer is providing a means for protecting the security of the encryption keys. Kerberos offers a methodical process for distributing keys to the communicating hosts and verifying the credentials of a client requesting access to a service.

The Kerberos system uses a server called the **Key Distribution Center (KDC)** to manage the key distribution process. The Kerberos authentication process results from a relationship of three entities:

- ▶ **The client:** A computer requesting access to a server
- ▶ **The server:** A computer offering a service on the network
- ▶ **The KDC:** A computer designated to provide keys for network communication

The Kerberos authentication process is shown in Figure 11.18. Note that this process presupposes that the KDC already has a shared secret key it can use to communicate with the client and a shared secret key it can use to communicate with the server. These keys are used to encrypt a new session key, which the client and server will use to communicate with each other. The separate keys used by the KDC to encrypt data for the client and server are called long-term keys. The long-term key is typically derived from a secret shared by the KDC and the other computer. Commonly, the client long-term key is derived from a hash of the user's logon password, which is known to both the client and the KDC.

FIGURE 11.18
The Kerberos
authentication
process.

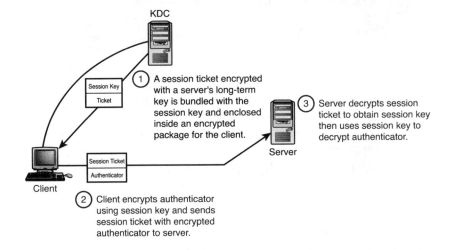

The process is as follows. As you read through this process, keep in mind that Kerberos normally uses conventional (symmetric) encryption rather than public key (asymmetric) encryption. In other words, the same key is used at both ends of each exchange:

1. The client wants to access a service on Server A. The client sends the KDC a request for access to the service on Server A. (In some cases, the client has already undergone an authentication process and received a separate session key for encrypting communication with the ticket granting service on the KDC.)

2. The KDC performs the following steps:

    a. The KDC generates a session key that will be used to encrypt communication between the client and Server A.

b. The KDC creates a session ticket. The session ticket includes a copy of the session key generated in step 2a. The ticket also contains time stamp information and information about the client that is requesting access, such as client security settings.

c. The KDC encrypts the session ticket using Server A's long-term key.

d. The KDC bundles the encrypted session ticket, a copy of the session key, and other response parameters for the client and encrypts the whole package using the client's key. The response is then sent to the client.

3. The client receives the response from the KDC and decrypts it. The client obtains the session key necessary for communicating with Server A. Also included in the package is the session ticket, which is encrypted with the server's long-term key. The client cannot read the session ticket, but it knows it must send the ticket to the server to be authenticated. The client creates an authenticator (a string of authentication parameters) and encrypts it with the session key.

4. The client sends Server A an access request. The request includes the session ticket (encrypted with the server's long-term key) and the authenticator (encrypted with the session key). The authenticator includes the user's name, network address, time stamp information, and so forth.

5. Server A receives the request. Server A uses its long-term key to decrypt the session ticket (see step 2c). Server A extracts the session key from the session ticket and uses the session key to decrypt the authenticator. Server A verifies that the information in the authenticator matches the information included in the session ticket. If so, access to the service is granted.

6. As an optional final step, if the client wants to verify the credentials of Server A, Server A encrypts an authenticator with the session key and returns this authenticator to the client.

The Kerberos system is gradually becoming more popular as a means of providing a unified logon system for a network. Kerberos 4 used DES encryption, which, as this hour has already noted, is considered unsecure by many encryption experts. The latest version of Kerberos (Kerberos 5—described in RFC 41201510) supports AES and other encryption types.

> **Three Heads?**
>
> If you've ever read a description of Kerberos, you probably know the standard description of where Kerberos got its name. In Greek mythology, Kerberos (also called Cerberus) is a three-headed hound that guards the gates of the underworld. The story now is that the three heads are the three elements of the Kerberos authentication process (the client, the server, and the KDC). The original intent for the name, however, is a little murkier. In his book *Network Security Essentials, Fourth Edition* (Prentice Hall, 2010), William Stallings points out that the Kerberos system was originally intended to guard the gates of the network with the three heads of authentication, accounting, and audit, but the latter two heads (accounting and audit) were never implemented. The security community apparently found it easier to realign the metaphor than to rename the protocol for an equivalent one-headed canine.

Summary

The Internet has millions of users, and a significant number of them are devoted to making mischief. If you want to preserve your privacy and protect your resources, you need to take an active role in protecting your network. This chapter examined some important security concepts. You learned about firewalls and studied some intrusion techniques. This chapter also examined encryption and some security features that depend on encryption, such as digital certificates, TLS, IPsec, and VPNs.

Q&A

Q. *What is the benefit of a stateful firewall?*

A. By monitoring the state of a connection, a stateful firewall can watch for certain DoS attacks, as well as invalid packets and tricks that hijack or manipulate the session.

Q. *What is the purpose of a DMZ?*

A. The purpose of a DMZ is to provide an intermediate security zone that is more accessible than the internal network but more protected than the open Internet.

Workshop

The following workshop is composed of a series of quiz questions and practical exercises. The quiz questions test your overall understanding of the current material. The practical exercises give you the opportunity to apply the concepts discussed during the current hour and to build on the knowledge acquired in previous hours of study. Take time to complete the quiz questions and exercises before continuing. Refer to Appendix A, "Answers to Quizzes and Exercises," for answers.

Quiz

1. How does a proxy server improve response time for a web browser?

2. Why is it important to install updates?

3. Ellen must figure out a way to make several legacy network applications work on a Windows XP computer. She has been instructed to provide confidentiality for communication using these ancient apps. Should she use TLS/SSL or IPsec?

4. What happens if an intruder tricks a Kerberos client into sending a session ticket to the wrong server?

Exercises

1. Look for a personal firewall configuration page for your computer. In Windows 7, look for the Windows Firewall icon in the control panel. On Mac OS, choose the Security preferences dialog and select Firewall. Linux has several personal firewall options. On recent Ubuntu systems, choose System, Administration, Firewall configuration.

2. Go to the U.S. government's Cyber Security Bulletins page (http://www.us-cert.gov/bulletins). Select a vulnerability summary for a recent week. Study the descriptions and look for some of the concepts discussed in this hour, such as buffer overflow and denial of service.

Key Terms

Review the following list of key terms:

▶ **Advanced Encryption Standard (AES):** A symmetric encryption algorithm that supports key lengths of 128, 192, and 256 bits.

▶ **Asymmetric encryption:** An encryption technique that uses different keys for encryption and decryption.

▶ **Back door:** A hidden pathway for gaining entry to a computer system.

▶ **Blowfish:** A symmetric encryption algorithm that supports key lengths of up to 448 bits.

▶ **Buffer overflow:** An attack method that lets the attacker deliver malicious commands to a system by overrunning an application buffer.

▶ **Certificate authority (CA):** A central authority that oversees the certificate creation and delivery process.

▶ **Data Encryption Standard (DES):** A symmetric encryption algorithm that was once popular but is now considered unsecure due to the small 56-bit key length.

▶ **Denial-of-service attack (DoS):** An attack design to cripple the victim's system by consuming system resources.

▶ **Digital certificate:** An encrypted data structure used to distribute a public key.

▶ **Digital signature:** An encrypted string used to verify the identity of the sender and the integrity of the data.

▶ **DMZ:** An intermediate space inhabited by Internet servers that falls behind a front firewall and in front of a more restrictive firewall protecting an internal network.

▶ **Encryption:** The process of systematically altering data to make it unreadable to unauthorized users.

▶ **Encryption key:** A value (usually kept secret) used with the encryption algorithm to encrypt or decrypt data.

▶ **Firewall:** A device or application that restricts network access to an internal network.

- ► **IPsec (IP Security):** A security protocol system consisting of extensions to the IP protocol.

- ► **KDC (Key Distribution Center):** A server that manages the key distribution process on Kerberos networks.

- ► **Kerberos:** A network authentication system designed for secure access to services over hostile networks.

- ► **Packet filter:** A firewall that filters by port number or other protocol information indicating the purpose of the packet.

- ► **Phishing:** Using a fake link, message, or web page to entice the user into initiating a connection with a fraudulent website.

- ► **Private key:** A key used in asymmetric encryption that is kept secret and not distributed on the network.

- ► **Proxy server:** A computer or application that requests services on behalf of a client.

- ► **Public key:** A key used in asymmetric encryption that is distributed over the network.

- ► **Reverse proxy:** A computer or application that receives inbound requests from the Internet and forwards them to an internal server.

- ► **Root access:** The highest level of access to a computer system. Root access offers nearly unlimited control of the system.

- ► **Rootkit:** A set of tools used by an intruder to expand and disguise his control of a system.

- ► **Script kiddies:** Young, usually adolescent Internet intruders who work mostly with ready-made scripts and tools available on the Internet.

- ► **Session hijacking:** An attack method that lets the attacker insert malicious packets into an existing TCP session.

- ► **SSL (Secure Sockets Layer):** A security protocol system originally developed by Netscape that operates above the TCP protocol. SSL has officially been replaced by TLS.

- ► **Stateful firewall:** A firewall that is aware of the state of the connection.

▶ **Symmetric encryption:** Encryption technique in which the encryption key and the decryption key are the same or trivially related.

▶ **TLS (Transport Layer Security):** A secure transport-layer protocol based on SSL.

▶ **Trojan horse:** A program that purports to do one thing but actually takes other unseen and malicious actions behind the scenes.

▶ **X.509:** A standard that describes the digital certificate process and format.

HOUR 12

Configuration

What You'll Learn in This Hour:

▶ Dynamic address assignment

▶ DHCP

▶ NAT

▶ Zeroconf

In the old days, every client computer held a static IP address defined somewhere within a configuration file, and to change the configuration, the system administrator had to go change the file. Networks today, however, require a more versatile and convenient approach, and most computers operate through some form of dynamic or automatic configuration. This hour looks at some common techniques for configuring TCP/IP networking.

At the completion of this hour, you will be able to

▶ Describe DHCP and the benefits it provides

▶ Describe the process of leasing an IP address through DHCP

▶ Describe the purpose of Network Address Translation

▶ Show how computers use the zero-configuration protocols

Getting on the Network

The interplay of protocols described in the previous hours might seem intimidating, but today's operating systems have gotten very good at handling the details automatically. The user component of TCP/IP configuration comes down to a few simple choices during the installation.

Although different systems ask it in different ways, the most basic choice is which of the following you would prefer to do:

▶ Configure a static IP address

▶ Configure the computer to receive a dynamic IP address through DHCP

In most cases, you are asked to choose a name to serve as an identifier for the computer on the network. (See Hour 10, "Name Resolution," for more on hostnames, domain name system [DNS], and NetBIOS name resolution.)

As you learn later in this hour, even if your computer isn't successfully configured with a static or dynamic address, some systems can still perform a kind of rudimentary TCP/IP networking through the zero-configuration techniques that have become popular in the past few years.

When it comes to pointing and clicking in the user interface once the system is installed, every version of every operating system requires slightly different steps, but the basic concepts are fairly constant. This hour takes a look at TCP/IP configuration in recent Windows, Mac OS, and Ubuntu Linux systems. See your vendor documentation for more on setting up TCP/IP for your system.

At the conceptual level, static TCP/IP configuration is self-explanatory in that there isn't much more to it than inputting the address, hostname, subnet mask, and gateway router. Dynamic addressing is even easier to configure, but when you tell your computer to "receive a dynamic IP address," you are actually calling for a series of interactions that will take place behind the scenes using the important **Dynamic Host Configuration Protocol (DHCP)**. This hour starts with a look at DHCP.

The Case for Server-Supplied IP Addresses

Every computer, as you learned in a previous hour, must have an IP address to operate on a TCP/IP network. The IP addressing system was originally designed for the logical condition in which each computer is preconfigured with an IP address. This condition is known as static IP addressing. Each computer knows its IP address from the moment it boots and can use the network immediately. Static IP addressing works well for small, permanent networks, but on larger networks that are subject to reconfiguration and change (such as new computers coming and going from the network), static IP addressing has some limitations.

The principal shortcomings of static IP addressing are as follows:

▶ **More configuration:** Each client must be configured individually. A change to the IP address space or to some other parameter (such as the DNS server address) means that each client must be reconfigured separately.

▶ **More addresses:** Each computer uses an IP address whether it is currently on the network or not.

▶ **Reduced flexibility:** A computer must be manually reconfigured if it is assigned to a different subnetwork.

As an answer to these limitations, an alternative IP addressing system has evolved in which IP addresses are assigned on request using DHCP. DHCP was developed from an earlier protocol called **BOOTP**, which was used primarily to boot diskless computers. (A diskless computer receives a complete operating system over the network as it boots.) DHCP has become increasingly popular in recent years because of the dwindling supply of IP addresses and the growth of large, dynamic networks.

It is quite likely that the majority of all computers with Internet access receive their configurations through DHCP. The small router/firewall device that brings the Internet to your home network is probably also acting as a DHCP server.

What Is DHCP?

DHCP is a protocol used to automatically assign TCP/IP configuration parameters to computers. DHCP was originally described in RFC 1531 and later updated in RFCs 1534, 1541, 2131, and 2132. The current standard is RFC 2131, which has received updates in RFCs 3396, 4361, and 5494. A DHCP server can supply a DHCP client with a number of TCP/IP settings, such as an IP address, a subnet mask, and the address of a DNS server.

Because the DHCP server is assigning the IP addresses, only the DHCP server must be configured with static IP address information. The only networking parameter you need to configure on the client end is an option for the client to receive IP address information from a DHCP server. The rest of the TCP/IP configuration is transmitted from the server. If some aspect of the TCP/IP configuration changes on the network, the network administrator needs to update just the DHCP server, instead of updating each client manually.

Furthermore, each client receives a lease of finite duration for the address. If the client is no longer using the address when the lease expires, the address can be assigned to another client. The effect of DHCP's leasing feature is that a network will not usually need as many IP addresses as it has clients.

DHCP is especially important in today's environment, in which many employees carry notebook computers between offices of a large corporation. If a laptop computer is configured with a static IP address, it must be reconfigured each time the traveling employee plugs into a different network. If the computer is configured to receive an IP address through DHCP, the laptop automatically receives a complete TCP/IP configuration each time the user attaches to a network with a DHCP server.

How DHCP Works

When a **DHCP client** computer is started, the TCP/IP software is loaded into memory and starts to operate. However, because the TCP/IP stack has not been given an IP address yet, it is incapable of sending or receiving directed datagrams. The computer can, however, transmit and listen for broadcasts. This capability to communicate via broadcasts is the basis for how DHCP works. The process of leasing an IP address from the **DHCP server** involves four steps (see Figure 12.1):

1. **DHCPDISCOVER:** The DHCP client initiates the process by broadcasting a datagram destined for UDP port 67 (used by BOOTP and DHCP servers). This first datagram is known as a DHCP Discover message, which is a request to any DHCP server that receives the datagram for configuration information. The DHCP discover datagram contains many fields, but the one that is most important contains the physical address of the DHCP client.

2. **DHCPOFFER:** A DHCP server configured to lease addresses for the network on which the client computer resides constructs a response datagram known as a DHCP offer and sends it via broadcast to the computer that issued the DHCP discover. This broadcast is sent to UDP port 68 and contains the physical address of the DHCP client. Also contained in the DHCP

FIGURE 12.1
A DHCP server provides the network client with an IP address.

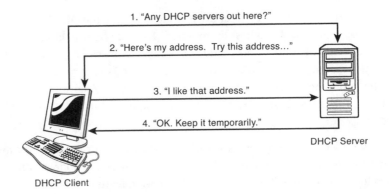

1. "Any DHCP servers out here?"
2. "Here's my address. Try this address…"
3. "I like that address."
4. "OK. Keep it temporarily."

DHCP Server

DHCP Client

offer are the physical and IP addresses of the DHCP server, as well as the values for the IP address and subnet mask that are being offered to the DHCP client.

At this point it is possible for the DHCP client to receive several DHCP offers, assuming there are multiple DHCP servers with the capability to offer the DHCP client an IP address. In most cases, the DHCP client accepts the first DHCP offer that arrives.

3. **DHCPREQUEST:** The client selects an offer and constructs and broadcasts a DHCP request datagram. The DHCP request datagram contains the IP address of the server that issued the offer and the physical address of the DHCP client. The DHCP request performs two basic tasks. First it tells the selected DHCP server that the client requests it to assign the DHCP client an IP address (and other configuration settings). Second, it notifies all other DHCP servers with outstanding offers that their offers were not accepted.

4. **DHCPACK:** When the DHCP server from which the offer was selected receives the DHCP request datagram, it constructs the final datagram of the lease process. This datagram is known as a **DHCP ack** (short for *acknowledgment*). The DHCP ack includes an IP address and subnet mask for the DHCP client. Optionally, the DHCP client is often also configured with IP addresses for the default gateway, several DNS servers, and possibly one or two WINS servers. In addition to IP addresses, the DHCP client can receive other configuration information such as a NetBIOS node type, which can change the order of NetBIOS name resolution.

Three other key fields are contained in the DHCP ack, all of which indicate time periods. One field identifies the length of the lease. Two other time fields, known as T1 and T2, are used when the client attempts to renew its lease.

Relay Agents

If both the DHCP client and the DHCP server reside on the same network segment, the process proceeds exactly as previously indicated. If the DHCP client and DHCP server reside on different networks separated by one or more routers, the process becomes more complicated. Routers typically do not forward broadcasts to other networks. For DHCP to work, a middleman must assist the DHCP process. The middleman can be another host on the same network as the DHCP client, but often it is the router itself. In any case, the process that performs this middleman function is called either a **BOOTP relay agent** or a **DHCP relay agent**.

A relay agent is configured with a fixed IP address and also contains the IP address of the DHCP server. Because relay agents have configured IP addresses, they can always send and receive directed datagrams to the DHCP server. Because the relay agent resides on the same network as the DHCP client, it can communicate with the DHCP client via broadcasts (see Figure 12.2).

FIGURE 12.2
A relay agent helps the client reach a DHCP server beyond the local network segment.

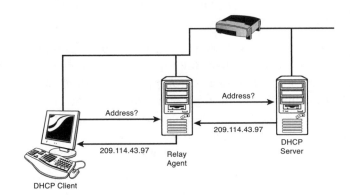

Relay agents listen for broadcasts destined for UDP port 67; when the relay agent detects a DHCP request, it retransmits the request to the DHCP server. When the agent receives a response from the DHCP server, the response is rebroadcast on the local segment. This explanation has eliminated a few details for brevity but conveys the essence of the function performed by a relay agent.

The popular practice of placing a DHCP server on the router itself has reduced the need for DHCP relay services on most networks. For more on relay agents, you can read RFC 1542.

DHCP Time Fields

DHCP clients lease IP addresses from DHCP servers for a fixed period of time. The actual lease length is typically configured on the DHCP server. The T1 and T2 time values sent with the DHCP ack message are used during the lease renewal process. The T1 value indicates to the client when it should begin the process of renewing its lease. T1 is typically set to one-half of the actual lease time. Assume in the following example that leases are issued for a period of 8 days.

Just 4 days into the lease, the client sends a DHCP request to attempt to renew its IP address lease with the DHCP server that issued the lease. Assuming the DHCP server is online, the lease typically is renewed using a DHCP ack. Unlike the DHCP request and ack explained earlier in the four-step process, these two datagrams are not

broadcast but are sent as directed datagrams. This is possible because both computers at this time contain valid IP addresses.

If the DHCP server is not available when the DHCP client issues the first request at
50% (4 days), the client waits and attempts to renew the lease at 75% of the lease
period, or 6 days into the lease. If this request also fails, the DHCP client tries a third
time at 87.5%, or seven-eighths of the lease. Up to this point, the DHCP client has
attempted to renew its lease with the DHCP server that issued the lease by sending
directed datagrams. If the DHCP client is incapable of renewing its lease by 87.5% of
the total lease, the T2 time period comes into effect. The T2 time allows the DHCP
client to begin broadcasting requests for any DHCP server. If the DHCP client is incapable of either renewing its lease or obtaining a new lease from another DHCP server by the time the lease expires, the client must stop using the IP address and stop
using TCP/IP for normal network operations.

DHCP Server Configuration

Unless you are a system administrator on a mid- to large-size network, you probably
won't ever have occasion to configure a computer to act as a DHCP server, and if
you do, you probably have access to other documentation that is far more attuned
to the peculiarities of your configuration than this book is. Windows provides a GUI-
based utility called DHCP Manager for configuring the DHCP server.

Linux systems provide DHCP services through dhcpd, the DHCP daemon.
Instructions for installing dhcpd vary according to the vendor. DHCP configuration
information is stored in the configuration file /etc/dhcpd.conf.

The /etc/dhcpd.conf file contains the IP address configuration information that the
DHCP daemon will assign to clients. /etc/dhcpd.conf also contains optional settings
such as the broadcast address, domain name, DNS server address, and the addresses
of routers. A sample /etc/dhcpd.conf file follows:

```
default-lease-time 600;
max-lease-time 7200;
option domain-name "macmillan.com";
option subnet-mask 255.255.255.0;
option broadcast-address 185.142.13.255;
subnet 185.142.13.0 netmask 255.255.255.0 {
range 185.142.13.10 185.142.13.50;
range 185.142.13.100 185.142.13.200;
}
```

As mentioned previously in this hour, DHCP service is often handled through a network device such as a router/firewall system. See the user manual for your home

router for more on configuring DHCP. Router devices typically provide a web configuration interface (see Figure 12.3). Log in to your router's configuration page to modify the DHCP configuration. In most cases, reconfiguration of DHCP isn't necessary.

FIGURE 12.3
Configuring
DHCP on a
home router
device.

You might occasionally want to ensure that a device maintains a permanent
address even though the rest of the network uses dynamic addressing. For instance,
you might want to maintain a permanent address for a network printer so that the
computers using it don't have to keep relearning the address. Some routers provide a
feature called **IP Reservation** that lets you associate a specific IP address with a specific physical (MAC) address. This feature ensures that the device will always receive
the same IP address.

Network Address Translation

Some experts began to notice that, if a DHCP server is providing the client with an
IP address, there is no real reason why this address has to be an official, unique
"legal" Internet address. As long as the router itself has an Internet-ready address, it
can act as a proxy for clients on the network—receiving requests from clients and
translating the requests to and from the Internet address space. Many router/DHCP
devices today also perform a service known as Network Address Translation (NAT).

A NAT device obscures all details of the local network and, in fact, hides the existence of the local network. Figure 12.4 shows a NAT device. The NAT device serves as
a gateway for computers on the local network to access the Internet. Behind the
NAT device, the local network can use any network address space. When a local
computer attempts to connect to an Internet resource, the NAT device makes the

connection instead. Any packets received from the Internet resource are translated into the address scheme of the local network and forwarded to the local computer that initiated the connection.

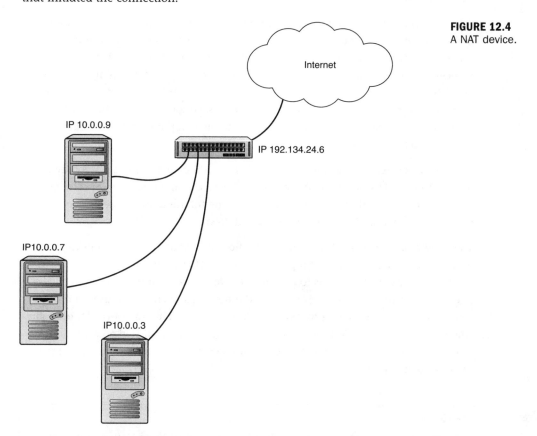

FIGURE 12.4
A NAT device.

A NAT device improves security because it can prevent an outside attacker from finding out about the local network. To the outside world, the NAT device looks like a single host connected to the Internet. Even if an attacker knew the address of a computer on the local network, the attacker would not be able to open a connection with the local network because the local addressing scheme is not contiguous with the Internet address space. As you learned in Hour 4, "The Internet Layer," a few IP address ranges are reserved for "private" networks:

10.0.0.0 to 10.255.255.255

172.16.0.0 to 172.31.255.255

192.168.0.0 to 192.168.255.255

(As you will learn later in this hour, the 169.254.0.0 to 169.254.255.255 address range is also a non-routable address block that is used for autoconfigured link-local addresses and isn't used by NAT.)

NAT devices typically assign IP addresses from the private address ranges. These addresses aren't even routable in the conventional sense, so the *only* way to reach the NAT client computer is through the address translation process. NAT also reduces the number of Internet-compatible addresses required for an organization. Only the router serving as a NAT device requires a true Internet-ready address. The economies of configuring fewer Internet addresses, coupled with the inherent security of a private network, make NAT devices extremely popular on both home and corporate networks.

Security, of course, is often not what it seems. Even the seemingly foolproof security of a NAT device is susceptible to breach. NAT devices sometimes have special features for providing administrative access from the Internet, and those features can introduce vulnerabilities if they aren't locked down.

The growth of NAT has led to a further development of attack techniques to get around the natural defenses of a private network. One common way for attackers to get inside a private network is to get the client to invite them in. Modern intruders often send out links to fake web pages and other traps to entice the user to initiate a connection to a subversive server system. Attacks of this kind are part of the reason why computer users are advised not to click on links in unsolicited email messages. Modern web browsers can sometimes spot attacks launched through cross site scripting or web attack methods.

> **IPv6 and NAT**
>
> The next-generation IPv6 protocol provides some additional link-local addressing features that might eventually render the kinds of NAT devices used on today's networks unnecessary. See Hour 13, "IPv6: The Next Generation," for more on IPv6.

Zero Configuration

You might be wondering what happens if the network clients are all configured to use DHCP, and the DHCP server goes offline. A circle of client computers could be alive and waiting to communicate, but without static addresses or a way to obtain dynamic addresses through DHCP. In another case (although this is rarer than it once was), a user might want to set up a small workgroup of networked PCs without the need for Internet access or a special DHCP/routing device.

Several OS vendors have explored techniques for letting the computers on a local network get connected without either a static configuration or a DHCP-based dynamic configuration. Previous LAN protocols like NetBEUI (on Windows systems) and AppleTalk (on Apple networks) offered this out-of-the-box configurationless connectivity, and vendors have searched for a way to return to it with TCP/IP.

The first step along this path was a concept called **link-local addressing** (IPv4LL). Link-local addressing has been a part of Apple systems since OS 9, and it has been included in Windows since Windows 98.

Microsoft calls the Windows version of IPv4LL **Automatic Private IP Addressing** (APIPA). If a Windows computer doesn't have a static IP address and can't receive a dynamic address, it assigns itself an IP address in the (nonroutable) address range 169.254.0.0 to 169.254.255.255. If other computers on the local network are in a similar situation, they assign themselves unused address within this same range, and the computers are then in a position to communicate successfully on the local network. Of course, because the address is not routable, the computers can't reach the Internet or access resources beyond the local network.

The whole point of APIPA is that it doesn't require configuration, so there isn't much to say about configuring it. Most Windows versions include a registry key for *turning off* APIPA. Consult your Windows documentation.

APIPA does create some troubleshooting issues. For instance, if the other computers of the network are configured normally and one is strangely unreachable, check to see whether this computer lost sight of the DHCP server and assigned itself an APIPA address that is incompatible with the local address space.

A more recent technology known as **Zeroconf** provides a far more powerful and complete configurationless environment. Zeroconf extends the philosophy of IPv4LL to provide the possibility of a largely complete networking environment for small local networks. The Zeroconf system is implemented in Apple Macintosh systems under the name Bonjour. Recent Windows systems versions have incorporated a similar zero-configuration technology using a slightly different system of protocols. Avahi, a Zeroconf implementation for Linux and UNIX systems, is similar to the Apple version.

This new zero-configuration environment has three important components:

- ▶ **Link-local addressing:** Computers assign themselves IP addresses in the private address range 169.254.0.0 to 169.254.255.255 (see the preceding discussion of IPvLL).

- ▶ **Multicast DNS:** DNS name resolution without a server or a preconfigured hosts file. Names are resolved to IP addresses (and addresses are resolved to names) through queries to a specific IP address and port number. Other devices listen for requests sent to this address and respond with information.

▶ **DNS Service Discovery:** A means for clients to learn about services available on the network.

The interplay of these components creates an environment where a computer can start up without any previous TCP/IP configuration, receive a locally compatible, nonroutable IP address, register its hostname with other computers on the local network, and browse for available network services (such as file and print servers) through a Network-Neighborhood-like, point-and-click style file browser for easy access.

Apple began to develop technologies surrounding multicast DNS and **DNS service discovery** when they knew they would need to find a DNS equivalent for the easy, simple AppleTalk network environment, which offered a similar zero-configuration approach to browsing and accessing network services and devices. These enhanced DNS services work together to provide a convenient view of the local network, but note that these techniques do not scale well to large networks. They are intended for smaller networks inhabiting a single LAN segment.

A computer that supports multicast DNS (mDNS) keeps its own internal table of DNS resource records and uses the table to resolve names to IP addresses. As shown in Figure 12.5, if the computer encounters a name that isn't listed in the table, it sends a message to the multicast address 224.0.0.251. Other computers that support multicast DNS are configured to listen at this address for DNS queries. A computer that is able to complete the query returns information showing the correct name-to-IP address mapping.

FIGURE 12.5
In multicast DNS, each computer keeps its own DNS table. (In a real situation, the computers pass and save other DNS information in addition to the basic name-to-IP address.)

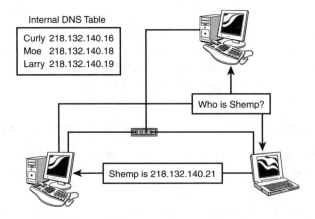

Internal DNS Table

Curly 218.132.140.16
Moe   218.132.140.18
Larry 218.132.140.19

Who is Shemp?

Shemp is 218.132.140.21

DNS Service Discovery (DNS-SD) offers a means for computers and devices to advertise their services through DNS. The new age of many small gadgets promises to rely heavily on DNS service discovery and other similar techniques that allow a device to come online quickly and discover services such as printers, music players, and so on with no previous configuration.

DNS-SD relies on queries to the SRV resource record, which identifies a service provided within the domain. For instance, on a conventional DNS network, an SRV record for a domain might hold the hostname and port number for an FTP server or Active Directory domain controller. DNS-SD extends this capability to a smaller scale and makes strategic use of other record types to complete the process. First, a variation of the DNS PTR pointer record (used in reverse lookups) points to available instances of services running on the network. The query might return the following information:

- ▶ **Instance:** A specific instance of the service. (It is possible for several servers to be offering the same service on the same network.)

- ▶ **Service:** The name of the service. (A master registry of DNS-SD service types is kept at http://www.dns-sd.org.)

- ▶ **Domain:** The domain that is home to the service.

By assembling the responses to this query, the DNS-SD client creates a browse list of available services and service instances on the network.

When the user or client application selects a specific service instance in this browse list, a DNS query for an associated SRV record returns the hostname and port number necessary for accessing the service on the network. DNS-SD also uses the TXT resource record to return additional information about the service.

DNS service discovery is designed to work with multicast DNS to provide a complete, zero-configuration DNS environment, but DSN-SD will also work with conventional DNS services with some minimal preliminary configuration.

Microsoft defines an alternative protocol for multicast DNS called **Link-Local Multicast Name Resolution (LLNR)**. Microsoft's **Simple Service Discovery Protocol (SSDP)** provides service discovery. SSDP is based on HTTP rather than on traditional DNS, which matches the trend for increased emphasis on URL-based services but provides some discontinuity with the conventional DNS infrastructure. The Universal Plug and Play (uPnP) protocol system, which provides a service browsing infrastructure similar to DNS-SD, relies on SSDP.

Microsoft, Apple, and other vendors participate in common discussions of zero-configuration TCP/IP networking, but the big players are at work on slightly different systems. The biggest difference appears to be in the service discovery protocols.

Another service discovery option known as Service Location Protocol (SLP) is used with HP printers and many other devices.

The zero-configuration protocols have appeared in various informational RFCs, and a parallel system is built in to the design of IPv6. The next few years will undoubtedly bring increased emphasis on zero-configuration technologies.

Zeroconf Options

Just because a major OS vendor might back a specific protocol option doesn't mean it is the only option that will work with that OS. Application developers are free to adopt whatever protocols they want to use. Apple has even developed a version of their Bonjour Zeroconf system for Windows.

Configuring TCP/IP

As this hour has already mentioned, most contemporary computers require very little networking configuration, and most of the necessary steps can take place during the installation or through some kind of "first boot" configuration wizard. As long as you enter the computer name and specify whether the computer will have a static or dynamic address, the operating system handles the rest. However, sometimes you might need to check network settings, or in other cases, you might need to change a configuration option after your computer becomes operational. The following sections show how to find the TCP/IP configuration settings on representative Windows, Mac OS, and Ubuntu Linux systems.

This discussion of how to configure and troubleshoot network connection on all three of these operating systems could easily fill a whole book just by itself. The following sections are not intended as a complete configuration manual or troubleshooting guide. The intent is to provide a brief orientation to the basic configuration environment and to demonstrate how the GUI acts as a window for managing settings for the underlying networking protocols. See the vendor documentation for more on configuring networking in these systems or look online for additional networking information.

Windows

Windows network settings are stored in the Windows Registry, which is a dangerous place to poke around unless you are really sure of what you are doing. The preferred method for configuring networking in Windows is through the GUI tools provided with the Windows user interface. As if often the case with Windows, the various configuration dialogs can sometimes be reached through more than one point-and-click procedure. Windows 7 and Windows Vista both manage the network configuration through a tool called the Network and Sharing Center. To reach the Network and Sharing Center, click the Windows Start button and choose Control Panel. In the Control Panel Home view, select Network and Internet, and then click the Network and Sharing Center link.

The Network and Sharing Center displays the current network connection at the top of the window, with configuration options on the left. The Windows Vista version includes a handy summary of current sharing and discovery settings (Figure 12.6). The default Windows 7 configuration omits the sharing and discovery summary to provide additional configuration options.

FIGURE 12.6
The Windows Network and Sharing Center.

Windows treats each preconfigured connection as a separate logical entity. To view the currently configured connections, select Manage Network Connections in Vista or choose Change Adapter Settings in Windows 7. In each case, you see one or more icons for connections to a local network, wireless network, and so forth. Right-click the icon and choose Properties to view the Connection Properties dialog box (Figure 12.7).

As you can see in Figure 12.7, the Connection Properties dialog lists a number of so-called items currently installed in the networking configuration. The word *item* might seem needlessly vague, but readers of this book will quickly notice that these "items" are actually optional components of the TCP/IP networking stack. The items at the top (the top three entries shown in Figure 12.7) are network client and service components corresponding to the TCP/IP Application layer.

To view the current TCP/IP configuration (assuming your system is using IPv4, which is still the case for the vast majority of computers), choose the component labeled Internet Protocol Version 4 (TCP/IPv4) and click the Properties button.

FIGURE 12.7
The Connection
Properties dia-
log box.

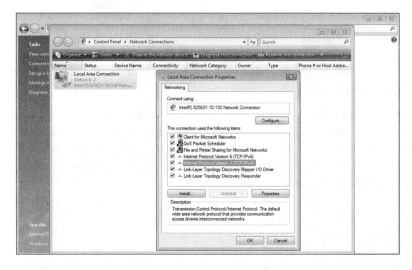

In the IPv4 Properties dialog (Figure 12.8), you can make the fundamental choice of
whether the connection should receive an IP address assigned automatically
through DCHP or whether you would like to configure a static TCP/IP connection. If
your computer is set up to receive an address dynamically, and if it is working now,
you are better off just keeping this setting unchanged. If you want to configure the
network manually, click the Use the following IP address button and enter the
address, subnet mask, and default gateway. (This addressing information has to be
consistent for your network; see Hour4, "The Internet Layer," and Hour 5,
"Subnetting and CIDR," for more on IP addresses and subnet masks.)

FIGURE 12.8
Configuring
IPv4 properties
in Windows.

The Advanced button (shown in Figure 12.8) takes you to additional dialogs for manually configuring DNS and WINS name service options (see Hour 10).

The advantage of treating network connections as separate, logical entities is that you can set up different connections for different situations. If your computer is just acting as an ordinary DHCP client, this probably isn't necessary. Just plug it into the network, and it will find a configuration. If you have a portable computer that moves between two different networks with dissimilar configurations (for instance, one requires DHCP and one requires a static configuration), however, you can create different connections for the different locations. To set up a new connection or define a new network, choose Set up a new connection or network in the Network and Sharing Center. Another window will let you choose to launch a wizard to set up a LAN, wireless, dial-up, or virtual private network (VPN) connection. In each case, the computer looks for available undefined network connections to let you choose an available network or device.

As you have already learned in previous hours, wireless networking is no different from other forms of TCP/IP networking once you get above the Network Access layer. However, the nature of wireless networks calls for a few differences in how you configure and access them.

A Windows system with wireless hardware typically configures wireless networking automatically. Depending on your configuration, however, it might not automatically open a wireless networking connection at boot time. To view available wireless networks, click the wireless icon (with several vertical bars forming a triangular shape) in the lower-right corner of the screen (Figure 12.9). A list of available networks will appear. Choose a network and click the Connect button. You must provide the required security information to start the connection, such as a security set identifier (SSID).

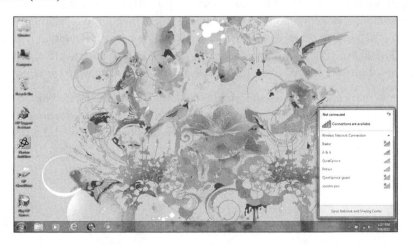

FIGURE 12.9
Choosing a wireless network in Windows.

In Windows 7, you can set up a network profile with a bundle of configuration set-tings for a specific wireless network. The Windows 7 Network and Sharing Center offers a Manage wireless networks option. In the Manage wireless networks window, click the Add button to define the settings for manually connecting to a wireless net-work (Figure 12.10).

FIGURE 12.10
Connecting Windows to a wireless net-work.

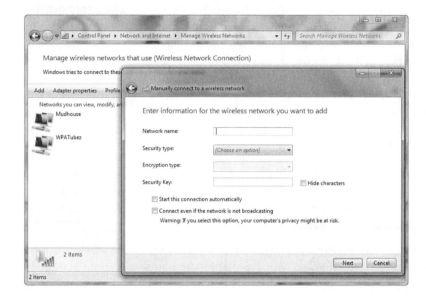

Mac OS

Like Windows, Mac OS is good at finding the available wired (or wireless) network and getting itself connected if it is configured to use DHCP. To reach the networking configuration, choose System Preferences in the Apple menu and select the Network icon. The Network Preferences window (Figure 12.11) is a central point for configur-ing TCP/IP in Mac OS. In the network list on the left, choose Ethernet to access set-tings for a conventional wired LAN, and select AirPort for wireless networking.

In the Ethernet configuration window, pull down the Configure menu box (to select DHCP or a manual configuration; see Figure 12.11). If you choose a manual config-uration, enter the address, subnet mask, router address (gateway), and the DNS serv-er. Click Apply to save the changes.

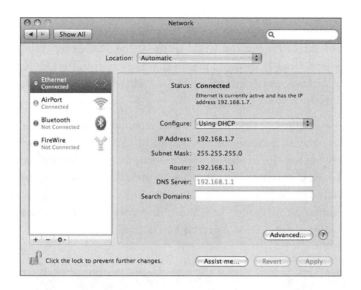

FIGURE 12.11
Configuring
TCP/IP settings
in Mac OS.

In the AirPort configuration dialog (Figure 12.12), click the button in the upper right
to turn wireless networking on and off. From the Network Name menu box, you
select an available network to connect to. You can also choose to Join a Network, in
which case you must provide the password, SSID, or other security information. The
Create a Network option lets you set up an ad hoc network with another wireless
computer or device.

Mac OS also provides a convenient, easy-access toolbar icon for choosing a wireless
network and launching other configuration options.

FIGURE 12.12
Configuring
AirPort, Apple's
pet name for
wireless net-
working.

Linux

Ubuntu is a popular Linux variant based on the Debian Linux distribution. The Ubuntu developers recently changed the desktop system from the Gnome desktop to the new Unity desktop, which has changed some of the configuration information, but the concepts are similar.

Like Windows and Mac OS, Ubuntu has a small icon in the toolbar that provides quick access to network information (see Figure 12.13). Click the icon with the up/down arrow to view the available network options. Select Edit Connections to reach the Network Connections window (see Figure 12.14). Note that the various tabs let you view information on wired, wireless, VPN, digital subscriber line (DSL), or mobile broadband connection. To add a connection, select the tab for the type of connection you want to add and click the Add button.

FIGURE 12.13
Adding and accessing connections from the Ubuntu 11.04 toolbar.

The Edit Connection dialog provides tabs for entering the MAC (physical) address as well as IPv4 and IPv6 configuration settings. On the IPv4 Settings tab (see Figure 12.15), you can select DHCP or a manual configuration. If you select Manual, enter the address, mask, and gateway information.

If you click the Wireless tab in the Network Connections window and click the Add button, you enter a dialog that lets you enter the SSID and wireless security settings and IP address configuration information.

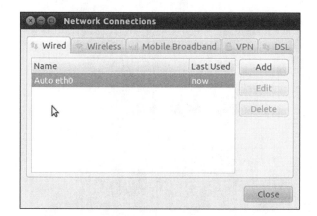

The Network Tools app provides a quick view of the current TCP/IP configuration and serves as an interface for launching some of the network diagnostic tools you learn about in Hour 14, "TCP/IP Utilities," such as ping, traceroute, and Netstat. To reach the Network Tools app, click the Ubuntu icon in the upper-left corner, select More Apps, and click the Linux in the Installed section of Display More Apps. Search for the Network Tools app and click it.

The Network Tools window (see Figure 12.16) shows the current IP configuration. Choose Ethernet Interface in the Network device drop-down menu. The IPv4 address, IPv6 address, network mask, and other settings appear in the window.

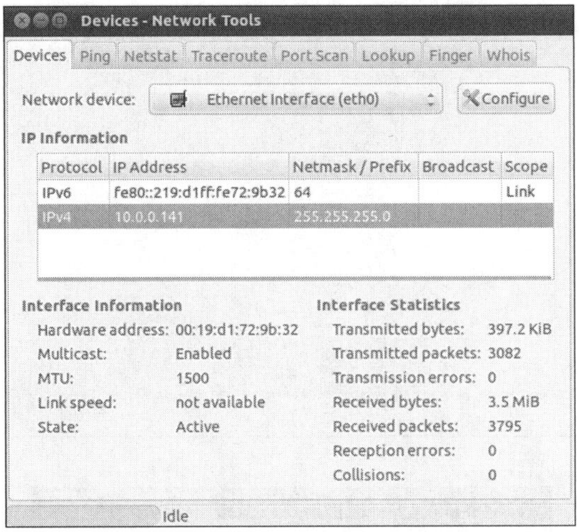

FIGURE 12.16
Viewing current
address infor-
mation in the
Ubuntu Network
Tools window.

The nature of Linux is that if you are using a different Linux variant (or even an older version of Ubuntu) the configuration dialogs might look quite different. However, all these dialogs actually just act as GUI interfaces to the network configuration files. Of particular importance is the /etc/network/interfaces file, which holds IP address information and other important settings.

Within the /etc/network/interfaces file, a static address configuration for the eth0 interface (the first ethernet card) is defined as follows:

```
iface eth0 inet static
address 203.121.14.13
netmask 255.255.255.0
gateway 203.121.14.1
```

The /etc/network/interfaces entry for a network interface configured for DHCP looks like this:

```
auto eth0
iface eth0 inet dhcp
```

The /etc/network/interfaces file can contain many other settings defining the configuration. See your Linux documentation.

Unlike Windows and Mac OS, the command line is still alive and well with Linux. Many users prefer to configure and troubleshoot network settings using the command utilities you learn about in Hour 14.

Because of problems with obtaining timely information on hardware drivers and other complications of working with an open source system, wireless networking sometimes requires some troubleshooting. If you are working with Ubuntu, try the

Ubuntu Wireless Troubleshooting Guide (https://help.ubuntu.com/community/WifiDocs/WirelessTroubleShootingGuide). The Linux Wireless Project is another good source for general information on wireless in Linux (http://linuxwireless.org/).

Summary

This hour began with a discussion of DHCP, an essential protocol that offers an easy way to configure IP addresses and other settings. A DHCP server provides an IP address (and sometimes other configuration information) to the DHCP client. DHCP is so common now that it is actually the normal operating mode for most TCP/IP networks. When you configure a computer to receive a dynamic IP address, you are configuring it to act as a DHCP client.

This hour also examined NAT and zero-configuration protocols, and ended with some examples showing how to configure TCP/IP on typical Windows, Mac OS, and Linux systems.

Q&A

Q. *How does a DHCP client communicate with a DHCP server when it is first started?*

A. By broadcasting and receiving broadcasts.

Q. *How does NAT improve security?*

A. Because a NAT address is discontiguous and nonroutable, an outside intruder can't communicate with the local network. Note that this important feature is still no guarantee of secure networking. Intruders have discovered several techniques for gaining access to NAT networks.

Workshop

The following workshop is composed of a series of quiz questions and practical exercises. The quiz questions test your overall understanding of the current material. The practical exercises give you the opportunity to apply the concepts discussed during the current hour and to build on the knowledge acquired in previous hours of study. Take time to complete the quiz questions and exercises before continuing. Refer to Appendix A, "Answers to Quizzes and Exercises," for answers.

Quiz

1. What is required to enable a DHCP client on one network to lease an IP address from a DHCP server on another network?

2. DNS-SD primarily relies on which DNS records?

Exercise

If your computer isn't connecting to the network, one common remedy is to renew the DHCP lease. If you own a Mac and your system uses DHCP, pull down the Apple menu and choose System Preferences. In the System Preferences window, open the Network application (as described earlier in this hour). Choose Ethernet if you have a LAN-based wired ethernet connection or select AirPort if you are using wireless networking.

The current IP address will appear in the window. Now click the Advanced tab. In the Advanced Network window, make sure TCP/IP is selected at the top, and then click the Renew DHCP Lease button. Your computer will release its IP address configuration and receive a new address from the DHCP server. (Depending on your DHCP server and how it is configured, it is possible that the new address is the same as the old address.)

To try this exercise in Windows, you need administrator privileges. Right-click the command prompt icon in the Accessories menu and select Run as Administrator. You'll need to enter a password, or if you're already logged in as Administrator, approve the action.

Open the command-line window and enter the following for the current IP address:

```
ipconfig
```

Now enter the following to release the IP address:

```
ipconfig /release
```

Try the following again:

```
ipconfig
```

You should see that the IPv4 address is gone. Now enter the following to renew the address:

```
ipconfig /renew
```

One last visit to the `ipconfig` command shows you that your address has been restored.

You learn more about ipconfig and other troubleshooting configuration and commands in Hour 14.

Key Terms

Review the following list of key terms:

▶ **Automatic Private IP Addressing (APIPA):** A link-local addressing technique used on some Microsoft systems.

▶ **BOOTP:** A protocol used primarily to assign addresses to diskless clients.

▶ **DHCP:** Dynamic Host Configuration Protocol. A protocol that provides dynamic assignment of IP addresses.

▶ **DHCP client:** A computer that receives a dynamic IP address through DHCP.

▶ **DHCP server:** A computer that distributes TCP/IP configuration parameters to client computers through DHCP.

▶ **DNS-SD:** DNS Service Discovery. A means for clients to learn about services on a zero-configuration network.

▶ **Link-local addressing:** A technique for zero-configuration IP address assignment.

▶ **LLNR:** Link-Local Multicast Name Resolution. An alternative zero-configuration name resolution technique developed by Microsoft.

▶ **Multicast DNS:** A DNS name resolution technique that doesn't require a server or a preconfigured hosts file.

▶ **SSDP:** Simple Service Discovery Protocol. A service discovery technique sponsored by Microsoft that uses HTTP rather than DNS. SSDP is the service discovery protocol associated with Universal Plug and Play (uPnP).

▶ **Zeroconf:** A collection of protocols designed to deliver TCP/IP services with zero configuration.

IPv6: The Next Generation

What You'll Learn in This Hour:

▶ The reasons for IPv6
▶ IPv6 header format
▶ IPv6 addressing
▶ Subnetting
▶ Multicasting
▶ Neighbor discovery
▶ IPv6 tunnels

Because the Internet keeps changing, the protocols that govern Internet communication must also keep changing. The Internet Protocol (IP), which defines the all-important IP address system, has been poised for an upgrade for years. This hour looks at what's ahead for the next generation of IP.

At the end of this hour, you will be able to

▶ Discuss the reasons why a new IP address system is necessary

▶ Describe the fields of the IPv6 header

▶ Apply the conventions for writing and simplifying IPv6 address

▶ Map existing IPv4 addresses to the IPv6 address space

▶ Understand IPv6 multicasting and neighbor discovery

▶ Describe some popular IPv6 tunnel options

Why a New IP?

The IP addressing system described in Hour 4, "The Internet Layer," has served the Internet community for nearly a generation, and those who developed it are justifiably proud of how far TCP/IP has come. But the Internet community has one big problem: The world is running out of addresses. This looming address crisis might seem surprising, because the 32-bit address field of the current IP format can provide over three billion possible host IDs. But it is important to remember how many of these three billion addresses are actually unusable.

A network ID is typically assigned to an organization, and that organization controls the host IDs associated with its own network. Recall from Hour 4 that IP addresses were originally intended to fall within address classes determined by the value of the first octet in the address field. The address classes and their associated address ranges are shown in Table 13.1, which also shows the number of possible networks within an address class and the number of possible hosts on each network. A Class B address can support 65,534 hosts. Many Class B organizations, however, do not have 65,534 nodes and therefore assign only a fraction of the available addresses. The 127 Class A networks can support 16,777,214 addresses, many of which also go unused. It is also worth noting that the 16,510 Class A and B networks are reportedly all taken. The Class C networks that remain face a limitation of only 254 possible addresses. (Refer to Hour 4, "The Internet Layer," and Hour 5, "Subnetting and CIDR," for more on the anatomy of IP addresses.)

TABLE 13.1   Number of Networks and Addresses for IP Address Classes

Class	First Octet	Number of Networks	Possible Addresses per Network
A	0–126	127	16,777,214
B	128–191	16,384	65,534
C	192–223	2,097,152	254

Fortunately, the use of Network Address Translation (NAT) has reduced the need for Internet-ready addresses, and the classless interdomain routing (CIDR) address system described in Hour 5 has found homes for many of the lost addresses. At the same time, however, other recent developments, such as the rise of mobile networking, have placed renewed pressure on the address space.

Internet philosophers have discussed a transition to a new addressing system for some time. And, because the system was due for an overhaul anyway, they also proposed additional enhancements to IP to add new features and integrate new technologies. This new system eventually crystallized into IP version 6 (**IPv6**), which is sometimes called **IPng**, for **IP next generation**. The current IPv6 specification is RFC 2460, which appeared in December 1998. (Several other preliminary RFCs set the stage for RFC 2460, and many newer RFCs continue to discuss issues relating to IPv6.)

The IP address format in IPv6 calls for 128-bit addresses. Part of the reason for this larger address space is supposedly to support one billion networks. As you learn later in this hour, this large address size is also spacious enough to accommodate some compatibility between IPv4 addresses and IPv6 addresses.

Some of the goals for IPv6 are as follows:

▶ **Expanded addressing capabilities:** Not only does IPv6 provide more addresses, it also provides other improvements to IP addressing. For instance, IPv6 supports more hierarchical addressing levels. IPv6 also improves address auto-configuration capabilities and provides better support for **anycast addressing**, which enables an incoming datagram to arrive at the "nearest" or "best" destination given a group of possible targets.

▶ **Simpler header format:** Some of the IPv4 header fields have been eliminated. Other fields have become optional.

▶ **Improved support for extensions and options:** IPv6 includes some header information in optional extension headers. This approach increases the range of possible information fields without wasting space in the main header. In most cases, these extension headers are not processed by routers; this further streamlines the transmission process.

▶ **Flow labeling:** IPv6 datagrams can be marked for a specific flow level. A **flow level** is a class of datagrams that requires specialized handling methods. For instance, the flow level for a real-time service might be different from the flow level of an email message. The flow level setting can be useful for ensuring a minimum quality of service for the transmission.

▶ **Improved authentication and privacy:** IPv6 extensions support authentication, confidentiality, and data-integrity techniques.

As of this writing, IPv6 has been ready for more than 10 years, yet very few networks have actually implemented it as a complete system. Part of the problem is that this change to the next generation requires a transition in which both IPv4 and IPv6 are simultaneously supported, and so long as IPv4 is working, admins have no compelling reason to stop using it. As of now, all major operating systems and most routers offer IPv6 support. Most organizations, however, do not expend the overhead to actively maintain both systems (although an IPv6 stack might be running by default).

Even if an organization wants to implement a native IPv6 network at the local level, they might run into problems finding an Internet service provider that offers native IPv6 support. Internet IPv6 service is often available through IPv6 tunnel brokers. As you learn later in this hour, a tunnel broker encapsulates IPv6 packets within an IPv4 tunnel. This approach does indeed provide IPv6 connectivity at the endpoints, but supporting IPv6 through an IPv4 tunnel reduces the effect of the advanced routing and quality-of-service features built in to IPv6.

IPv6 Header Format

The IPv6 header format is shown in Figure 13.1. Note that the basic IPv6 header is actually simpler than the corresponding IPv4 header. Part of the reason for the header's simplicity is that detailed information is relegated to special extension headers that follow the main header.

FIGURE 13.1
The IPv6 header.

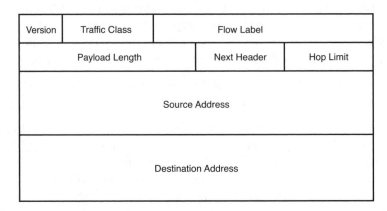

Version	Traffic Class	Flow Label	
Payload Length		Next Header	Hop Limit
Source Address			
Destination Address			

The fields of the IPv6 header are as follows:

- **Version (4 bit):** Identifies the IP version number (in this case, version 6).

- **Traffic Class (8 bit):** Identifies the type of data enclosed in the datagram.

- **Flow Label (20 bit):** Designates the flow level (described in the preceding section).

- **Payload Length (16 bit):** Determines the length of the data (the portion of the datagram after the header).

- **Next Header (8 bit):** Defines the type of header immediately following the current header. See the discussion of extension headers later in this section.

- **Hop Limit (8 bit):** Indicates how many remaining hops are allowed for this datagram. This value is decremented by one at each hop. If the hop limit reaches zero, the datagram is discarded.

- **Source Address (128 bit):** Identifies the IP address of the computer that sent the datagram.

- **Destination Address (128 bit):** Identifies the IP address of the computer that receives the datagram.

As this hour has already mentioned, IPv6 provides for bundles of optional information in separate extension headers between the main header and the data. These extension headers provide information for specific situations and at the same time allow the main header to remain small and easily manageable.

The IPv6 specification defines the following extension headers:

- ▶ Hop-by-Hop Options
- ▶ Destination Options
- ▶ Routing
- ▶ Fragment
- ▶ Authentication
- ▶ Encrypted Security Payload

Each header type is associated with an 8-bit identifier. The Next Header field in the main header or in an extension header defines the identifier of the next header in the chain (see Figure 13.2).

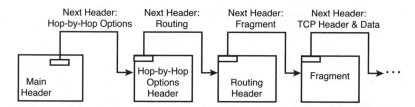

FIGURE 13.2
The Next
Header field.

Of the extension headers described in the preceding list, only the Hop-by-Hop Options header and the Routing header are processed along the transmission path by intermediate nodes. Routers do not have to process the other extension headers; they just pass them on.

The following sections discuss each of these extension header types in greater detail.

Hop-by-Hop Options Header

The purpose of the Hop-by-Hop Options header is to relate optional information for routers along the transmission path.

The Hop-by-Hop Options header, like the Destination Options header discussed in the next section, was included in the specification largely to provide the industry with a format and a mechanism for developing future options.

The specification includes an option type designation and some padding options for aligning the data. One option that is defined explicitly in the specification is the **jumbo payload** option, which is used to transmit a data payload longer than 65,535 bytes.

Destination Options Header

The purpose of the Destination Options header is to relate optional information to the destination node. Like the Hop-by-Hop Options header, the Destination Options header is included primarily as a framework for developing future options.

Routing Header

The Routing header is used to specify one or more routers that the datagram routes through on the way to its destination.

The Routing header format is shown in Figure 13.3.

FIGURE 13.3
The Routing header.

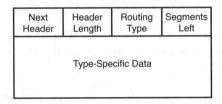

The data fields for the Routing header are as follows:

▶ **Next Header:** Identifies the header type of the next header following this header.

▶ **Header Length (8 bit):** Specifies the length of the header in bytes (excluding the Next Header field.

▶ **Routing Type (8-bit):** Identifies the routing header type. Different routing header types are designed for specific situations.

▶ **Segments Left:** Indicates the number of explicitly defined router segments before the destination.

▶ **Type-Specific Data:** Identifies data fields for the specific routing type given in the Routing Type field.

Fragment Header

Each router along a message path has a setting for the **maximum transmission unit (MTU)**. The MTU setting indicates the largest unit of data the router can transmit. In IPv6, the source node can discover the **path MTU**—the smallest MTU setting for any device along the transmission path. The path MTU represents the largest unit of data that can be sent over the path. If the size of the datagram is larger than the path MTU, the datagram must be broken into smaller pieces so that it can be delivered across the network. The Fragment header contains information necessary for reassembling fragmented datagrams.

Authentication Header

The Authentication header provides security and authentication information. The Authentication field provides a means of determining whether a datagram was altered in transit.

Encrypted Security Payload Header

The Encrypted Security Payload header (ESP) provides encryption and confidentiality. Using IPv6's ESP capabilities, some or all of the data being transmitted can be encrypted. Using tunnel-mode ESP (which is designed for VPN tunnels), an entire IP datagram is encrypted and placed in an outer, unencrypted datagram. In transport mode, only the payload and ESP trailer are encrypted.

IPv6 Addressing

IPv6 addresses, like IPv4 addresses, are assigned by a central Internet authority and distributed through a system of Internet service providers (ISPs) and other bandwidth providers. As shown in Table 13.2, certain address ranges are reserved for specific activities such as multicasting and link-local addressing (which is similar to the IPv4 zero-configuration system described in Hour 12, "Configuration"). Another special range of addresses is reserved for mapping IPv4 addresses to the IPv6 address space.

TABLE 13.2 IPv6 Address Ranges per RFC 4291

Address Type	Binary Prefix	IPv6 Notation	Description
Unspecified	0...00 (all 0s)	::/128	Must never be assigned. Indicates the absence of an address.
Loopback	0...01 (127 0s)	::1/128	Diagnostic address used for a host to send a packet to itself.
Mapped IPv4	0...0:FFFF (80 0s)	::FFFF/96	IPv6 equivalent for existing IPv4 address.
Multicast	11111111	FF00::/8	Identifies a group of hosts.
Link-local uni-cast	1111111010	FE80::/10	Use for automatic address con-figuration.
Gobal unicast	(Everything else)		

The 128-bit IPv6 address is taxing for the memory no matter how you express it. As you'll recall from Hour 4, 32-bit IPv4 addresses are commonly shown in dotted-decimal notation, in which each byte is expressed as a decimal number of up to three digits. This string of 12 decimal digits is much easier to remember than the 32 binary digits of the actual binary address, and it is possible, if you try, to even remember a dotted-decimal address. This method for humanizing works for a 32-bit address, but it is utterly useless for remembering a 128-bit address. A few conventions have evolved to simplify the intimidating IPv6 address.

An IPv6 address is typically shown as eight colon-separated groups of four hexadecimal (base 16) digits, with leading 0s omitted:

`2001:DB8:0:0:8:800:200C:417A`

A shorthand trick is to eliminate multiple consecutive blocks of 0s and replace them with a double colon. The preceding address would then appear as follows:

`2001:DB8::8:800:200C:417A`

Only one double colon is allowed in any address. The rules for IPv6 address assignment often lead to long strings of 0 bits, which makes the double colon especially useful. For instance, the address

`FF01:0:0:0:0:0:101`

Can simply be written as

`FF01::101`

Like IPv4 addresses, IPv6 addresses begin with a prefix representing the network. An equivalent to the CIDR system (see Hour 5) lets you represent a block of addresses by specifying the first address in the block along with a decimal number representing the number of network bits. According to RFC 4291, "IPv6 Addressing Architecture," to show the block of addresses with the 60-bit network prefix 20010DB80000CD3, you could write the following:

`2001:0DB8:0000:CD30:0000:0000:0000:0000/60`

Or you could write this:

`2001:0DB8:0:CD30::/60`

Eventually, IPv6 network configuration software will allow the user to define a default network prefix so that manual configuration at the client will require only reference to the host portion of the address. IPv6 also provides sophisticated auto-configuration features, which reduces the need for typing long addresses at the keyboard.

It's too early to predict how network administrators will accommodate the formidable IPv6 address, but you can certainly bet name resolution will play an important role on IPv6 networks.

Subnetting

As you learned in Hour 5, some of the bits of IPv4 address can be used to represent the network or subnet, and some of the bits can represent the host ID. In recent years, the old address class system has been replaced with the CIDR shorthand. In CIDR notation, a slash after the address, followed by a number, represent the number of bits in the 32-bit address associated with the network and subnet: 205.123.196.183/25.

As the preceding section mentions, IPv6 also uses this CIDR-style notation to mark the bits associated with the network portion of the address. But the larger address space and advanced technology of IPv6 leads to a whole new approach to subnetting. The 128 bits of an IPv6 address leaves lots of room for the network and host portions of the address. In IPv6, the subnetting is supposed to take place in the first 64 bits of the address, leaving the remaining 64 (or more) for the range of host IDs available for the subnet. This range of billions of hosts is plenty for anyone's network, meaning that the old concept of subdividing the address space to conserve the address space will likely be unnecessary. Thousands of nodes could easily coexist on the same network subnet.

However, for performance and traffic management reasons, admins might still want to divide large networks with routers and use subnetting to deliver packets to the different network segments. In that case, the first 64 bits of the address space will provide plenty of room for the network and subnet portions of the address. For instance, if the network is assigned a /48 address range, they would have 16 bits for subnetting and still provide the 64 space for host IDs.

Multicasting

IPv4 was designed around the idea of network broadcast. A message sent to a broadcast address, such as the 255.255.255.255 (all 1s) address, would be read by all the hosts on the subnet. This concept worked well for its time, but more efficient solutions have developed since the design of IPv4. A new approach known as **multicasting** provides an intermediate option between single delivery (unicast) and delivery to everybody (broadcast). Multicasting was introduced during the IPv4 era, but it receives renewed interest and considerable attention with IPv6. In fact, multicasting is built into the very fabric of IPv6. In multicasting, hosts participate in multicast "groups" that share a single multicast address. A host that isn't part of the group doesn't have to bother with the message, and this makes multicast more efficient than broadcast.

Several different types of IPv6 multicast addresses are defined for IPv6. For instance, link-local multicast, which you learn more about later in this hour, has the multicast address prefix ff02::/16.

Multicasting finds its way into many background discovery processes within IPv6 networking. Application developers can also use multicasting for efficient delivery to multiple hosts over IPv6 networks.

Link Local

IPv6 addresses with the prefix fe80::/10 are link-local addresses. Link-local addresses do not pass through routers and are used only for communication on local network segments. That makes a link-local address similar to the private address ranges used on IPv4 networks. (See Hour 4 for more on special private address ranges in IPv4.)

As you learn later in this hour, these link-local addresses play a role in IPv6's elaborate automatic configuration system. The link-local address allows computers to communicate on a local network segment without the need for manual configuration steps (and without the need for automatic configuration through a Dynamic Host Configuration Protocol [DHCP] server). Of course, because these link-local addresses are not routable, they do not provide connectivity with a greater network beyond the local segment. To connect with the rest of the world, the host needs its own routable IP address, or it needs access to an IPv6-ready DHCP device to receive a dynamic address.

Neighbor Discovery

What? No Address Resolution Protocol (ARP)? As you learned in Hour 4, ARP provides a means for mapping IPv4 addresses to the physical (MAC) addresses associated with network adapter hardware. ARP supplies the link between the logical addressing of the Internet layer and the hardware-based addresses at the Network Access layer. On IPv6 networks, this mapping of IP addresses to physical addresses occurs through a process known as **neighbor discovery**.

Internet Control Message Protocol version 6 (ICMPv6) provides neighbor discovery services. A host that wants to resolve an IPv6 address on the local network first calculates a solicited node multicast address associated with the address. (The solicited mode multicast address follows a format described in the IPv6 documentation, including a prefix in the multicast range with the final host bits corresponding to the IPv6 unicast address.) The host then sends a neighbor solicitation packet to the solicited multicast address that includes the IPv6 address the sender wants to resolve, asking for the owner of the address to respond. The sender also sends its own physical address to use as a destination address for the response. The owner of the IPv6 address responds with a neighbor advertisement packet that includes its own physical and link-local address.

Through this process, the hosts on the network build a neighbor cache, which corresponds to the Arp table used with IPv4 networks.

Autoconfiguration

Autoconfigured addresses in the 169.254.0.0/16 address range have appeared in recent years on IPv4 networks. (See Hour 12 for more on autoconfiguration in IPv4.) The autoconfiguration technique is intended to assign an IP address to a computer even if it can't find a DHCP server and doesn't have a manually configured address. This nonroutable "zero-configuration" address is at least enough for the computer to connect with a printer or other local networking peers, or to discover local devices through domain name system (DNS) service discovery.

The IPv6 stateless autoconfiguration feature provides similar functionality in a more fool-proof way. IPv6 autoconfiguration assigns a link local address to the computer based on a hash of the physical (MAC) address. Because physical addresses are all unique, the link local address will most likely be unique, thus preventing some of the address collision problems that occur on IPv4 zeroconf networks. The 48-bit physical address is transformed into a 64-bit string using a standard transformation, and the 64-bit result is appended onto the end of the fe80::/10 link-local prefix (padded with the necessary 0 bits) to form a complete link-local address.

Through another process known as duplicate address detection (DAD), the host checks to be sure that the address is not already in use on the local segment, and if not, the host assumes the autoconfigured address.

IPv6 and Quality of Service

IPv6 addresses another challenge that has recently faced the aging IPv4 infrastructure: the need for uniform quality of service (QoS) levels.

In the old days, when the Internet primarily was used for email and File Transfer Protocol (FTP)-style downloads, no one thought much about prioritizing data transmission. If an email message didn't arrive in 2 seconds, it would arrive in 2 minutes (or possibly in an hour). No one really cared about specifying or limiting the time interval in which the message could arrive. In contrast, today's Internet supports many different types of transmissions, some with rigid delivery requirements. Internet video and television and other real-time applications cannot operate properly with long delays as packets wind their way through router buffers. Even a small delay in an Internet phone connection can have the effect of distorting the speech of the participants.

In the Internet of the future, it will be possible to prioritize IP datagrams as they wait for delivery. A datagram from an interactive video application could move to the top of the queue as it waits in a router buffer, whereas an email datagram might pause for a momentary delay.

IPv6 is designed to support prioritizing through differentiated service levels. The Traffic Class and Flow Label fields of the IPv6 header provide a means for specifying the type and priority of data enclosed in the datagram (refer to Figure 13.1).

> **Differentiated Service**
>
> Some vendors and engineers have experimented with using the IPv4 Type of Service field for differentiated service information. The IPv6 Traffic Class field is intended to support continued experimentation with differentiated service.

IPv6 with IPv4

The only way IPv6 will ever take hold, of course, is if it phases in gradually. A full-scale retooling of the Internet isn't going to happen, so engineers designed IPv6 so that it could coexist with IPv4 over a long-term transition.

The intention is that an IPv6 protocol stack will operate beside the IPv4 protocol stack in a multiprotocol configuration, just as IPv4 once coexisted with IPX/SPX, NetBEUI, or other protocol stacks.

The IPv6 addressing system provides a means for accommodating existing IPv4 addresses within the address space. The original plan was to map every valid IPv4 address to a 128-bit IPv6 address by simply preceding the original address by 96 zero bits. This form, which is known as the **IPv4-compatible IPv6 address**, was deprecated with RFC 4291 in favor of an alternative technique, known as the **IPv4-mapped IPv6 address**, which consists of eighty 0 bits, followed by sixteen 1 bits (or FFFF in hexadecimal) followed by the original 32-bit IPv4 address.

For example, the IPv4 address

169.219.13.133

Maps to the following IPv6 address

`0000:0000:0000:0000:0000:FFFF:A9DB:0D85`

Or simply

`::FFFF:A9DB:0D85`

Because the prefix clearly places this address in the range for mapped IPv4 addresses, the IPv4 portion is sometimes just left in the familiar dotted-decimal format:

`::FFFF:169.219.13.133`

IPv6 Tunnels

Experts have been talking about the planned transition to IPv6 for years, and yet the full IPv6 Internet is still several steps away from reality. Over the past couple years, however, the pace has stepped up. The assignment of the last IPv4 address blocks in spring 2011 has brought the address depletion problem into the spotlight, and the IETF is taking steps to make sure ISPs and admins tune in to the need to implement IPv6 functionality.

Everyone always knew that no one would ever be able to throw a switch and magically toggle the whole Internet from an IPv4 network to an IPv6 network. Over the past several years, a collection of technologies has evolved to provide for a gradual transition from IPv4 to IPv6. The idea is for networks and Internet providers to retain IPv4 connectivity while they slowly implement and test the various components of the IPv6 infrastructure.

According to a migration plan published by the IETF in 2007, the transition to IPv6 was supposed to occur between 2010 and 2011, with IPv6 support mandatory in 2012 and beyond. As of this writing, this ambitious adoption plan seems to have fallen a bit off track, but the move to IPv6 is definitely underway.

Most computer systems offer some form of IPv6 compatibility. A typical scenario is for the computer to support both IPv4 and IPv6 in a dual-stack configuration. A dual-stack computer has the necessary networking software to communicate through either IPv4 or IPv6.

Of course, seamless access to the complete Internet through IPv6 requires universal IPv6 implementation, which is not yet possible. Engineers have therefore developed several methods for connecting the IPv6 islands within the greater IPv4 Internet.

The most common approach for achieving remote IPv6 connectivity is to use an IPv6 tunnel broker. The idea of an **IPv6 tunnel** is to encapsulate IPv6 traffic within

IPv4. A tunnel server at the end point of the tunnel receives an IPv6 packet and encloses it within an IPv4 header, transmitting it to another end point, where the original IPv6 packet is extracted and forwarded to the destination IPv6 network (Figure 13.4). This kind of tunneling lets IPv6 networks talk to other IPv6 networks. Admins can implement and test a complete IPv6 configuration on the home network and on a branch network and use the tunnel broker to connect the pieces.

FIGURE 13.4
Tunnel brokers operate the tunnel servers that let IPv6 networks connect over IPv4 networks.

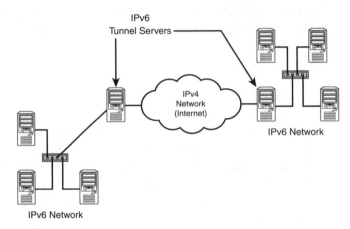

Sometimes networks contract directly with a tunnel broker to support IPv6 traffic, and sometimes the ISP contracts with the broker behind the scenes and then offers a package to the end-user network that provides IPv6 support.

A few other variations on this tunnel concept are discussed in the following sections, including 6to4 and Teredo.

Note that all these tunneling techniques are designed to connect deliberately configured IPv6 hosts with other deliberately configured IPv6 hosts. This will provide a means for implementing some of the benefits of IPv6, such as advanced multicasting and quality of service, and it will allow the IT staff to get some experience working with IPv6, but the rest of the Internet will remain as before until the thousands of web servers, mail servers, and other Internet-connected services make the transition to IPv6 support.

6to4

The **6to4** mapping technique provides a means for automatically mapping IPv4 to IPv6 addresses. 6to4 is similar to the address mapping strategy described earlier in this chapter, but the 6to4 system reserves a specific part of the IPv6 address space, creating an IPv6 address that is automatically recognizable as a 6to4 address.

6to4 provides a means for threading IPv6 packets through an IPv4 network even when the IPv6 network doesn't have an arrangement with a tunnel provider or ISP with IPv6 support. In some cases, 6to4 might be used by the tunnel broker as a tunneling technique.

The idea behind 6to4 is to embed the IPv4 destination address within the IPv6 address. IPv6 addresses with the prefix 2002::/16 are reserved for 6to4. The 32-bit IPv4 address is then appended to this prefix, meaning that the first 48 bits of the IPv6 address signal that the address is a 6to4 address, specify the IPv6 subnet, and provide the IPv4 destination address for routing across the IPv4 network.

A 6to4 relay server receives this doctored-up IPv6 address, extracts the IPv4 address, and encapsulates the IPv6 packet within an IPv4 packet, which is sent to the destination address (Figure 13.5). At its destination, the packet is sent to a 6to4 relay operating at the anycast address 192.88.89.1, where the original IPv6 packet is extracted and delivered.

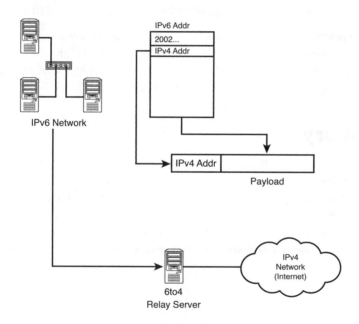

FIGURE 13.5
A 6to4 relay server receives an IPv6 packet with the 2002::/16 prefix, extracts the embedded IPv4 address, and creates an IPv4 packet for delivery over an IPv4 network.

Teredo

The 6to4 tunneling technique is a powerful and popular means for providing connectivity for IPv6 nodes over IPv4 networks, but it has one big problem. The IPv4 destination address must be an Internet-ready, routable address. A nonroutable, private networking address won't work. Unfortunately, vast numbers of Internet users now operate on private networks hidden behind Network Address Translation (NAT) devices. **Teredo** was developed as an alternative technique that could work around NAT devices.

Teredo, described in RFC 4380, uses the User Datagram Protocol (UDP) transport protocol, which is better at getting past NAT devices than the connection-oriented TCP. The IPv6 prefix for Teredo is 3FFE:831F::/32, and Teredo uses UDP port 3544.

A Teredo client computer, operating behind an IPv4 NAT, can use Teredo to communicate through IPv6. A Teredo server maintains information on client computers behind the NAT. The server does not actually participate in forwarding packets, but it is aware of the client and the Teredo relay and participates in establishing the connection.

The IPv6 address assigned to the client is a mash-up of pertinent information necessary to deliver the message. Following the Teredo prefix (3FFE:831F::/32) is the 32-bit IPv4 address of the Teredo server. Also embedded in this IPv6 address are the IPv4 address of the NAT device that serves as a public interface for the private network and a UDP port number that is mapped to the Teredo client behind the NAT device.

Teredo is a powerful technique, and some networks are already using it, but it is still somewhat experimental, and like all tunneling techniques described in this hour, it is temporary. When the Internet achieves full IPv6 connectivity, these strategies for interfacing IPv4 with IPv6 will no longer be necessary.

Summary

IPv6, the next-generation IP protocol, is slowly making its way into the real world. The IPv6 addressing system is totally different from the system you learned in Hour 4. The 128-bit address space will accommodate an almost unlimited number of addresses. IPv6 also offers a simplified header, a bigger payload, and several enhancements related to security and quality of service. The transition to IPv6 has already begun. Various tunnel services provide connectivity services over existing IPv4 networks.

Q&A

Q. Why do many IP addresses go unused?

A. An organization that is assigned an Internet address space often doesn't use all the host IDs associated with that address space.

Q. What is the advantage of placing header information in an extension header instead of in the main header?

A. The extension header is included only if the information in the header is necessary. Also, many extension headers are not processed by routers and therefore won't slow down router traffic.

Q. *How will IPv6 help real-time applications such as video conferencing?*

A. The Traffic Class and Flow Level fields of the IPv6 header provide a means for specifying the type and priority of data.

Workshop

The following workshop is composed of a series of quiz questions and practical exercises. The quiz questions test your overall understanding of the current material. The practical exercises give you the opportunity to apply the concepts discussed during the current hour and to build on the knowledge acquired in previous hours of study. Take time to complete the quiz questions and exercises before continuing. Refer to Appendix A, "Answers to Quizzes and Exercises," for answers.

Quiz

1. Why is multicast more efficient than broadcast?

2. Why is IPv6 autoconfiguration more reliable than IPv4 zeroconf autoconfiguration?

3. What IPv6 address prefix is reserved for 6to4?

4. I want to connect to a remote IPv6 network, but my computer is behind an IPv4 NAT device. What kind of tunnel should I use?

Exercise

Several IPv6 calculators are available on the Internet. For instance, the calculator at Subnet Online (http://www.subnetonline.com/pages/subnet-calculators/ipv4-to-ipv6-converter.php) converts IPv4 addresses to IPv6 addresses. Enter your IPv4 address and click IPv6 button to convert the address to IPv6 format.

Depending on your address and the network mask, you might recognize the address as a mapped 6to4 address beginning with the 2002::/16 prefix.

Experiment with other IP addresses and network masks to understand how IPv4 names map to IPv6.

Key Terms

Review the following list of key terms:

▸ **6to4:** A popular IPv6 tunneling technique.

▸ **Anycast:** An addressing technique that delivers the datagram to the nearest or best destination.

▸ **Flow level:** A designation for an IPv6 datagram specifying special handling or a special level of throughput (for example, real time).

▸ **IPv6 (or IPng for "IP Next Generation"):** A new standard for IP addressing that features 128-bit IP addresses. The intent of IPv6 designers is for IPv6 to phase in gradually over the next several years.

▸ **IPv6 tunnel:** An Internet connection that is capable of delivering IPv6 traffic over an IPv4 network.

▸ **Jumbo payload:** A datagram payload with a length exceeding the conventional limit of 65,535 bytes. IPv6 enables jumbo payload datagrams to pass through the network.

▸ **Maximum transmission unit (MTU):** The largest unit of data a router can transmit.

▸ **Multicasting:** A technique for sending a transmission to a group of users on a network segment.

▸ **Neighbor discovery:** The process for mapping IPv6 addresses to physical (MAC) addresses on an IPv6 network.

▸ **Path MTU:** The smallest MTU setting for any device along the transmission path. The path MTU represents the largest unit of data the transmission path can deliver.

▸ **Teredo:** An IPv6 tunneling technique designed to work around NAT devices.

PART IV

Tools

HOUR 14

TCP/IP Utilities

What You'll Learn in This Hour:

▶ Protocol problems
▶ Line problems
▶ Name resolution problems
▶ Network performance problems

The TCP/IP environment includes a number of standard utilities for configuring, managing, and troubleshooting network connections. These TCP/IP utilities date back to the days before the birth of the modern graphical user interface, and many of them are designed to operate from the command line. A command-line interface might sound old fashioned, but many seasoned network admins still find that working from the command prompt is faster, simpler, and more effective than clicking a mouse and shuffling through windows.

This hour looks at some utilities you can use to troubleshoot and configure TCP/IP. You will find these tools indispensable when you need to identify connectivity problems, test communication between network nodes, and check the TCP/IP settings of computers on your network.

At the completion of this hour, you will be able to

▶ Identify and describe common TCP/IP connectivity utilities
▶ Use connectivity utilities to troubleshoot problems

Connectivity Problems

A protocol, as described in earlier hours, is a standard for communication. That standard is then implemented by a software vendor into a software module that performs the operations described in the standard. A human installs and configures the protocol software, either directly or by installing an operating system that supports the protocol software. As you might guess, once the software is up and running, the network still might not work. Sometimes certain services function and others do not. Other times, a computer can connect to one remote PC and not to another. Once in a while, a computer appears to have no network access at all, as if it weren't even connected.

Network dysfunction typically results from one of a handful of common problems. The TCP/IP community has developed a number of utilities for uncovering these problems and tracing each problem to its source. This hour discusses some of the common network problems and the tools you can use to solve them.

The top four network connectivity problems are typically some variation of the following:

▶ **Protocol dysfunction or misconfiguration:** The protocol software doesn't work or (for whatever reason) isn't configured to operate properly on the network.

▶ **Line problems:** A cable isn't plugged in or isn't working. A hub, router, or switch isn't working.

▶ **Faulty name resolution:** Domain Name System (DNS) or NetBIOS names can't be resolved. Resources are accessible by IP address but not by hostname or DNS name (www.sun.com).

▶ **Excessive traffic:** The network appears to be working, but it is working slowly.

The following sections discuss tools and techniques for addressing these common connectivity problems.

Protocol Dysfunction and Misconfiguration

Like any software, TCP/IP protocol software sometimes doesn't get installed properly. Even after it is installed, it might stop working because of a corrupt file or some change to the system configuration. For example, even if the software is working, the computer might not be able to connect to other computers because its IP address and subnet mask are incorrect.

The TCP/IP protocol suite provides a number of useful utilities that help you determine whether TCP/IP is functioning and properly configured, such as

▶ **ping:** This utility is an extremely useful diagnostic tool that initiates a simple test of network connectivity and reports on whether the other computer responds.

▶ **Configuration information utilities:** Each OS vendor provides some form of utility that displays TCP/IP configuration information and lets you check whether the IP address, subnet mask, DNS server, and other parameters are configured properly.

▶ **arp:** This utility lets you view and configure the contents of the Address Resolution Protocol (ARP) cache (see Hour 4, "The Internet Layer"), which associates IP addresses with physical (Media Access Control [MAC]) addresses.

These utilities come standard with TCP/IP implementations for all operating systems. The following sections discuss these important TCP/IP configuration tools.

Ping

If you notice that your computer can't complete a network operation, the first question you should ask is whether it can complete any other network operation. In other words, is your computer currently functioning as a member of the network? The ping utility initiates the most minimal test of network connectivity. It sends a message to another computer that says "Are you there?" and waits for the other computer to respond.

By the Way

Ping the Name

The name *ping* was originally based on the sound made by the sonar equipment used in submarines and ships to locate other objects. The word *ping* is also an acronym for Packet Internet Groper.

The basic form of a ping command is

ping *IP_address*

where *IP address* is the address of the computer to which you want to connect. Like other utilities, ping offers a number of additional command-line options. These options differ, depending on the implementation and the operating system.

The ping utility sends a message to the recipient computer using the Internet Control Message Protocol (ICMP) Echo Request command. (For more information on ICMP, see Hour 4.) If the recipient computer is present and operational, it responds using the ICMP Echo Reply message.

When the sending computer receives the reply, it outputs a message stating that the ping was successful.

Successful completion of the ping command verifies that both the pinging and the pinged computers are on the network and able to communicate. However, keep in mind that ping is a minimal application. It requires only that the bottom two layers of the TCP/IP stack (the bottom three layers of the Open Systems Interconnection [OSI] stack) are operational. You could have problems with Transport Control Protocol (TCP), User Datagram Protocol (UDP), or applications in the upper layers and ping would still operate. If ping operates correctly, you can largely rule out problems with items such as the Network Access layer, network adapter, cabling, and even routers.

Ping offers a number of options that make it particularly useful for troubleshooting network problems. You can

▶ Ping the local IP software using a special IP address called the loopback address: 127.0.0.1. If the command ping 127.0.0.1 is successful, your TCP/IP protocol software is functioning properly.

▶ Ping your own IP address (in other words, ping yourself). If you can ping the IP address assigned to your network adapter, you know that the adapter is properly configured and interfaced with the TCP/IP software.

▶ Ping by hostname. Most systems let you substitute a hostname for the IP address in the ping command. If you can ping a computer by IP address, but you can't ping the same computer by its hostname, you know that the problem is related to name resolution.

In a typical troubleshooting scenario, a network administrator performs the following ping commands:

1. Ping the loopback address (127.0.0.1) to verify that TCP/IP is working properly on the local computer.

2. Ping the local IP address to verify that the network adapter is functioning and the local IP address is configured.

3. Ping the default gateway to verify that the computer can communicate with the local subnet and to verify that the default gateway is online.

4. Ping an address beyond the default gateway to verify that the gateway is successfully forwarding packets beyond the local network segment.

5. Ping the local host and remote hosts by hostname to verify that name resolution is functioning.

Some admins prefer to apply these steps in reverse order—start with Internet and work backwards to the loopback address. In either case, the goal is the same: to isolate the point where the communication breaks down. The preceding steps are a good beginning for searching out a network problem. You might not find an answer, but at least you'll get a clue about where to look.

Looking Closer at Ping Output

By the Way

The output for the ping command varies according to the implementation. In some systems, such as Solaris, the output is a single line stating *ip_address* is alive. Some versions of Linux (by default) send ICMP packets and output packet response information continuously until you press Ctrl+C. Windows systems typically send four ICMP Echo Requests and output four responses. It is not uncommon to receive three or even fewer responses to those four Echo Requests. You should not consider the occasional dropped datagram a failure, though, because ICMP does not guarantee delivery. However, missing responses could be an indication of an overcrowded network. Dropped packets notwithstanding, the most common responses to a ping are that all requests were successful (indicating that the connection is working) or that all requests were unsuccessful (indicating that the connection isn't working).

Some versions of the ping utility display the time in milliseconds from the time the Echo Request message is sent until the Echo Reply message is returned. Short response times indicate that a datagram does not have to pass through too many routers or through slow networks. If ping responses are returning with a Time To Live (TTL) value near 0, it might be an indication that the connection is near the TTL threshold and some packets are getting lost or re-sent.

Configuration Information Utilities

All modern operating systems offer a utility that lets you view the current TCP/IP configuration. These utilities output information such as the IP address, subnet mask, and default gateway for the local computer. You can use these utilities to verify that the IP address information for the computer is what you expect. With the recent popularity of Dynamic Host Configuration Protocol (DHCP), you can't always determine the IP address information from configuration files or setup dialog boxes. The configuration information utilities tell you the address that the computer is actually using. If your computer is configured for DHCP, you might even discover that the computer has no IP address, indicating a problem with the DHCP server connection.

Of course, these utilities don't tell what your IP address and subnet mask should be. They just tell what address and mask your computer is using. It is then up to you to verify that the address parameters are consistent with the IP addressing scheme for your network (see Hour 5, "Subnetting and CIDR," and Hour 6, "The Transport Layer").

UNIX and Linux systems use the ifconfig command to display address information. As you will recall from earlier hours, the IP address is actually associated with a network interface (such as a network adapter card) rather than with the computer itself. If a computer has two network interfaces, it will have two IP addresses. The ifconfig command displays address information associated with each network interface.

To display IP address information using ifconfig, enter

```
ifconfig interface_name
```

where interface_name is the name of the network interface for which you want to display address information. (In UNIX and Linux, each network interface is assigned a name by the configuration file that defines the interface and is referenced by that name.) For example

```
ifconfig eth0
```

displays the current IP address and netmask (and other parameters depending on the UNIX/Linux version) for the interface called eth0.

ifconfig also lets you directly configure IP address information for a network interface by typing the IP address and netmask directly at the command line:

```
ifconfig eth0 IP_address netmask netmask
```

where IP_address is the address of the interface and netmask is the network mask of the interface.

The ifconfig up and down options let you enable and disable the network interface. For example

```
ifconfig eth0 up
ifconfig eth0 down
```

Other `ifconfig` options are also available. Options vary with the version. Consult the `ifconfig` man page on your UNIX/Linux system for more on `ifconfig`:

`man ifconfig`

Windows systems use the `ipconfig` command to display local TCP/IP configuration settings.

For a list of `ipconfig` options, type `ipconfig /?`. Important options include the following:

▶ **Default (no options):** When `ipconfig` is used without options, it displays the IP address, subnet mask, and default gateway values for each configured interface, as shown in the upper portion of Figure 14.1.

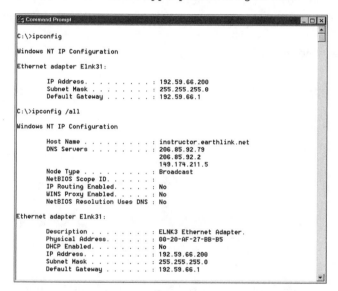

▶ **all:** When the all option (`ipconfig /all`) is used, `ipconfig` displays additional information such as the IP addresses for the DNS and WINS servers it is configured to use, as well as the physical address (MAC address) burned into local network adapters. If addresses were leased from a DHCP server, `ipconfig` displays the IP address of the DHCP server and the date the lease is scheduled to expire.

▶ **release** or **renew:** These optional parameters work only on computers that lease their IP address from a DHCP server. If you enter `ipconfig /release`, the leased IP addresses for all interfaces are released back to the DHCP servers. Conversely, if you enter `ipconfig /renew`, the local computer attempts to contact a DHCP server and lease an IP address. Be aware that in many cases the network adapters will be reassigned the same IP addresses previously assigned.

Release and Renew

A variation on the `release` and `renew` options can be used to release or renew one adapter at a time in a computer that contains multiple network adapters. Assuming one of the computer adapters is named Elnk31, this one adapter can be released or renewed by using the command `ipconfig /release Elnk31` or `ipconfig /renew Elnk31`.

Mac OS X displays network configuration information through the Network applications in System Preferences (see Figure 14.2). Because Mac OS X is actually a form of UNIX system, you can also view the network configuration by typing `ifconfig` in the Terminal window.

FIGURE 14.2
The Mac OS X Network application offers a view of the network configuration.

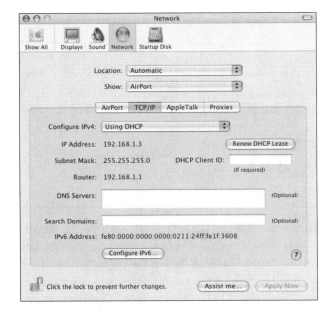

Address Resolution Protocol

Address Resolution Protocol (ARP) is a key TCP/IP protocol used to determine the physical (MAC) address that corresponds to an IP address. Each host on a TCP/IP network maintains an ARP cache—a table used to correlate IP addresses to physical addresses. The `arp` command enables you to view the current contents of the ARP cache of either the local computer or another computer. In most cases, the protocol software takes care of updating the ARP cache, and cases in which you need to use the arp command to troubleshoot a network connection are rare. However, the arp command is occasionally useful for tracing subtler problems related to the association of IP addresses with physical addresses.

The arp command also enables you to enter desired physical/IP address pairs manually. System administrators sometimes enter arp information manually for commonly used hosts such as the default gateway and local servers. This approach helps reduce traffic on the network (although it typically isn't necessary on small networks).

Entries in the ARP cache are dynamic by default: Entries are automatically added to the cache whenever a directed datagram is sent and a current entry does not exist in the cache of the destination computer. The cache entries start to expire as soon as they are entered. Therefore, don't be surprised if there are few or no entries in the ARP cache. Entries can be added by performing pings of another computer or router. The following arp commands can be used to view cache entries:

▶ **arp -a:** Use this command to view all ARP cache entries.

▶ **arp -g:** Use this command to view all ARP cache entries.

Displaying ARP Cache Entries

You can use either arp -a or arp -g. The -g option has for many years been the option used on UNIX platforms to display all ARP cache entries. Windows uses arp -a (think of -a as *all*), but it also accepts the more traditional -g option.

By the Way

▶ **arp -a *IP address*:** If you have multiple network adapters, you can see just the ARP cache entries associated with one interface by using arp -a plus the IP address of the interface, for example, arp -a 192.59.66.200.

▶ **arp -s:** You can add a permanent static entry to the ARP cache manually. This entry remains in effect across boots of the computer, and is updated automatically if errors occur using manually configured physical addresses. For example, to add an entry for a server manually using IP address 192.59.66.250 with a physical address of 0080C7E07EC5, enter arp -s 192.59.66.250 00-80-C7-E0-7E-C5.

▶ **arp -d *IP address*:** Use this command to delete a static entry manually. For example, enter arp -d 192.59.66.250.

See Figure 14.3 for examples of arp commands and responses.

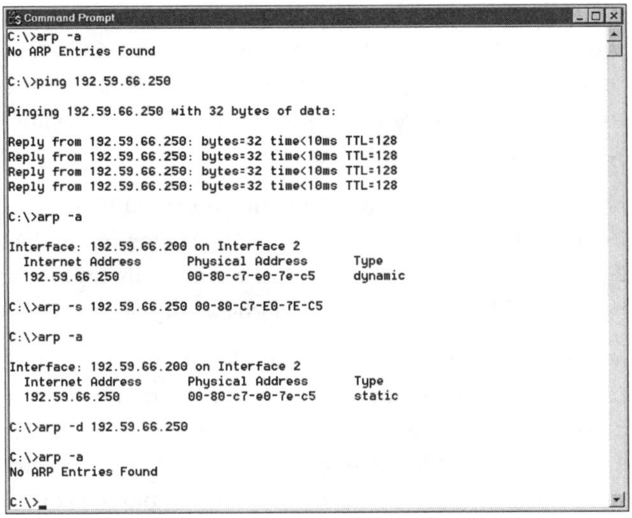

FIGURE 14.3
arp commands
and responses.

```
Command Prompt                                                    _ □ ×
C:\>arp -a
No ARP Entries Found

C:\>ping 192.59.66.250

Pinging 192.59.66.250 with 32 bytes of data:

Reply from 192.59.66.250: bytes=32 time<10ms TTL=128
Reply from 192.59.66.250: bytes=32 time<10ms TTL=128
Reply from 192.59.66.250: bytes=32 time<10ms TTL=128
Reply from 192.59.66.250: bytes=32 time<10ms TTL=128

C:\>arp -a

Interface: 192.59.66.200 on Interface 2
  Internet Address      Physical Address      Type
  192.59.66.250         00-80-c7-e0-7e-c5     dynamic

C:\>arp -s 192.59.66.250 00-80-C7-E0-7E-C5

C:\>arp -a

Interface: 192.59.66.200 on Interface 2
  Internet Address      Physical Address      Type
  192.59.66.250         00-80-c7-e0-7e-c5     static

C:\>arp -d 192.59.66.250

C:\>arp -a
No ARP Entries Found

C:\>_
```

Line Problems

A problem with a network hub or cable is not really a TCP/IP problem. However, you can still use TCP/IP diagnostic utilities such as ping to diagnose line problems. In general, if the network used to work and has stopped working suddenly, a line problem is often the cause. Make sure all network cables are properly plugged in. Most network cards, hubs, switches, and routers have display lights that indicate whether the unit is on and ready to receive data. Each port of a hub, router, or switch has a **link status** light that shows whether an active network connection is operating through the port. Several tools exist for testing network cabling. If you don't have access to a cable testing tool, you can always unplug a suspicious cable and plug a new cable into its place to see if that solves the problem.

You can use ping (described in an earlier section) to isolate line problems. If a computer can ping its own address but cannot ping any other addresses on the network, the trouble might be in the cable segment that connects the computer to the local subnet.

Name Resolution Problems

A name resolution problem occurs when a hostname to which a message is addressed cannot be resolved on the network. A name resolution problem is (arguably) not a connectivity problem because it doesn't necessarily mean that the source computer cannot connect with the target. In fact, as was mentioned in an earlier section, the most common symptom of a name resolution problem is that the source computer can reach the target by IP address but can't reach the target host-name. Even though a name resolution problem isn't a connectivity problem in the strictest sense, as a practical matter, resources on today's networks are referenced by hostname or NetBIOS name, and your first attempt to connect to a host will proba-bly be by name. If that attempt fails, you can begin the problem-solving steps dis-cussed in the "Ping" section earlier in this hour. If you can still connect by IP address, you probably have a problem with name resolution.

Many common name resolution problems are obvious when you consider the process of name resolution (see Hour 10, "Name Resolution"). Some common causes are

- ▶ The hosts file is missing or incorrect.

- ▶ The name server is offline.

- ▶ The name server is referenced incorrectly in the client configuration.

- ▶ The host you are trying to reach does not have an entry in the name server.

- ▶ The hostname used in the command is incorrect.

If you can't connect to a computer by hostname, try connecting to a different com-puter. If you can connect to Computer A by hostname and you can't connect to Computer B, chances are the problem has something to do with Computer B and how it is referenced by the name service. If you can't connect to either Computer A or Computer B, chances are the problem is a more general failure of the name serv-ice infrastructure.

If you are experiencing name resolution problems on a network that uses a name server, it is a good idea to ping the name server to make sure it is online. If the name server is beyond the local subnet, ping the gateway to ensure that name resolution requests can reach the name server. Double-check the name you entered to ensure that it is the correct name for the resource. If none of these measures lead you to a solution, you can use the nslookup utility to query the name server about specific entries. See Hour 10 for more on nslookup and other DNS tools.

If you are working at a computer and you don't know its hostname, use the hostname command. hostname is a simple command available on most operating systems that returns the hostname of the local computer. Just enter the command hostname and view the one-word response.

Network Performance Problems

Network performance problems are problems that cause your network to respond slowly. Because TCP/IP protocols commonly use TTL settings limiting the age of a packet on the network, slow performance can cause lost packets and, therefore, loss of connectivity. Even if you don't lose connectivity, slow network performance can be an irritation and a source of lost productivity. A common cause for poor network performance is excessive traffic. Your network might be experiencing heavy traffic because there are too many computers on the network, or the cause might be a malfunctioning device such as a network adapter creating unnecessary traffic on the network in what is known as a **broadcast storm**. Sometimes the cause for poor network performance is a downed router that has stopped forwarding traffic and caused a bottleneck somewhere else in the network.

TCP/IP offers a number of utilities that let you see where packets are going and display statistics related to network performance. The following sections discuss these utilities.

Traceroute

The traceroute utility is used to trace the path taken by datagrams as they travel from your computer through multiple gateways to their destinations. The path traced by this utility is just one path between the source and destination; there is no guarantee or assumption that datagrams will always follow this path. If you are configured to use Domain Name System (DNS), you can often determine the names of cities, regions, and common carriers from the responses. traceroute is a slow command; you need to give it as much as 10 to 15 seconds per router.

The traceroute (or tracert if you are using Windows) utility makes use of the ICMP protocol to locate each router that stands between your client computer and the destination computer. The TTL value tells you the number of routers or gateways that a packet has passed through. By manipulating the TTL value that is used in the original outgoing ICMP Echo message, traceroute can find each router along the path, as follows:

1. An ICMP Echo message is sent to the destination IP address with a TTL value set to 1. The first router subtracts 1 from the TTL value, which results in a new TTL value of 0.

2. Because the TTL value is now set to 0, the router knows that it should not make any attempt to forward the datagram and simply discards it. The datagram's TTL value has expired. The router sends an ICMP Time Exceeded—TTL Expired In Transit message back to the client computer.

3. The client computer that issued the traceroute command displays the name of this router and then sends out another ICMP Echo message with the TTL value set to 2.

4. The first router subtracts 1 from the TTL value and, if it can, forwards the datagram to its next hop along the path. When the datagram reaches the second router, the TTL value is again decremented by 1, resulting in a 0 value.

5. The second router, like the first, simply discards the packet and returns an ICMP message to the sender in the same way the first router did.

6. This process continues, with `traceroute` incrementing the TTL value and routers decrementing this value until the datagram finally reaches its intended destination.

7. When the destination computer receives the ICMP `Echo` message, it sends back an ICMP `Echo Reply` message.

In addition to locating each router or gateway the datagram travels through, the `traceroute` utility also records the round-trip time that it takes to reach each router. Depending on the implementation, `traceroute` might actually send more than a single `Echo` message to each router. For example, in the Windows version of this utility (`tracert`), two additional `Echo` messages are sent to each router so that it can better judge the round-trip time.

However, you shouldn't use this round-trip time value to judge your network's performance precisely. Many routers simply give a lower priority to ICMP traffic and spend most of their processing time forwarding more important datagrams.

The syntax for the `traceroute` command is simply `traceroute` followed by an IP address, a DNS name, or even a URL:

```
traceroute 198.137.240. 91
traceroute www.whitehouse.gov
tracert yahoo.com (on a Windows system)
```

`traceroute` and `tracert` are useful for showing you the path a datagram traverses on the way to its destination. These helpful commands can also provide some diagnostic capabilities.

Route

As you learned in Hour 8 "Routing," each computer and each router contains a routing table. Most routers use special routing protocols to exchange routing information and dynamically update their tables periodically. However, there are many times when it is necessary to add entries manually to route tables on routers and host computers.

The `route` command has many uses in TCP/IP networking. You can use `route` to display the routing table in cases where packets from a host are not being routed efficiently. If the `traceroute` command reveals an abnormal or inefficient path, you might be able to use `route` to determine why that path is being used and possibly to configure a more efficient route.

The `route` command is also used to add, delete, and change entries in routing tables manually. Some options include the following:

▶ **route print:** This form of the `route` command displays the current entries in the routing table. See Figure 14.4 for an example of output from a `route print` command. As you can see, several entries refer to various networks (for example, `0.0.0.0`, `127.0.0.0`, and `192.59.66.0`), some are used for broadcasting (`255.255.255.255` and `192.59.66.255`), and others are for multicasting (`224.0.0.0`). All of these entries were added automatically as a result of configuring network adapters with IP addresses.

FIGURE 14.4
A **route print** command displays the current information in the routing table.

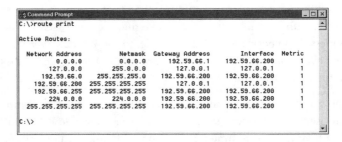

▶ **route add:** Use this form of the `route` command to add a new routing entry to a routing table. For example, to specify a route to a destination network 207.34.17.0 that is five router hops away and passing first through a router with an IP address on the local network of 192.59.66.5 and the subnet mask of 255.255.255.224, you would enter the following command:

```
route add 207.34.17.0 mask 255.255.255.224 192.59.66.5
metric 5
```

> **Only Temporary**
>
> The route information added in this way is volatile and is lost if the computer or router reboots. Often a series of `route add` commands is contained in startup scripts so that it is reapplied every time the computer or router boots.

▶ **route change:** You can use this syntax to change entries in the routing table. The following example changes the routing of the data to a different router that has a more direct three-hop path to the destination:

```
route change 207.34.17.0 mask 255.255.255.224 192.59.66.7 metric 3
```

▶ **route delete:** Use this command syntax to delete an entry from the routing table:

```
route delete 207.34.17.0
```

Netstat

The netstat utility displays statistics related to the IP, TCP, UDP, and ICMP protocols. The statistics display numeric counts for items such as datagrams sent, datagrams received, and a wide variety of errors that could have occurred.

You should not be surprised if your computer occasionally receives datagrams that cause errors, discards, or failures. TCP/IP is tolerant of these types of errors and automatically resends the datagram. Discards occur when a datagram is delivered to the wrong location. If your computer acts as a router, it will also discard datagrams when TTL reaches zero on a routed datagram. Reassembly failures occur when all the fragments fail to arrive within a time period based on the TTL value in received fragments. Again, like errors and discards, occasional reassembly failures should not be a reason for concern. In all three cases, accumulated counts that are a significant percentage of the total IP packets received or that rapidly accumulate should cause you to investigate why this is occurring.

The following list describes various netstat command options:

▶ **netstat -s:** This option displays statistics on a protocol-by-protocol basis. If user applications such as web browsers seem unusually slow or are incapable of displaying data such as web pages, you might want to use this option to see what information is displayed. You can look through the rows of statistics for the words *error*, *discard*, or *failure*. If the counts in these rows are significant relative to the IP packets received, this should prompt further investigation.

▶ **netstat -e:** This option displays statistics about ethernet. Items listed include total bytes, errors, discards, number of directed datagrams, and number of broadcasts. These statistics are provided for datagrams both sent and received.

▶ **netstat -r:** This option displays routing table information similar to what is seen with the route print command. In addition to the active routes, current active connections are also displayed.

▶ **netstat -a:** This option displays the list of all active connections, including both established connections and those that are listening for a connection request.

The following three options provide subset information of what is displayed with the -a option:

- **netstat -n:** This option displays all established active connections.

- **netstat -p TCP:** This option displays established TCP connections.

- **netstat -p UDP:** This option displays established UDP connections.

Figure 14.5 shows an example of the statistics displayed by netstat -s.

FIGURE 14.5
The **netstat** command displays protocol-by-protocol statistics.

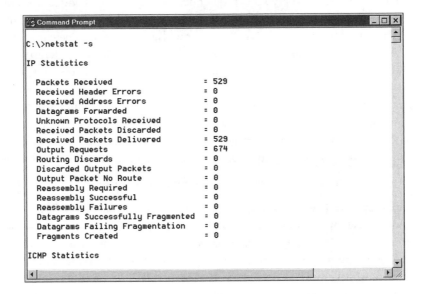

Nbtstat

As you learned in Hour 10, NetBIOS is a name resolution system used on many legacy Windows networks. The nbtstat (NetBIOS over TCP/IP statistics) utility provides statistics about NetBIOS over TCP/IP. nbtstat allows you to view the NetBIOS name table on the local computer or on a remote computer.

The following command options are used in relation to the local computer:

- **nbtstat -R:** This command causes the NetBIOS name cache to be purged and reloaded. This is done to load recently added entries from the LMHosts file. (LMHosts entries are covered in Hour 10.)

- **nbtstat -n:** This command displays the names and services registered on the local computer.

▶ **nbtstat -c:** This command displays the contents of the NetBIOS name cache that holds the NetBIOS names to IP address pairs of other computers with which this computer has had recent communication.

▶ **nbtstat -r:** This command lists the count of registrations and resolved names of other computers and whether they were registered or resolved by broadcast or by a name server.

Figure 14.6 shows an example of nbtstat output.

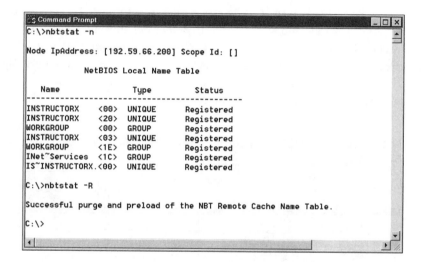

FIGURE 14.6
nbtstat commands and responses.

The nbtstat command can also be used to view the NetBIOS name table of remote computers. The output is similar to nbtstat -n on the local computer:

▶ **nbtstat -A *IP address*:** Displays the name table including physical addresses from another computer by using its IP address.

▶ **nbtstat -a *NetBIOS name*:** Displays the name table including physical addresses from another computer by using its NetBIOS name.

Similarly, two other nbtstat command options enable you to view the list of NetBIOS connections that a remote computer has open. This list is called a connections table:

▶ **nbtstat -S *IP address*:** Displays the NetBIOS connections table of another computer using its IP address.

▶ **nbtstat -s *NetBIOS name*:** Displays the NetBIOS session table of another computer using its NetBIOS name.

Protocol Analyzers

Utilities known as **protocol analyzers** or **packet sniffers** capture data from the network into a buffer or a file. After the data is captured, you can display the contents one frame or datagram at a time. Protocol analyzers are useful for analyzing subtle problems with network traffic. You can also use protocol analyzers to find the source of corrupt packets that might have come from a malfunctioning device. You can trace an ethernet frame by its physical address. You can analyze header information from any protocol level.

Figure 14.7 shows the sequence of 10 datagrams that was initiated by entering a ping command. The top window shows the 10 datagrams starting with an ARP request and an ARP reply followed by four ICMP request/reply pairs. The middle window decodes the ICMP header, and in the bottom frame you can see the 32 bytes of data in the datagram. The data includes the complete alphabet followed by the letters abcdef, for a total of 32 bytes of data.

FIGURE 14.7
A view of traffic following a **ping** command.

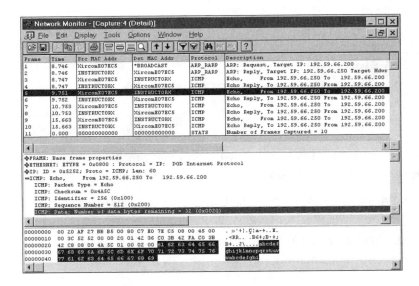

Protocol analyzers are highly sophisticated tools used by network professionals. As you can see in Figure 14.7, they are much more elaborate than the command-line utilities described in the rest of this hour; however, they perform a significant role in troubleshooting network problems and therefore deserve mention in this hour. Microsoft's Network Monitor is a native protocol analyzer for Windows systems. UNIX and Linux users have several options, including Wireshark and TCP dump.

Summary

The toolkit of TCP/IP connectivity utilities helps users configure and troubleshoot network connections. Each utility displays only a small amount of information. However, a user who knows how to operate these tools can quickly zero in on problems and spot potential headaches ahead. This hour looked at connectivity issues caused by protocol dysfunction and misconfiguration, line problems, faulty name resolution, and excesses traffic and how to address these problems with tools such as ping, ifconfig, ipconfig, and arp. The hour also examined some tools for troubleshooting performance problems, including traceroute and tracert, route, netstat, nbtstat, and performance analyzers.

Q&A

Q. *Which utility displays a path taken by datagrams?*

A. `traceroute`, which is known as `tracert` on Windows systems.

Q. *I'm experiencing a slow network as I surf the web, and I want to find out whether a high percentage of web traffic is resulting in discarded packets. Which utility should I use?*

A. `netstat`

Q. *I want to see if I can connect to a host with the address 192.168.1.18. Which utility should I use?*

A. `ping`

Q. *The `traceroute` command revealed an inefficient path to the remote computer. I want to check the entries in the routing table to see if there is a problem. Which utility should I use?*

A. `route`

Workshop

The following workshop is composed of a series of quiz questions and practical exercises. The quiz questions are designed to test your overall understanding of the current material. The practical exercises are intended to afford you the opportunity to apply the concepts discussed during the current hour, as well as build upon the knowledge acquired in previous hours of study. Please take time to complete the quiz questions and exercises before continuing. Refer to Appendix A, "Answers to Quizzes and Exercises," for answers.

Quiz

1. You are surfing the web when suddenly pages stop loading. What should be your troubleshooting tool of first resort?

2. What command should you use to see the contents of the ARP cache?

3. How can you see what hosts you are connected to via TCP?

4. Some versions of route do not have an option to print the routing table. What other utility can you use?

5. Network Monitor, TCPdump, and Wireshark are examples of what type of utility?

Exercises

Execute the following commands and view the responses on your computer:

`ipconfig /all` or `ifconfig -a` (Not all TCP/IP stacks implement these.)

`ping 127.0.0.1`

`ping w.x.y.z` (Replace `w.x.y.z` with the IP address of your computer.)

`ping w.x.y.z` (Replace `w.x.y.z` with the IP address of another local computer.)

`ping w.x.y.z` (Replace `w.x.y.z` with the IP address of your default gateway.)

`ping w.x.y.z` (Replace `w.x.y.z` with the IP address of a remote computer.)

`ping localhost`

`ping http://www.whitehouse.gov` (if you are connected to the Internet and have a DNS server)

`hostname`

`ping hostname` (Replace *hostname* with your actual hostname.)

`arp -a` or `arp -g` (One or both might work. Wait a few minutes, and then repeat.)

Key Terms

Review the following list of key terms:

▶ **arp:** A utility that configures and displays the contents of the Address Resolution Protocol (ARP) table.

▶ **broadcast storm:** Excess traffic caused by a malfunctioning network adapter.

▶ **hostname:** A utility that outputs the hostname of the local host.

▶ **ifconfig:** A UNIX/Linux utility that displays TCP/IP configuration information.

▶ **ipconfig:** A Windows utility that displays TCP/IP configuration information.

▶ **nbtstat:** A utility that provides statistics and other diagnostic information on NetBIOS over TCP/IP.

▶ **netstat:** A utility that provides statistics and other diagnostic information on TCP/IP protocols.

▶ **ping:** A diagnostic utility used to check connectivity with another host.

▶ **Protocol analyzer (or packet sniffer):** A class of diagnostic applications or hardware devices that can capture and display the contents of network packets.

▶ **route:** A utility that configures and displays the contents of a routing table.

▶ **traceroute:** A utility that displays the router path a packet takes from its source to its destination.

▶ **tracert:** The Microsoft equivalent of the traceroute utility.

Monitoring and Remote Access

What You'll Learn in This Hour:

- ▶ Telnet
- ▶ Berkeley r* utilities
- ▶ SSH
- ▶ Remote control
- ▶ Network management
- ▶ SNMP
- ▶ RMON

Networks are for sharing resources remotely, so almost anything you do on a network could fall within the definition of remote access. Still, by tradition, a few TCP/IP utilities are classified as remote access utilities. These remote access utilities grew up around UNIX, but many have been ported to other operating systems. The purpose of these utilities is to give a remote user some of the capabilities a local user might have. Other tools have evolved through the years to help network administrators manage computers and devices from across the network. In this hour, you learn about Telnet, Secure Shell (SSH), remote control, and network management protocols.

At the completion of this hour, you will be able to

- ▶ Explain the purpose of Telnet

- ▶ List some of the Berkeley r* utilities and their successors in the SSH suite

- ▶ Describe some common network management protocols

Telnet

Telnet is a set of components that provide terminal-like access to a remote computer. Telnet was once the most common means for achieving command-line access to
a remote computer. In recent years, however, the more-secure SSH protocol, which
you learn about later in this hour, has become the standard for terminal access.
Telnet is still around, though, and no book on TCP/IP networking is complete without some mention of it.

A Telnet session requires a Telnet client that will serve as the remote terminal and a
Telnet server, which receives the connection request and allows the connection. This
relationship is depicted in Figure 15.1.

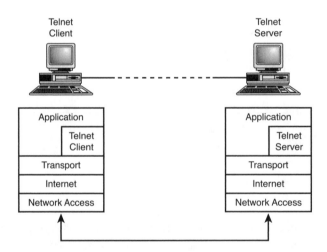

Telnet is also a protocol—a system of rules defining the interactions between Telnet
servers and clients. The Telnet protocol is defined in a series of Requests for
Comment (RFCs). Because Telnet is based on a well-defined open protocol, it can be
and has been implemented on a wide range of hardware and software systems. The
basic purpose of Telnet is to provide a means by which keyboard commands typed
by a remote user can cross the network and become input for a different computer.
Screen output related to the session then crosses the network from that different
computer (the server) to the client system (see Figure 15.2). The effect is that the
remote user can interact with the server as if he were logged in locally.

On UNIX systems, the `telnet` command is entered at the command prompt, as
follows:

```
telnet hostname
```

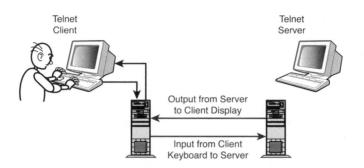

FIGURE 15.2
Network input
and output with
Telnet.

where *hostname* is the name of the computer to which you'd like to connect. (You can also enter an IP address instead of a hostname.) The preceding command launches the Telnet application. When Telnet is running, the commands you enter are executed on the remote computer. Telnet also provides some special commands that you can use during a Telnet session, as follows:

▶ **close:** Use this command to close the connection.

▶ **display:** Use this command to display connection settings, such as the port or terminal emulation.

▶ **environ:** Use this command to set environment variables. Environment variables are used by the operating system to provide machine-specific or user-specific information.

▶ **logout:** Use this command to log out the remote user and close the connection.

▶ **mode:** Use this command to toggle between ASCII or binary file transfer mode. ASCII mode is designed for efficient transfer of text files. Binary mode is for other types of files, such as executable files and graphic images.

▶ **open:** Use this command to connect to a remote computer.

▶ **quit:** Use this command to exit Telnet.

▶ **send:** Use this command to send special Telnet protocol sequences to the remote computer, such as an abort sequence, a break sequence, or an end-of-file sequence.

▶ **set:** Use this command to set connection settings.

▶ **unset:** Use this command to unset connection parameters.

▶ **?:** Use this command to print Help information.

On graphics-based platforms such as Microsoft Windows, a Telnet application might have its own icon and run in a window, but the underlying commands and processes are the same as with a text-based system. Consult your vendor documentation.

Security Matters

Telnet was once an extremely useful tool, but in recent years it has been replaced by more secure options such as SSH, which you learn about later in this hour. One problem is that Telnet gives network intruders what they want more than anything (direct access to a terminal session on a remote server), and although the Telnet standard supports password authentication, passwords are usually transported as clear text.

Berkeley Remote Utilities

The Berkeley Systems Design (BSD) UNIX implementation, known as BSD UNIX, was a major step in UNIX's development. Many innovations that began with BSD UNIX are now standard on other UNIX systems and have been incorporated into other operating systems in the world of TCP/IP and the Internet.

One of the innovations of BSD UNIX was a small set of command-line utilities designed to provide remote access. This set of utilities became known as the Berkeley r* utilities, because the name of each utility begins with an r for *remote*. Versions of the Berkeley r* utilities are still available for UNIX, Linux, and Windows systems, although, like Telnet, these tools are now somewhat anachronistic in light of modern security concerns. Fortunately, as you learn in the next section, many of the r* utilities appear in a new, more secure form in the SSH protocol suite.

Some of the Berkeley r* utilities are as follows:

- **Rlogin:** Allows users to log in remotely
- **Rcp:** Provides remote file transfer
- **Rsh:** Executes a remote command through the rshd daemon
- **Rexec:** Executes a remote command through the rexecd daemon
- **Ruptime:** Displays system information on uptime and the number of connected users
- **Rwho:** Displays information on users who are currently connected

The r* utilities were designed in an earlier and simpler time for TCP/IP networking. The creators of these utilities expected that only trusted users would access these utilities. Today, many admins reject the whole concept of a "trusted" user. The r* utilities are generally considered too risky for today's open and interconnected networks and, even on an internal network, you must be careful about how and when to use these utilities. The r* utilities do have a rudimentary security system that, if implemented properly, offers a measure of protection in restricted and trusted environments.

The r* utilities use a concept called **trusted access**. Trusted access allows one computer to trust another computer's authentication. In Figure 15.3, if Computer A designates Computer B as a trusted host, users who log in to Computer B can use the r* utilities to access Computer A without supplying a password. Computer A can also designate specific users who will be trusted users. Trusted hosts and users are identified in the /etc/hosts.equiv file of the remote machine to which the user is attempting to gain access. The rhosts file in each user's home directory can also be used to grant trusted access to the user's account.

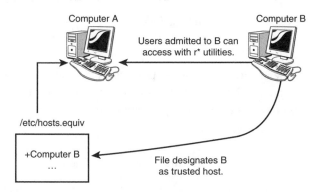

FIGURE 15.3
UNIX trusted access.

Hunting for Hosts

Because the /etc/hosts.equiv file and the rhosts file grant access to system resources, they are a major target for network intruders. The vulnerability of the hosts.equiv file and the rhosts file is one reason why the r* utilities are no longer considered secure.

By the Way

The following sections discuss some of the Berkeley r* utilities.

Rlogin

Rlogin is a remote login utility. You can use rlogin to connect with a UNIX host that is running the server daemon rlogind (*d* stands for *daemon*). Rlogin serves the same purpose as Telnet, but rlogin is considerably less versatile. Rlogin is designed specifically to provide access to UNIX systems, whereas Telnet, which is covered under a TCP/IP standard, can have a broader application. Also, rlogin does not provide some of the configuration negotiation features available with Telnet.

A significant feature of rlogin is that, because it uses the r* utilities security model, it supports remote login without a password. No-password access is a property of all r* utilities, but some users consider a passwordless terminal session a little more unsettling than some of the other functions achievable through the r* utilities. Nevertheless, the r* utilities' security model does limit access to trusted users.

> **Alternative Access**
>
> It is important to keep in mind that many network operating systems also provide methods for passwordless access to network resources after the user has achieved some form of initial authentication. For instance, the Kerberos authentication scheme, described in Hour 11, "TCP/IP Security," provides passwordless access to network resources on UNIX/Linux, as well as Windows, networks. Many of the benefits of the r* utilities can now be achieved through other, more secure methods.

The syntax for the rlogin command is as follows:

```
rlogin hostname
```

where *hostname* is the hostname of the computer to which you want to gain access. If no username is specified, the username defaults to the user's username on the local computer. Otherwise, you can specify a username as follows:

```
rlogin hostname -l username
```

where *username* is the username you want to use for the login.

The server daemon rlogind, which must be running on the server machine, then checks host.equiv and rhosts files to verify host and user information. If this authentication is successful, the remote session begins.

Rcp

The Rcp utility provides remote file access. Rcp is not as versatile or as widely used as FTP, but it is still sometimes used for file transfer.

Rsh

Rsh lets you execute a single command on a remote computer without logging in to the remote computer. Rsh is short for *remote shell*. (A **shell** is a command interface to the operating system.) The rshd daemon, running on the remote computer, accepts the rsh command, verifies the username and hostname information, and executes the command. Rsh is useful when you want to enter one command and don't need or want to establish a terminal session with the remote computer.

The format for the rsh command is

```
rsh -l username hostname command
```

where *hostname* is the hostname of the remote computer, *username* is the name to use when accessing the remote computer, and *command* is the command you want to execute.

The username (preceded by the -l) is optional. If you do not include a username, it defaults to the name on the local host as follows:

```
rsh hostname command
```

Rexec

Rexec is like rsh in that it instructs the remote computer to execute a command. Rexec uses the rexecd daemon.

The syntax for the rexec command is as follows:

```
rexec hostname -l username command
```

where *hostname* is the name of the host, *username* is the user account name on the remote computer, and *command* is the command you want to execute. If you omit -l *username*, the username defaults to the username on the local computer.

Ruptime

Ruptime displays a summary of how many users are logged in to each computer on the network. Ruptime also lists how long each computer has been up (hence the name "r-up-time") and displays some additional system information.

To generate a ruptime report, you need only enter

```
ruptime
```

Both ruptime and rwho (see the next section) use the rwhod daemon. Actually, each computer on the network has an rwhod daemon that broadcasts regular reports of user activity. Each rwhod daemon receives and stores the reports from other rwhod daemons for a networkwide view of user activity.

Rwho

Rwho reports on all users who are currently logged in to network computers. Rwho lists usernames, the computer each user is logged in to, the time of login, and the time elapsed since login.

The syntax of the rwho command is simply

rwho

The default report excludes users whose terminals have been inactive more than an hour. For a report on all users, use the -a option:

rwho -a

Rwho, like ruptime, uses the rwshod daemon.

Secure Shell

As you have probably learned already from this chapter, classic TCP/IP remote-access utilities such as Telnet and the r* tools are not safe for security-conscious environments. The r* utilities are fast disappearing. Telnet persists in some limited uses, such as dial-up access, but most IT professionals wouldn't dream of using Telnet on the open Internet.

At the same time, the evolution of the Internet has placed even more emphasis on networking and remote access. On today's networks, remote shell sessions are typically managed through a suite of protocols and utilities that fall under the collective name **Secure Shell (SSH)**. SSH is essentially equivalent to an implementation of the Berkeley r* utilities only with public key encryption. The principal components of the SSH suite are

- ▶ **SSH:** A remote shell program that replaces rlogin, rsh, and telnet

- ▶ **scp:** A file transfer utility that replaces Rcp

- ▶ **sftp:** A file transfer utility that replaces FTP

The most popular implementation of SSH is the free OpenSSH project, which is available for UNIX, Linux, Windows, and Mac OS. OpenSSH comes with several additional utilities for managing key signing and encryption. The server side of the SSH connection is handled by the sshd (SSH daemon), which is also included in the OpenSSH package.

After you have logged in to a remote system using OpenSSH

ssh user@host_name

and supplied a password at the prompt, you can operate as you would with a local command shell. SSH is much safer than its predecessors on the Internet, where its built-in encryption prevents most forms of spying and spoofing. Many firewalls provide a feature that supports outside access to the internal network through an SSH connection, so a network administrator can use SSH to log in to the internal network from across the Internet.

In addition to offering secure remote shell connections, SSH also supports a form of port forwarding so that other nonsecure applications can operate securely through SSH-based encrypted connections.

By the Way

Need a Server

If you feel like experimenting, keep in mind that SSH is a client/server application. Most modern computer systems come with an SSH client utility, but you won't be able to connect to a remote computer unless the SSH service is running on the remote system. If the service is running, you need the necessary login credentials.

Remote Control

Many system administrators and power users prefer to operate from the command shell, where a single line of text maps neatly to a single response. The command shell is also easy to extend to a remote execution environment, using SSH and similar tools. However, most users don't operate from the shell prompt anymore. Most users like to operate by clicking with a mouse in a graphical user interface (GUI).

A number of remote access protocols and utilities let the user control a remote system using ordinary graphic desktop operations with the keyboard and mouse. The task of providing remote access through a GUI is a bit more complicated, but the philosophy is the same (see Figure 15.4). A software component operating at the Application layer of Computer A intercepts keyboard input and redirects it through the protocol stack to Computer B. Screen output data from Computer B is then sent back through the network to Computer A. The effect is that the keyboard and mouse of Computer A act as a keyboard and mouse for Computer B, and the screen of Computer A displays a view of the Computer B desktop. In short, a user at Computer A can see and operate Computer B by remote control.

GUI-based remote access was originally popularized by third-party tools such as Symantec's pcAnywhere and Netopia's Timbuktu. Recent versions of Mac OS and Windows have built remote-access capability directly in to the operating system with tools such as Apple Remote Desktop and Windows Remote Desktop Connection. UNIX/Linux systems have always had a rudimentary version of this functionality through the basic architecture of the X Server graphics environment; however, recent tools such as Virtual Network Computing (VNC) and NoMachine's NX have added convenience and brought remote access to the end user.

FIGURE 15.4
GUI-based remote access tools redirect keyboard and mouse commands.

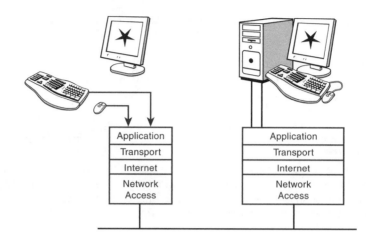

Remote system administrators and IT help desks often use remote control tools to configure and troubleshoot desktop PCs.

Network Management

Many users are glad for the chance to connect to a remote computer and type some commands or click through a configuration dialog, but IT specialists who manage dozens (or hundreds) of computers need a more efficient alternative. Network management tools let the user configure, monitor, and manage remote systems and devices from a single user interface. These tools don't just wait for the user to figure out there is a problem. Agent applications running on the remote system send back status information automatically, and the system will even alert the user through email or a text message if disk space, resource usage, or network performance cross a predefined threshold.

Several network management tools and protocols exist today. Many management tools are still based on the venerable **Simple Network Management Protocol (SNMP)** and **Remote Monitoring (RMON)** protocols described later in this hour. However, since the development of tools like SNMP, the Distributed Management Task Force (DMTF), an organization supported by many network hardware and software companies, has unveiled standards such as the Web-Based Enterprise Management (WBEM) and the Common Information Model (CIM) to provide a more general solution that lets developers and hardware vendors build drivers that communicate with network management tools. Microsoft's Windows Management Instrumentation (WMI) and Red Hat's OpenPegasus system are both implementations of WBEM.

Simple Network Management Protocol

The purpose of a protocol is to facilitate communication, and whenever a particular *type* of communication has distinctive and definable characteristics, you are likely to find a corresponding protocol. SNMP is a protocol designed for managing and monitoring remote devices on a network. SNMP supports a system that enables a single network administrator operating from a single workstation to remotely manage and monitor computers, routers, and other network devices.

Figure 15.5 shows the principal components of the SNMP architecture:

▶ **Network monitor:** A management console, sometimes called a manager or a network management console (NMS), provides a central location for managing devices on the network. The network monitor is typically an ordinary computer with the necessary SNMP management software.

▶ **Nodes:** Devices on the network.

▶ **Community:** A group of nodes in a common management framework.

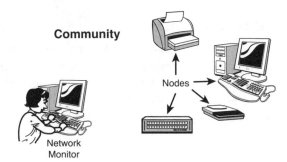

Community

Nodes

Network
Monitor

FIGURE 15.5
An SNMP community consists of one or more network monitors and a collection of nodes.

As you've learned elsewhere in this book, a protocol provides a scheme for communication, but the actual interaction occurs between applications running on the communicating devices. In the case of SNMP, a program called an **agent** runs on the remote node and communicates with the management software running on the network monitor (see Figure 15.6).

The monitor and the agent use the SNMP protocol to communicate. SNMP uses User Datagram Protocol (UDP) ports 161 and 162. Older versions of SNMP did not require any form of user logon security. Security was provided by the community name, which is referred to as the **community string**. (You had to know the community string to connect.) In some cases, you could also configure the agent to receive only data from specific IP addresses. This type of security, however, is considered weak by contemporary standards. The most recent version of SNMP, SNMP v3, addresses these concerns, providing authentication, privacy, and better overall security for the system.

FIGURE 15.6
An agent program running on the remote node sends information on the node to the network monitor and receives requests for changes to configuration settings.

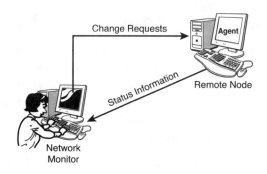

You might be wondering what the monitor and the agent communicate *about*. What kind of data passes between the monitor and the agent through SNMP? As you learn in the next section, SNMP defines a vast collection of management parameters. The network monitor uses the parameters of this **Management Information Base (MIB)** to request information from the agent and change configuration settings.

The SNMP Address Space

The SNMP process is predicated on both the monitor and agent software being capable of exchanging information regarding specific addressable locations within the MIB. The MIB, shown in Figure 15.7, allows the monitor and agent to exchange information accurately and unambiguously. Both the monitor and the agent require identical MIB structures, because they must be capable of uniquely identifying a specific unit of information.

FIGURE 15.7
A small portion of the MIB.

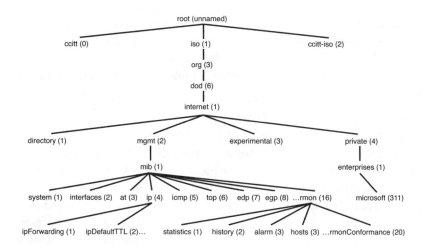

The MIB is a hierarchical address space that includes a unique address for each piece of information. Note that MIB addresses aren't like network addresses in that they don't represent a location or an actual device. The MIB is a collection of parameters arranged hierarchically into an address space. This hierarchical address arrangement ensures that all SNMP devices refer to a specific setting the same way. This approach also allows for convenient decentralization. For instance, a specific vendor can define the MIB settings (often referred to simply as MIBs) that apply to the vendor's products, or a standards organization can manage the part of the MIB tree devoted to its standard. The MIB uses dotted notation to identify each unique address within the MIB object.

MIB

The MIB has been described in several RFCs, including RFC 1158 and RFC 1213. You'll find the official description of SNMP in RFC 1157. The latest version is described in RFC 3418 and a number of other RFCs.

By the Way

The majority of the addressable locations within the MIB refer to counters, which are obviously numeric. An example of a counter is ipForwarding, shown in Figure 15.7, or ipInReceives (not shown), which counts the number of inbound IP datagrams received since either the networking software was started or the counter was last reset.

MIB information could be in any of several forms: numeric, textual, IP addresses, and so on. Another example of MIB configuration information is ipDefaultTTL. The ipDefaultTTL setting holds the numeric value of the TTL (Time To Live) parameter inserted into every IP datagram that originates on a computer.

The MIB structure is addressed by always starting at the root and progressing down through the hierarchy until you have uniquely identified the setting you want to read. For example, to address the ipDefaultTTL and ipInReceives MIBs, the SNMP monitor would send the following MIB addresses to the SNMP agent:

```
.iso.org.dod.internet.mgmt.mib.ip.ipDefaultTTL
.iso.org.dod.internet.mgmt.mib.ip.ipInReceives
```

Every location of the MIB tree also has an equivalent numeric address. You can refer to an MIB by either its alphanumeric string or by its numeric address. In fact, it's the numeric form that the network monitor uses when querying information from the agent:

```
.1.3.6.1.2.1.4.2
.1.3.6.1.2.1.4.3
```

The MIB address provides a common nomenclature to ensure that the monitor and the agent can reliably refer to specific parameters. These MIB parameters are then included in commands, as described in the next section.

SNMP Commands

The network monitoring agent software responds to three commands: get, getnext, and set. These commands perform the following functions:

- **get:** The get command instructs the agent to read and return one specific unit of information from the MIB.

- **getnext:** The getnext command instructs the agent to read and return the next sequential unit of information from the MIB. This command could be used to read a table of values, for example.

- **set:** The set command instructs the agent to set a configurable parameter or to reset an object such as a network interface or a specific counter.

SNMP software actually works in several different ways, depending on the needs of the network administrator. Different types of SNMP behavior are described in the following list:

- A network monitor agent always operates in a query/response manner where it can receive requests from and send responses to the monitor. The agent receives either a get or getnext command and returns the information from one addressable location.

- Although optional, agents are often configured to send unsolicited messages to the network monitor when unusual events occur. These unsolicited messages are known as **trap messages** or **traps**; they occur when the agent software traps some unusual occurrence.

- For example, SNMP agent software usually operates in a mode where it monitors for established thresholds to be exceeded. These thresholds are established using the set command. In the event that a threshold is exceeded, the agent traps the occurrence and then constructs and sends an unsolicited message to the network monitor identifying the IP address of the machine where the trap occurred, as well as which threshold was exceeded.

- Agents can also receive requests from the monitor to perform certain actions, such as to reset a specific port on a router or to set the threshold levels that are used in trapping events. Again, the set command is used for setting configurable parameters or resetting counter or interfaces.

The following example illustrates query and response commands used by SNMP. This example uses a diagnostic utility called snmputil, which allows a technician to simulate a monitor. Through the utility, a technician can issue commands to the agent. In this case, the agent is located on a computer with an IP address of 192.59.66.200, and the agent is a member of a community named public. Notice the .0 at the end of the first two commands; this is used as a suffix when reading simple variables such as counters:

```
D:\>snmputil get 192.59.66.200 public .1.3.6.1.2.1.4.2.0
Variable = ip.ipDefaultTTL.0
Value    = INTEGER - 128

D:\>snmputil getnext 192.59.66.200 public .1.3.6.1.2.1.4.2.0
Variable = ip.ipInReceives.0
Value    = Counter - 11898
```

Change the Name

The default community name on many SNMP systems is public. The admin in this example should have changed the name to something else. You give an attacker a head start when you use a default name.

By the Way

SNMP is useful to network administrators, but it is not perfect. Some of the shortcomings of SNMP are as follows:

▶ **Cannot see lower layers:** SNMP resides at the Application layer above UDP, so it cannot see what is happening at the lowest layers within the protocol stack, such as what is happening at the Network Access layer.

▶ **Requires an operational protocol stack:** A fully operational TCP/IP stack is required for an SNMP monitor and agent to communicate. If you're having network problems that prevent the stack from operating correctly, SNMP cannot help troubleshoot the problem.

▶ **Can generate heavy network traffic:** The query response mechanism used by SNMP causes a great deal of network traffic. Although unsolicited traps are sent when significant events occur, in actuality network monitors generate a constant amount of network traffic as they query agents for specific information.

▶ **Provides too much data and too little information:** With the literally thousands of address locations within an MIB, you can retrieve many small pieces of information. However, it requires a powerful management console to analyze these minute details and to be capable of providing useful analysis of what is occurring on a specific machine.

▶ **Provides a view of the machine but not the network:** SNMP is designed to provide information on a specific device. You can't look directly at what is occurring on the network segment.

Remote Monitoring

RMON is an extension to the MIB address space and was developed to allow monitoring and maintenance of remote local area networks (LANs). Unlike SNMP, which provides information retrieved from a single computer, RMON captures data directly from the network media and, therefore, can provide insight on the LAN as a whole.

The RMON MIB begins at address location .1.3.6.1.2.1.16 (as shown in Figure 15.7) and is currently divided into 20 groups, for example .1.3.6.1.2.1.16.1 through .1.3.6.1.2.1.16.20. RMON was developed by the IETF to address shortcomings with SNMP and to provide greater visibility of network traffic on remote LANs.

There are two versions of RMON: RMON 1 and RMON 2.

▶ **RMON 1:** RMON 1 is oriented toward monitoring ethernet LANs. All groups within RMON 1 are concerned with monitoring the bottom two layers, for example, the Physical and Data Link layers of the OSI reference model (corresponding to the Network Access layer in the TCP/IP model). RMON 1 is described in several RFCs, including 2819, 1757, and the original RFC 1271, originally published in November 1991.

▶ **RMON 2:** RMON 2 provides the functionality of RMON 1 and also lets you monitor the upper five layers of the OSI reference model (corresponding to the Internet, Transport, and Application layers of the TCP/IP model). The specifications for RMON 2 appeared in 1997 with RFC 2021 which was later updated with RFC 4502.

Because RMON 2 listens to higher layers of the protocol stack, it can provide information on higher-level protocols, such as IP, TCP, and NFS.

The purpose of RMON is to capture network traffic data. An RMON agent (or **probe**) listens on a network segment and forwards traffic data to an RMON console. If the network includes several segments, a different agent listens on each segment. RMON information is gathered in groups of statistics that correlate to different kinds of information. The RMON 1 group names are as follows:

▶ **Ethernet Statistics:** The Statistics group holds statistical information in the form of a table for each network segment attached to the probe. Some of the counters within this group keep track of the number of packets, the number of broadcasts, the number of collisions, the number of undersize and oversize datagrams, and so on.

▶ **Ethernet History:** The Ethernet History group holds statistical information that is periodically compiled and stored for later retrieval.

▶ **History Control:** The History Control group includes controls for managing the sampling of data.

▶ **Alarm:** The Alarm group works in conjunction with the Event group (described later). Periodically the Alarm group examines statistical samples from variables within the probe and compares them with configured thresholds; if these thresholds are exceeded, an event is generated that can be used to notify the network manager.

▶ **Hosts:** The Hosts group maintains statistics for each host on the network segment; it learns about these hosts by examining the source and destination physical addresses within datagrams.

▶ **Host Top n:** The Host Top n group is used to generate reports based on statistics for the top defined number of hosts in a particular category. For instance, a network manager might want to know which hosts appear in the most datagrams, or which hosts are sending the most oversized or undersized datagrams.

▶ **Matrix:** The Matrix group constructs a table that includes the source and destination physical address pairs for every datagram monitored on the network. These address pairs define conversations between two addresses.

▶ **Filter:** The Filter group allows the generation of a binary pattern that can be used to match, or filter, datagrams from the network.

▶ **Packet Capture:** The Capture group allows datagrams selected by the Filter group to be captured for later retrieval and examination by the network manager.

▶ **Event:** The Event group works in conjunction with the Alarm group to generate events that notify the network manager when a threshold of a monitored object has been exceeded.

RMON 2 provides additional groups related to its oversight of the upper-level protocols.

Summary

This hour covered some of the TCP/IP remote-access utilities that have evolved around TCP/IP. You learned about Telnet, r* utilities, and SSH. You can use these utilities to execute commands and access information on a remote computer.

You also learned that the SNMP protocol is integral to providing centralized monitoring and maintenance of distant remote networks. By using a network management console and a central site, a network manager learns when abnormal events occur and can view network traffic status as reported by agents operating on routers, hubs, and servers. The network management console also lets the network manager perform functions such as resetting ports on routers or even resetting remote equipment in the event that less drastic measures don't cure a problem.

Many newer network devices include embedded RMON features. RMON can greatly reduce network traffic normally associated with SNMP and does not require a powerful network management console to interpret the data. However, when using RMON, a significant amount of processing occurs on the RMON agent, or probe, that is capturing the network traffic.

Q&A

Q. *Is Telnet a server application, a client application, or a protocol?*

A. The term *Telnet* could refer to either the server or the client Telnet application, or it could refer to the Telnet protocol.

Q. *Which file should you use if you want to designate a host as a trusted host?*

A. Use the /etc/hosts.equiv file or the rhosts file in a user's home directory to designate a trusted host.

Q. *What utility would tell me if the user Ethelred is currently logged in to the network?*

A. The rwho utility displays information on current users.

Q. *The SNMP protocol uses which transport protocol and which ports?*

A. SNMP mostly uses UDP port 161; port 162 is used for SNMP traps.

Q. *What is the name of the message that an SNMP agent can send in an unsolicited manner when an event occurs?*

A. A trap message.

Q. *What layer of the TCP/IP model does RMON 1 address?*

A. The Network Access layer.

Q. *What layers of the TCP/IP model does RMON 2 address?*

A. RMON 2 addresses all layers of the protocol stack.

Q. *I want to monitor cyclical changes in the traffic level on my network. Should I use SNMP or RMON?*

A. SNMP is used primarily to monitor network devices. RMON captures data directly from the network media and, therefore, is usually a better choice for monitoring network traffic.

Workshop

The following workshop is composed of a series of quiz questions and practical exercises. The quiz questions are designed to test your overall understanding of the current material. The practical exercises are intended to afford you the opportunity to apply the concepts discussed during the current hour, as well as build upon the knowledge acquired in previous hours of study. Please take time to complete the quiz questions and exercises before continuing. Refer to Appendix A, "Answers to Quizzes and Exercises," for answers.

Quiz

1. Why should you prefer SSH to Telnet?

2. Which set of utilities has the concept of "trusted access?"

3. Which protocol uses a MIB to organize its data?

4. In what sense does SNMP provide a limited view?

5. What functionality does RMON 2 add to RMON 1?

Exercises

1. List three ways to log in to a remote machine. List them in order of security.

2. Referring to Figure 15.7, find the MIB address for information about interfaces.

3. Referring to Figure 15.7, find the MIB address of the RMON Alarm group.

4. List some of the shortcomings of SNMP.

5. Use SSH to log in to a remote machine. If you don't have access to a remote machine, log in to your own machine.

Key Terms

Review the following list of key terms:

▶ **Agent:** The SNMP software loaded on to a host that can read the MIB and respond to a monitor with the desired results. Agents have the capability to transmit unsolicited messages to the monitor when significant abnormal events occur.

▶ **Community string:** The name associated with an SNMP network or monitoring group.

▶ **Management Information Base (MIB):** A hierarchical address space used by SNMP monitors and agents. Specific parameters within the MIB are located by using dotted notation from the top of the MIB structure down to the MIB address you want.

▶ **Probe:** Another name for an agent. The term is often used in situations involving RMON.

▶ **rcp:** A remote file transfer utility.

▶ **Remote Monitoring (RMON):** A service and MIB extension that provides enhanced capabilities over traditional SNMP functions. To store data in the RMON MIB, the agent or probe must include RMON software.

▶ **Rexec:** A remote command-execution utility.

▶ **Rlogin:** A remote login utility.

▶ **Rsh:** A remote command-execution utility.

▶ **Ruptime:** A utility that displays system information on uptime and the number of connected users.

▶ **Rwho:** A utility that displays information on currently connected users.

▶ **Secure Shell (SSH):** A collection of utilities that form a secure, encrypted remote shell access solution.

▶ **Shell:** A command interface to the operating system.

▶ **Simple Network Management Protocol (SNMP):** A protocol used for managing resources on a TCP/IP network.

▶ **Telnet:** A once-popular remote terminal utility that has largely been replaced by the more-secure SSH.

▶ **Trap:** Unsolicited message from an SNMP agent announcing an event.

▶ **Trusted access:** A weak security system in which a system administrator designates remote hosts and users who are trusted to access the local system.

PART V

The Internet

HOUR 16

Classic Services

What You'll Learn in This Hour:

- ▶ FTP
- ▶ TFTP
- ▶ NFS
- ▶ SMB and CIFS
- ▶ LDAP

You have probably learned by now that the TCP/IP protocol suite is an extremely versatile system for network communication. If you are willing to write a server application, write a client application, and string some network cable, you can create tools for a vast range of purposes. Most people, however, prefer to rely on tools that are already written.

At an earlier and more experimental age, a wider range of more primitive services played an important role on the Internet. The first edition of this book even included descriptions of some of these services, such as Archie, Veronica, and Gopher, all of which have disappeared and been replaced by the super-versatile Hypertext Transfer Protocol (HTTP) service at the heart of what we know as the World Wide Web. This hour rounds up some of the most important standard services that are at work right now on TCP/IP networks. In terms of the TCP/IP protocol system, these services all operate at the Application layer and listen for service requests through the Transport layer ports. These tools make up a vast portion of Internet activity, and they command a large share of attention from IT professionals. You'll learn about

- ▶ HTTP
- ▶ Email
- ▶ FTP file transfer

► File and print services

► LDAP

► IRC and IM messaging

As you will learn in later hours, many of the tools that appear as separate activities on the Web, such as social networking and streaming, are often extensions of the web infrastructure supported by HTTP. Hour 18, "HTTP, HTML and the World Wide Web," takes a closer look at HTTP and the World Wide Web. Email is also a hugely important Internet activity that requires a separate discussion to describe in detail. See Hour 21, "Email," for more information about email.

This hour primarily focuses on services available to users who are already connected and making choices about their network activities. Equally important are background services the user doesn't see, such as domain name system (DNS) (see Hour 10, "Name Resolution") and DHCP (see Hour 12, "Configuration"), and troubleshooting tools such as ping (see Hour 14, "TCP/IP Utilities").

HTTP

Many of the activities that once took place through myriad separate tools on the early Internet, as well as many of the more innovative developments to appear in recent years, now all happen within the scope of the ubiquitous and very versatile Hyper Text Transfer Protocol (HTTP). HTTP, which is the engine at the heart of the phenomenon we know as the World Wide Web, is essentially an Application layer protocol for transferring and requesting data and images in Hyper Text Markup Language (HTML) format.

HTTP is too big of a topic to cover in this short summary. You learn about HTTP and HTML in Hours 18, 19, and 20, all of which are devoted to this important service and the technologies surrounding it. For the purposes of this hour, keep in mind that anything with the word *web* in it is really about HTTP. A web server is primarily an HTTP server. A website is a directory of files, links, and other resources accessible through HTTP. A webmaster is one who understands how to work with HTTP, HTML, and other components used to glue websites together. Blogs and social networking sites use HTTP. Present-day content management systems (CMSs) rescue the user from the tedious details of hard-coding HTML tags, but at the core, they still operate through HTTP.

See later hours for more on the important topic of HTTP.

Email

Electronic mail is one of the most important services on the Internet. A vast number of Internet users send dozens of email messages every day (at home and at work).

Like other Internet services, email depends on the interaction between a client application (typically an email reader on your personal computer) and a server application. Actually, standard email depends on a pair of server systems, which is why you need to configure an "incoming server" and an "outgoing server" in your email reader configuration interface. The outgoing server (which uses the Simple Mail Transfer Protocol [SMTP]) receives outgoing messages from you and forwards them through a network of other SMTP servers to the destination address. The incoming mail server (which typically uses POP or IMAP protocol) receives messages addressed to your email account and waits for requests from your mail reader to connect and access the messages.

Most mail servers are operated by Internet service providers or by corporations, agencies, and organizations that provide email connectivity for members and employees.

See Hour 21 for a complete discussion of email over TCP/IP.

FTP

The **File Transfer Protocol (FTP)** is a widely used protocol that enables a user to transfer files between two computers on a TCP/IP network. A file transfer application (typically also called ftp) uses FTP to transfer files. The user runs an FTP client application on one computer, and the other computer runs an FTP server program such as ftpd (FTP daemon) on a UNIX/Linux computer, or an FTP service on other platforms. Many FTP client programs are command-line based, but graphical versions are available as well. FTP is used primarily to transfer files, although it can perform other functions such as creating directories, removing directories, and listing files.

By the Way

FTP and the Web

FTP is also widely used on the World Wide Web, and the FTP protocol has been integrated into most web browsers. Sometime when you're downloading a file through a web browser, you might notice the URL in the address box begins with ftp://.

FTP uses the TCP protocol and, therefore, operates through a reliable, connection-oriented session between the client and server computers. The standard FTP daemon (on the server) listens on TCP port 21 for a request from a client. When a client sends a request, a Transport Control Protocol (TCP) connection is initiated (see Hour 6, "The Transport Layer"). The remote user is then authenticated by the FTP server, and a session begins. A classic text-based FTP session requires the remote user to interact with the server through a command-line interface. Typical commands start and stop the FTP session, navigate through the remote directory structure, and upload or download files. Newer GUI-based FTP clients offer a graphic interface (rather than a command interface) for navigating directories and moving files.

By the Way

Daemon and Service

In the UNIX world, a daemon is a process that runs in the background and performs a service when that service is requested. A daemon is called a *service* in the Windows world.

On most computers, you start a text-based FTP session by entering ftp followed by the hostname or IP address of the FTP server. FTP then prompts you for a user ID and a password, which are used by the FTP server to validate you as an authorized user and determine your rights. For example, the user account you log on with might be assigned read-only access, or it might be configured for both read and write operations. Many FTP servers are available for public use and allow you to log on with a user ID called anonymous (usually for read-only access). When the anonymous account is used as the user ID, you can enter virtually any password. However, it is customary to enter your email account name as the password. When FTP servers are not intended for general public use, the servers are configured to not allow anonymous access. In that case, you must enter a user ID and password to gain access. The user ID and password are typically set up and provided by the FTP server administrator.

Many FTP client implementations allow you to enter either UNIX-based commands or DOS-based commands. The actual commands available depend on the client software being used. When you transfer files using FTP, you must specify to FTP the type of file that you are about to transfer; the most common choices are binary and ASCII. Choose ASCII when the type of file you want to transfer is a simple text file. Choose binary when the type of file you want to transfer is a program file, a word processing document, or a graphics file. The default file transfer mode is ASCII.

Be aware that many FTP servers reside on UNIX and Linux computers. UNIX and Linux are case sensitive—that is, they distinguish between uppercase and lowercase letters. So, you must match the case exactly when entering filenames. The current directory on the local computer from which you start an FTP session is the default location where files are transferred to or from.

The following is a list of commonly used FTP commands and explanations of the commands:

▶ **ftp**: The ftp command is used to start the FTP client program. You can enter ftp by itself, or you can follow it with an IP address or domain name. In Figure 16.1, an FTP session to rs.internic.net was started by typing ftp rs.internic.net.

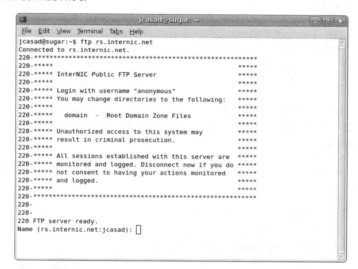

FIGURE 16.1
Starting an FTP session.

▶ **user**: The user command is used to change the user ID and password information of the current session. You will be prompted to enter a new user ID and password, exactly as when you use the ftp command. This command is effectively the same as quitting FTP and starting again as a new user.

▶ **help**: The help command displays the ftp commands that are available on your FTP client (see Figure 16.2).

▶ **ls or dir**: The UNIX/Linux ls or ls -l command or the Windows dir command lists the contents of a directory. The response from these commands lists the filenames and directory names contained within the current working directory on the FTP server. Between the two system messages (the lines preceded by 150 and 226) is the actual directory listing, which contains all of the files and subdirectories within the current working directory. The ls -l command is similar to the ls command but lists additional details such as read and write permissions and file creation dates.

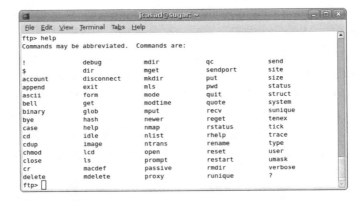

▶ **pwd**: The pwd command prints the name of the current working directory. This is the directory on the remote server, not the directory on your local computer.

▶ **cd**: The cd command changes the current working directory on the FTP server.

▶ **mkdir**: The UNIX/Linux mkdir command creates a directory on the FTP server inside the current working directory. This command is typically not allowable during an anonymous FTP session.

▶ **rmdir**: The UNIX rmdir command removes a directory on the FTP server from the current working directory. This command is typically not allowable during an anonymous FTP session.

▶ **binary**: The binary command switches the FTP client to binary transfer mode from the default ASCII transfer mode. Binary mode is useful when transferring binary files, such as programs and graphics, using the get, put, mget, and mput commands.

▶ **ascii**: The ascii command switches the FTP client to ASCII transfer mode from binary mode.

▶ **type**: The type command displays the current mode (ASCII or binary) for file transfer.

▶ **status**: The status command displays information about the various settings on the FTP client. Such settings include the mode (binary or ASCII) the client is set to and whether the client is set to display verbose system messages.

▶ **get**: The get command retrieves a file from an FTP server to an FTP client. Using the get command followed by a single filename will copy that file from the FTP server to the working directory on the FTP client. If the get command is followed by two filenames, the second name is used to designate the name of the new file created on the client.

- ▶ **mget**: The mget command is similar to the get command except that it lets you retrieve multiple files.

- ▶ **put**: The put command transfers a file from the FTP client to the FTP server. Using the put command followed by a single filename will copy the file from the FTP client to the FTP server. If the put command is followed by two filenames, the second name designates the name of the new file created on the server.

- ▶ **mput**: The mput command is similar to the put command, except that it enables you to transfer multiple files with one command.

- ▶ **open**: The open command allows you to establish a new session with an FTP server. This is essentially a shortcut to quitting FTP and starting it again. The open command can be used to open a session with an entirely different FTP server or to reopen a session with the current server.

- ▶ **close**: The close command ends the current session with an FTP server. The FTP client program remains open, and you can start a new session with the server by using the open command.

- ▶ **bye** or **quit**: These commands close the current FTP session and terminate the FTP client.

Although the preceding list does not cover every FTP command, it gives you an idea of those used most often during an FTP session.

Most modern computer systems include support for FTP at the command line; however, a new generation of GUI-based FTP clients eliminates the need for command-line input. Users who access FTP frequently often opt for a graphical client that displays and manages file resources much like an ordinary file browser.

FTP is a relatively ancient protocol that evolved before the recent emphasis on secure networking. Later updates to the specification, such as RFC 2228, "FTP Security Extensions," have added important protections, such as more secure authentication, but FTP is still considered unsecure.

Despite these security concerns, FTP remains quite popular. FTP provides a convenient mechanism for uploading and downloading ordinary documents and files too big to circulate through email. One advantage of uploading a document through FTP rather than emailing it is that you can use FTP commands to check for the presence of the file on the server and, thus, verify that the file has reached its destination.

For those who need something more secure than garden-variety FTP, the SSH toolkit (see Hour 15, "Monitoring and Remote Access") includes the scp and sftp file transfer utilities.

Trivial File Transfer Protocol

The **Trivial File Transfer Protocol (TFTP)** is used to transfer files between the TFTP client and a TFTP server, a computer running the tftpd TFTP daemon. This protocol uses User Datagram Protocol (UDP) as a transport and, unlike FTP, does not require a user to log on to transfer files. Because TFTP does not require a user logon, it is often considered a security hole, especially if the TFTP server permits writing.

TFTP was designed to be small so that both it and UDP could be implemented on a PROM (programmable read-only memory) chip. TFTP is limited (hence the name *trivial*) when compared to FTP. TFTP can only read and write files; it cannot list the contents of directories, create or remove directories, or allow a user to log on as FTP allows. TFTP is primarily used in conjunction with the RARP and BOOTP protocols to boot diskless workstations and, in some cases, to upload new system code or patches to routers or other network devices. TFTP can transfer files using either an ASCII format known as netascii or a binary format known as octet; a third format known as mail is no longer used.

When a user enters a `tftp` statement on a command line, the computer initiates a connection to the server and performs the file transfer. At the completion of the file transfer, the session is closed and terminated. The syntax of the TFTP statement is as follows:

```
TFTP [-i] host [get | put] <source filename> [<destination filename>]
```

To learn more about the TFTP protocol, see RFC 1350.

File and Print Services

Utilities such as ftp and tftp are standalone applications operating at the Application layer of the TCP/IP protocol stack. These utilities were a great advance at the time of their appearance, and they are still useful in some contexts, but since then, vendors and Internet visionaries have looked for more versatile solutions. Their goal is to seamlessly integrate remote file access with local file access so that local and remote resources appear together within a common interface.

As you learned in Hour 7, "The Application Layer," part of this integrated network file access requires a *redirector* (or *requester*) on the client computer to interpret resource requests and route network-bound requests to the network. Another part of this solution is a general-purpose file-access protocol that forms a complete protocol layer through which GUI-based user interface tools and other applications can access the network. This file-access method is now the preferred approach for local area networks. The following sections introduce a pair of protocols that provide integrated network file access:

▶ **Network File System (NFS):** A protocol used on UNIX and Linux computers

▶ **Common Internet File System/Server Message Block (CIFS/SMB):** A protocol used to provide remote file access for Windows clients

These protocols demonstrate the power of the TCP/IP Application layer and the benefits of building a network system around a well-defined protocol stack, in which lower-level protocols form a foundation for more specialized protocols above.

Network File System

The Network File System (NFS) was originally developed by Sun but is now supported on UNIX, Linux, and many other systems. NFS allows users to access (read, write, create, and delete) directories and files located on a remote computer as if those directories and files were located on the local computer. Because NFS is designed to provide a transparent interface between local file systems and remote file systems, and because it is implemented within the operating system of both computers, it does not require any changes to application programs. Programs are capable of accessing both local files and remote files and directories via NFS without any recompilation or other changes. To the user, all files and directories appear and operate as if they existed only on the local file system.

The original implementation of NFS used the UDP protocol for its transport and was intended for use on a LAN. However, later revisions allow use of the TCP protocol; the additional reliability of TCP allows for expanded capabilities of NFS, which can now operate in a WAN.

NFS is designed to be independent of operating systems, transport protocols, and physical network architecture. This allows an NFS client to interoperate with any NFS server. This independence is achieved by using Remote Procedure Calls (RPCs) between the client and server computers. RPC is a process that enables a program running on one computer to make calls on code segments inside a program running on another computer. RPC has been around for many years and is supported on many operating systems. In the case of NFS, the operating system on the client issues a remote procedure call to the operating system on the server.

Before remote files and directories can be used on the NFS system, they must first go through a process known as mounting. After they are mounted, the remote files and directories appear and operate as if they were located on the local file system.

The latest version of the NFS protocol is version 4, which is covered in RFC 3530. For additional information about earlier versions of NFS, see RFC 1094 and RFC 1813. NFS implementations vary with the operating system. See the vendor documentation for more on how to configure NFS for your operating system.

Server Message Block and Common Internet File System

Server Message Block (SMB) is the protocol that supports the network-integrated tools of the Windows user interface, such as Explorer, Network Neighborhood, and the Map Network Drive feature. SMB is designed to operate above a variety of different protocol systems, including IPX/SPX (the legacy NetWare protocols stack), NetBEUI (an obsolete protocol for PC LANs), and TCP/IP.

Like other network protocols, SMB is designed around the concept of a client (a computer requesting services) and a server (a computer providing services). Every session begins with a preliminary exchange of information, in which an SMB dialect is negotiated and a client is authenticated and logged on to the server. The details of the authentication process vary depending on the operating system and the configuration, but as far as SMB is concerned, the logon is encapsulated in a sesssetupX SMB. (A protocol transmission under the SMB protocol is simply called an SMB.)

If the logon is successful, the client sends an SMB specifying the name of the network share it wants to access. If the share access is successful, the client may open, close, read from, or write to the network resource, and the server sends the necessary data to fulfill the request.

SMB is generally considered a Windows protocol, and it is true that the primary importance of SMB is its tight integration with the Windows client user interface. An open standard version equivalent of SMB is known as the **Common Internet File System (CIFS)**. The details of the SMB and CIFS protocols are well known to developers, and other operating systems support servers that speak SMB to Windows clients. A popular open source server called Samba (which is, if you'll notice, SMB with two vowels to make a dance) provides SMB file services for UNIX/Linux systems.

Whenever you configure file sharing in Windows, you are essentially configuring the computer to act as a CIFS server (see Figure 16.3). When you connect to a shared resource from another system, the system often identifies the resource as a Windows Network and connects to it using built-in SMB/CIFS client software.

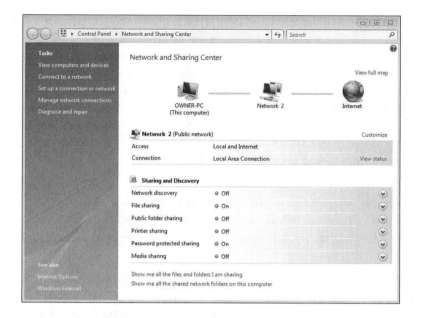

FIGURE 16.3
When you set up your Windows computer for file sharing, you are configuring it to use the SMB/CIFS protocols.

The versatility and universal support for SMB/CIFS make it a popular option for networks containing a mix of different operating systems. SMB is typically supported out of the box by Linux and Mac OS clients in addition to Windows clients, so it is a logical choice for small networks. On the server side, the free Samba server has become a sophisticated tool that performs well and integrates well with native Microsoft networking components. Linux server admins often opt for SMB/CIFS even without the need for Windows interoperability.

Lightweight Directory Access Protocol

Experts have grappled for years with the problem of how to store and retrieve information about users, systems, devices, and other network resources. On larger networks, the task of managing resource information in a uniform, efficient manner is increasingly difficult. **Lightweight Directory Access Protocol (LDAP)** was originally developed as a TCP/IP-based successor to the X.500 data model. LDAP is a **directory service**. An LDAP server maintains a directory of information on network resources organized in a logical, treelike hierarchy. LDAP operates at the TCP/IP Application layer and listens for requests on well-known TCP port 389. The LDAP protocol, data format, and syntax are spelled out in a series of Internet RFCs. LDAP v3 (the latest version) is spelled out in RFCs 4510 to 4519.

On modern networks, the security system is much more complicated than a simple list of usernames and passwords. For one thing, the network typically includes multiple servers, and it makes sense to provide the different systems with a common way to access information on the user's credentials. Also, the network needs a common way to assign, track, and verify access permissions for hardware resources like printers, as well as for files and directories. Once you have compiled this common network information directory, it makes sense to roll in other types of information also, such as employee contact information, emergency phone numbers for equipment manufacturers, and information on where employees are located (either geographically or within the company's organizational chart).

LDAP provides this common structure of network information in a way that operates easily over TCP/IP networks. Perhaps the most famous LDAP-based system is Microsoft's Active Directory. In the open source world, OpenLDAP is a popular equivalent.

The structure for an LDAP directory is defined in a schema. The schema spells out a collection of attributes that define the data that will reside in the directory. For instance, a directory of employee records might include attributes for the employee name, address, and userid. The individual entries in the directory then assign values to these attributes.

An LDAP directory is organized hierarchically, like a file directory structure. Each entry has a **distinguished name (DN)** that defines its position in the tree. The distinguished name consists of a **relative distinguished name (RDN)** that uniquely defines the entry within its container, plus a series of components defining the hierarchy of containers in which the entry resides (see Figure 16.4).

FIGURE 16.4
The LDAP DN consists of an RDN defining the object within the container, plus a series of components defining the hierarchy of containers.

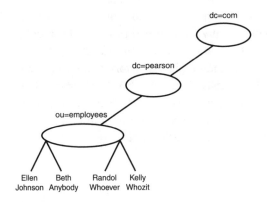

dn: cn=Ellen Johnson, ou=employees, dc=pearson, dc=com

dc=com

dc=pearson

ou=employees

Ellen Johnson   Beth Anybody   Randol Whoever   Kelly Whozit

A DN might look something like this:

```
dn: cn=Ellen Johnson, ou=employees,dc=pearson,dc=com
```

Note the two-letter attribute types (on the left of the equal sign) associated with the name values. LDAP predefines some standard attribute types used to define in building distinguished names, including the following:

- **domain component (dc)**: An entry in the chain of nested containers defining the directory hierarchy. In the preceding example, the dc entries refer to a DNS domain name (pearson.com). Basing the distinguished name around a domain name is a common approach for modern networks, but it is not required.

- **Organizational unit (ou)**: A container grouping entries for administrative convenience. An ou might define some logical group, such as a department, whereas a dc is more likely to reflect the structure of the network itself.

- **Canonical name (cn)**: A human-friendly name for the object that is unique for the container.

In the preceding example, the cn served as the RDN. It is also possible to use another distinguishing attribute, such as a userid or employee number, as the RDN element within the distinguished name:

```
dn: userid=ejohnson,ou=Employees,dc=pearson,dc=com
```

Other attributes associated with the schema can include any other parameters you want to associate with the entry:

```
dn: cn=Ellen Johnson, ou=employees,dc=pearson,dc=com
cn: Ellen Johnson
userid: ejohnson
phonemumber: 785-212-3311
employeeID: 3224177
...
```

LDAP is a binary format. Alphanumeric representations such as the preceding example are actually in **LDAP Data Interchange Format (LDIF)**, which is used for reading and reporting LDAP data.

References to directory information take the form of URLs passed to the LDAP server. (You'll learn more about URLs and URIs in Hour 17 "The Internet: A Closer Look.") Depending on the type of request, the URL might specify the distinguished name, the attributes associated with the query or update, the scope (domain) and filter criteria to define a search, or other extensions as described in the LDAP standards. The prefix (or scheme) ldap is used to associate the URL with the LDAP protocol.

The following URL:

```
ldap://ldap.pearson.com/userid=ejohnson,ou=Employees,dc=pearson,dc=com
```

refers to all attributes at ldap.pearson.com associated with the following distinguished name:

```
userid=ejohnson, ou=employees,dc=pearson,dc=com
```

To specify a specific attribute, enclose it in question marks:

```
ldap://ldap.pearson.com/userid=ejohnson,ou=Employees,dc=pearson,dc=com
?phonenumber?
```

See RFC 4516 for more on LDAP URLs. Each LDAP implementation has a set of tools for querying and updating the LDAP directory. Many UNIX and Linux systems include support for the ldapsearch, ldapmodify, and ldapdelete command-line utilities. Microsoft's Active Directory includes an extensive set of user interface tools for interacting with the directory.

The possibilities for storing and retrieving data through LDAP are nearly endless. You can create your own schema to organize your LDAP directory however you like.

Because the LDAP directory stores information on users and resources, it is a logical candidate to participate in networkwide authentication service. LDAP is sometimes combined with other authentication tools to provide a secure means for users to authentic against the LDAP data store. For instance, Active Directory is integrated with Kerberos authentication, which you learned about in Hour 11 "TCP/IP Security." UNIX/Linux admins can combine LDAP with Kerberos or the Pluggable Authentication Module (PAM) system.

Mass LDAP infrastructures like Active Directory provide ready-made schema options and a set of user interface tools for entering and accessing LDAP information. LDAP services also typically provide a replication system that copies and synchronizes the data store across a collection of multiple servers. Replication provides fault tolerance and improves performance, especially on large, multisite networks.

In addition to supporting the standard user and resource management services offered by ready-made systems like Active Directory, LDAP is also easily adaptable to custom applications. Any scenario that requires network lookup from a common data store, and that benefits from a directory-style data structure rather than a flat file or SQL-style database, is a candidate for LDAP. LDAP's schema framework fits in easily with object-oriented programming methods, and many programming environments offer application programming interfaces (APIs) and other tools for supporting LDAP queries.

Summary

Network services operating at the Application layer create the rich, vibrant user environment we know as the Internet. This hour described some important network services, including FTP, NFS, SMB and CIFS, and LDAP. This hour also briefly mentioned HTTP and email, which you learn more about in later hours.

Q&A

Q. *What is the default representation (transfer type) for FTP?*

A. ASCII.

Q. *What FTP commands typically are not allowed when a user is connected using the anonymous account?*

A. The anonymous account is usually configured for read-only access. Commands that write to a file or change the directory structure on the FTP server are not allowed. These commands include `put`, `mkdir`, `rmdir`, and `mput`.

Q. *What is the primary role for LDAP on most modern networks?*

A. LDAP maintains a directory of network and user information that is easily accessible over TCP/IP.

Workshop

The following workshop is composed of a series of quiz questions and practical exercises. The quiz questions test your overall understanding of the current material. The practical exercises give you the opportunity to apply the concepts discussed during the current hour and to build on the knowledge acquired in previous hours of study. Take time to complete the quiz questions and exercises before continuing. Refer to Appendix A, "Answers to Quizzes and Exercises," for answers.

Quiz

1. What is the difference between FTP's put and mput commands?

2. Can you list the files in the directory using TFTP?

3. What file service protocol is used with the UNIX/Linux Samba file server?

Exercise

Try your luck with a real anonymous FTP server.

1. Open a terminal or command prompt tool on your Internet-connected computer. On Windows, find the Command Prompt icon in the main menu or in the Accessories menu. On Mac OS, look for the Terminal tool in the Utilities menu. The Terminal of Bash Prompt is also readily accessible in Linux; consult your vendor documentation.

2. In the terminal window, type ftp ftp.gnu.org to access the FTP server for the GNU Free Software project. If prompted for a username, type anonymous. As of this writing, the site did not prompt for a password; if it does, or if you decide to try this on another anonymous FTP site, type your email address as the password. If the login fails, or if you mistyped something and need to start over, be sure to quit the FTP> prompt before you try the preceding command again; enter quit at the prompt. Or, to connect to the site from within the FTP> prompt, use the open command: open ftp.gnu.org.

3. Once you have logged in, enter the command ls to list the contents of the current directory.

4. To download the README file, enter get README. To make sure the README landed correctly on your home computer, use the ! character with the directory listing command used on your local system: !ls or !dir, depending on your operating system.

5. To move to the gnu directory, enter cd ./gnu.

6. To check whether the change directory operation was successful, type pwd to list the current working directory.

7. When you are finished exploring the FTP site, enter close to close the connection. Then enter quit to leave the FTP> prompt.

Key Terms

Review the following list of key terms:

▶ **Common Internet File System (CIFS):** An open standard version of the SMB file service protocol originally popularized by Microsoft and now used with all common operating systems.

▶ **Directory service:** A type of information service used on many networks that organizes and manages user and resource information in a hierarchical, tree-like structure.

▶ **Distinguished name (DN):** A name that uniquely identifies an object in an LDAP database. The distinguished name consists of a relative distinguished name followed by a concatenation of identifiers describing the hierarchy of containers in which the object resides.

▶ **File Transfer Protocol (FTP):** A client/server utility and protocol used to transfer files between two computers. In addition to transferring files, the FTP utility can create and remove directories and display the contents of directories.

▶ **Lightweight Directory Access Protocol (LDAP):** A protocol designed to allow easy access to a directory service over TCP/IP.

▶ **LDAP Data Interchange Format (LDIF):** A human-readable format used to display LDAP data.

▶ **Network File System (NFS):** NFS allows the user on an NFS client computer to access files located on a remote NFS server computer transparently.

▶ **Relative distinguished name (RDN):** An attribute included with the LDAP object definition that uniquely identifies an LDAP object within its container. The canonical name is often used as an RDN, although another attribute with a unique value could also be used.

▶ **Server Message Block (SMB):** SMB is an Application layer protocol that enables Windows clients to access network resources such as files and printers.

▶ **Trivial File Transfer Protocol (TFTP):** A UDP-based client/server utility and protocol used for simple file transfer operations.

The Internet: A Closer Look

The ever-expanding Internet is the world's biggest example of a TCP/IP network. This hour provides a brief overview the Internet's structure. This discussion of the Internet continues over the next 3 hours, which cover the World Wide Web (Hour 18, "HTTP, HTML, and the World Wide Web"), HTML 5 (Hour 19, "The New Web"), and web services (Hour 20, "Web Services").

At the end of this hour, you'll be able to

▶ Briefly describe the structure of the Internet

▶ Recognize and describe the components of a uniform resource identifier

How the Internet Looks

You'll have to look hard to find a description of what the Internet really is. Most descriptions of the Internet, unfortunately, favor simplicity over detail, and the reader is left with little more than the vague impression that the Internet is "a highway for data."

In fact, the details of Internet topology are so complex that few professional network administrators can tell you precisely what happens to the data that leaves their lines. Nor is it necessary for them to know. The stability and versatility of TCP/IP make it possible for a datagram to enter the cloud of the Internet and emerge without oversight in exactly the right place on the other side of the Earth. Where does the datagram go when it enters that cloud?

The original ARPAnet that gave rise to the Internet was based on a backbone network that carried traffic among the various participating institutions. As long as you were connected to the backbone, you could share information with any other network connected to the backbone (refer to Figure 8.9). The U.S. National Science Foundation's NSFNET replaced the original ARPAnet in 1987, adding power and greatly expanding the capacity. The Internet was still on a much smaller scale than it is today, mostly inhabited by universities and research institutions, and NSFNET was based on an extended version of the same basic backbone system.

As the Internet started to capture the world's imagination, the backbone eventually became inefficient and resistant to further expansion. In the mid-1990s, another, more decentralized system emerged. Today's Internet is a massive collection of mostly private networks sharing and selling access to other networks. At the heart of the system is a circle of what are called **Tier 1 networks**. Verizon, Sprint, AT&T, and Qwest all operate Tier 1 networks. Every Tier 1 network has a **peering** arrangement that provides free transit for traffic from every other Tier 1 network (at least in theory; the actual contractual arrangements between the networks usually are not public knowledge, because most Tier 1 networks are operated by private companies). The vast spaces spanned by the huge Tier 1 networks provide the Internet with much of its global connectivity, but Tier 1 is only part of the picture.

A system of **Tier 2 networks** operates around the edges of the Tier 1 networks. A Tier 2 network might lease access to a Tier 1 provider, but it might also have peering relationships with other Tier 2 providers to form a regional backbone and offer redundant pathways for downstream clients. By definition, a Tier 2 network operates with a combination of transit-free peering and leased IP transit. Tier 2 networks make their money by leasing Internet access to **Tier 3 networks**.

A Tier 3 network is what most of us would recognize as a typical Internet service provider (ISP). Tier 3 networks purchase access from an upstream provider (typically, a Tier 2 network) and make their money by selling Internet access to individual homes and businesses. Tier 3 ISPs lease what is called a **point of presence (POP)** connection (see Figure 17.1) to provide the subscribers on their lines with access to the greater Internet.

Phone Connection

It should come as no surprise that telephone companies such as Sprint and AT&T are major players in the Internet topology. The presence of these long-distance carriers underscores the fact that the Internet, like the phone system, is built from lots and lots and lots of cable strung over vast distances.

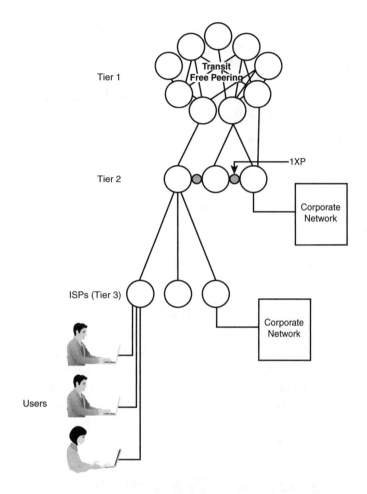

FIGURE 17.1
Today's Internet is a multitiered system of public and private networks.

Tier 1 and Tier 2 networks across the Internet (as well as some ISPs) intersect at large switching facilities called **Internet exchange points (IXPs)**. Verizon's MAE East (in the Washington, D.C., area) and MAE West (in the San Jose, California, area) are two of the busiest IXPs in the United States. IXPs are large facilities. Dozens, or sometimes hundreds, of participating networks can connect at a single exchange point. The IXP does not provide routing services. Instead, the member networks supply and maintain their own routers within a secure space made available at the IXP facility. The IXP facility itself is a local network, and traffic across the local net within the IXP facility that serves as an interface between the member networks is typically managed through switches operating at the Network Access layer (OSI Data Link layer).

The Internet, therefore, consists of thousands of intertwined business arrangements, covering lines, connections at the end of lines, bandwidth leases, and thousands of ISPs offering services for users, businesses, and organizations. You can see why the Internet is often depicted as a cloud: From a distance, it looks like a single object, but as you move closer, you can never really find the center, because it is everywhere around you, however you look at it.

The fact that the Internet is a single cohesive entity is not because of its physical connectivity, but because

▶ It has a common set of rules.

▶ It is managed and maintained by a common collection of organizations.

▶ It speaks a common language.

In Hour 1, "What Is TCP/IP?," you learned about the organizations governing the Internet, including the Internet Advisory Board (IAB) and the Internet Engineering Task Force (IETF). The language of the Internet is, of course, TCP/IP, but it is worth highlighting a significant element of the TCP/IP infrastructure that provides for Internet messaging on a global scale: the common naming and numbering system overseen by Internet Corporation for Assigned Names and Numbers (ICANN). The domain name system (DNS) naming system is more than the name resolution protocols described in Hour 10, "Name Resolution." Name service on a global scale requires an enormous human effort to manage the lower-tier organizations that manage the orderly assignment of Internet names. Without the powerful DNS naming system, the Internet would not be the pervasive force in daily life it is today.

What Happens on the Internet

The Internet really is a big TCP/IP network, and if you're not worried about security or time delays, you can use the Internet for almost anything you can do on a routed corporate local area network (LAN). Of course, the security considerations are substantial. You definitely *should not* use the Internet for anything you could do on a routed corporate LAN, but you could if you wanted to.

It is important to remember that all computers participating in a networking activity (on the Internet or on any other network) have one thing in common: They are running software that was designed for the activity in which they are engaged. Networking doesn't just happen. It requires protocol software (such as the TCP/IP software described in Hours 2 through 7), and it also requires applications at each end of the connection that are specifically designed to communicate with each other. As shown in Figure 17.2, most computers on the Internet can be classified as either clients (computers that request services) or servers (computers that provide services). A client application on the client computer was written specifically to interact with the server application on the server computer. The server application was written to listen for requests from the client and to respond to the requests.

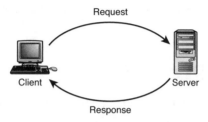

FIGURE 17.2
On the Internet, a computer typically acts as a client or a server.

Figure 17.3 shows the whole teaming ecosystem at a glance. A user sitting at a single computer anywhere in the world can connect to any of thousands of servers elsewhere in the world. A hierarchy of DNS servers resolves the target domain name to an IP address (in a process that is invisible to the user), and the client software on the user's computer establishes a connection. The server might provide web pages for the user to browse and view, instant messaging, or files to download with File Transfer Protocol (FTP). Or perhaps the user is connecting to a mail server to download incoming messages.

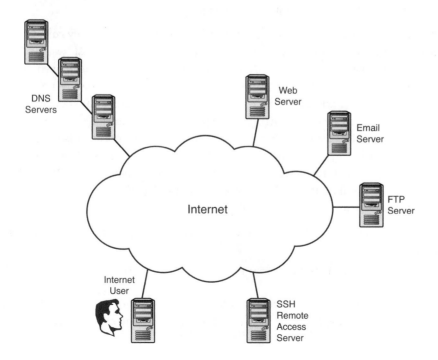

FIGURE 17.3
The Internet is a vast sea of services accessible from anywhere on Earth.

From the simple beginning of a few networked mainframes, the Internet has morphed into a sprawling jumble of services that the original professors and researchers couldn't have imagined. In addition to sending email and surfing the web, a new generation of Internet users can make phone calls, connect webcams, watch television, download music, listen to podcasts, and blog their deepest emotions—all through the miracle of TCP/IP. You'll learn more about many of these new web technologies in later hours.

URIs and URLs

As shown in Figure 17.3, the Internet is a gigantic mass of client systems requesting resources and server systems providing resources. If you look closer at the process, though, you'll realize that the protocol addressing rules discussed earlier in this book are not enough to support the rich array of services available on the Internet. The IP address or domain name can locate a host. The port number can point to a service running on the host. But what is the client requesting? What is the server supposed to do? Is there input for which the client is requesting output?

Experts have long understood the importance of providing a standard format for requesting Internet resources. Some have argued, in fact, that the presence of a unified request format is another reason why the Internet seems like a single big, cohesive essence rather than just a jumble of computers.

The request format most familiar to Internet users is what is commonly called a **uniform resource locator (URL)**. The URL is best known for the classic web address format: http://www.mercurial.org. URLs are so common now that they appear with little or no explanation on TV commercials and bubble gum wrappers. What we think of as a URL is actually a special case of a more general format known as a **uniform resource identifier (URI)**. The two acronyms are sometimes used interchangeably, but the distinction is important. Recent Internet documents have attempted to converge the terms. RFC 3986, "Uniform Resource Identifier Generic Syntax," states that future documents should use the more general term URI rather than URL. The term *identifier* is better than *locator* for the general case because every request doesn't actually point to a location.

The specification for the structure of a URI is over 60 pages, but the basic format is as follows:

```
scheme://authority/path?query#fragment
```

The **scheme** identifies a system for interpreting the request. The scheme field is often associated with a protocol. Table 17.1 shows some of the schemes used on the

Internet today. The classic http scheme is used with web addresses. Although alternative schemes such as gopher are less important than they once were, others, such as the ftp scheme, are still in common usage.

TABLE 17.1 URI Schemes

Scheme	Description	Reference
file	A file on the host system	RFC 1738
ftp	File Transfer Protocol	RFC 1738
gopher	The Gopher protocol	RFC 4266
http	Hypertext Transfer Protocol	RFC 2616
https	Hypertext Transfer Protocol Secure	RFC 2818
im	Instant Messaging	RFC 3860
ldap	Lightweight Directory Access Protocol	RFC 4516
mailto	Electronic mail address	RFC 2368
nfs	Network File System protocol	RFC 2224
pop	Post Office Protocol v3	RFC 2384
telnet	Telnet Interactive session	RFC 4248

The **authority**, which begins with a double slash (//), defines the user, host, and port associated with the request. A full expression of the authority component might look like this:

```
//joeyesterday8042
```

As you learned in Hour 6, "The Transport Layer," a default port number is often associated with the protocol, so the port number is typically omitted. The username is necessary only if the user must provide credentials to access the resource, which is uncommon for the Web but more common with a protocol like FTP.

By the Way

Logging In

Even if the user is required to provide credentials, you still might not need to specify a user in the URI. Many services prompt for a user ID and password after the initial request.

Without the user and the port, the authority field looks more like the basic web address we all appreciate:

```
//www.bonzai.com
```

Or coupled with the scheme component:

```
http://www.bonzai.com
```

In this example, the host is expressed as a DNS domain name, but you can also refer to a host by its IP address.

The path component points down through a hierarchy of directories to a file that is the subject of the request. In the case of the http scheme, if the path is omitted, the request points to a default web page for the domain (the home page). The default filename for a web page is typically index.html. Most users by now are also familiar with the practice of typing additional directory and filenames after the domain name:

```
http://www.bonzai.com/trees/LittleTrees.pdf
```

The query and fragment components of the URI are rarely typed or interpreted by humans. The precise meaning of these components can vary depending on the scheme, and some schemes don't even support the query and fragment components. The easiest way to observe the query field in the wild is to type a search request into a search engine like Google and then examine the URI that appears in the address bar.

The preceding example considers the URI in the context of the hugely popular Hypertext Transfer Protocol (HTTP) used on the World Wide Web. (You learn more about HTTP and its companion markup language, Hypertext Markup Language (HTML) in Hour 18, "HTTP, HTML, and the World Wide Web.") Keep in mind, though, that each of the different scheme specifications can define how to interpret the information in the URI. The generic URI specification is intentionally kept separate from the details defined in the specifications for each of the schemes so that the schemes can evolve without requiring a change to the basic format. Table 17.1 also lists the RFCs associated with each scheme.

Summary

The Internet consists of computers all over the world requesting and providing services. The networks that make up the Internet fall into three basic categories. Tier 1 networks have free-transit peering relationships with other Tier 1 networks. Tier 2 networks operate through a combination of peering and purchased IP-transit arrangements. Tier 3 networks (such as a typical local ISP) purchase Internet connectivity from an upstream provider and sell access to businesses and individual users.

The URI format offers a standard means for identifying and locating those resources. All these protocols are different, however, and the details of communication vary depending on the service. Later hours introduce you to some of the critical services at work on the Internet today.

Q&A

Q. *Why do Internet authorities want to replace the popular term URL?*

A. Uniform resource locator (URL) is a special case of the general term uniform resource identifier (URI). Experts prefer the more general term URI because the identifier sometimes doesn't just specify a location but might also include additional information.

Q. *Why have some Asian and Eastern European countries suggested starting their own independent alternatives to DNS and the URI format?*

A. The restriction of the Latin character set is unintuitive for users who speak languages with non-Latin characters.

Workshop

The following workshop is composed of a series of quiz questions and practical exercises. The quiz questions test your overall understanding of the current material. The practical exercises give you the opportunity to apply the concepts discussed during the current hour and to build on the knowledge acquired in previous hours of study. Take time to complete the quiz questions and exercises before continuing. Refer to Appendix A, "Answers to Quizzes and Exercises," for answers.

Quiz

1. What is the difference between a Tier 1 and Tier 2 network?
2. What part of the URI is the scheme?
3. Where is the scheme located in the URI?
4. What are four schemes in common use on the Internet?
5. What file will most web servers send by default if the filename is omitted from the destination directory in the URI?

Exercises

1. Enter a search term in Google or Bing and study the URI of the result. The major search engines are getting better about returning explicit results, so you might have to experiment a little to find a fully aggregated, search URI. Try misspelling a word and then click the "Did you mean" link. When you turn up a search URI, identify the scheme, path, and query components. Look for a fragment component.

2. If there is a website or FTP site where you typically log in by entering your credentials in a dialog box, try sending your user name as part of the URI. (This doesn't always work, depending on the server configuration.)

Key Terms

Review the following list of key terms:

▸ **Authority:** The portion of the URI identifying the host, users, and port.

▸ **Internet exchange point (IXP):** A facility that provides access to the Internet.

▸ **Peering:** A free-transit arrangement between a pair of Internet provider networks. The participating networks agree to share traffic across the connection for no charge.

▸ **Point of presence (POP):** An attachment point to the Internet leased by an ISP.

▸ **Scheme:** The portion of the URI that identifies the protocol or system for interpreting the rest of the URI.

▸ **Tier 1 network:** One of several large networks at the core of the Internet that participate in a system of mutual peering arrangements.

▸ **Tier 2 network:** A midlevel network in the Internet infrastructure that might purchase or sell access to some networks and participate in peering relationships with others.

▸ **Tier 3 network:** A retail-level Internet network that sells Internet access to businesses and end users and purchases access from an upstream provider (typically a Tier 2 network). Many local ISPs are Tier 3 networks.

▸ **Uniform resource identifier (URI):** An alphanumeric string used to identify an Internet resource.

▸ **Uniform resource locator (URL):** A type of URI that locates a resource. A common URL form is web addresses (www.sams.com).

HOUR 18

HTTP, HTML, and the World Wide Web

What You'll Learn in This Hour:

▶ HTML

▶ HTTP

▶ Web browsers

The World Wide Web began as a universal graphic display framework for the Internet. Since its inception, the Web has come to dominate public perceptions of the Internet, and it has revolutionized the way we think about application interfaces. This hour provides an introduction to HTTP, HTML, and the Web.

At the completion of this hour, you will be able to

▶ Show how the World Wide Web works

▶ Build a basic web page using text and HTML tags

▶ Discuss the HTTP protocol and describe how it works

What Is the World Wide Web?

The view of the web page you see through the window of your web **browser** is the result of a conversation between the browser and a web server computer. The language used for that conversation is called **Hypertext Transfer Protocol (HTTP)**. The data delivered from the server to the client is a finely crafted jumble of text, images, addresses, and formatting codes rendered to a unified document through an amazing versatile formatting language called **Hypertext Markup Language** (HTML).

The basic elements of what we know today as the World Wide Web were created by Tim Berners-Lee in 1989 at the CERN research institute in Geneva, Switzerland. Berners-Lee created a subtle and powerful information system by bringing together three technologies that were already in development at the time:

- **Markup language:** A system of instructions and formatting codes embedded in text

- **Hypertext:** A means for embedding links to documents, images, and other elements in text

- **The Internet:** (As you know by now) A global computer network of clients requesting services and servers providing services through TCP/IP

Markup languages began in the 1960s as a means for adding formatting and typesetting codes to the simple text used by early computers. At the time, text files were used throughout the computing world for configuration files, online help documents, and electronic mail messages. When people started using computers for letters, memos, and other finished documents, they needed a way to specify elements such as headlines, italics, bold font, and margins. Some of the early markup languages (such as TeX, which is still in use today) were developed as a means for scientists to format and typeset mathematical equations.

By the time modern-day word processing programs began to emerge, vendors had developed numerous systems (many of them proprietary) for coding formatting information into a text document. Some of these systems used ASCII-based codes. Others used different digital markers to denote formatting information.

| **Compatibility** |
| Of course, these formatting code systems work only if the application that writes the document and the application that reads the document agree on what each code means. |

Berners-Lee and other HTML pioneers wanted a universal, vendor-neutral system for encoding format information. They wanted this markup system to include not just typesetting codes but also references to image files and links to other documents.

The concept of hypertext (a live link within text that switches the view to the document referenced in the link) also evolved in the 1960s. Berners-Lee brought the hypertext concept to the Internet through the development of the uniform resource locator (URL) (or uniform resource indicator [URI]; see Hour 17, "The Internet: A Closer Look"). Links let the reader view the online information in small doses. The reader can choose whether to link to another page for additional information. HTML documents can be assembled into unified systems of pages and links (see Figure 18.1). A visitor can find a different path through the data depending on how the visitor traverses the links. And the web developer has almost unlimited ability to define where a link will lead. The link can lead to another HTML document in the same directory, a document in a different directory, or even a document on a different computer. The link might lead to a totally different website on another computer across the world.

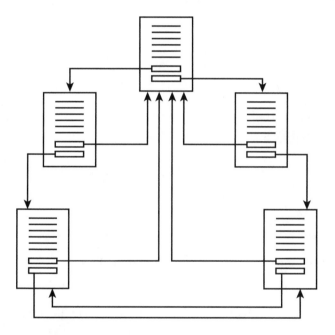

FIGURE 18.1
A website is a unified system of pages and links.

As you learned in Hour 17, the form of URL most associated with the Web is

http://www.dobro.com

It is also common to see a path and filename appended to the URL:

http://www.dobro.com/techniques/repair/fix.html

A web browser navigates by URLs. You access a web page by entering the URL of the page in the address box of the browser window (see Figure 18.2). When you click a link, the browser opens the web page specified in the link's URL.

FIGURE 18.2
Enter the URL in the address box of the browser window.

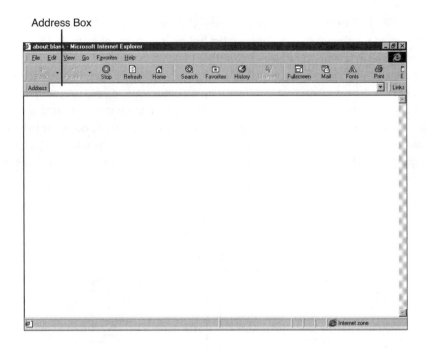

To summarize this brief introduction, a basic HTML document contains some combination of

- Text

- Graphics

- Text formatting codes (font and layout information)

- References to secondary files such as graphics files

- Links to other HTML documents or to other locations in the current document

To visit a website, the user enters the URL of the website into the web browser window. The browser initiates a connection to the web server specified in the URL. The server sends the HTML data across the network to the web browser. The web browser interprets the HTML data to create the view of the web page that appears in the browser window.

Understanding HTML

HTML is the payload that is transmitted through the processes of HTTP. As you learned earlier in this hour, an HTML document includes text, formatting codes, references to other files, and links. When you inspect the contents of a basic HTML document using a text processing application such as Windows Notepad or UNIX's vi, you'll find that the document is actually an ordinary text file. The file contains any text that will appear with the page, and it also includes a number of special HTML codes called **tags**. Tags are instructions to the browser. They do not appear as written on the web page, but they affect the way the data appears and the way the page behaves. The HTML tags supply all the formatting, file references, and links associated with a web page. Some important HTML tags are shown in Table 18.1.

TABLE 18.1   Some Important HTML Tags

Tag	Description
<HTML>	Marks beginning and end of HTML content in the file.
<HEAD>	Marks the beginning and end of the header section.
<BODY>	Marks the beginning and end of the body section, which describes the text that will appear in the browser window.
<H1>, <H2>, <H3>, <H4>, <H5>, and <H6>	Marks the beginning and end of a heading. Each heading tag represents a different heading level. <H1> is the highest level.
<B>	Marks the beginning and end of a section of bold text.
<U>	Marks the beginning and end of a section of underlined text.
<I>	Marks the beginning and end of a section of italicized text.
<FONT>	Marks the beginning and end of a section with special font characteristics. See Table 18.2 for some of the available font attributes.
<A>	Defines an anchor—typically used to mark a link. The link destination URL appears inside the first <A> tag as a value for the HREF attribute (as described later in this section).
<IMG>	Specifies an image file that should appear in the text. The file URL appears in the tag as a value for the SRC attribute. (You'll learn more about attributes later in this section.)

Of course, there is much more to HTML than a single table can convey. Many tags apply to a block of text. If so, the tag appears at the beginning and the end of the block. The tag at the end of the block includes the slash character (/) to signify that it is an end tag. In other words, the callout for an H1 heading would be tagged as follows:

```
<H1>Dewey Defeats Truman</H1>
```

An HTML document is supposed to begin with a <!DOCTYPE> declaration. The !DOCTYPE defines the version of HTML used for the document. For HTML 4.0, the !DOCTYPE command is as follows:

```
<!DOCTYPE HTML PUBLIC "-//W3C/DTD HTML 4.0//EN">
```

(Web pages that use special browser extensions might specify a different document type.)

Most browsers don't require the !DOCTYPE statement, and many HTML tutorials don't even discuss the !DOCTYPE.

Following the !DOCTYPE statement is the <HTML> tag. The rest of the document is enclosed between the <HTML> tag and a corresponding </HTML> tag at the end of the file. Within the beginning and ending <HTML> tags, the document is divided into the following two sections:

▶ The head (enclosed between the <HEAD> and </HEAD> tags) contains information about the document. The information in the head does not appear on the web page, although the <TITLE> tag specifies a title that will appear in the title bar of the browser window. The <TITLE> is a required element. Other elements of the <HEAD> section are optional, such as the <STYLE> tag for information on document styles. See an HTML text for more on <STYLE>.

▶ The body (enclosed between the <BODY> and </BODY> tags) is the text that actually appears on the web page and any HTML tags related to that text.

A simple HTML document is as follows:

```
<!DOCTYPE HTML PUBLIC "-//W3C/DTD HTML 4.0//EN">
<HTML>
<HEAD>
<TITLE> Ooh This is Easy </TITLE>
</HEAD>
<BODY>
Easy!
</BODY>
<HTML>
```

If you save the preceding HTML to a text file and then open the file with a web browser, Easy! appears in the browser window. (Depending on your browser and operating system, you might have to save this file with an .htm or .html extension or open it as an HTML file.) The title bar includes the title Ooh This is Easy (see Figure 18.3).

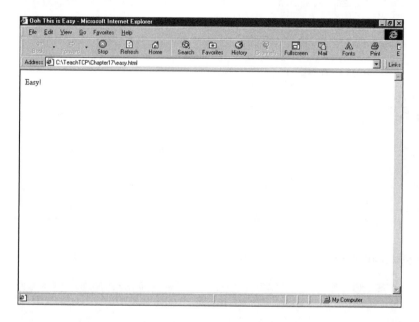

FIGURE 18.3
A very easy web page example.

You can spice up the page with additional text and formatting in the body section. The following example adds the <H1> and <H2> tags for headings, the <P> tag for a paragraph, the <B> tag for bold, the <I> tag for italics, and the <FONT> tag for font information. Note that the <FONT> tag includes an attribute. Attributes are parameters enclosed within the tag that provide additional information. See Table 18.2 for other font attributes.

```
<!DOCTYPE HTML PUBLIC "-//W3C/DTD HTML 4.0//EN">
<HTML>
<HEAD>
<TITLE> Ooh This is Easy </TITLE>
</HEAD>
<BODY>
<H1>The Easy and Hard of HTML</H1>

<P><U>Webster's Dictionary</U> defines HTML as <I>"a small snail found
originally in the Canary Island and ranging now to the Archipelago of
Parakeets."</I> I borrow from this theme in my consideration of HTML as a
language that is both easy and hard.
</P><H2>HTML is Easy</H2>
```

```
<P>HTML is easy to learn and use because everyone reacts to it
energetically. You can walk into a bar and start speaking HTML, and the
man beside you will <B>happily</B> tell you his many accomplishments.</P>
<H2>HTML is Hard</H2>

<P>HTML is hard because the options are bewildering. You never know when
to use <FONT SIZE=1>small text</FONT> and when to use <FONT SIZE=7>big
 text</FONT>.</P>
</BODY>
</HTML>
```

TABLE 18.2   HTML <FONT> Tag Attributes

Attribute	Description
SIZE	Relative font size setting. Values vary from 1 to 7: <FONT SIZE=7>.
LANG	Language code denoting the language in which the text is written.
FACE	Typeface setting: <FONT FACE="Arial">.
COLOR	Color of the text: <FONT COLOR="RED">.

The preceding example appears in the browser as shown in Figure 18.4.

FIGURE 18.4
Expanding the
easy example.

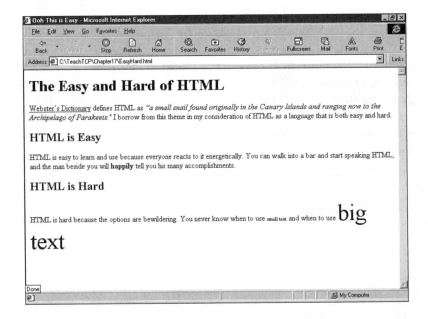

As you learned earlier in this hour, the hypertext link is an important element of web design. A link is a reference to another document or another part of the current document. If the user clicks the highlighted text of the link, the browser immediately opens the document referenced in the link. The effect is that the user appears to lilt through an endless garden of colorful and informative content.

What is a Browser?

As you lilt through this colorful garden, pause occasionally to consider that the term *browser* originally referred to a giraffe or a large dinosaur eating leaves out of trees.

By the Way

A link appears in the HTML file as a tag. The simplest form of a link uses the <A> tag with the URL of the link destination given as a value for the HREF attribute. For instance, in the preceding example, if you would like the words "Archipelago of Parakeets" to appear as hypertext with a link to a website that tells about the archipelago, enclose the words within <A> tags as follows:

```
ranging now to the <A HREF="http://www.ArchipelagoParakeets.com">
Archipelago of Parakeets</A>. I borrow from this theme
```

The versatile HTML format includes many additional options. You can place a hotspot link inside a picture. You can create your own style sheets with special tags for preformatted paragraph styles. You can structure the web page with tables, columns, forms, and frames. Or you can add radio buttons, check boxes, and pull-down menus. In the early days of HTML, designers coded all the HTML directly into their documents using text editors (as described in the preceding examples). Professional web designers now work with special web development applications, such as Adobe Dreamweaver or Microsoft FrontPage, that hide the details of HTML and let the designer view the page as it will appear to the user. New tools such as wikis and content management systems (CMSs) provide additional options for effortless web design.

Static, preformed HTML documents like those described in this section are still widely used, but many websites today use dynamic HTML techniques to generate the web content at the time of the request.

Captialization

With classic HTML tags, capitalization is not significant; however, later standards such as Extensible Markup Language (XML) and XHTML pay more attention to capitalization. XML is case sensitive, and XHTML requires lowercase element and attribute names.

By the Way

Understanding HTTP

As you learned earlier, web servers and browsers communicate using the Hypertext Transfer Protocol (HTTP). HTTP (1.1) is described in RFC 2616, and later documents have extended HTTP functionality. The purpose of HTTP is to support the transfer of HTML documents. HTTP is an application-level protocol. The HTTP client and server applications use the reliable TCP transport protocol to establish a connection.

HTTP does the following:

▶ Establishes a connection between the browser (the client) and the server

▶ Negotiates settings and establishes parameters for the session

▶ Provides for the orderly transfer of HTML content

▶ Closes the connection with the server

Although the nature of web communication has become extremely complex, most of that complexity relates to how the server builds the HTML content and what the browser does with the content it receives. The actual process of transferring the content through HTML is relatively uncluttered.

When you enter a URL into the browser window, the browser first checks the scheme of the URL to determine the protocol. (Most web browsers support other protocols besides HTTP.) If the browser determines that the URL refers to a resource on an HTTP site, it extracts the domain name system (DNS) name from the URL and initiates the name resolution process. The client computer sends the DNS lookup request to a name server and receives the server's IP address. The browser then uses the server's IP address to initiate a TCP connection with the server. (See Hour 6, "The Transport Layer," for more on TCP.)

> **Persistence**
>
> In older versions of HTTP (before version 1.1), the client and server opened a new TCP connection for each item transferred. Recent versions of HTTP allow the client and server to maintain a persistent connection.

After the TCP connection is established, the browser uses the HTTP GET command to request the web page from the server. The GET command contains the URL of the resource the browser is requesting and the version of HTTP the browser wants to use for the transaction. In most cases, the browser can send the relative URL with the GET request (rather than the full URL) because the connection with the server has already been established:

```
GET /watergate/tapes/transcript HTTP/1.1
```

Several other optional `field:value` pairs might follow the `GET` command, specifying settings such as the language, browser type, and acceptable file types.

The server response consists of a header followed by the requested document. The format of the response header is as follows:

```
HTTP/1.1 status_code reason-phrase
field:value
field:value...
```

The status code is a three-digit number describing the status of the request. The reason-phrase is a brief description of the status. Some common status codes are shown in Table 18.3. As you can see, the leftmost digit of the code identifies a general category. The 100s are informational, the 200s denote success, the 300s specify redirection, the 400s show a client error, and the 500s specify a server error. You might be familiar with the famous 404 code, which often appears in response to a missing page or a mistyped URL. Like the client request, the server response can also include a number of optional `field:value` pairs. Some of the header fields are shown in Table 18.4. Any field that is not understood by the browser is ignored.

TABLE 18.3   Some Common HTTP Status Codes

Code	Reason-Phrase	Description
100	Continue	Request is in process.
200	OK	Request is successful.
202	Accepted	Request accepted for processing but not finished.
301	Moving Permanently	Resource has a new address.
302	Moving Temporarily	Resource has a new temporary address.
400	Bad Request	Server doesn't recognize the request.
401	Unauthorized	Authorization failed.
404	Not Found	Resource requested doesn't exist.
406	Not Acceptable	Content will not be acceptable to browser.
500	Internal Server Error	Server encountered error.
503	Service Unavailable	Server is overloaded or not working.

TABLE 18.4   Examples of HTTP Header Fields

Field	Value Must Be	Description
`Content-Length`	integer	Size of the content object in octets
`Content-Encoding`	`x-compress x-gzip`	Value representing the type of encoding associated with the message
`Date`	Standard date format defined in RFC 850	Date in Greenwich mean time when the object was created
`Last-modified date`	Standard date format defined in RFC 850	Date in Greenwich mean time when the object was last modified
`Content-Language`	Language code per ISO 3316	The language in which the object was written

As you can see from Table 18.4, some of the header fields are purely informational. Other header fields might contain information used to parse and process the incoming HTML document.

The `Content-Length` field is particularly important. In the earlier HTTP version 1.0, each request/response cycle required a new TCP connection. The client opened a connection and initiated a request. The server fulfilled the request and then closed the connection. In that situation, the client knew when the server had stopped sending data because the server closed the TCP connection. Unfortunately, this process required the increased overhead necessary for continually opening and closing connections. HTTP 1.1 allows the client and server to maintain the connection for longer than a single transmission. In that case, the client needs some way of knowing when a single response is finished. The `Content-Length` field specifies the length of the HTML object associated with the response. If the server doesn't know the length of the object it is sending—a situation increasingly common with the appearance of dynamic HTML—the server sends the header field `Connection:close` to notify the browser that the server will specify the end of the data by closing the connection.

HTTP also supports a negotiation phase in which the server and browser agree to common settings for certain format and preference options.

Scripting

The web page has evolved tremendously in the last 20 years, and most professional web pages today are quite unlike the ideal described earlier in this hour of a simple text file embedded with static HTML tags.

Modern web pages are often a complex pastiche of objects, scripts, and machine-generated code produced on-the-fly in response to user input and back-end data. The versatile HTML makes it easy to insert data or additional instructions into the page as it is delivered, or to add code that will execute after the page arrives.

Web browsers have become very adept at interpreting and manipulating this incoming code. As you'll learn in the next hour, special tools called content management systems run on the web server, obscuring the details of HTML code generation to provide a simple interface for the web developer.

> ▶ Two fundamental techniques for autogenerating web code are **server-side scripting** and **client-side scripting**.

As you will learn later in this hour, the collection of plug-in and add-on applications running on the client system add another dimension to the activities that can be triggered from a web page. For more about advanced web techniques see Hour 19, "The New Web," and Hour 20, "Web Services."

Most of these technologies are actually programming topics. The end user doesn't really have to know whether the image or table embedded in a web page comes from a static callout or a script. However, a brief introduction to some of the concepts will provide some insights on how HTML is used on today's Internet.

Server-Side Scripting

Server-side scripting lets the server accept input from the client and process that input behind the scenes. A common server-side scripting scenario is shown in Figure 18.5. The process is as follows:

1. The user browses to a page that includes a form for purchasing a product or entering visitor information.

2. The server generates the form based on user choices and transmits the form to the browser.

3. The user enters the necessary information into the form, and the browser transmits the form back to the server. (Note that the HTML form feature reverses the usual process. The browser sends content to the server at the server's request.)

4. The server accepts the data from the browser and uses a programming interface to pass the data to programs that process the user information. If the user is purchasing a product, these behind-the-scenes programs may check credit card information or send a shipment order to the mail room. If the user is adding his name to a mailing list or joining a restricted online site, a program may add the user information to a database.

FIGURE 18.5
A server-side scripting scenario.

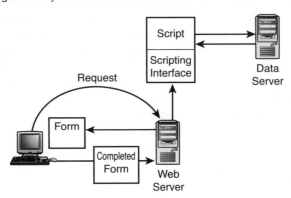

Several programming languages and environments have evolved to help developers build server-based web applications. One method for interfacing a program or script with a web page is through the **Common Gateway Interface (CGI)**. CGI was developed to accept form-based input from a web user, process that input, and then generate output in the form of HTML. CGI scripts are commonly written in the Perl language, but CGI is compatible with other languages, including C.

PHP is also becoming increasingly popular as a language for web development. A simple PHP script is often embedded within an HTML tag:

```
<?php code here... ?>
```

Or defined using the `<script language>` tag:

```
<script language="php"> code here ... </script>
```

A web server that supports PHP parses and executes the code between the brackets, inserting the output of the PHP command set in place of the tag as the page is delivered to the client.

Microsoft's Active Server Page (ASP) and the later ASP.NET technologies are also popular server-side web techniques. ASP.NET has been very influential for web development in recent years. As of this writing, however, it appears that HTML5 and other recent technologies might figure more importantly into the next generation of websites. Hour 19 discusses HTML5 in more detail.

The concept of a web interface to a custom, server-side application has led to a whole paradigm for programming known as the web services environment. Many of the leading hardware and software vendors, including IBM, Microsoft, and others, have developed sophisticated infrastructures to support web service programming. See Hour 20 for more about web service technologies and techniques.

Client-Side Scripting

Another way to integrate scripts with the web environment is on the client side (that is, on the local client computer system that is running the web browser application). Whereas a server-side script is executed on the server and the output of the script is embedded in the page, a client-side solution transfers the embedded script along with the rest of the HTML code and text, and the script is executed by the browser.

JavaScript and VBScript are two common client-side scripting technologies. The script file is often referenced through the HTML:

```
<script src="/script.js" type="text/javascript"></script>
```

The tag can reference the actual instructions, or it can refer to an external file containing the code. In either case, this technique only works if the client computer includes support for the scripting language referenced in the code.

For certain types of applications, client-side scripting is a more efficient alternative. An interpreter executing the script on the client has a much more detailed view of the local environment. Also, confining interactive elements to the client reduces network traffic and improves performance.

AJAX (which is sometimes billed as an acronym for Asynchronous JavaScript and XML) is a collection of technologies that use client-side scripting to provide for seamless update of web content without a full refresh of the web page. Other common client-side techniques offer interactive options for the user, invoke animations or other multimedia effects, or respond to information on the state of the client system.

Client-side scripting is extremely common, but as you can imagine, it poses some security challenges. What intruder would not love the chance to execute code on the client system? Most systems now take measures to restrict the privileges of code executing on the browser, and, as you will learn in the next section, users have some freedom to limit the use of browser-launched scripts. As is often the case with network-related software, the best precaution is often to keep your system up to date and install security patches whenever they are available.

Web Browsers

As you probably already know, the whole business of the World Wide Web depends on a very special and versatile application known as a web browser. In the client-server model discussed earlier in this book, the web browser is the client. Early, simple browsers originally just rendered the early, simple, static HTML files discussed in earlier hours. When web data arrived from the server, browsers interpreted the tags, formatting the text with the specified fonts, links, and photos.

As web data became more complex, the web browser evolved with it, and as the web became the center of Internet commercial activity, the browser became a major source of competition and corporate leverage among leading software companies in an era that is now known as the "browser wars."

Why declare a war over browsers, which have no market value in their own right and are mostly given away as free software (either bundled with the OS or downloadable at no charge)? Big companies like Microsoft and Netscape (and later Google) knew that by controlling the browser they could control a whole range of technologies surrounding Internet activity, not just web servers but also the lucrative and influential business of providing development tools and application programming interfaces (APIs) that interact with the operating system.

At one point, Microsoft even said it had embedded its browser Internet Explorer into the operating system itself in a way that could not be separated (an argument that was later rejected by the courts). Microsoft wanted to extend its control of the OS market to control of the browser market so that they could control the development environment and build pathways back into the operating system to ensure the continued dominance of their OS projects.

From the user's perspective, the browser is the focal point for everything that happens on today's Internet. The purpose of the HTML and HTTP standards is to ensure that any standard-compliant browser can communicate with any standard-compliant server. However, the big vendors have a tendency to use the standard as a minimum and to add their own enhancements, which has the same effect of locking in the user who has invested in building custom tools for a proprietary development environment. Microsoft was forced through legal action to open its APIs, which has largely addressed this issue. Even so, there are still custom web tools out in the world that will work only with Internet Explorer.

To fully participate in today's Internet, a browser must support the client-side scripting described earlier in this hour through support for JavaScript or some other scripting technology. Depending on the browser and system, this support might take the form of a browser plug-in or add-on or it might be implemented through the operating system. A full-featured browser also must provide support for digital signatures and certificates to allow the user to engage in secure transactions and communication through Secure Sockets Layer/Transport Layer Security (SSL/TLS) encryption with Hypertext Transfer Protocol Secure (HTTPS). (For more about encrypted communication, see Hour 11, "TCP/IP Security.")

Modern browsers can launch other applications if necessary to open files or execute procedures. Using other applications for these extended capabilities keeps the browser itself from getting too big and cumbersome, and it allows application developers to concentrate on their own area of specialty. These external applications are typically referred to as add-ons, plug-ins, or helper applications.

Browsers are often smart enough to recognize a missing plug-in and ask whether you want to install it if it is needed to open a file or start a video. Most browsers also provide a means for manually adding, removing, and managing the plug-ins included within the configuration. For instance, in Internet Explorer, select Manage Add-ons in the Tools menu (Figure 18.6).

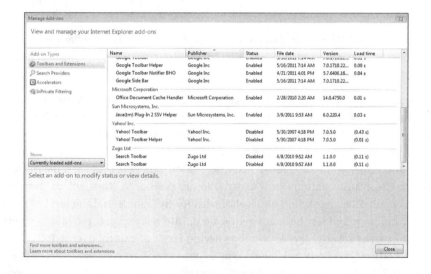

FIGURE 18.6
Managing add-ons in Internet Explorer.

Classic examples of browser plug-ins are Adobe tools such as the Acrobat reader and the Flash player. When a browser encounters a reference to a link or reference to a PDF file, it calls the appropriate Acrobat plug-in to open the file and displays the contents in a browser window.

Some plug-ins provide other forms of extensions and enhanced capabilities. For instance, Firefox provides an extensive collection of add-ons for alerts, social networking, and privacy (see Figure 18.7).

FIGURE 18.7
Firefox offers
add-ons for
social network-
ing, privacy,
alerts, and
other uses.

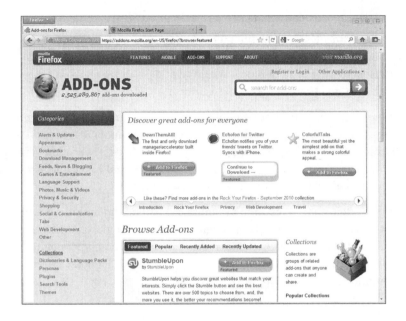

As you learn in the next hour, the recent HTML5 standard might reduce the importance of certain plug-ins such as Flash by offering direct support for video codecs
within the browser.

The other critical component of browser configuration, in addition to extending
what the browser can do, is limiting what the browser can do. With new threats
appearing on the Internet every day, and old threats continuing to succeed despite
the continuing efforts of the authorities, the security configuration becomes an
important aspect of the browser environment. Most browsers provide a means for
defining the security settings for web activities, in essence to "turn on" or "turn off"
certain capabilities depending on level of trust for the source and the level of privacy
and security required for the user environment. Internet Explorer provides a sliding
scale of Internet security levels, offering varying levels of control over scripts,
ActiveX controls, and other elements that might appear on a website (see Figure
18.8). Click the Custom level button to choose your own cocktail of available security settings.

In the simplified world of Mac OS, the Safari browser offers a means for enabling
and disabling Java and JavaScript, blocking pop-ups, and configuring other aspects
of the security environment. Choose Preferences in the Safari menu and select the
Security option to configure Safari security settings (see Figure 18.9). Firefox,
Chrome, Opera, and other browsers offer similar features. Many browsers also let
the user predefine a list of trusted sites that are allowed to operate with fewer security restrictions.

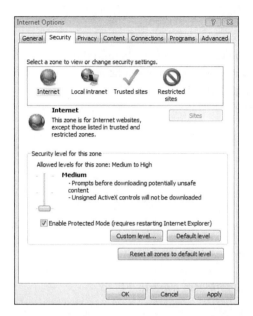

FIGURE 18.8
Most browsers have a way to fine-tune the security level. A more secure browser is safer, but a high security setting can block legitimate web activity.

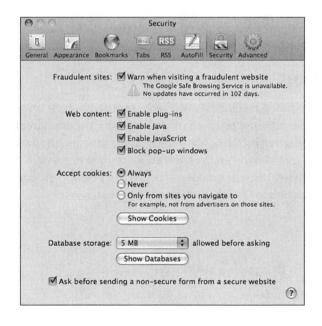

FIGURE 18.9
Safari's simpler interface lets you enable JavaScript and define a cookie policy.

Summary

This hour described the processes at work behind the famous Internet service known as the World Wide Web. You learned about how the Web works. You also learned about HTML documents and about HTTP. This hour also introduced the concept of dynamic HTML. You learn more about dynamic HTML and other web techniques in Hours 19 and 20.

Q&A

Q. *What HTML tag changes the color of text?*

A. To change the color of text, use the <FONT> tag with the COLOR attribute:

```
<FONT COLOR="RED"> red text </FONT>
```

Q. *What HTML tag defines a hypertext link?*

A. For a hypertext link, use the <A> tag with the HREF attribute:

```
<A HREF="www.ElvisIsDiseased.com">I'm All Shook Up</A>
```

Workshop

The following workshop is composed of a series of quiz questions and practical exercises. The quiz questions test your overall understanding of the current material. The practical exercises give you the opportunity to apply the concepts discussed during the current hour and to build on the knowledge acquired in previous hours of study. Take time to complete the quiz questions and exercises before continuing. Refer to Appendix A, "Answers to Quizzes and Exercises," for answers.

Quiz

1. Why does HTTP support a negotiation phase?

2. What are the major sections of an HTML document?

3. Consider a website that includes a back-end database with book titles and pricing information. Should you use a server-side or client-side script to provide this information for users?

4. Suppose you just installed a new system and it is working very well, but when you go to your favorite website and click a PDF file, it doesn't open. How would you fix this?

Exercise

Open a web browser and go to a popular commercial website of your choice (for example, http://www.cnn.com or www.slashdot.org). Select the browser menu option for showing the web page source. For instance, in Internet Explorer, choose the View menu and select Source. In Safari, choose the View menu and select View Source. In Firefox, choose Web Developer in the Firefox menu and choose View Page Source.

A separate window opens, showing the HTML associated with the page. You will find many of the elements described in this hour. Look for some ordinary static HTML, with text that displays in the main view of the page. Look for headings with <H1>, <H2>, or <H3> tags. Look for paragraphs with <P> tags. Look for a hypertext link. Now search for the term *JavaScript*. Find the JavaScript code. Try to determine the effect of each block of code on the finished view of the site you see in the browser window.

Key Terms

Review the following list of key terms:

▶ **Body:** The section of the HTML document that contains the text that will actually appear in the browser window. The body section is enclosed between the <BODY> and </BODY> tags.

▶ **Browser:** An HTTP client application. Most modern browsers can also process other protocols, such as FTP.

▶ **Client-side scripting:** A type of script that executes on the client computer (the browser system).

▶ **CGI (Common Gateway Interface):** A programming interface that lets a designer integrate scripts and programs with a web page.

▶ **Head:** The beginning section of an HTML document containing the title of the document and other optional parameters. The head section is enclosed between the <HEAD> and </HEAD> tags.

▶ **Hypertext link:** A highlighted portion of a web page. When the user clicks on the link, the browser goes to an alternative document or location specified as a URL in the link definition.

▶ **Hypertext Markup Language (HTML):** A markup language used for building web pages. HTML consists of text and special codes describing formatting, links, and graphics.

▶ **Hypertext Transfer Protocol (HTTP):** The protocol used to transmit HTML content between the server and client.

▶ **PHP:** A popular programming language used in web development.

▶ **Server-side scripting:** A form of script that executes on the server system (the web server).

▶ **Tag:** An HTML instruction.

The New Web

What You'll Learn in This Hour:

▶ The new Web
▶ Peer-to-peer networking
▶ IRC and IM
▶ The semantic Web
▶ XHTML
▶ HTML5

New ideas abound on the Web, leading to a variety of new forms and formats, but what looks new from the outside might just be the artful coordination of existing tools and services. This hour describes the view from the new Web.

At the completion of this hour, you'll be able to

▶ Discuss blogs, wikis, and social networking sites

▶ Explain the purpose of XHTML

▶ Understand how a peer-to-peer network works

▶ Describe IRC and IM messaging

▶ Explain the purpose of the semantic Web

Web 2.0

The World Wide Web has recently taken on a new look, with a new generation of smarter, more interactive websites serving a new generation of users. These technologies collectively fall under the name **Web 2.0**.

The components of the new Web look different from old-style websites, and they are quite revolutionary from the viewpoint of human interaction and communal experience, but behind the scenes, the Web 2.0 technologies are a logical development based on many of the same components used with the web services infrastructure:

▶ **Database systems:** A separate system for storing and managing data

▶ **Design elements:** Predefined standard elements

▶ **Layout:** A structure for the site

▶ **Scripting:** A means for generating Hypertext Markup Language (HTML) code by injecting data into the predefined structure

Web wonders such as **blogs**, **wikis**, and **social networking** sites hide these details, so the user is free to craft a web identity through images, sounds, and written language without ever having to worry about pesky details like HTML.

Content Management Systems

It didn't take long for web developers and users to discover that the tedious task of entering HTML tags into text files was an inefficient use of expensive talent. Also, the explosion of web development into the commercial space led to a new generation of web designers who were oriented more as graphic artists or editors than as classic computer programmers. This need to simplify web development and extend it to a new class of non-technical (or not-as-technical) professionals led to a collection of web editing tools that obscured the details of the HTML and let the user work within the a simple graphical interface that lets the developer view the page as if seeing it in its final form. This concept came to be known as a **WYSIWYG** editing interface. This expansive acronym, which is usually pronounced *wizzy-wig*, stands for What You See Is What You Get. In other words, you can manipulate text, images, and other features in a context that appears like it will appear for the user.

The WYSIWYG concept isn't really as radical as it sounds—it is pretty much what a word processor does, and web development tools such as Dreamweaver have offered this feature for years. In fact, these WYSIWYG editors have been a fixture of the web development world for long enough that you could ask why they even deserve mention in an hour devoted to "the new Web." The reason for mentioning them now is that they are a logical step in the evolution toward a new class of tools: the **content management system (CMS)**.

A web editor like Dreamweaver lets the user build content from a graphic interface, then outputs the result to an HTML file (plus other supporting files). The developer then takes the HTML-based content generated by the web editor tool and posts it to a web server, as one would post any other HTML file.

The ever-inventive and ever-restless programming community soon realized that they could automate this process still further. The next logical step was to merge the creation of this web content with the actual process of posting and providing the information for web visitors. In other words, they wanted a way to interface this GUI-based design interface with the web server itself, so the content could be created and posted (or *published*) on a live web server from the same tool. At the same time, developers were also working on some of the web service technologies you'll learn about in the next hour, with back-end databases and other data management features. This convergence of the web server with back-end services and the WYSIWYG user interface led to the development of the CMS, which is now the most widely used means of managing content on commercial web servers.

A CMS is essentially an extension of the web server. It typically runs on the web server machine, and users interact with it through a web interface from a remote client workstation. The web content managed through the CMS is stored and managed as a system of attribute values, through Extensible Markup Language (XML) or some form of back-end database (see Figure 19.1).

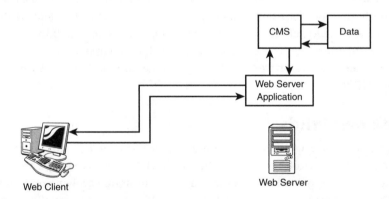

FIGURE 19.1
A CMS runs above the web server, providing a friendly configuration interface. Content data typically resides in a back-end database or XML-based data store.

The CMS interface is often itself built from standard server-side web scripting components through PHP, Perl, Java, or ASP.NET. Dozens of CMS applications are in use today, including free tools such as Drupal and Wordpress, as well as proprietary applications like Microsoft SharePoint.

Although a good CMS handles a wide range of web scenarios, CMS systems are most advantageous for web content that consists of multiple instances following a standard pattern, such as blog or a web zine where each entry includes a collection of predefined elements (title, author, description, body, and so on).

In addition to providing an easy interface for managing and posting content, many CMS tools offer standard web design templates and components, making it easy to create a customized look without having to separately create each of the elements.

Social Networking

Although the phenomenon of social networking is an extremely broad topic, covering an extremely broad range of technologies and tools that drift quite far afield from the basic topic of TCP/IP, it is worth pausing to point out that a social networking website like Facebook represents a further evolution of the CMS concept discussed in the previous section. Facebook and its equivalents merge the CMS and web viewing experience into a single tool.

The owner of a Facebook page can log in to a secure space where the interface basically acts as a CMS, letting the owner enter text and post pictures that will appear to visitors of the site. The idea is that a bundle of attributes associated with the user are stored in a database, and when the page is requested, software running on the server merges the user-specific data with a general template defining the structure of the site to form the page the viewer sees.

To a user who visits the page, the page looks like an ordinary website, albeit with a distinctively Facebook look and feel. Other technologies such as live chat create a richer user experience, but under all the application layers and application programming interfaces (APIs), a Facebook page is still a web application in which a web server and a browser-based client communicate through Hypertext Transfer Protocol (HTTP).

Blogs and Wikis

A **blog** (short for *weblog*) is an e-zine or online journal where new stories are added at the top and older stories scroll down in a vertical list. The revolving, chronological nature of a blog gives the impression that it is constantly evolving and transforming, which keeps readers coming back. Some bloggers are essentially keeping online diaries, but the form is also used by commentators, reporters, and corporate spokespeople. Many blogs are news sites, such as the Slashdot.org site, which is a favorite for high-tech news and commentary (see Figure 19.2).

Most blogs are basically a specialized form of CMS, and many standard CMS tools offer built-in blogging support. The blogging software used for Slashdot is a tool called Slash, which is actually an open source application available for free download through the SourceForge site (http://sourceforge.net/projects/slashcode/). Microsoft provides the Windows Live Writer desktop blogging application.

FIGURE 19.2
Slashdot.org is a popular blog stop.

One way to study how a blog works is to view the source code sent to the client. Most web browsers offer a feature for viewing the source code associated with a web document. In the case of Slashdot, you'll find that the different new entries are created through a series of nested HTML <div> tags. The <div> tag denotes a division or section within a document. The code that you view from your browser is the finished HTML code that arrives at the client. On the server side, an application or script (the Slash application, in the case of Slashdot), generates the code, inserting attribute values for elements such as the story title, description, introduction, image, and so on, taken from a data record associated with the news story.

A wiki is a website that serves as a space for easy collaboration and information sharing. The point of a wiki is to provide a place for users to post notes, documents, and other important information. Ideally, a wiki is easy to expand. Users can easily create new pages and link them to existing pages. Some wikis provide version control, which means that editorial revisions from different users can be tracked separately.

The largest wiki in the world is the huge online encyclopedia Wikipedia (see Figure 19.3). Wikipedia users can post their own entries, and users can edit existing entries. (Click the Recent Changes link in the Wikipedia menu to view the changes to an entry.)

Wikis are used extensively by companies and other organizations as a means for planning, coordinating work, and organizing documents. MediaWiki, the software used on the Wikipedia site, is also a freely available open source application (http://www.mediawiki.org/wiki/MediaWiki).

FIGURE 19.3
Wikipedia is a
huge wiki that
anyone can
edit.

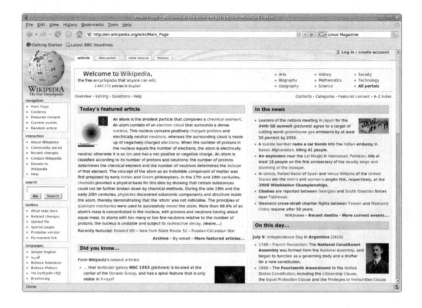

The design of wiki systems can vary, but you can think of a wiki page or entry (such as an entry in Wikipedia) as a collection of values assigned to standard attributes. An XML schema or similar data structure might define a series of values associated with the entry, such as

▶ **Title:** The heading that accompanies the entry

▶ **Category:** Hierarchical classification of the entry by topic

▶ **Language:** The language in which the entry is written

▶ **Contents:** The complete HTML code associated with the entry

Revisions to the text could also be tracked through extensions of this structure. When the page is requested, the data is merged with layout tags and other formatting information to form the code that appears in the browser.

Peer to Peer

A new information sharing technique that emerged through Internet music-sharing communities such as Napster is called **peer to peer (P2P)**. The term *peer to peer* is actually borrowed from a related configuration on local area networks (LANs), in which services are decentralized and every computer acts as both a client and a server. The Internet peer-to-peer form allows computers throughout the network to share data in data-sharing communities. In other words, the data doesn't come from a single web server serving requests from a multitude of clients. Instead, the data resides on ordinary PCs throughout the community.

If you have read this book carefully, you might be wondering how this peer-to-peer scenario I've just described is any different from ordinary networking. All I really said in the preceding paragraph is that each peer must be capable of acting as both a client (requesting data) and a server (fulfilling requests). The short answer is that, after the connection is established, peer-to-peer networking *is* just ordinary networking. The long answer is the reason why peer-to-peer networking is considered somewhat revolutionary.

The Internet was created with diversity as a goal, and it is theoretically possible for any Internet-ready computer to establish a connection with any other compatible, Internet-ready computer that has the necessary services. However, consider that ordinary PCs are not always turned on. Also consider that most computers connected to the Internet do not have a permanent IP address but instead receive a dynamic address through Dynamic Host Configuration Protocol (DHCP) (see Hour 12, "Automatic Configuration"). On a conventional TCP/IP network, it is impossible for other computers to know how to contact a computer that has no permanent IP address or domain name.

The designers of the peer-to-peer technique knew their vision of a diverse, music-sharing community would not work unless they solved these problems. Their solution was to provide a central server to dispense connection information that the clients could then use to establish connections with each other. As shown in Figure 19.4, a user at Computer A logs on to the Internet. The client software on the user's PC registers the user's presence with the server. The server keeps a record of the client's IP address and any files the client has made available to the community. A user at Computer B connects to the server and discovers that a desired file is available on Computer A. The server gives Computer B the necessary information to contact Computer A. Computer B contacts Computer A, establishes a direct connection, and downloads the file.

The best part about peer-to-peer communities is that the details of requesting the IP address and establishing the connection are handled within the software. The user stays within the user interface of the peer-to-peer application and doesn't need to know anything about networking.

FIGURE 19.4
A peer-to-peer computer registers its address and a list of its resources. Other computers then access those resources through a direct connection.

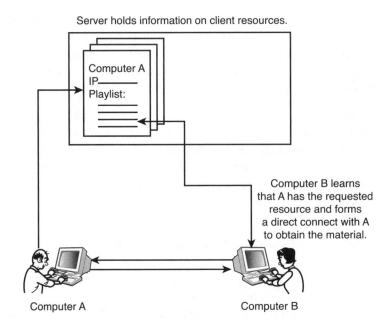

Server holds information on client resources.

Computer A
IP_____
Playlist:

Computer B learns that A has the requested resource and forms a direct connect with A to obtain the material.

Computer A   Computer B

Peer-to-peer networking has come under fire, but not because of the technology. The problems are purely legal. One of the reasons for the development of P2P was to facilitate the untraceable (and sometimes illegal) exchange of copyrighted materials.

IRC and IM

Real-time text messaging systems have been around for years. In fact, the concept predates the Internet as we know it today. In recent years, however, Internet-based chat has gained popularity with a new generation of users. Many users prefer messaging to the other interactive alternative of talking on the telephone. One can chat while working at a computer screen, and text is often less intrusive than sound, lending itself more readily to multitasking. Some users can even manage multiple messaging sessions simultaneously, which is difficult to do with phone calls.

Several forms of messaging exist today—some proprietary and some open. The popular form known as **Internet Relay Chat (IRC)** is actually described through a series of Internet RFCs (beginning with RFC 1459; see also RFCs 2810–2813).

IRC is actually a protocol operating at TCP/IP's Application layer. The IRC protocol was officially assigned TCP port 194, but servers typically run at higher port numbers to avoid the need to operate with root privileges. An IRC network is a collection of IRC servers configured to communicate with each other to support interactive chat sessions for network users.

A chat session occurs on what is called an IRC channel. Multiple users from any-where in the network can connect to the channel and communicate in real time (see Figure 19.5). Channel groups can form around a common hobby or professional interest, as well as around family or social connections. One user, who is designated as the channel operator, or "channel op," is theoretically in charge of the channel, with the power to ban users or moderate the content.

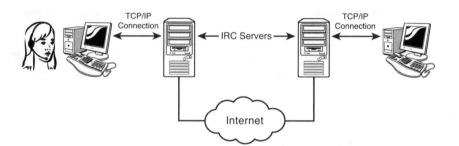

FIGURE 19.5
IRC servers receive connec-tions from users and communicate with other servers on the network.

A client program lets the user connect to an IRC server and join a chat channel. Text-based clients communicate through a series of text commands. More-recent GUI tools eliminate the importance of this command syntax, allowing the user to type the text as if in conversation.

Many IRC networks exist throughout the world. The largest IRC networks, such as EFnet, reportedly support up to 30,000 users at once.

IRC networks are easy to join, sometimes requiring little more than an online nick-name to sign up and sign in. Some have attempted to impose more vigorous securi-ty; however, no matter how you go about it, IRC was never intended to be particu-larly secure.

Instant messaging (IM) is conceptually similar to chat, but it is less standardized and often offers a wider range of options. The user typically just has to sign up, download a client application, and exchange contact information with friends who are also part of the network. IM systems are often proprietary, and the networks are managed by large Internet companies. The largest instant messaging network is the AOL Instant Messenger (AIM) network, with an estimated 50 million active users. Other proprietary systems include the Windows Live Messenger Network and the Yahoo! Network.

One popular open source instant messaging variant is based on the **Extensible Messaging and Presence Protocol (XMPP)**, which is used on the Jabber network. XMPP is an XML-based protocol for exchanging chat messages. The Jabber network has an estimated 40 million users throughout the world.

The Semantic Web

A promising area of research that truly might cause another Internet revolution is an ambitious concept known as the **Semantic Web**. The Semantic Web, which has the full support and advocacy of World Wide Web creator Tim Berners-Lee, is designed as a universal technique for linking web data with real semantic meaning as a human understands it. In other words, the goal is to somehow encode the meaning of web information in a way that is easily accessed and processed by a computer.

To understand the purpose of the Semantic Web, one must start with some sense of how little knowledge is truly present on a web page. For instance, consider the following lines of text, which might be present at a typical website:

A Streetcar Named Desire

Lawrence Community Theater

Saturday, October 12, 2008

7:30 PM

A human who looks at this text knows immediately that it is a notice of an event that will occur at the Lawrence Community Theater at 7:30 on October 12. Many readers will also recognize the name *A Streetcar Named Desire* as a famous play, but those who don't recognize the title will still infer that the event is a play or movie because it is associated with a theater.

A computer, on the other hand, will just read those lines as alphanumeric text. The computer doesn't really know anything about the meaning of the text. It doesn't know what a theater is, and it doesn't know that the third line is a date unless you specifically tell it so. For that matter, a search engine will even call up this page for a user who is searching for a streetcar schedule.

The tools of the Semantic Web will one day help the web developer encode semantic information so that an automated process will know that this page is about a play and not about a ticket for a tram ride. Because this semantic information will be encoded along with the page itself, the creator of the site won't need any advance knowledge of how the reader will use the information. Anyone can come along later and create a tool that searches for information on plays, and the tool will find the notice of this play. Different websites can present the information differently, with no standard format or style, and the play finder application will still find the plays—as long as the semantic information defines the meaning of the text.

Resource Description Framework

Semantic Web techniques are still experimental, although several strategies have appeared in the publications of the World Wide Web Consortium (W3C). One semantic tool that has received considerable attention in the web community is called the **Resource Description Framework (RDF)**. RDF is a framework for expressing relationships that give an indication of meaning. The fundamental unit of RDF is a statement consisting of three parts, which is called a triple in RDF parlance. A triple is structured like a basic sentence, which has a subject, a predicate, and an object.

For instance, in the sentence "The play has the title *A Streetcar Named Desire,*" the subject is "The play," the object is "*A Streetcar Named Desire,*" and the predicate is "has the title."

RDF triples can take on several forms, but the idea is that each element is expressed as a URI, and the URIs are concatenated in a colon-separated list. The Dublin Core Metadata Initiative maintains a database of standard predicates referenced in RDF triples. For instance, the following callout

```
<http://purl.org/dc/elements/1.1/title>
```

refers to the predicate "has the title."

RDF and other semantic web techniques might someday lead to smarter search tools.

Microformats

RDFs are an extremely powerful tool for adding meaning to text; however, a fierce debate is going on within the Internet community over whether the RDF concept is too complex and too much effort to fit in with the methods of ordinary web developers. An alternative approach, which is less ambitious but, most likely, more manageable and accessible for working web professionals, is **microformats**.

Unlike RDFs, microformats do not attempt to represent complete sentence structures and syntactic constructs. The goal of a microformat is simply to flag a section of text to associate it with a predefined meaning, so that a browser or other web application that visits the site will get a clue about the purpose of the text.

Microformats are not part of any official Internet specification, although the practice relies on the existing tags and concepts underpinning HTML. The microformat community has arisen independently, partly under the sponsorship of the nonprofit CommerceNet, which is interested in promoting opportunities for Internet commerce.

A microformat is a specific vocabulary of name/value pairs designed to serve a specific purpose. Microformat vocabularies have been developed for uses such as the following:

```
calendars (hCalendar)
business cards (hCard)
recipes (hRecipe)
copyright information (rel-license}
```

When a block of text is associated with a microformat (such as a resume, which can be identified with the hResume microformat) the surrounding text elements can then be associated with the various elements that make up a resume (such as experience, skill, affiliations, publications).

Perhaps the most common microformat in use today is the hCard microformat, which is used for business cards. hCard is a later incarnation of the vCard format, a MIME type originally described in RFC 2426.

A simple example of HTML data tagged with the hCard microformat is as follows:

```
<div class="vcard">
<div class="fn"> Abraham Lincoln</div>
<div class="org">Former Presidents USA</div>
<div class="tel">785-842-5115</div>
<a class="url"
href="http://former_presidents.org">http://former.presidents.org/</a>
</div>
```

Of course, other settings are also available for specifying a street address and email address, as well as to specify whether the telephone number is a home, work, cell, or fax number. If text on a web page is tagged with these hCard settings, a browser that arrives at the site immediately knows how to treat the information. Microformat-aware browsers automatically format the data as a business card.

See the microformats.org website for more on the microformats movement, including specifications for specific microformats and even some tools that automatically generate microformat data. As you learn later in this hour, a similar concept known as microdata is now into the official Internet lexicon with the arrival of HTML5.

XHTML

Many tools of the new Web, as well as many other websites on today's Internet, rely on another development that is quite technical for the purposes of this hour but is nevertheless worth mentioning. The **XHTML** standard is an effort to bridge between old-fashioned HTML and the realities of the XML-based web environment. (See Hour

20, "Web Services," for more about XML.) XHTML is essentially a formulation of HTML functionality that conforms to XML syntax. The XHTML format provides all the expressive power of HTML within the machine-readable confines of an XML schema.

Although the concepts of XHTML are similar to HTML, XHTML is much more finicky about sloppy or nonstandard coding practice. Certain declarations occur differently, or more formally, and the nesting of tags must be more structured and precise. The goal of expressing HTML as an XML schema is to provide flexibility for developers building scripts and other programs that generate and interpret the code. XHTML also lends itself more readily to dynamic interpretation or modification by the receiving entity. For instance, the small screen of a mobile device might not be able to display a standard HTML page as specified, but a client-side application receiving the page as XHTML could readily modify the text for the smaller screen.

Many believe the emergence of HTML5 (described in the next section) reduces the importance of XHTML.

HTML5

One of the most important changes taking place on the Internet today is the adoption of a new HTML standard. HTML5 has been in discussion for several years, and it is finally making its way to the practical side of the everyday Internet.

One who looks at the HTML5 feature list will see that many of its traits reflect the new role of HTML as a tool for building the mobile revolution. The HTML5 standard includes many features designed to support web browsing from mobile devices. However, other features simply reflect a further evolution of the web environment and incorporate functionality once provided by add-ons and extensions directly into the HTML.

New important new features of HTML5 include the following:

- Local storage and offline application supporting
- Drawing
- Embedded audio and video
- Geolocation
- Semantic Elements

The following sections describe these important new developments in HTML5. The HTML5 standard also includes other improvements, such as a drag-and-drop API and improved support for forms. In many ways, HTML5 marks the further evolution of HTML to something more like a development environment for web applications. Developers have long used HTML and its surrounding technologies to build web-based client/server applications, but much of the functionality required additional components and third-part extensions. HTML5 builds more of the functionality directly into the HTML. In the rapidly evolving world of mobile device programming, developers have begun to use HTML5 to build cross-platform mobile applications that will run on Android, iPhone, and other platforms with only minor modifications.

Of course, the adoption of the HTML5 standard by a standards committee doesn't guarantee its adoption by the larger Internet community. Several popular browsers already provide HTML5 support, and web servers are also getting connected with the newest HTML. However, until web developers start building ordinary web pages that incorporate HTML5 elements, you won't see the benefits of HTML5 in your everyday web surfing experience.

HTML5 Local Storage and Offline Application Support

A cookie is a small bundle of persistent data stored on the remote client system by the web server. Cookies have been part of the web scene for years, and you'll find configuration options in most web browsers that let you manage how cookies are stored and saved. Web servers use cookies to restore a previous application state or save information on the user's previous activities. Cookies are a very useful tool that most web developers (and most web users) are familiar with; however, they have some limitations. The cookies storage size of 4KB is barely enough room for a few basic bits of data about the user and session history, but today's web programmers see the need for much more local storage.

HTML5 comes with a local storage feature that greatly expands and enhances how web browsers can store and retrieve information on the local system. HTML5 storage (which is also called web storage or DOM storage) lets the browser store values for settings defined within the web application. This local storage provides a number of benefits. For instance, a script executing on the client side can stash temporary results in the storage area, thus improving performance by reducing the need for communication with the server over the network. The storage space can also save a more complete view of the current session state, so that a web-based game or other interactive application can be restored (and, in some cases, keep operating temporarily) if the server crashes or the connection is lost.

The local storage capabilities of HTML5 lead to another important improvement: offline application support. A web browser that supports the offline application feature can keep going when the network is disconnected.

As shown in Figure 19.6, a web application that supports offline processing includes a cache manifest, which names the files and other resources required for operating offline. When the browser first connects to the website, the files provided in the cache manifest are downloaded to the client system.

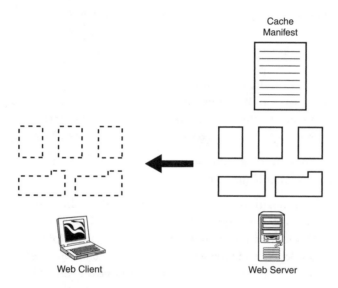

Cache
Manifest

Web Client   Web Server

FIGURE 19.6
The cache manifest lists the resources necessary for offline processing. The client downloads the required files and can therefore operate even when the connection is lost.

When the network is inaccessible, the web application still operates through the offline versions of the files listed in the cache manifest. This might not sound so impressive at a glance. (Of course, every application works if all the files it accesses are present on the system.) The problem is that the files downloaded to the client will soon become out-of-date. However, the interesting part of the HTML5 offline application feature is that the browser system automatically updates the files on the local system when the connection is restored and saves all offline changes back to the server. Thus, the files referenced in the cache manifest stand a better chance of being current at the time the system goes offline, and the client seamlessly synchronizes its changes through the restored connection without additional effort by the user.

HTML5 Drawing

Internet users are accustomed to seeing image files with photographs and diagrams embedded in web pages. This technique of embedding graphic images greatly enhances the power and beauty of the Web. However, web designers and developers want more from their pages, including the ability to draw images programmatically or create small animations that will unfold while the user is watching. Previous HTML versions add this functionality through third-party add-on tools, such as Adobe Flash.

HTML5 rolls out its own drawing capabilities through a pair of important new elements: the <canvas> element, for bitmap images; and the <svg> element, for Scalar Vector Graphics (SVG) images.

The <canvas> element simply defines an area of the screen that will serve as a drawing surface:

```
<canvas id="picture1" width="350" height="250"></canvas>
```

The web developer then draws on this "canvas" using drawing commands written in JavaScript. The ID used in the definition creates an identifier for relating the JavaScript to the canvas definition (through the DOM or Document Object Model definition, which is used by web programmers to manage the objects in a website).

Each page can have more than one canvas, and can even contain a mix of canvas elements and conventional graphics.

Scalar graphics is a means for drawing using shapes, lines, and other geometric elements rather than points on a grid. HTML5 offers scalar graphics through the <svg> element. Because scalar graphic images are built from shapes and other predefined elements, web developers and browser vendors need a common set of definitions for those shapes and the parameters that affect their shape and orientation.

The <svg> tag needs to refer to an XML namespace that defines the graphic elements used in the drawing. The World Wide Web consortium has defined its own namespace at http://www.w3.org/2000/svg, which is intended as a reference for HTML5 scalar images:

```
<svg xmlns="http://www.w3.org/2000/svg> </svg>
```

Information about the shape, size, color, and orientation of the image can also fall within the brackets of the <svg> element. For more information, see the World Wide Web consortium's Scalar Vector Graphics page: http://www.w3.org/Graphics/SVG/.

HTML5 Embedded Audio and Video

Embedded video has become increasingly popular on the Web. Surf to a site and click a video link to start up a tiny little TV-like window that plays the video.

Although video is now prevalent all over the Web, the fact is, the video support typically happens through a third-party tool like Flash or QuickTime. Prior to HTML5, the standard web specifications did not offer support for embedded video.

HTML5 rolls out a new <video> element, which tells the browser the file referenced with the tag is a video file. At the same time, HTML5 provides direct support for referencing video and audio codecs. (A codec basically provides a recipe for decoding a multimedia file.) If the browser is aware the file is a video, and it has access to the necessary codec for playing that file, the whole process can take place through the browser itself without the need for additional third party applications.

Some believe that HTML5's built-in video features will someday make tools like Flash (which is currently used with many online animations, as well by video sites such as YouTube) obsolete.

HTML5 Geolocation

The global GPS satellite system lets an electronic GPS device determine its current location in standard geographical coordinates. Travelers use GPS devices to track their location. GPS tools are also increasingly common in industry, with central dispatch systems charting the activities of delivery trucks and taxicabs. **Geolocation** functionality is also built in to most mobile phones, and end users have gotten accustomed to mobile applications that will reveal the nearest coffee shop or restaurant based on location data supplied through the device's onboard GPS functionality.

HTML5's geolocation API provides a standard way for applications to query the device to obtain geolocation data. The programmer can use the geolocation API to determine the location of the device and to process other geolocation data to map coordinates or find the path to nearby services.

HTML5 Semantics

HTML5 builds on some semantic concepts at play elsewhere in the Internet community (see the section "Semantic Web," earlier in this hour). One way that HTML5 uses semantics is through a series of predefined HTML elements that provide meaning to the text (see Table 19.1). You can use these elements to mark text that is intended for a particular purpose.

Note that the interesting thing about the Semantic Web is you don't have to know exactly why a user or application might actually need this information. The meaning is encoded into the page, and the viewer can decide how to display or interpret this information.

TABLE 19.1   HTML5 Semantic Elements

Element	Description
`<article>`	A section of the text that can be broken off as a self-contained article
`<aside>`	A sidebar or other boxout with content that is related but separable from the main discussion
`<footer>`	Basic information on a section, such as the author name and related links
`<header>`	Introductory information and navigational information, such as a table of contents
`<hgroup>`	Heading for a section
`<mark>`	Text marked for reference
`<nav>`	A block of the page designed as a navigation tool, with general links to other parts of the document
`<section>`	A chapter or other thematic division of the document
`<time>`	A reference for a date or time

The other important semantic concept included in the HTML5 specification is **microdata**. Microdata is an extension of the microformat concept discussed earlier in this hour. The microdata feature lets you build specialized vocabularies to assign meaning to text strings. Some basic vocabularies for important themes (such as persons, events, or organizations) are already defined (see http://data-vocabulary.org). It is also possible to create your own microdata vocabulary and reference the vocabulary source as a URL within the HTML.

Like microformats, microdata takes the form of a series of name/value pairs. One driving force behind the development of microdata has been the search engine industry. Google, for instance, has been instrumental in crafting the draft standard and defining microdata vocabularies. The search engines believe the widespread use of microdata will provide their search algorithms with additional information that will help them deliver better results.

Summary

This hour described some tools and technologies of the new Web. You learned how blogs, wikis, and social network sites use components such as databases and dynamic HTML. You learned how XHTML provides HTML functionality through a uniform XML schema. This hour also looked at peer-to-peer networking, messaging services, and the Semantic Web.

Q&A

Q. Why use a wiki instead of a conventional website?

A. A wiki is easy to expand and modify, and it is designed to support collaboration. Many wikis have a built-in version control system that tracks revisions from different users.

Q. What well-known port is assigned to IRC?

A. Port 194.

Q. Why do some IRC chat servers use a higher port number?

A. On most UNIX/Linux systems, programs using port numbers below 1024 run with root privileges. Using a higher port number allows a more restrictive security context. Note that this is a fairly limited security measure on today's networks; it is not a replacement for a complete security system, but it does offer an extra obstacle for the intruder, and it might make the channel a bit harder to reach for private chat groups who are not seeking outside connections.

Q. What is the advantage of coding for the Semantic Web?

A. Semantic information allows more sophisticated interpretation of the data by search engines and other tools.

Workshop

The following workshop is composed of a series of quiz questions and practical exercises. The quiz questions test your overall understanding of the current material. The practical exercises give you the opportunity to apply the concepts discussed during the current hour and to build on the knowledge acquired in previous hours of study. Take time to complete the quiz questions and exercises before continuing. Refer to Appendix A, "Answers to Quizzes and Exercises," for answers.

Quiz

1. Why are CMS tools usually accessed through a web browser?

2. What is the distinguishing characteristic of a peer-to-peer network?

3. What are the three parts of an RDF triple?

4. Why do some experts believe Adobe Flash and similar tools will lose influence in the next few years?

Exercises

1. Visit the http://www.microformats.org website. In the menu at the top, click code&tools. When you get to the code&tools page, select hCard creator. The hCard creator lets you interactively generate the microformat code for an online business card. Enter the business card information in the form on the left. The microformat code appears in the box on the right. Examine the code to gain a deeper understanding of microformats. The code&tools page also lets you experiment with other microformat types, such as the hCalendar or hReview microformats.

2. Browse to http://www.html5.com. This website provides a score for how well your browser supports HTML5. Scroll down through the subscore sections to view the support score for various HTML5 features.

Key Terms

Review the following list of key terms:

▶ **Blog (or weblog):** A website that posts periodic updates or new entries in a revolving, vertical queue of messages.

▶ **Content management system (CMS):** A GUI-based tool that provides an easy-to-use interface for building and managing websites.

▶ **Geolocation:** The act of locating geographical points on the Earth, typically using a GPS-like electronic device or cell phone.

▶ **Instant messaging (IM):** A real-time messaging technique.

▶ **Internet Relay Chat (IRC):** A protocol and network service for real-time text messaging.

▶ **Microdata:** An implementation of the microformat concept within HTML5.

▶ **Microformat:** A semantic structure within an HTML document that defines the purpose for a block of text (such as a business card or recipe) and labels the parts of the data (such as an address or ingredients) as a series of name/value pairs.

▶ **Peer to peer (P2P):** A system for establishing direct connections between Internet users for purposes of sharing files.

▶ **Resource Description Framework (RDF):** A Semantic Web framework.

▶ **Semantic Web:** A set of technologies designed to provide information on the meaning of web data.

▶ **Social networking:** One of several services that supports blogging, messaging, and other activities from a personal website.

▶ **Web 2.0:** A collection of tools that reflect a new vision of the interactive Web.

▶ **Wiki:** A form of easily edited, interactive websites designed to support collaboration.

▶ **WYSIWYG (What You See Is What You Get):** A form of editing tool that displays a page as it will appear to the user.

▶ **XHTML:** An expression of HTML through XML schema.

▶ **XMPP (Extensible Messaging and Presence Protocol):** An open source messaging protocol used with Jabber messaging technology.

PART VI

TCP/IP At Work

HOUR 20

Web Services

What you'll learn in this hour:

▶ Web services
▶ XML
▶ SOAP
▶ WSDL
▶ REST
▶ Web transactions

The technologies of the Web have led to a new revolution in software development. The web service architecture lets the programmer leverage the tools of the Web for complex tasks never envisioned by the creators of Hypertext Markup Language (HTML). This hour examines the web services infrastructure. You'll also get a quick look at how e-commerce websites process web transactions.

At the completion of this hour, you will be able to

▶ Discuss the web service architecture

▶ Understand the role of XML, SOAP, WSDL, and REST in the web service paradigm

▶ Describe how e-commerce websites process monetary transactions

Understanding Web Services

Now that almost every computer has a web browser, and web servers are widely understood, visionaries and software developers have been hard at work devising new ways to use the tools of the Web. In the old days, a programmer who wanted to write a network application had to create a custom server program, a custom client program, and a custom syntax or format for the two applications to exchange information. The effort of writing all this software was a huge expense of time and brain space, but with the rising importance of computer networking, the goals of data integration and centralized management were driving the demand for client/server applications. Network program interfaces existed of course—otherwise, many of the classic applications described in this book would have never evolved—but network programming typically required some significant, high-priced coding at the network interface.

An easier solution that emerged over time is to use the existing tools, technologies, and protocols of the Web as a basis for creating custom network applications. This approach, which is supported by big companies such as IBM and Microsoft, as well as open source advocates and development tool vendors around the world, is known as the **web services architecture**.

The idea behind the web services architecture is that the web browser, web server, and TCP/IP protocol stack handle the details of networking so that the programmer can concentrate of the details of the application. In recent years, this technology has outgrown the original vision of the Web as a manifestation of the global Internet. This web services architecture is regarded now as an approach to building any sort of network application, whether or not that application is actually connected to the Internet. Large and powerful vendors have invested enormous resources in building component infrastructures to support this web services vision.

The Hypertext Transfer Protocol (HTTP) delivery system is only part of what we know as web services. Also significant is the arrival of component architectures that provide ready-made classes, functions, and programming interfaces for working within a web-based environment.

Web service applications are often used in situations that require a simple client connection to a server that maintains inventory or processes orders. For instance, a manufacturing company might use a web services program to place orders, track deliveries, and maintain up-to-date information on the contents of the warehouse.

Almost any big company has a need for software that tracks appointments, orders, and inventory. A web service framework is good for gluing together disparate services and transactions into a single, unified environment.

Figure 20.1 shows a complete web services scenario. On the front end (the left side of Figure 20.1), the programmer can take advantage of the preexisting web infrastructure, which handles data transmission and also provides a user interface through the web browser application on the client computer. On the back end, the programmer relies on the preexisting data storage system provided by an SQL database. The programmer is left to concentrate on the center section of Figure 20.1, where the ready-made components of the web services platform further simplify the task of programming.

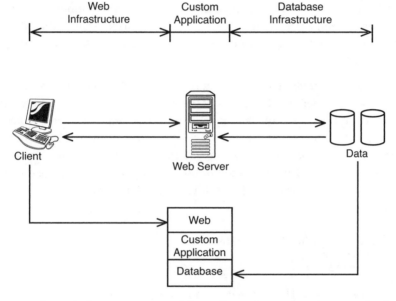

FIGURE 20.1
The web services programming model.

Data passes through the components of the web services system in a standard markup format—typically **Extensible Markup Language (XML)**, although alternatives such as JavaScript Object Notation (JSON) are gaining popularity with some developers.

XML is an efficient, universal means for assigning values to attributes. The powerful web service paradigm has led to many innovations and later developments. As you learn in this hour, some experts decided that the system would work even better if they could use the XML format to actually invoke services or generate responses over the network. **Simple Object Access Protocol (SOAP)** offers a standard method for passing XML-based data between web service processes. SOAP also describes how to use the XML and HTTP to invoke remote procedures. As you learn later in this hour, SOAP messages pass to and from network services defined through the **Web Services Description Language (WSDL)**.

Other experts advocated a back-to-basics approach, with a carefully structured system designed to operate through standard HTTP commands. The **Representational State Transfer (REST)** architecture reflects this emphasis on simplified design.

XML

As soon as users, vendors, and web designers became accustomed to Hypertext Markup Language (HTML), they started to ask for more. The growth of server-side and client-side programming techniques caused many experts to wonder if there might be a way to extend the rigid tag system of HTML. Their goal was to get beyond the conception of a markup language as a means for formatting text and graphics and to employ the language simply as a means for transmitting data. The result of this discussion was a new markup language called Extensible Markup Language, or XML.

The meaning and context for HTML data is limited to what you can express through a set of predefined HTML tags. If the data is enclosed in <H1> tags, it is interpreted as a heading. If the data is enclosed in <A> tags, it is interpreted as a link. XML, on the other hand, lets users define their own elements. The data can signify whatever you want it to signify, and you can invent the tag you will use to mark the data. For instance, if you follow horse racing, you could create an XML file with information on your favorite horses. That file might contain entries such as the following:

```
<horses>
    <horse_name="winky" breed="Thoroughbred">
        <sex="male" />
        <age="3" />
    </horse>
     <horse_name="Goddess" breed="Arabian">
        <sex="female" />
        <age="3" />
    </horse>
    <horse_name=""Gecko" breed="Uncertain">
        <sex="male" />
        <age="14" />
    </horse>
 </horses>
```

XML format looks a little like HTML, but it certainly isn't HTML. (Can you imagine how much your browser would choke if you tried to pass off <horse_name> as an HTML tag?) You can use whatever tag you want to use in XML, because you aren't preparing the data for some specific, rigidly predefined application like a web browser. The data is just data. The idea is that whoever creates the structure for the file will come along later to create an application or style sheet that will read the file and understand what the data means.

A separate document contains the XML **schema** (the roadmap used to format and interpret the XML data). The presence of the schema document makes it easy to check the validity of XML data, and it makes it easy to create new client applications that parse and process the XML data.

XML is an extremely powerful tool for passing data between applications. It is easy for a script or homegrown application to create XML as output or read XML as input. Even though a browser can't read XML directly, XML is still used extensively on the Web. In some cases, the XML data is generated on the server side and then converted to display-ready HTML before it is transmitted to the browser. Another technique is to provide an accompanying file called a Cascading Style Sheet (CSS) that tells how to interpret and display the XML data. However, XML is not limited to the Web. Programmers now use XML for other contexts that require a simple, convenient format for assigning values to attributes.

XML now reaches far beyond the ordinary Web as a format for storing and transmitting data. As long as the application that writes the XML data and the application that reads the data agree on the meaning of the elements, the data passes easily and economically between the applications through the miracle of XML.

XML is often described as a "markup language for creating markup languages."

By the Way

Schema

The term *schema* is sometimes used generically with a number of schema languages used to provide a structure for XML. W3C also provides an official specification called XML Schema Language that is used to create W3C-compliant XML Schema Document (XSD) schema files, which have the .xsd file extension.

SOAP

XML defines a universal format for exchanging application data. The universal XML specification alone, however, is not enough to provide developers with the infrastructure they need to create easy and elegant web services. Although XML provides an efficient format for reading and writing program data, XML alone does not provide a standard format for structuring and interpreting that data. The SOAP specification fills that role. SOAP is a standard protocol for exchanging XML-based messages that pass between the web-service client and server.

SOAP is designed to support communication between so-called SOAP nodes. (A SOAP node is basically a computer or application that supports SOAP.) The SOAP specification defines the structure of a message that passes from the SOAP sender to the SOAP receiver. Along the way, the message might pass through intermediate nodes that process the information in some way (see Figure 20.2). An intermediate node might provide logging, or it might modify the message somehow in transit to its final destination.

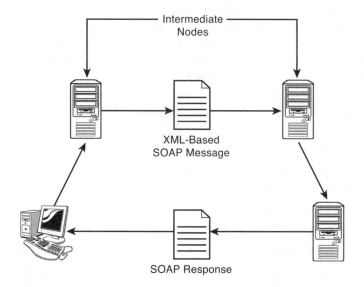

At the conceptual level, a SOAP message from the client says, "Here is some input. Process this and send me the output." The functionality of the application derives from a series of these XML-based SOAP messages in which the endpoints send information and receive responses. The formal structure of the SOAP message allows the software developer to easily create a SOAP-based client application that interacts with the server. For instance, a rental company that provides car rental reservations through a web-based server application could easily make the specifications available for a developer to write a custom client application that could connect to the server and reserve a car.

The structure of a SOAP message consists of an optional header and a message body. The header contains callouts, definitions, and meta-information that will be used by any node along the message path. The body includes data intended for the message recipient. For example, in the case of the car reservation service, the message body might contain data from the client describing the car the customer would like to rent and the date the vehicle must be available.

WSDL

The Web Services Description Language (WSDL) provides an XML format for describing the services associated with the web service application. According to the W3C's WSDL specification, "WSDL is an XML format for describing network services as a set of endpoints operating on messages containing either document-oriented or procedure-oriented information." WSDL is a format for defining the services that exchange information through SOAP messages.

A WSDL document is primarily a set of definitions. The definitions within the document specify information on the data being transmitted and the operations associated with that data, as well as other data related to the service and the service location.

WSDL is not confined to SOAP but is also used with other web service communication protocols. In some cases, WSDL is used directly with HTTP to simplify the design and restrict the actions to more fundamental GET and POST-style operations at the heart of HTTP.

Web Service Stacks

Armed with XML, SOAP, WSDL, and the underlying components of TCP/IP and web service frameworks, a developer can easily create light and simple client and server applications that communicate through a web interface. Like TCP/IP itself, a web service environment consists of a stack of components. Major vendors have their own web service stacks that they provide to customers. The complete system forms a package of server software, developer tools, and even computer hardware that is provided to the client, along with consulting services and, sometimes, made-to-order custom applications.

Linux vendors and developers often talk about the **LAMP** stack, a collection of open source components that is easily tailored for web service environments. The memorable acronym LAMP spells out the principal components of the stack:

- **Linux:** An operating system that supports server applications running on the server system

- **Apache:** A web server that serves up XML-based SOAP messages

- **MySQL:** A database system that provides access to back-end data services

- **PHP (or Perl or Python):** A web-ready programming language used to code the details of the custom web service application

Proprietary web service infrastructures provide similar features. The Java programming language is often used with web services—not just by Oracle/Sun (the creators of Java), but also in IBM's WebSphere and other systems. Microsoft provides equivalents to Java through the tools of the .NET Framework.

REST

The power of XML and the client/server model can lead to an endless variety of applications sharing requests and transferring data. It is possible for a custom server to provide almost any kind of custom information to almost any kind of custom client application in almost any kind of format. When developers started building web services applications, however, they began to discover that an intricate, highly specialized, nonstandard interaction between the client and the server could lead to a number of problems. For instance, a client application that must have specialized knowledge of the server's methods and structure is difficult to write (and difficult to port to other platforms). On the other end, a server that must undergo complex, multistep interactions with the client passes through a series of state changes that can lead to complications and unintended problems. In recent years, developers have settled on a design philosophy known as **Representational State Transfer (REST)** to address these problems.

REST was actually developed around the time of HTTP 1.1. The REST concept was originally defined in 2000 by Roy Fielding in his doctoral dissertation "Architectural Styles and the Design of Network-based Software Architectures." In recent years, REST has seen a rise in popularity, and it is now a dominant principle used in millions of local web apps and thousands of the world's highest-traffic websites.

Unlike SOAP, REST is not a protocol in itself; instead, it is a design philosophy for creating simple, clean, and portable web-based applications. The REST system boils the communication process down to a few very basic elements:

▶ **Resources:** The target of the request (the thing the client wants). This could be a web page, a database record, or other programmatic object.

▶ **Resource identifiers:** A URI naming the resource.

▶ **Representations:** The response from the server conveying the resource within a finished format. Note that the resource isn't necessarily stored in the representational form delivered to the client. The object might be assembled dynamically on the server side into the representation delivered to the client.

By the Way

Metadata

In addition to the primary REST elements (resources, resource identifiers, and representations), various forms of resource and representational metadata can pass with the message to clarify the nature of the data.

The important part of the REST system is that the client doesn't tell the server to do things; it just says what it wants. REST rejects the conventional sense of an application programming interface (API), where a client invokes processes on the server. Instead, the client simply sends a resource identifier in the form of a URI identifying the resource it wishes to add, view, or modify and provides the necessary information within the body of the URI to complete the request.

The only actions specified through a basic REST request are the standard HTTP methods:

- ▶ **GET:** Obtain a resource from the server.

- ▶ **PUT:** Create or modify a resource directly.

- ▶ **POST:** Submit data for the server to modify the resource.

- ▶ **HEAD:** Obtain metadata associated with the resource.

- ▶ **DELETE:** Delete the resource.

Confining the set of available methods to standard HTTP requests known to all web programmers and available on all web servers further simplifies the REST system, ensuring portability.

The difference between the POST and PUT commands is worth a moment's reflection. PUT replaces the entire contents of a resource. POST submits information for the server to use in updating the resource, with no presumption about how that update will occur (see Figure 20.3). PUT is said to be idempotent, which means that the same action leads to the same result no matter how many times it is executed. POST makes no such guarantee. For instance, the POST command might append a line of text to the end of a document, and if you execute the command multiple times, the outcome will differ each time because you will accumulate multiple copies of the same appended line. REST design principles place the emphasis on using idempotent methods if possible, but the POST method is included for cases where it is necessary. This emphasis on idempotent operations is a defining feature of REST systems. SOAP-based systems, for instance, tend to make more extensive use of nonidempotent POST operations, which can actually be more efficient in terms of minimizing data transfer and network bandwidth. REST makes a definitive statement for clarity and simplicity, even at the occasional expense of marginal performance benefits.

Data passed into the server is typically in XML format, although REST services sometimes support JavaScript Object Notation (JSON) as well as ordinary HTML. Ideally, the data returning from the server is in a representational form, which is typically HTML or some other format that is easily processed with a web browser.

FIGURE 20.3
The HTTP **PUT** method updates a complete resource. The **POST** method supplies information that is used for the update, which might include appending text or modifying an existing resource.

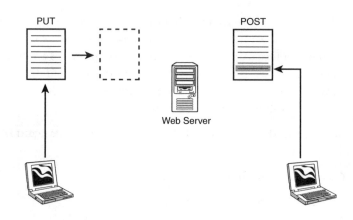

As you might guess, a major concern in REST systems is the structure of the URI. URIs are hierarchical and point to objects (resources). Of course, an intermediate layer of the URI could point to a collection of objects. In that sense, the structure of a REST URI often looks similar to the structure of a directory path, progressing through an ever-more granular series of containers or collections to a record ID at the end of the string. This approach might seem obvious (since the original intent of a URI was to point down through a directory path to a filename), but this back-to-basics approach is in contrast to other developments in the web service model, in which the URI came to include complex command strings passed to the server for execution.

In addition to providing simplicity and portability, the REST model is thought to offer better and more uniform security because it obscures all server operations inside the server and away from the interface. The alternative technique of passing commands to the server through the URI, which was popular in the early days of web services, was prone to a range of intrusion techniques that are not possible through a secure and well-designed REST system. It is no wonder high-traffic sites such as Amazon, eBay, and YouTube make use of REST design principles.

> **Get RESTful**
>
> A website, service, or development framework designed around the REST paradigm is said to be RESTful.

E-Commerce

An e-commerce site is not necessarily an implementation of the web service paradigm described earlier in this hour; however, it still might use some web-service techniques, especially on the back end. E-commerce is a high-profile example of the way applications and components can be combined together using the tools of the Web.

Vendors and advertisers began to notice early on that the Web is a great way to get people to buy things. It is no secret that many websites look like long, intricate advertisements. Despite the hype, which is enough to make anyone doubt the validity of the design, the fact is that the Web is a convenient and cost-effective way to shop. Instead of sending thousands of catalogs by direct mail, a vendor can simply post the catalog on the Web and let the customers find it through searches and links.

The business of buying over the Web did not really get started until vendors solved the security issues related to sending credit card information over the open Internet. In fact, Internet sales would not even be possible without the secure networking techniques. Most browsers are now capable of opening a secure communications channel with the server. This secure channel makes it impossible for a cyber thief to listen for passwords or credit card information.

A typical web transaction scenario is shown in Figure 20.4. The process is as follows:

1. A web server provides an online catalog accessible from the Web. A user browses through the product offerings from a remote location across the Internet.

2. The user decides to buy a product and clicks a Buy This Product link on the web page.

3. The server and browser establish a secure connection. (See Hour11, "TCP/IP Security," for more on Secure Sockets Layer [SSL] and other secure communication techniques.) At this point, the browser sometimes displays a message that says something like "You are now entering a secure area...." Different browsers have different methods for indicating a secure connection.

4. After the connection is established, some form of authentication usually follows. On some transaction sites, the buyer establishes some form of user account with the vendor. This is partly for security reasons and partly for convenience (so that the user can track the status of purchases). The user account information also lets the vendor track the behavior of the user and correlate the user's demographic information and purchase history. This logon step requires the web server to contact some form of back end database server—either to establish a new account or to check the credentials

for logon to an existing account. An alternative approach that has gained popularity recently is to provide credit information directly within the session without logging in.

5. The server (or some application working on the server back end) must verify the credit card information and register the transaction with some credit card authority that oversees the tasks associated with executing and verifying the credit card information (often called a *payment gateway*). This credit card authority is typically a commercial service.

6. If the transaction is approved, notice of the purchase and mailing information is transmitted to the vendor's fulfillment department, and the transaction application attends to the final details of confirming the purchase with the user and updating the user's account profile.

FIGURE 20.4
A typical web transaction scenario.

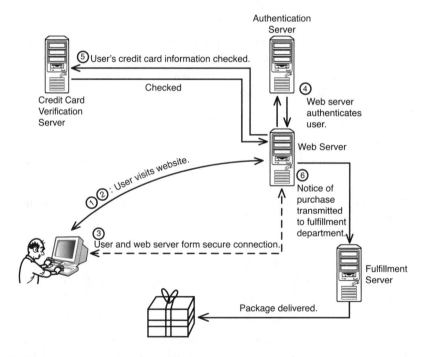

System vendors such as Oracle, IBM, and Microsoft offer transaction server applications to assist with the important task of processing orders over the Web. Because web transactions are highly specialized, and because they require an interface with existing applications on the vendor's network, application frameworks often provide special tools to assist with the task of constructing a transaction infrastructure.

Note that Figure 20.4 omits the role of the firewall within the transaction infrastructure. A large-scale commercial network might include a firewall behind the web server, protecting the network, and another firewall in front of the web server that blocks some traffic but leaves the server open to web requests. Also, on high-volume websites, you're more likely to find a collection of web servers sharing the load, rather than a single server.

Connections from the web server to the back-end servers could be across a protected internal network. Alternatively, the connection to the back end could be through a dedicated line that is separate from the main network. The credit card verification server is often an off-site service provided by a different company and accessed through a secure Internet connection.

Summary

The tools of the Web provide a backdrop for many kinds of application development. In addition to simple web pages and web forms, developers are putting together complex applications that place reservations, track inventory, and process purchase orders. This hour described some of the technologies at the heart of the web service paradigm. You learned about the web service infrastructure and why it is important. This hour also discussed three important web service components (XML, SOAP, and WSDL) and described the REST web services architecture. Lastly, this hour took a look at the structure of web-based transactions.

Q&A

Q. *What is the advantage of the web service model over conventional client-server programming?*

A. The web service model is design to integrate standard components that are already present on most networks, such as web server and web browser applications.

Q. *Why is the web service model based on XML rather than HTML?*

A. HMTL is a predefined collection of tags intended specifically as a markup language for web pages. XML has nearly unlimited capacity for defining new elements and assigning values to variables.

Q. *Considering that countless vendors all have their own languages and components for supporting web services, what is the benefit of uniform standards like SOAP and WSDL?*

A. Standards like SOAP and WSDL provide a common format so that components written for different vendor environments can easily interact.

Workshop

The following workshop is composed of a series of quiz questions. The quiz questions test your overall understanding of the current material. Take time to complete the quiz questions before continuing. Refer to Appendix A, "Answers to Quizzes and Exercises," for answers.

Quiz

1. What is the XML schema?

2. What is the difference between the HTTP PUT and POST methods?

3. Why does REST emphasize PUT?

4. Why do many experts consider REST more secure than other comparable web services architectures?

Key Terms

Review the following list of key terms:

▶ **LAMP:** An open source web service stack consisting of the Linux operating system, the Apache web server, the MySQL database system, and any of three programming languages that start with *P* (PHP, Perl, or Python).

▶ **Representational State Transfer (REST):** A design philosophy for building simple and portable web applications.

▶ **Simple Object Access Protocol (SOAP):** A message exchange protocol for web applications.

▶ **Web services architecture:** A paradigm for building custom network applications around web components.

▶ **Web Services Description Language (WSDL):** An XML-based format for describing network services.

▶ **Extensible Markup Language (XML):** A markup language used for defining and transmitting program data in a web service application.

HOUR 21

Email

You don't have to be a computer professional to notice that email has become an extremely common feature of the modern world. Both professional and personal relationships now depend on email for fast, reliable communication across great distances. This hour introduces some important email concepts and shows how electronic mail services operate on a TCP/IP network.

At the completion of this hour, you will be able to

▶ Describe the parts of an email message

▶ Discuss the email delivery process

▶ Describe how an SMTP transmission works

▶ Discuss the mail retrieval protocols POP3 and IMAP4

▶ Describe the role of an email application

What Is Email?

An email message is an electronic letter composed on one computer and transmitted across a network to another computer (which might be nearby or on the other side of the world). Email developed early in the history of networking. Almost as soon as computers were linked into networks, computer engineers began to wonder if humans as well as machines could communicate across those same network links.

The current Internet email system dates back to ARPAnet days. Most of the Internet's email infrastructure derives from a pair of documents published in 1982: RFC 821 ("Simple Mail Transfer Protocol") and RFC 822 ("Standard for the Format of ARPA Internet Text Messages"). Later documents have refined these specifications, including RFC 2821, which defined a new version of SMTP that was later updated again with RFC 5321, and RFC 2822 "Internet Message Format," which was revised with RFC 5322. Other proposed email formats have developed through the years (such as the X.400 system, as well as several proprietary formats), but the simplicity and versatility of SMTP-based electronic mail have made it the dominant form and the de facto standard for the Internet.

Electronic mail was invented in the days of the text-based user interface, and the original purpose of email was to transmit text. The email message format is designed to transmit text efficiently. The original email specifications did not include provisions for sending binary files. One of the primary reasons for the efficiency of email is that ASCII text is light and simple to transmit. But emphasis on ASCII text ultimately proved limiting. In the 1990s, the email format was extended to include binary attachments. An attachment can be any type of file, as long as it doesn't exceed the maximum size allowed for the email application. As you learn in this hour, these attachments are typically encoded in **Multipurpose Internet Mail Extensions (MIME)** format. Users today attach graphics files, spreadsheets, word processing documents, and other files to their email messages.

Email Format

Your email client application assembles a message into the format necessary for Internet transmission. An email message sent over the Internet consists of two parts: the **header** and the **body**.

Like the body of the message, the header is transmitted as ASCII-based text. The header consists of a series of keyword field names followed by one or more comma-separated values. Most of the mail header fields are familiar to anyone who has worked with email. Some of the important header fields are given in Table 21.1.

Following the header is a blank line, and following the blank line is the body of the message (the actual text of the electronic letter).

Users often want to send more than just text with an email message. A number of methods have emerged for transmitting binary files through email. Early strategies involved converting the binary bits into some ASCII equivalent. The resulting file looks like ASCII text—in fact, it is ASCII text—but you can't read it because it is just a jumble of letters representing the original binary code. The BinHex utility (originally developed for the Macintosh) and the Uuencode utility (originally developed for UNIX) use this method. You or your email client must have the necessary decoding utility to convert the file back to its binary form.

TABLE 21.1 Some Important Email Header Fields

Header Field	Description
To	Email address(es) of mail recipient(s).
From	Email address of sender.
Date	Date and time the message was sent.
Subject	A brief description of the message subject.
Cc	Email addresses of other users who will receive a copy of the message.
Bcc	Email addresses of users who will receive a blind copy of the message. A blind copy is a copy of the message that the other recipients don't know about. Any email address listed in the Bcc field will not appear in the header received by the other recipients.
Reply-To	Email address that will receive replies to this message. If this field is not given, replies will go to the address referenced in the From field.

A more general and universal solution for sending binary files through email has emerged through the MIME format. MIME is a general format for extending the capabilities of Internet email. A MIME-enabled email application encodes the binary attachment into MIME format before transmission. When the message is downloaded to the recipient, a MIME-enabled email application on the recipient's computer decodes the attachment and restores it to its original form.

MIME brings several innovations to Internet mail, including the following:

▶ Expanded character sets. MIME is not limited to the standard 128-character ASCII set. This means you can use it to transmit special characters and characters that aren't present in American English.

▶ Unlimited line length and message length.

▶ Standard encoding for attachments.

▶ Provisions for integrating images, sound, links, and formatted text with the message.

Most email client applications support MIME. MIME format is described in several RFCs.

How Email Works

Like other Internet services, email is built around a client/server process. However, the email process is a bit more complicated. To put it briefly, the computers at both ends of the email transaction act as clients, and the message is passed across the network by servers in between. The email delivery process is shown in Figure 21.1. An **email client** application (sometimes called an email reader) sends a message to an email server. The server reads the address of the intended recipient and forwards the message to another email server associated with the destination address. The message is stored on the destination email server in a mailbox. (A **mailbox** is similar to a folder or queue of incoming mail messages.) The user to whom the message is addressed occasionally logs on to the email server to check for mail messages. In the past, the standard process called for a client application on the user's computer to download the messages waiting in the user's mailbox. The user could then read, store, delete, forward, or reply to the email message. Although this approach is still common, newer techniques such as **Internet Message Access Protocol (IMAP)** and webmail let the user manage the mail on the server without ever downloading it.

FIGURE 21.1
The email delivery process.

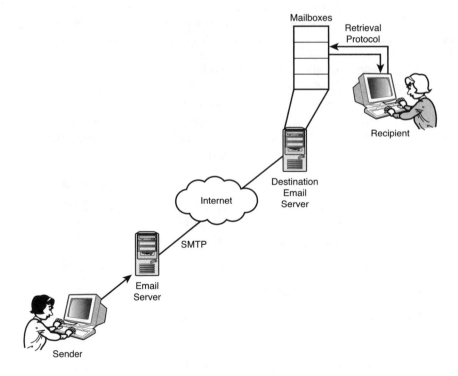

As you learn later in this hour, a client application tends to the details of sending outgoing mail and logging in to the server to download incoming mail. Most users interact with the email process through the interface of an email client. The process of sending a message and forwarding it between servers is managed by an email protocol called **Simple Mail Transfer Protocol (SMTP)**.

The email address gives the addressing information the server needs to forward the message. The format of the ever more popular Internet email address is as follows:

> user@server

or (for example)

> BillyBob@Klondike.net
>
> SallyH@montecello.com
>
> cravenprof@harvard.edu

In this standard format, the text after the @ symbol is the name of the destination email server. The text before the @ symbol is the name of the recipient's **mailbox** on the email server.

Email and DNS

The text after the @ symbol usually represents the domain name of the default email server on the recipient domain. The Domain Name System (DNS) servers for the domain hold an MX resource record that associates a mail server with the domain name. See Hour 10, "Name Resolution," for more on DNS.

By the Way

The format of the email address underscores an important observation about email on the Internet: The destination of an email message is not the recipient's computer but the recipient's mailbox on the email server. The final step of transferring waiting email messages from the email server to the computer of the recipient is actually a separate process. You learn later in this hour that this final step is managed through a mail retrieval protocol such as **Post Office Protocol (POP)** or Internet Message Access Protocol (IMAP).

Some networks use a hierarchy of email servers for more efficient delivery. In this scenario (see Figure 21.2), a local email server forwards messages to a relay email server. The relay email server then sends the mail to another relay server on the destination network, and this relay server sends the message to a local server associated with the recipient.

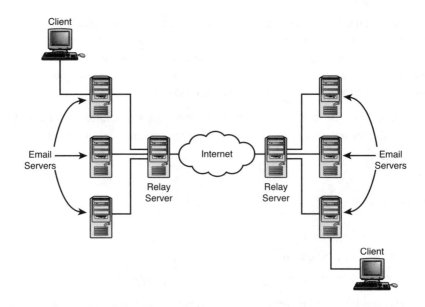

Simple Mail Transfer Protocol

SMTP is the protocol that email servers use to forward messages across a TCP/IP net-work. The client computer that initiates an email message also uses SMTP to send that message to a local server for delivery.

A user never has to speak SMTP. The SMTP communication process goes on behind the scenes. However, it is occasionally important to know a little about SMTP to interpret error messages for undelivered mail. Also, programs and scripts sometimes access SMTP directly to send email warnings and alerts to network personnel.

Like other TCP/IP application services, SMTP communicates with the network through the TCP/IP protocol stack. The duties of the email application are kept sim-ple because the application can count on the connection and verification services of the TCP/IP protocol software. By default, SMTP communication occurs through a TCP connection to port 25 on the SMTP server. The dialog between the client and server consists of standard four-character commands (and data) from the client interspersed with three-digit response codes from the server. Table 21.2 shows some SMTP client commands. The corresponding server response codes are shown in Table 21.3.

TABLE 21.2 SMTP Client Commands

Command	Description
HELO	Hello. (Client requests a connection with the server.)
MAIL FROM:	Precedes email address of sending user.
RCPT TO:	Precedes email address of receiving user.
DATA	Announces an intention to start transmitting the contents of the message.
NOOP	Asks the server to send an OK reply.
QUIT	Asks the server to send an OK reply and terminate the session.
RESET	Aborts the mail transaction.
220	<domain> service ready.
221	<domain> service closing transmission channel.
250	Requested action completed successfully.
251	User is not local. Message will be forwarded to <path>.
354	Start sending data. End data with the string <CRLF>.<CRLF> (which signifies a period on a line by itself).
450	Action was not taken because mailbox is busy.
500	Syntax error: Command not recognized.
501	Syntax error: Problem with parameters or arguments.
550	Action was not taken because mailbox was not found.
551	User is not local. Try sending the message to <path>.
554	Transaction failed.

The process of sending a message to the email server is roughly as follows. As mentioned earlier in this hour, this process is used to send a message from the initiating client to the local email server and also to forward the message from the local server to the destination server or to another server on the relay path:

1. The sending computer issues a HELO command to the server. The domain name of the sender is included as an argument.

2. The server sends back the 250 response code.

3. The sender issues the MAIL FROM: command. The email address of the user who sent the message is included as an argument.

4. The server sends back the 250 response code.

5. The sender issues the RCPT TO: command. The email address of the message recipient is included as an argument.

6. If the server can accept mail for the recipient, the server sends back the 250 response code. Otherwise, the server sends back a code indicating the problem (such as the 550 code, which indicates that the user's mailbox wasn't found).

7. The sender issues the DATA command, indicating that it is ready to start sending the contents of the email message.

8. The server issues the 354 response code, instructing the sender to start transmitting the message contents.

9. The sender sends the message data and ends with a period (.) on a line by itself.

10. The server sends back the 250 response code, indicating that the mail was received.

11. The sender issues the QUIT command, indicating that the transmission is over and the session should be closed.

12. The server sends the 221 code, indicating that the transmission channel will be closed.

The network uses this SMTP communication process to pass the email message to the user's mailbox on the destination email server. The message then waits in the user's mailbox until the user logs in to view the mail. Depending on the protocol or the type of email client, the message is either downloaded to the user's computer for viewing and processing, or the user edits and manages the message directly on the server.

Retrieving the Mail

The SMTP delivery process described in the preceding section is not designed to deliver mail to a user but only to deliver mail to the user's mailbox. The user must then access the mailbox to view the mail. This additional step might complicate the process, but it offers the following advantages:

▶ The server continues to receive mail for the user even when the user's computer is not on the network.

▶ The email delivery system is independent of the recipient's computer or location.

The latter advantage is a feature with which many email users are well acquainted. This feature enables the user to check email from multiple locations. Theoretically, any computer with access to the Internet and an email client application can be configured to check the user's mailbox for messages. You can check your mail from home, from an office, or from a hotel room. This process of accessing the mailbox and downloading messages requires a mail retrieval protocol. In the following sections, you learn about POP and IMAP. You also learn about webmail, a more recent alternative that lets users access their mailbox through an ordinary web browser.

Email and Network Security

In reality, network security structures, such as firewalls, sometimes prevent the user from checking and sending email from unfamiliar locations.

By the Way

The email server that holds user mailboxes typically must support both the SMTP service (for receiving incoming messages) and a mail retrieval protocol service (for giving users access to the mailbox). This process is depicted in Figure 21.3. This interaction requires coordination and compatibility between the SMTP service and the mail retrieval service so that data doesn't become lost or corrupt when the services access the same mailbox simultaneously.

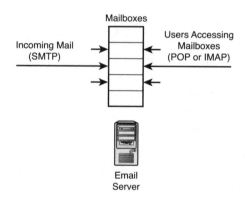

FIGURE 21.3
The SMTP service application and the mail retrieval service application must coordinate access to the mailbox.

POP3

Post Office Protocol version 3 (POP3) is a widely used message-retrieval protocol. POP3 is described in RFC 1939, and later RFCs have offered extensions and refinements. The client initiates a TCP connection to the POP3 server application on the email server. By default, the POP3 server listens for connections on TCP port 110. After the connection has been established, the client application must send username and password information to the email server. If the login credentials are accepted, the user can access the mailbox to download or delete messages.

Like the SMTP client, the POP3 client uses a series of four-character commands for communicating with the server. The server responds with a small number of alphabetic responses, such as +OK (indicating that the command was executed) and -ERR (indicating that the command resulted in an error). The responses might also include additional arguments or parameters. Each message in the mailbox is referenced by a message number. The client sends a RETR (retrieve) command to the server to download a message. The DELE command deletes a message from the server.

The messages sent between the POP3 client and server are invisible to the user. These commands are issued by the email client application as a response to the user's activities within the email client user interface.

One disadvantage of POP3 is the limited number of functions that can take place at the server. The user can only list the messages in the mailbox, delete messages, and download messages. Any manipulation of the message contents must occur on the client side. This limitation can cause delays and increase network traffic as messages are downloaded from the server to the client. The newer and more sophisticated IMAP was developed to address some of these shortcomings.

IMAP4

Internet Message Access Protocol version 4 (IMAP4) is a message-retrieval protocol similar to POP3. IMAP4, however, offers several new features that aren't available with POP3. With IMAP4, you can browse server-based folders and move, delete, and view messages without first copying the messages to your local computer. IMAP4 also allows you to save certain settings such as client window appearance or search messages on the server for a specified search string. You can also create, remove, and rename mailboxes on the server computer.

Most recent email clients support both POP3 and IMAP4. Although POP3 currently has a wider user base, the many advantages of IMAP ensure that email installations will continue converting to IMAP4.

Email Clients

An email client application runs on a user's workstation and communicates with an email server. As you learned earlier in this hour, the local workstation does not form a direct connection with the recipient of an email message. Instead, the workstation sends the message to an email server using an email client. The server sends the message on to the email server assigned to the recipient. In a conventional email scenario, the user who receives the message accesses a personal mailbox on the email server, and the message is downloaded to the user's workstation. The first step and the last step in this process (sending the message to the original server and downloading the message from the receiving server) are typically performed by an email client application.

The email client serves three functions:

▶ Sends outgoing messages to an outgoing email server using SMTP

▶ Collects incoming email messages from an email server using POP3 or IMAP

▶ Serves as a user interface for reading, managing, and composing mail messages

The email client must be capable of serving as both an SMTP client and a mail retrieval (POP or IMAP) client.

The email protocols discussed earlier in this hour provide a clear roadmap for electronic mail communication and, for that reason, email clients are all similar. The details of how to configure an email client may vary but, if you are familiar with the processes described in this hour, it usually isn't difficult to figure out how to get it working. (One caveat to the preceding sentence: Security features related to authentication and encryption provide an additional layer of complexity beyond mere networking. Consult your ISP or email administrator for information on the appropriate security settings for your mail account.) Like other network client applications, an email client communicates with the network through the protocol stack. The computer with the email client must have a working TCP/IP implementation, and it must be configured so that the email application can reach the network through TCP/IP.

After you have established that your computer is functioning properly as a client on a TCP/IP network, you need to obtain a few additional parameters from an official of your network to configure an email client on your system. If you are a home user, obtain this information through your ISP. If you are a corporate user, obtain this information from your network administrator.

You need to know the following:

▶ The fully qualified domain name of the email server to use for outgoing mail. This server often receives the hostname SMTP followed by the domain name (for example, SMTP.rosbud.org).

▶ The fully qualified hostname of the POP or IMAP server.

▶ The username and password of an email user account on the POP or IMAP server.

The task of configuring an email client is largely a matter of obtaining these parameters and entering them into the email client application.

Email client applications have gradually become integrated into the standard desktop environment for most operating systems. Windows users access mail through the Windows Mail or Outlook mail client. Apple Mail is standard on Mac OS X systems. Linux systems typically come with a popular open source mail client such as Evolution or Mozilla Thunderbird.

Email clients are often integrated with other related tools that offer calendar, scheduling, and address book features. Mail clients can also interpret filename extensions (.doc, .txt, .pdf, .jpg) and launch the appropriate viewer application to read incoming attachments. This kind of integration with other applications is convenient if used appropriately, but it has also spawned a whole new generation of macro **viruses** and **worms**—mostly affecting Windows systems—delivered through email attachments. A typical macro virus might access the user's address book to learn new email addresses and then automatically email itself to the other users in the address book (see Figure 21.4). Recent Windows systems employ additional safeguards to prevent this kind of breach, but email-borne worms and viruses were a major problem in the Windows 95 and Windows XP eras.

FIGURE 21.4
An email virus.

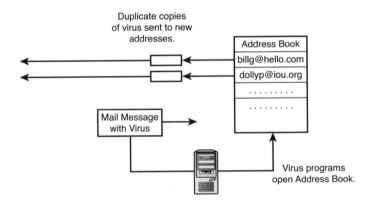

By the Way

Watch What You Click

Email-borne worms and viruses have caused considerable damage in the past, although the problem has gotten more manageable in recent years due to better public awareness and effective antivirus techniques. The important point is that accepting attachments and clicking links delivered through email creates a risk for your system. Consult your OS vendor documentation for recommendations on how to configure your system to minimize that risk.

Webmail

The rise of the World Wide Web has led to a whole new category of email designed around web technology. These web-based (or **webmail**) email tools do not require a full-featured email client application as discussed earlier in this hour. The user simply visits the website with an Internet browser and accesses the email through a web interface. The user's email is, therefore, accessible from any computer that can reach the Internet. Hotmail, Yahoo! Mail, and Google's Gmail are examples of webmail services. These services are often free—or almost free—because the provider makes enough money on advertising to support the whole infrastructure.

Webmail is versatile and easy to use. The option is a good choice for nontechnical home users who are accustomed to the web and don't want to have to configure and troubleshoot an email application. Some corporations now use webmail in certain situations because their firewalls permit HTTP traffic and prevent SMTP. Webmail might seem insecure at a glance. Anyone on the Internet knows how to reach the Yahoo! site and can probably figure out how to reach the Yahoo! mail site. But it is important to remember that traditional email isn't that secure either, unless you take steps to secure it. Anyone who has your username and password can probably check your mail. The major webmail sites provide secure login and other safeguards. If you're considering a small, local, webmail service, it is a good idea to find out about security for the system.

The biggest complaint about webmail is usually its performance. Because the mail system has no real presence on the client computer (other than a web browser), all the details of composing, opening, and moving messages take place across the bottleneck of a network connection. By contrast, a traditional email client downloads any new messages at the beginning of a session, and all actions related to composing and storing messages take place on the client. Despite the performance penalty, the extreme convenience of webmail ensures that it will remain an important option for many Internet users.

By the Way

> **It's Still Email**
>
> The primary purpose of webmail is to provide a user with a means of sending and receiving messages. Although webmail might seem like a whole new concept, it isn't so different from the ordinary email system depicted in Figure 21.1. The difference is that, with webmail, the software for reading and sending email resides on the email server and the recipient accesses that software through a web interface. Behind the scenes, webmail systems still use SMTP for transmitting email messages across the network.

Spam

No recent development in email technology has had more impact than the rise of spam. **Spam** is the nickname for the mass-mail email messages that clutter the mailboxes of millions of Internet users. The messages advertise bank loans, dietary aids, charity scams, and various products and services on the theme of ephemeral gratification. Technologically, spam is just email—that's why it works. The email servers routing a message don't know whether the message was generated by an odious automation scheme or by a loved one of the recipient.

Luckily, the receiver has some options for identifying and eliminating spam. Some of the techniques used for fighting spam are based on TCP/IP principles and are therefore relevant to this book. However, as you will see, the creators of spam are good at finding their way around the antidotes, so no solution lasts forever. Newer techniques focus primarily on analyzing the text of the email message.

When the spam industry started, recipients began to realize that much of the spam came from a few specific email addresses. Spam foes have accumulated large lists of addresses that are thought to be associated with spam. These lists are called **blacklists**. Firewalls, mail servers, or client programs can scan incoming messages for evidence of a blacklisted address.

Spammers, however, often change IP addresses and domain names to avoid the blacklist. A blacklist is considered a good first line of defense, but it is not adequate for completely controlling spam. In fact, conventional blacklists are becoming increasingly irrelevant because spammers have perfected the technique for getting around them. One strategy is to use the mail server of other unsuspecting companies to forward spam messages. As you learned earlier in this hour, an SMTP mail server simply waits for a message from a client and forwards it. The idea, of course, is that only the owners of the mail server use it to forward messages, but a mail server that isn't properly locked down can be used by *anybody*, including spammers at another location (see Figure 21.5). Sometimes legitimate companies and totally innocent individuals find themselves on email blacklists because spammers are using their server as a relay.

Spam foes have struck back against this tactic with their own remedy. By placing the mail server inside the corporate firewall and blocking incoming SMTP requests at the firewall (see Figure 21.6), an organization protects itself from becoming a spam relay. As shown in Figure 21.6, mail clients from inside the firewall can use the mail server to forward messages, but clients located outside cannot reach the mail server. This technique is useful for controlling spam. However, it does create some limitations. A user from the home network who is traveling with a laptop or checking mail from some outside location might find it impossible to send messages without reconfiguring the email client to point to a different SMTP server. (As you learn in Hour 11, a virtual private network (VPN) connection eliminates this problem by allowing the laptop user to connect directly to the local network from a remote location.) A more versatile solution that is gaining popularity is to keep the SMTP server outside of the firewall but to require authentication by the email client. Most contemporary email client applications support authentication settings for outgoing mail.

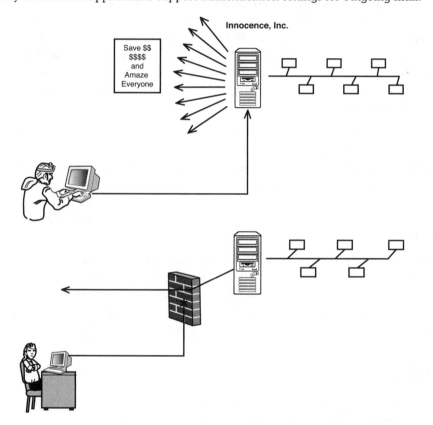

FIGURE 21.5
Spammers can sometimes use someone else's unsecured and unsuspecting email server to send their messages.

FIGURE 21.6
Placing the SMTP server behind a firewall and blocking incoming SMTP requests protects the server from misuse by spammers.

Some spammers even break into the computers of innocent users and configure the systems to send spam. These spambots can often send thousands of messages before they are ever detected. Some network admins have fought back by using a **whitelist**—a list of addresses that *are allowed* to send mail to the domain. This technique can be effective, but it is prohibitively restrictive for many organizations.

Another defense is known as a **graylist**. A graylist system temporarily rejects messages from an unknown source. If the message is legitimate, the sending server retransmits the message; however, spam servers are typically automated tools that are not designed to retransmit in the case of failed deliveries. If the server doesn't retransmit, the message is assumed to be spam. By the time a spam server does get around to retransmitting, there is a good chance the Internet's blacklisting services might have already picked up the spamming address. Graylisting is, therefore, often used in conjunction with blacklisting.

Many tools for fighting spam rely on analysis of the message content. Certain terms and phrases occur more frequently in spam headers and messages. Some spam filters impound messages based on rules. For instance, a filter might impound curse words or other terms associated with gratuitous anatomical descriptions. More sophisticated methods, such as Bayesian spam filtering, use probabilistic techniques to analyze the word use within the message and assign a score that indicates the likelihood that a message is spam. The weird word choice and cryptic language of some spam messages reflects the spammer's desire to slip through the net of these content-based probabilistic filters.

Some of these filtering tools have a tendency to create false positives, in which legitimate messages are impounded for exhibiting a spamlike profile. The best techniques offer a means for "training" the filter, by showing it any mistaken positives so that it can recalculate the probabilities and not make the same mistake twice.

Summary

This hour described what happens to an email message after it leaves your computer. You looked behind the scenes at the email delivery process. You learned about SMTP and the mail retrieval techniques such as POP3, IMAP4, and webmail. This hour also discussed the role of the email client application and described the ongoing struggle to control and contain spam email messages.

Q&A

Q. *I can send messages but I can't connect to my mail server to download new messages. What should I check?*

A. Your email client application uses SMTP to send messages and a mail retrieval protocol (probably POP or IMAP) to check the server for incoming messages. You might have a problem with the transmission of your mail retrieval protocol. Many networks use different servers for incoming and outgoing messages. Your POP or IMAP server might be down. Look for a configuration dialog box in your email client application that gives the name of your POP or IMAP server. Try to ping the server and see whether it responds.

Q. *A Turkish accounting firm ordered 14 computers from my company. They insist that the email applications included with the computers support MIME. Why are they so adamant?*

A. Email was originally designed to support the ASCII character set, a collection of characters developed for users who write in English. Many characters used in other languages are not present in the ASCII set. MIME extends the character set to include other non-ASCII characters.

Workshop

The following workshop is composed of a series of quiz questions and practical exercises. The quiz questions are designed to test your overall understanding of the current material. The practical exercises are intended to afford you the opportunity to apply the concepts discussed during the current hour, as well as build upon the knowledge acquired in previous hours of study. Please take time to complete the quiz questions and exercises before continuing. Refer to Appendix A, "Answers to Quizzes and Exercises," for answers.

Quiz

1. What is MIME and what is it used for?

2. What protocol is used to send email messages?

3. Which protocols are used to retrieve email messages from the user's mailbox?

4. What is the largest complaint about webmail?

5. What are the advantages of webmail?

Exercises

1. If you have an Internet account, open the email client you use for sending and viewing email. Try to figure out where the SMTP server (for outgoing mail) and the POP or IMAP server (for incoming mail) are configured.

2. If you're feeling really adventurous, ask a close friend whether you can configure an email client on the friend's computer to check your email account. Some email applications support multiple email accounts. Or you might be able to configure a built-in email tool that your friend isn't currently using.

By the
Way

> **SMTP Protection**
>
> You might find that you can check your mail from your friend's ISP network but you can't send outgoing mail from your friend's network to the SMTP server on your own ISP's network. Many ISPs do not allow external email messages to bounce off their SMTP server.

Key Terms

Review the following list of key terms:

▶ **Blacklist:** A list of servers that aren't allowed to forward mail messages to the domain.

▶ **Email body:** The section of an email message that includes the text of the message.

▶ **Email client (Email reader):** A client email application that is responsible for sending mail, retrieving mail, and managing the user interface through which the user interacts with the mail system.

▶ **Email header:** The preliminary section of an email message, consisting of informational fields and associated values.

▶ **Graylist:** A system for detecting spam servers by rejecting the initial delivery and waiting to see if the server resends the message.

▶ **Internet Message Access Protocol (IMAP):** An enhanced mail retrieval protocol that provides several features not available with POP. For instance, you can access mail messages without first downloading the messages from the server.

▶ **Mailbox:** A location on an email server where incoming messages are stored for a user.

▶ **Multipurpose Internet Mail Extensions (MIME):** An email format that extends the capabilities of Internet mail.

▶ **Post Office Protocol (POP):** A popular mail retrieval protocol used on the Internet. POP enables the user to log in to an email server and download or delete waiting messages.

▶ **Simple Mail Transfer Protocol (SMTP):** A protocol used for sending mail on TCP/IP networks.

▶ **Webmail:** A system that lets the user access email messages through an ordinary web browser.

▶ **Whitelist:** A list of addresses that are allowed to forward mail messages to the domain.

HOUR 22

Streaming and Casting

What You'll Learn in This Hour:

▶ Streaming protocols

▶ Multimedia links

▶ Podcasting

▶ Voice over IP

The Internet wasn't created for playing music and watching old TV shows. New ideas and new protocols were necessary to usher in the era of Internet streaming. This hour looks at multimedia technologies for the Internet.

At the completion of this hour, you will be able to

▶ Describe RTP and its helper protocols

▶ Discuss the Transport layer alternatives SCTP and DCCP

▶ Describe how a multimedia file is played from a web link

▶ Explain what podcasting is and how it works

▶ Describe some important VoIP protocols

The Streaming Problem

With all those network connections, transmission media, video monitors, and PC speakers pointing at all those users around the world, the next question was whether the Internet would ever make TV channels, telephones, and radio stations obsolete. Could the Internet support voice communications? Could providers stream multimedia programming to users on demand (or even live)?

Experts and entrepreneurs have talked about a combination TV/computer system for years, but early models always came up short—partly for lack of Internet bandwidth but also because home computer hardware was not quite to the mark.

The TV/computer box is now a reality for users who want to pay for it, and Internet phone service is becoming quite common. Online services such as Hulu and YouTube offer access to an endless play list of feature films, TV shows, and home video, while Facebook pages and even ordinary websites provide convenient links to embedded audio and video. These developments wouldn't have happened without advances in hardware and Internet infrastructure, but the new world of multimedia on demand also required some enhancements to the TCP/IP protocol system.

Multimedia streaming poses several problems for the protocol system, but perhaps the most significant problem is quality of service (QoS). The Internet was designed for transferring files and finite messages, not for interactive or continuous service. Datagrams follow their own paths based on decisions made at routers, and there is no guarantee they will arrive in a uniform, continuous stream. Streaming requires high performance, but also performance that is consistent and continuous enough to make voices and videos seem natural.

To illustrate this problem, consider the two primary protocols of the Transport layer (see Hour 6, "The Transport Layer"). The User Datagram Protocol (UDP) is fast, but it is not versatile or reliable. The Transport Control Protocol (TCP), on the other hand, is reliable, but this reliability comes at the expense of performance. The reliability of TCP is achieved through rituals of verification and retransmission, which adds uncertainty and interferes with the notion of continuous delivery.

Several new members of the TCP/IP protocol family were added to address issues related to streaming delivery. You learn about Real-time Transport Protocol (RTP) and some of other streaming protocols in this hour.

One important thing to notice is that the streaming problem is relevant to several different tasks. You can stream audio (such as FM radio or a **Voice over IP** [VoIP] telephone call), video (such as a live webcast or movie on demand), and even graphic animations.

Another means for transmitting multimedia content, of course, is just to save it in a file and transmit the file through email, web link, Really Simple Syndication (RSS) feed, or a music-sharing application. This hour also looks at multimedia links and how they work, but these techniques are not so different from any other file transfer scenario and therefore do not pose the same kind of challenge to the protocol system. The majority of this hour focuses on issues related to streaming.

Multimedia Environments

The problem of multimedia delivery concerns much more than just networking protocols. Server and client applications must be able to communicate vast amounts of information to stream and capture multimedia. Most of this data is carried within the payload of the network connection and thus isn't directly relevant to TCP/IP networking.

Until recently, much of the video on the Internet was based on Adobe's Flash video format and its surrounding technologies. Apple's QuickTime and Microsoft's Windows Media Services also provide ecosystems for streaming, including server-side applications, client-side media players, and file formats. Microsoft's Silverlight framework was intended as a full-scale alternative to the rich web development environment offered by Flash. As you learned in Hour 19, "The New Web," the Hypertext Markup Language version 5 (HTML5) specification provides built-in support for streaming that could make frameworks like Flash obsolete. HTML5 offers direct access to a variety of multimedia protocols and formats, including the RTP family protocols described in this hour.

Real-time Transport Protocol

Several solutions have appeared for the problem of timely, reliable delivery, but perhaps the most important solution to the Internet streaming puzzle is **Real-time Transport Protocol (RTP)**. RTP defines a packet format and a standard method for transmitting audio and video streams over TCP/IP. The name announces RTP as a transport protocol, but the reality is a bit more complex. RTP does not replace the primary transport protocols but is, instead, built on top of UDP (see Figure 22.1) and uses UDP ports to reach the Internet.

You might be wondering how RTP gets away with using UDP, considering the reliability issues related to UDP transmission. As you learned in Hour 6, developers can write their own reliability mechanisms to go along with UDP. In the case of RTP, an accompanying protocol called **Real-Time Control Protocol (RTCP)** monitors the QoS for an RTP session. This allows the application to make adjustments to the stream (by varying the flow rate or perhaps switching to a less-resource-intensive format or resolution). This approach doesn't completely eliminate the problem, but it does provide additional options for monitoring the flow of packets.

FIGURE 22.1
RTP uses UDP
to provide net-
work streaming.

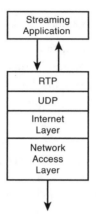

RTP was originally described in RFC 1889, which has since been superseded by RFC 3550 and later updates. The RTP header is shown in Figure 22.2. The fields in the header are

- **Version:** The version of RTP.

- **Padding:** Signals whether the packet contains one or more padding octets.

- **Extension:** Signals the existence of a header extension.

- **CSRC count:** Number of CSRC identifiers that follow the fixed header.

- **Marker:** Marks frame boundaries and other significant points in the packet stream.

- **Payload type:** Format of the payload.

- **Sequence number:** A number representing the place in the session that increments by one with each packet. This parameter can be used to detect lost packets.

- **Timestamp:** The sampling instant of the first octet in the payload.

- **SSRC:** Identifies a synchronization source.

- **CSRC:** Identifies contributing sources for the packet payload.

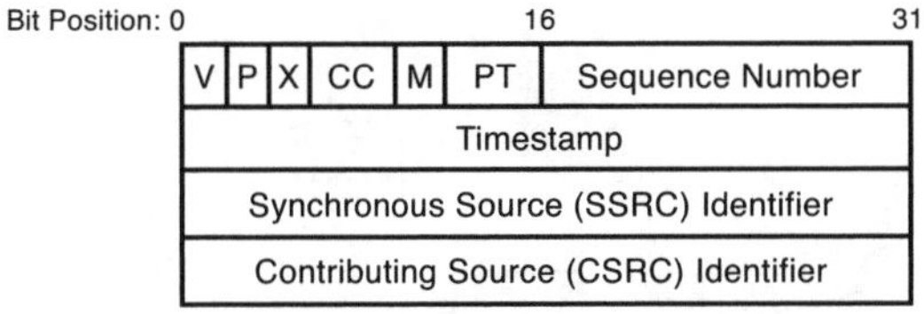

Bit Position: 0   16   31

V	P	X	CC	M	PT	Sequence Number

Timestamp

Synchronous Source (SSRC) Identifier

Contributing Source (CSRC) Identifier

FIGURE 22.2
RTP header
format

An optional RTP extension header allows individual application developers to experiment with modifications to improve performance and quality of service. Some vendors have rolled out their own versions of RTP—with varying degrees of compatibility.

The audio applications using RTP (or any other streaming protocol for that matter) must provide some form of buffering to ensure a steady stream of audio or video output. A buffer is a block of memory used for temporarily storing data as it is received. Buffering allows the application to process input at a steady rate even though the arrival rate might vary. As long as the buffer is never totally empty or totally full, the application receiving the data can process input at a constant rate.

The RT family also provides another protocol called **Real-Time Streaming Protocol (RTSP)**. RTSP sends commands that let the remote user control the stream. You can think of RTSP as something like a television remote. RTSP does not participate in the actual streaming, but it lets the user send commands like pause, play, and record to the server application.

A typical streaming scenario is shown in Figure 22.3. In this case, audio input is received through an audio interface and transmitted to a computer application, where it is converted to a digital format. Streaming software breaks the stream into discrete packets that are transmitted through RTP and the TCP/IP protocol stack to a streaming client, where data is received into a buffer and then read continuously from the buffer by a music player application that outputs sound to a pair of stereo speakers. Meanwhile, RTCP provides QoS information to the applications participating in the session, and, if this were a prerecorded video or audio file instead of a real singer, the user on the client end could select options in the client application that send start or stop commands to the server through RTSP.

FIGURE 22.3
A streaming
scenario.

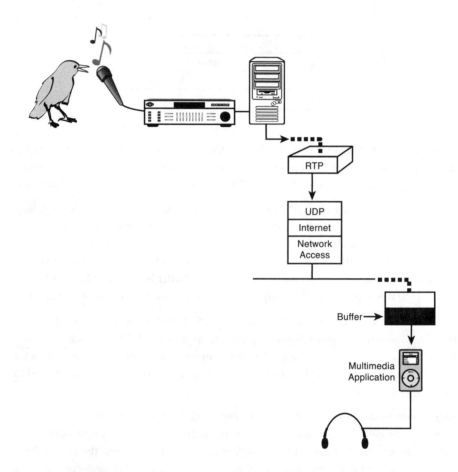

Transport Options

Despite the widespread use of RTP over UDP for audio and video streaming, the experts are still at work on Transport layer options that address the fundamental unsuitability of either TCP or UDP for streaming situations.

Stream Control Transmission Protocol (SCTP), which was first described in RFC 2000 and is now covered in RFC 4960, is a connection-oriented transport protocol (and thus more similar to TCP), but, like UDP, SCTP is more message oriented. SCTP also offers the capability to maintain several message streams in parallel through a single connection.

Datagram Congestion Control Protocol (DCCP), which is described in RFC 4340, also borrows features from both TCP and UDP. DCCP is connection oriented (like TCP), with fast but unreliable delivery (like UDP).

Both SCTP and DCCP perform something called congestion control. As you can see by the name, DCCP is especially interested in providing a congestion-control mechanism. Congestion control is a means for reducing the kinds of retransmission issues associated with TCP and providing more efficient use of the bandwidth. Algorithms used by the protocol adjust the characteristics of the data flow to optimize throughput and reduce the number of retransmitted packets.

Implementations of SCTP and DCCP are available now. SCTP has been around for a little longer, and is perhaps better known to developers, but DCCP shows promise.

Multimedia Links

You don't have to surf far to find video and audio images embedded in web pages. Click a link to hear a sound, watch video, or listen to a vocal track. You might be wondering what is actually happening when you click that link.

The answer, of course, depends on where the link goes. Many multimedia links are simply files. As you learned earlier in Hour 18, "HTTP, HTML, and the World Wide Web," an <a> tag with an HREF attribute is a reference to another resource. In previous examples, that resource was a web page. However, the reference can point to any type of file as long as the browser knows how to interpret the file's contents. Modern browsers can handle many different types of file formats. On Windows systems, the file extension (the part of the filename after the period, such as .doc, .gif, or .avi) tells the browser (or the operating system) what application to use to open the file. Some other operating systems can determine the file type independently of the file extension. If the browsing computer has the necessary software to open the video or audio file, and if the browser or operating system is configured to recognize the file, the web page can reference the file through an ordinary link, and the browsing computer executes the file when the link is clicked.

Common video file formats include

- ▶ **AVI (Audio Visual Interleave):** An audio/visual format developed by Microsoft.

- ▶ **MPEG (Motion Picture Experts Group):** A popular and high-quality digital video format.

- ▶ **SWF (Shockwave Flash):** A format used with screen animations and Flash videos.

- ▶ **MOV (QuickTime):** Apple originally developed the QuickTime format for Macintosh systems, but QuickTime is widely available for other systems.

YouTube accepts submissions in several different formats but converts most videos to a Flash Video (FLV)-formatted file embedded in a SWF file because Flash format is fast and the Flash player is readily available. Several audio file formats are also available on the Internet, but the proprietary MP3 format is by far the most popular for downloading and playing music files.

When you install multimedia software on the client computer (for instance, when you install the QuickTime viewer), the installer application typically registers the file extensions that the computer should use to open the application. In some cases, if the correct application or plug-in isn't available to play the file, the user is directed to a download site and the file is installed automatically.

Of course, there is much more to the process of recording, encoding, and viewing a multimedia file. However, the details are not actually the business of HTTP or TCP/IP. As far as the network is concerned, the browser simply downloads a file when a user clicks the link.

By the Way

Helper Apps

The fact that the browser sometimes uses other applications to open and execute files demonstrates that the whole HTTP ecosystem (HTTP, HTML, the web server, the web browser) is essentially a delivery method, much like the TCP/IP layers below.

Sometimes the link offers the option of connecting to an actual multimedia stream, as described earlier in this hour. Streaming servers located on the Internet stream audio and video content on demand to a user who clicks the link.

A common way to initiate a stream through a web browser is with RTSP, which you learned about earlier in this hour. As this hour has already described, RTSP does not actually participate in the streaming, but it provides a control system for starting and stopping the stream. A URL such as

rtsp://greatmovies.com/casablanca.mp4

might deliver a Bogart classic to your desktop—if your browser is configured with the correct software to process the connection.

To complicate matters, streams are sometimes obscured by web scripts or intentionally hidden from view. Sometimes the URL for a multimedia stream is actually enclosed in a small text file called a metafile. The resource referenced in the address bar might actually be the metafile, which might have an extension such as .pls, .ram, .asx, .wax, .wvx, and so on. If you're curious where the link leads, you can find several utilities on the Internet that can help you find the location of a hidden multimedia stream.

Podcasting

Between this duality of a multimedia file made available for download and a continuous stream on demand is an intermediate (or at least conceptually distinct) creature known as the podcast. **Podcasting** arose around Apple's famous iPod device, but the term now finds a more general use.

A podcast subscription delivers multimedia (usually audio) content through an RSS feed. RSS was originally developed to feed or channel news to the user, kind of like delivering the morning paper through the Internet. The user subscribes to an RSS news service, and stories are automatically delivered to the user's desktop. The important point is that the user doesn't have to go out and find the news on a website. After the subscription is established, new stories are "pushed" to the reader automatically (see Figure 22.4).

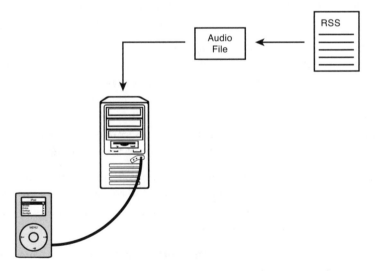

FIGURE 22.4
Podcasting delivers multimedia files over an RSS service.

The goal of the podcast phenomenon is to deliver multimedia files to the viewer directly using the tools of RSS. As it turns out, RSS provides a means of attaching a file to the news message. That attachment feature became the vehicle for podcasting.

Podcast client applications manage the podcast files and provide notice of updates. iTunes users can easily receive podcasts, and other music players also offer the feature. iPodder is an open source podcast client that works with Windows, Mac OS, Linux, and Berkeley Software Distribution (BSD) systems.

The whole purpose of the podcast is to receive periodic updates, which means that whoever is producing the podcasts on the server side needs to provide some kind of ongoing programming. Grassroots podcasts have become popular around the world, with regular interviews, how-to sessions, music videos, and comedy acts beaming out to subscribers through the miracle of RSS.

Voice over IP

Internet telephony is now quite common in many areas. TCP/IP phone service is often less expensive, and more versatile, than conventional phone service. In many ways, Internet phone calls are just another form of streaming audio, so it should be no surprise that RTP is the most popular protocol for transmitting Voice over IP (VoIP) communications. But the act of talking is only one piece of the puzzle. The business of finding a user, placing a call, setting up a session, and gracefully ending the session requires new tools and protocols.

If you expect your IP phone service to connect with the conventional phone network, you also face the problem of providing a control system that is compatible (or at least "interface-able") with equivalent controls used on conventional phone systems.

IP telephony can occur through an actual hardware phone device (which is similar to a telephone, but it is designed to work with TCP/IP), or it can happen with what is commonly called a soft phone—a computer program performing the function of a phone that receives audio input from a microphone device, sends audio output to speakers or a headset, and connects with the world through the computer's TCP/IP networking software. In either case, the phone sends signals over the network that must be received and interpreted by another phone at the end of the call.

Several protocols exist for initiating and managing VoIP phone calls. The International Telecommunication Union's H.323 protocol system is a large family of protocols for managing VoIP, teleconferencing, and other communications tasks. Many VoIP systems are designed for H.323.

Another more recent protocol that is simpler (and easy to describe) is known as the **Session Initiation Protocol (SIP)**.

SIP is an Application layer protocol for starting, stopping, and managing a communication session. SIP sends what is called an invitation to a remote user. In the context of VoIP, that invitation is equivalent to placing a call. In addition to initiating and terminating calls, SIP provides features such as conferencing, call forwarding, and **feature negotiation**.

When the call is established, the actual streaming voice communication occurs using a protocol such as RTP.

The other complication with IP telephony is reaching callers with old-fashioned land lines. A VoIP gateway device serves as an interface from the Internet to the phone network (Figure 22.5). VoIP callers can talk to each other directly over the Internet without the need for a gateway, but when they call a number on the conventional phone network, the call is routed to a VoIP gateway device. Internet telephony users can subscribe to a VoIP gateway service to gain access to a gateway. The option is also typically part of a VoIP phone contract, but the rates for connecting through a gateway are often much higher than calling a user through end-to-end Internet telephony. End-to-end calls across the Internet are often free (or nearly free) to anywhere in the world for users who pay the monthly subscription rate.

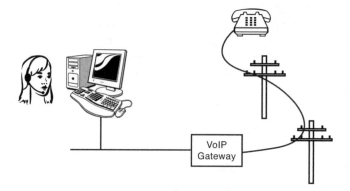

FIGURE 22.5
A VoIP gateway serves as an interface to the conventional phone network.

Summary

This hour looked at some of the technologies that provide multimedia streaming on the Internet. You learned about RTP, RTSP, and RTCP. This hour also looked at the SCTP and DCCP transport protocols and discussed how multimedia links play music and video with a mouse click. You also learned about podcasting, and the hour ended with a look at VoIP.

Q&A

Q. Why are the primary Transport layer protocols ill-suited for streaming?

A. UDP is fast but unreliable, and TCP is reliable, but the controls used to ensure delivery make it slow and prone to retransmission.

Q. *What is the purpose of RTP's two sister protocols, RTCP and RTSP?*

A. While RTP provides the streaming, RTCP monitors and reports on quality of service. RTSP is used for control commands to start or stop the stream.

Q. *Why does YouTube convert the videos submitted to Flash format?*

A. Flash is an efficient and reliable video format, and the Flash player is readily available.

Workshop

The following workshop is composed of a series of quiz questions and practical exercises. The quiz questions are designed to test your overall understanding of the current material. The practical exercises are intended to afford you the opportunity to apply the concepts discussed during the current hour, as well as build upon the knowledge acquired in previous hours of study. Please take time to complete the quiz questions and exercises before continuing. Refer to Appendix A, "Answers to Quizzes and Exercises," for answers.

Quiz

1. What is the purpose of buffering in RTP?

2. What is RTSP and what is it used for?

3. Are SCTP and DCCP connection oriented or connectionless?

4. What system are podcasts delivered by?

5. What is SIP and what is it used for?

Exercises

1. Locate and listen to a streaming radio station.

2. If you have access to VoIP, make a phone call and compare the call quality to a land line.

3. Locate and listen to a podcast. Podcast.com is a good place to look.

4. Watch a YouTube video and compare the quality to a show viewed on your television.

Key Terms

Review the following list of key terms:

▶ **Datagram Congestion Control Protocol (DCCP):** An alternative Transport layer protocol for streaming applications.

▶ **Feature negotiation:** A negotiation between applications or devices to arrive at a common set of features for the connection.

▶ **Podcasting:** A technique for delivering multimedia files over RSS feeds.

▶ **Real-Time Control Protocol (RTCP):** A protocol that provides quality of service monitoring for RTP.

▶ **Real-Time Streaming Protocol (RTSP):** A protocol that provides control commands for RTP.

▶ **Real-time Transport Protocol (RTP):** A popular streaming protocol.

▶ **Session Initiation Protocol (SIP):** A protocol for managing VoIP communications.

▶ **Stream Control Transmission Protocol (SCTP):** An alternative Transport layer protocol for streaming applications.

▶ **Voice over IP (VoIP):** Telephony services over TCP/IP networks.

HOUR 23
Living in the Cloud

What You'll Learn in This Hour:

- ▶ Software as a service
- ▶ Virtual hosting
- ▶ The elastic cloud
- ▶ Platform as a service

Everyone is talking about the cloud, but the term *cloud computing* can have different meanings depending on the context. This hour studies the cloud from the viewpoints of the end user and IT specialist.

At the completion of this hour, you'll be able to

- ▶ Explain why software as a service tools are gaining popularity in the mobile era

- ▶ Define cloud storage, cloud backup, and cloud printing

- ▶ Describe how data centers use virtualization

- ▶ Describe elastic hosting

- ▶ Explain how platform as a service differs from EC2-style elastic cloud services

What Is the Cloud?

The term **cloud computing** has recently emerged as the loudest buzz in an industry that loves buzzwords. IT companies, phone companies, advertisers, and everyday companies with overcrowded server rooms or overspent IT budgets are all betting on the cloud. But what is cloud computing, really? Like many buzzwords, cloud computing is a term chasing a meaning. It has come to mean different things to different people and different market segments, but for purposes of this discussion, the services that fall under the heading of cloud computing primarily inhabit the following realms:

▶ **Online user services:** Software as a service (SaaS) tools and other online applications that provide the end user with convenient access to simple and practical online services, such as storage, printing, and online versions of desktop productivity tools.

▶ **IT professional cloud services:** A system administrator who talks about the cloud is not referring to an online spreadsheet. IT cloud services provide a complete online replacement for everything within an IT server room, including the server hardware.

Although the experience of working with these technologies is quite different, behind the scenes, they are both embodiments of the same cloud principles.

The cloud computing revolution is about providing services on the Internet that used to have to happen on the local computer or local network. The cloud metaphor implies a lack of visibility. You cannot see exactly where these services come from or how they do what they do; you just know they are out there and available through the same Internet addressing rules you learned about in earlier hours.

As you read through this hour, you will notice that the cloud services model is yet another embodiment of the client/server architecture that has been a major theme throughout this book. However, in the world of the cloud, the lines between what is the server and what is the client—and what is the application—become blurred.

The rest of this hour describes the cloud as it appears within both end-user and IT services. Keep in mind, though, that IT cloud **data center** techniques such as virtual computing and cloud-based load balancing are probably at work behind the scenes with the SaaS-style cloud services, as well, just as they are a silent presence within the framework of many major websites, enterprise networks, and social networking services today.

The User's Cloud

As you learned in Hour 20, "Web Services," TCP/IP and the web infrastructure have become a platform for building and deploying network-based applications. When you visit a website today, you probably aren't reading a simple static HTML page.

Previous hours have discussed the practice of launching scripts or other programmatic elements over the Web. The modern concept of cloud-based services takes that concept even further. As you will learn in later sections, the cloud provides a complete user experience from within the browser window.

End users have surfed to websites for years now without having to hear about cloud-based services or the customer cloud paradigm. In one sense, the technologies have evolved gradually, but the term *cloud* has only emerged for end users with the rise of smartphones and the mobile app culture. By shifting application processing to the server and reducing the need for client resources to a minimum, vendors can provide a vastly greater array of services on vastly lighter systems. At the same time, economies of scale provide savings on the server end, where a large volume of users helps to minimize the per-user cost.

However, big vendors like Apple, Google, and Microsoft that support these user cloud environments have more on their mind than simple networking. It is no secret that the reason these vendors are enticing users into the cloud is to gain a captive audience that they can market to advertisers or monetize through the discovery and sale of demographic information.

The following sections describe some representative elements of the user cloud environment. You'll learn about

- SaaS
- Cloud storage and backup
- Cloud printing

Keep in mind that the goal of these services is to provide simple, unobtrusive integration of the computer or mobile device with the user's life so that a user can attend to the task at hand (finding a song or filing a picture) with minimal distraction from the electronics.

Software as a Service

The term **software as a service (SaaS)** applies to a broad range of user applications designed to run on web servers rather than on the user's desktop. Many of these applications fall along the lines of classic productivity tools, such as word processors, spreadsheets, and presentation software. But many other popular online applications also inhabit this category.

In the world of SaaS, the only client is the web browser; everything else runs on the server. For instance, the user can connect to an online word processing tool and write an essay with a web browser. One of the major benefits is that the user can then reach the same essay from any web browser. The user can log in from a computer at school or from a computer in a hotel room across the world and access the same online document. Also, the service vendor provides fault tolerance, so the user doesn't have to worry about losing the document with a hard drive crash.

SaaS tools have been around for years, but they have gained popularity recently with the appearance of tool suites such as Google Docs (see Figure 23.1). The online version of Apple's iWork suite provides a similar range of services for iPhone and iPad users.

FIGURE 23.1
Google Docs and other similar SaaS tools provide an online equivalent to classic desktop productivity tools such as word processors and spreadsheets.

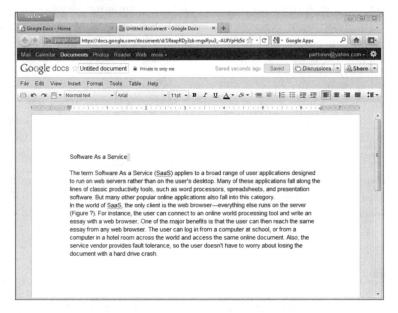

The spectrum of SaaS tools goes well beyond the classic productivity services offered by Google Apps. Some of the most common Internet tools today are theoretically classified as SaaS tools (for example, the iTunes music app, the Flickr photo manager, and even the Gmail webmail service). For a complete introduction to these tools, hunt them down online. For purpose of this discussion, the important thing to remember is that although these tools seem breathtakingly original and revolutionary from the viewpoint of the user experience, under the hood, they are built using a combination of the TCP/IP networking technologies you learned about in earlier hours, including the following:

▶ Encrypted login and access through Hypertext Transfer Protocol Secure (HTTPS) (Hour 11, "TCP/IP Security")

▶ Hypertext Markup Language (HTML) transmitted through HTTP (Hour 18, "HTTP, HTML, and the World Wide Web").

▶ AJAX, for efficient update of the client workspace and other client- and server-side scripting technologies (Hour 18)

▶ Extensible Markup Language (XML), to allow for efficient storage and retrieval of user data, along with Representation State Transfer (REST)- and Simple Object Access Protocol (SOAP)-based web service components (Hour 20, "Web Services").

▶ A content management system (CMS), in some cases, or other web server application that manages and maintains the client workspace and communicates with a back-end database or XML-based data store (Hour 19, "The New Web").

Of course, all communication occurs using the same TCP/IP protocols described throughout this book with resource location information transmitted through uniform resource identifiers (URIs) (Hour 17, "The Internet: A Closer Look").

Cloud Storage and Backup

Cloud-based storage and backup is a fast-growing application of the cloud paradigm that scales to all levels of use, from home users to large networks. Network backup techniques have existed for years and are routinely employed on corporate networks. As you learned in previous hours, the Internet is just another TCP/IP network, so these techniques are easily adapted to the Internet environment. The path for cloud-based storage and backup was cleared when engineers implemented the technologies necessary for its widespread adoption: a fast network and abundant, cheap online storage.

As described in the preceding section, online storage for user files and folders allows access from multiple locations. This concept is easily adapted to backup, a problem that has plagued users for years. Despite the pleas of experts to back up data on a regular basis, vast numbers of users don't take the time for it. A cloud backup service performs the task automatically. Most of these cloud backup tools take a similar approach. As Figure 23.2 shows, some form of backup agent program is located on the user's home system. At some regular interval (typically defined by the user), the operating system wakes up the client agent, which collects the files that have changed since the last backup (or all files, again depending on the user preference), connects to the backup service, and transfers the files to the server location. Most high-end services use some form of encryption for the backup and restore process.

Like the SaaS tools described in the preceding section, cloud-based storage offers the ability to access the data from other computers in other locations. The storage service also handles the problem of fault tolerance, and the fact that the data is stored offsite adds an additional layer of protection from loss due to fire or other calamity.

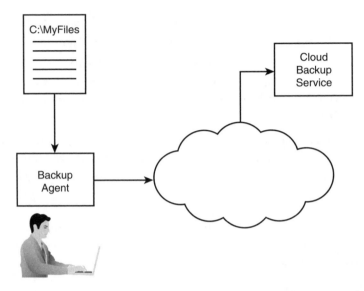

Online backup solutions are relatively inexpensive (as low as $5 per month in some cases, or even free when bundled with other services). One problem that many privacy advocates have mentioned in the past is that someone else has your data. Many of these services freely admit (or won't deny) that they scan through online data to obtain marketing and demographic information, and if you close your account, you don't have any guarantee they will delete your data.

Online storage with web-based SaaS tools is practically a necessity, however. Even with files stored using local applications, it is becoming an increasingly popular option, especially in a world of inexpensive portable computers and mobile devices, where storage space is limited and a convenient backup medium might not be available.

Cloud Print

Google's cloud printing is a new and still experimental technology that illustrates an exciting area for development in cloud services. This innovative service is a fitting place to end this brief summary of the user cloud environment, because techniques such as cloud printing might someday lead to a new generation of cloud-based control technologies that manage a vast assortment of appliances and devices around the home.

Google's idea is to manage printers through a form of cloud service. A user can associate printing devices with a Google account. When the user sends a print job to the printer, the computer accesses the Google printing service, which then puts the file in a print-ready format and sends it to the printer (see Figure 23.3).

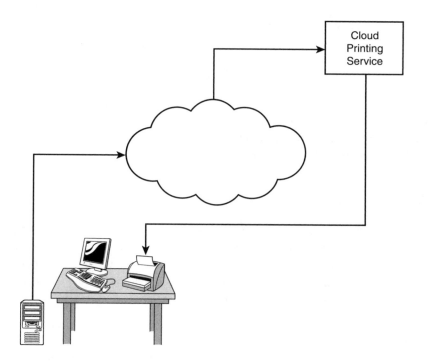

FIGURE 23.3
Google will even manage your printer through a cloud-based service.

At a glance, this concept might seem totally unnecessary. Google's print service is essentially acting as a print queue or print server, a role that ordinary household computers can easily fill without difficulty. However, Google's vision does offer some advantages.

According to Google, cloud printing eliminates the need for the user to get involved with the problems of installing and managing printer drivers, which would eliminate many common troubleshooting scenarios.

The global nature of the service provides benefit similar to the SaaS tools: The user can print to a home computer from a remote location, and friends or co-workers who have your permission can print to your home printer from remote locations.

Another Print Cloud

Hewlett-Packard (HP) has its own version of web-based printing, which differs slightly from cloud printing as it is defined by Google, but is emerging as an alternative option. HP printer models in HP's ePrint series have an email address, and the user can print a document by sending it to the printer through email.

By the Way

The full vision of Google's vision requires what they call a cloud-ready printer (CRP), which seems to be a network-ready printer with built-in TCP/IP support and the necessary software to participate in the Google cloud printing service. If the printer doesn't meet these requirements, it can still participate in the service if attached to a local computer that uses Google's Chrome browser.

If Google is successful with its vision of cloud printing, you can bet other vendors will adopt similar techniques and expand this concept to encompass other devices, such as home entertainment centers and even kitchen appliances.

The IT Cloud

To an IT professional, the technologies discussed earlier in this hour are nothing more than a practical extension of principles of conventional networking and web service techniques. The real cloud revolution, according to the experts, is what goes on behind the scenes. The IT cloud service model is already changing the way corporations and governments make decisions about IT services.

Today's IT cloud environment is a product of the convergence of two important developments:

▶ Virtualization

▶ The modern data center

The following sections describe these important new technologies and discuss some of the fundamental cloud service alternatives.

Understanding Virtualization

Virtualization is the act of re-creating some kind of real-world object or process within a computer. One common thing to virtualize within a computer is another computer. In other words, a process running on a computer performs the functions of a real computer and looks to the network like a real computer. This virtual computer (or virtual machine, as it is often called) can run applications, supervise external processes, and even communicate with remote computers through its own network address.

Figure 23.4 shows a typical virtualization scenario. The computer with the real-world hardware that is running the virtual machine is called the **host system**. The virtual computer running on the host is called the **guest system**.

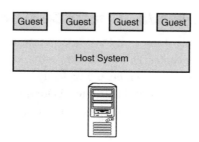

FIGURE 23.4
A single physi-
cal computer
can play host to
multiple virtual
guest systems.
Each guest
appears to the
network as a
real computer.

Various virtualization technologies have been around since the 1960s, but the concept has been viable in large-scale production settings only since computers have
become fast enough, and powerful enough, to support the intense processing load
associated with running a whole computer as an internal process. Of course, the host
system must be running software that provides a virtual environment for the guest
so that the guest behaves as if it were running on real hardware.

Various vendors provide virtualization software that is suitable for industrial settings,
including VMware, KVM, Xen, and Microsoft's Hyper-V. Virtualization techniques
have gained popularity in recent years for the following reasons:

▶ **Space:** By running multiple virtual computers on a single host, you reduce
the amount of floor space required for the server room. This can result in
significant savings and can provide a means for a company to expand even
if it can't expand its server room space.

▶ **Power:** Part of the virtualization trend is driven by utility costs. A single
host running several virtual systems uses much less power than a collection
of hardware-based servers.

▶ **Scalability:** New virtual systems can start and stop as the need arises.

▶ **Security:** The virtual space provides an additional layer of security to prevent intrusion, and if an attacker does gain entry to the guest system, a
sandbox-style security environment prevents access to the host. If a guest is
ever compromised, it can simply be deleted and replaced.

▶ **Compatibility:** Virtual systems can run programs that won't run on the
host. For instance, legacy applications created for previous Windows versions that will no longer run on a current Windows system will run inside a
virtual version of the previous system.

Once you start thinking of a complete computer system as something like a computer process, which doesn't take up space and can appear or disappear whenever the
need arises, it opens up a world of possibilities for how computers are deployed and
managed.

The Rise of the Modern Data Center

The availability of cheap file storage and fast Internet connections has led to a new concept known as the data center. Think of a data center as a place to store and process lots and lots of data. Data centers are typically big buildings full of servers and storage arrays. The prototypical data centers belong to giant Internet companies such as Google and Amazon who need to place huge amounts of data within easy reach of Internet users.

The data center holds racks of physical computer systems, each running multiple virtual computer systems. The infrastructure is carefully designed to provide fault tolerance and load balancing (see Figure 23.5). Virtual systems are distributed across the physical hardware to balance the server load. In some cases, the network can respond to overload or system distress by moving processes to other systems.

FIGURE 23.5
Within the data center, virtual machine instances are deployed across a collection of rack-mounted servers for a balanced workload.

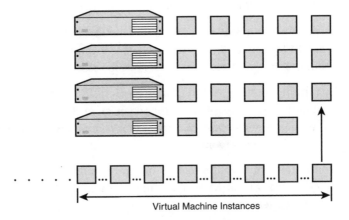

Virtual Machine Instances

Of course, the data center is connected to the Internet and systems placed within public access are reachable and addressable using TCP/IP. Internally, the local network of the data center often uses a proprietary, ultra-high-speed fabric network or other advanced technology for high-performance data sharing and storage.

The immense capacity of contemporary IT data centers provided a computing environment suitable for unleashing the IT cloud industry as it is known today.

The Hosting Context

IT cloud services help networks scale up their capacity, and in some cases they provide a complete solution for a company that doesn't want to invest in its own conventional server infrastructure.

To understand the evolution of cloud services, it is perhaps best to start with a look at the web-hosting industry. A major industry has developed over the past few years around the idea of hosting websites for companies and individuals. Instead of buying your own server and giving it an Internet-ready address, you can just pay a hosting company to host the site. This eliminates all the problems associated with configuring and managing the hardware (not to mention dealing with the Internet line fees and security issues). All you need to do is provide the web content.

The original goal was just to post the customer's HTML pages on the hosting company's web servers. With the new age of virtualization, however, the hosting company could offer a new option: virtual hosting. In a virtual hosting scenario, the customer leases a complete virtual computer system that runs somewhere inside the provider's data center. The user then has access to a complete virtual computer system without having to worry about the complications of managing real hardware. The first virtual hosting arrangements were typically for hosting web server systems. Because the customer is leasing a complete server system, however, this system can theoretically do whatever any other server can do. It could serve as a database server or provide some kind of web service solution. The customer has more control over how the system is used and can manage the system itself through internal IT staff, which is less expensive than paying the hosting company to manage it through conventional hosting; but the hardware, Internet connectivity, and fault tolerance are all managed by the hosting company.

These hosting techniques serve as the context for later developments that we now think of as the IT cloud.

Elastic Cloud

A few years ago, Amazon realized its data center had lots of extra capacity that went unused for most of the year. The center was designed for filling orders at peak usage times, such as the Christmas holidays, and the rest of year, some of the server capacity sat idle. To put that extra capacity to work, Amazon rolled out Amazon Web Services (AWS) in July 2006. AWS was instrumental in ushering in the new era of cloud IT.

At the heart of Amazon's AWS is a service known as the Elastic Compute Cloud (EC2). Amazon's EC2 **elastic cloud** service lets the user create and deploy virtual machine instances on an as-needed basis. The service is called "elastic" because it scales easily to accommodate spikes in the customer workload. Instead of users renting a virtual server on a monthly or yearly basis, EC2 makes various sizes of virtual servers available on an hourly basis. As the load picks up, you use more computer space, as it drifts back down, the virtual servers go offline and stop accumulating charges (see Figure 23.6).

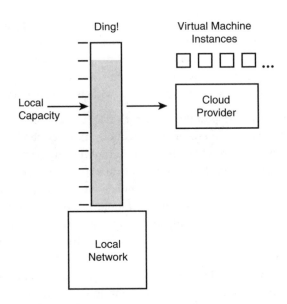

Several other cloud vendors now offer similar services. These services are extremely popular, and with good reason: The customer is charged only when the services are needed. Also, the customer's home network does not have to be designed for the maximum workload. The local network can downsize to the steady-state traffic level, and additional capacity for peak service is filled by the cloud.

Several tools have evolved for managing the process of spinning off these virtual machine instances and scaling the computer power to accommodate an expanding workload. Amazon has a collection of other services surrounding its EC2 cloud, including the Simple Queue service and the Simple Storage Service for online stor-age. Tools such as Eucalyptus provide a means to manage access to Amazon's cloud. Another example is Rackspace's OpenStack platform, which was originally used to support Rackspace's own cloud offerings. Several other vendors also now provide var-ious kinds of scalable cloud services.

Platform as a Service

On the other side of the cloud spectrum is a collection of services that are sometimes described as **platform as a service (PaaS)** tools. Unlike EC2, these tools don't exactly spin off whole virtual computers but simply provide a platform for the customer's application to execute in the cloud (see Figure 23.7). The details are invisible to the user (for example, what virtual machines you use and how many you need). The customer is basically provided with information on the application programming interfaces (APIs) for accessing the service, and most services support specific programming languages. For instance, Google's App Engine PaaS service supports Python and Java. Microsoft's Azure supports C#, Java, PHP, and Ruby.

Like the elastic cloud services, PaaS alternatives scale easily according to demand. However, these services are designed to work with specific programming tools and languages, usually with custom-built applications, and do not provide a general pro-gramming solution.

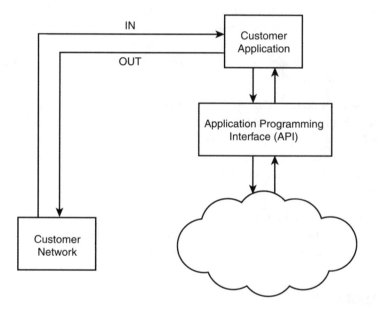

FIGURE 23.7
Platform as a Service: The customer's application runs in the cloud. As long as the application con-forms to the requirements of the API, the details are unimportant.

Cloud Alternatives

Other IT cloud alternatives cover the range of options between a pure PaaS option ("just give us your app and we'll do the rest") and a pure elastic cloud option of cre-ating and deploying virtual systems on-the-fly. These cloud computing alternatives share the characteristics of extreme scalability, reliance on data center technologies, and differing degrees of opacity (with the customer seeing only what is important).

> **Local Clouds**
>
> Although the impressive cloud architectures described in the preceding sections are designed for deployment through massive online service providers such as Amazon and Google, these technologies can also work on a private network. Some corporations are experimenting with deploying their own cloud services infrastructures without the need for a contract with an external cloud vendor.

Future of Computing

The widespread use of virtualization, data centers, and cloud technologies raises some interesting questions about the future of Internet computing. In the world of the cloud, the only application that really needs to run on the client computer is a web browser. All other apps, and even services such as printing, can be managed through cloud services.

The conventional notion of an operating system as a universal platform for running any arbitrary application and talking with devices might eventually fade in importance in favor of a client that is required to support only a browser and a server that does little more than run virtual machines. Guest systems running with specific applications could be slimmed down to only the components necessary to run the program.

With this diminished importance of the operating system, the only components that really matter will be the cloud, the browser, the APIs, and yes, the global network, with its elegant and very versatile protocol system: TCP/IP.

Summary

Cloud computing uses virtualization, high-bandwidth connections, and the power of the modern data center to provide application processing and sophisticated services over the Internet. The details are invisible to the user. This hour described some popular user cloud services, such as Google apps, as well as cloud-based storage and backup utilities. You also learned about experimental cloud services such as cloud printing. This hour also discussed IT cloud service models, such as the elastic cloud and the platform as a service model.

Q&A

Q. *What is the difference between a host system and a guest system?*

A. In a virtualization environment, a guest system is a virtual computer running as a process on another computer. The host system is the hardware-based computer that is executing the virtual system.

Q. *What is the difference between conventional web hosting and virtual hosting?*

A. In a conventional web-hosting scenario, the customer uploads HTML pages and related files to the hosting provider, and the provider manages the server systems. In virtual hosting, the hosting provider makes a complete virtual system available to the customer.

Workshop

The following workshop is composed of a series of quiz questions and practical exercises. The quiz questions test your overall understanding of the current material. The practical exercises give you the opportunity to apply the concepts discussed during the current hour and to build on the knowledge acquired in previous hours of study. Take time to complete the quiz questions and exercises before continuing. Refer to Appendix A, "Answers to Quizzes and Exercises," for answers.

Quiz

1. Why is SaaS gaining popularity in the mobile era?

2. A friend who is on vacation in Lithuania just printed his vacation photos directly to my home printer. How is this possible?

3. The traffic on my company's website sometimes exceeds the capacity of our in-house, local server farm. Should I employ an elastic cloud solution, or am I better off with a platform as a service alternative?

4. A massive Java application that runs constantly on our local system sucks up too much processing space. What cloud technology should I use?

Exercises

For a taste of the world of SaaS, try out the popular SaaS toolset known as Google Docs. Start by entering the following URL: http://docs.google.com.

At the Google Docs website, click the Try Google Docs Now button. The Google Docs demo site opens into the word processor. Click the Spreadsheet or Drawing button in the top menu bar to try the spreadsheet and drawing tools. Click the Get Started button in the upper-right corner to create your own Google Docs account.

Key Terms

Review the following list of key terms:

▶ **Cloud computing:** A broad collection of technologies providing online services with minimal complication for the user.

▶ **Data center:** A large facility for online data storage. The modern data center is an important component in the cloud computing industry.

▶ **Elastic cloud:** A cloud service designed to provide easily scalable processing power based on fluctuating demand.

▶ **Guest system:** A virtual system running as a process within another computer.

▶ **Host system:** A physical, hardware-based computer that acts as a host for virtual guest systems.

▶ **Platform as a service (PaaS):** A service that provides cloud-based execution of a customer application.

▶ **Software as a service (SaaS):** A range of online tools that offer services similar to ordinary desktop applications.

▶ **Virtualization:** The act of re-creating a real-world object or process within a computer.

Implementing a TCP/IP Network: 7 Days in the Life of a Sys Admin

---

What You'll Learn in This Hour:

▶ TCP/IP in action
▶ Life as a network admin

The preceding hours of this book introduced many of the important components that make up a TCP/IP network. In this hour, you witness many of these components in a real, although hypothetical, situation. At the completion of this hour, you'll be able to describe how the components of a TCP/IP network interact.

A Brief History of Hypothetical, Inc.

Hypothetical, Inc., is a large and ponderous company that began with nothing and has magnified that initial endowment many times. Since its birth in 1987, Hypothetical, Inc., has been devoted to the production and distribution of hypotheticals. The mission statement of the company is as follows:

> To make and sell the best hypotheticals any time and for any price the buyer will pay.

In keeping with trends throughout the economy, Hypothetical, Inc., has recently been in transition, and now the strategic focus of the company is to align itself such that a hypothetical is regarded not as a product but rather as a service. This seemingly innocuous change has brought forth severe and extreme measures with regard to implementation, and the tumultuous consequences of those measures have resulted in low employee morale and increased theft of petty business supplies.

A morale committee, consisting of the president, the vice president, the chief of operations, and the president's nephew (who is working in the mail room), analyzed the state of dissatisfaction and agreed the company's longstanding no-computer policy must end. (The no-computer policy, which was considered anachronistic even within the tepid backwaters of the hypotheticals industry, was a natural outgrowth of the company's official motto: "Everything I need to succeed in business was available in the stone age.")

The committee members, some of whom had gained their skills within the public sector, voted immediately to purchase a bulk lot of 1,000 assorted computers at a volume discount, assuming that any disparities of system or hardware would be resolved later.

They placed the 1,000 computers on desktops and countertops and in break rooms and boardrooms throughout the company and wired them together with whatever transmission media they could make fit with the assorted adapter ports. To their astonishment, the network's performance was not within a window of acceptability. In fact, the network did not perform at all, and the search began for someone to either fix the problem or assume the blame for the whole fiasco.

7 Days in the Life of Maurice

Maurice never doubted that he would find a job. As a baby, he had reprogrammed his Candy Kinetic Sing-and-Stomp dance mat to play Dvořák's New World Symphony, and ever since then, he had evidenced a singular capacity for achieving the improbable in cyberspace. But he didn't really think he would find a job so soon after graduating. He certainly didn't expect to be presented with an interview at the random corporate office where he had stopped to use the restroom. He was young enough and brash enough to accept the job of network administrator for Hypothetical, Inc., although in hindsight he should have realized that this was not a job for the upwardly mobile. He told the interviewers that he had no experience at all, but they didn't seem to mind and stated that his lack of experience was fine with them because it would allow them to pay him a lower salary. Instead of showing him the door, they immediately placed a W-4 form in front of him and handed him a pen.

Still, he had his library of fine computer books to guide him, including his copy of *Sams Teach Yourself TCP/IP in 24 Hours, Fifth Edition*, which provided him with an accessible and well-rounded introduction to TCP/IP.

Day 1: Getting Started

When Maurice arrived at work the first day, he knew his first goal must be to bring all the computers onto the network. A quick inventory of the computers revealed some DOS and Windows machines, some Linux computers, some Macintoshes, several UNIX machines, and some other computers that he didn't even recognize. Because this network was supposed to be on the Internet (several of the committee's morale-enhancing measures required visits to unnamed recreational websites), Maurice knew that the network would need to use TCP/IP. He performed a quick check to see whether the computers on the network had TCP/IP running. For example, he used the IPConfig utility to output TCP/IP settings on the Windows computers. On the UNIX and Linux machines, he used the `ifconfig` command.

In most cases, he found that TCP/IP was indeed running, but much to his surprise, he found complete disorganization in assignment of IP addresses. The addresses were seemingly chosen at random. No two addresses had any similar digits that might have served as a network ID. Each computer believed it was on a separate network, and because no default gateway had been assigned to any of the computers, communication within and beyond the network was extremely limited. Maurice asked his supervisor (the nephew who worked in the mail room) whether an Internet network ID had been assigned to the network. Maurice suspected that the network must have some preassigned network ID, because the company had a permanent connection to the Internet. The nephew said he did not know of any network ID.

Maurice asked the nephew whether the value-added retailers who sold them the 1,000 computers had configured any of the computers. The nephew said that they had configured one computer before abruptly leaving the office in a dispute over the contract. The nephew took Maurice to the computer the value-added retailers had configured. It had two computer cables leading from it: one to the corporate network and one to the Internet.

"A multihomed system," Maurice said. The nephew did not seem impressed. "This computer can serve as a gateway," Maurice told the nephew. "It can route messages to the Internet, that is, until we have time to buy something better."

The nephew tried to look impatient, hoping for a swift shift to a topic in which he and not Maurice held the greater knowledge. The computer appeared to be a legacy

Windows NT system. Maurice considered telling the nephew that he'd never heard of anyone using a multihomed Windows NT box as a corporate gateway and that many experts refer to this type of thing as a "really hokey configuration." It would have been better to purchase a gateway router. But it was his first day, so he didn't offer his advice. A computer, after all, is capable of acting as a router, as long as it is configured for IP forwarding. An ethernet cable led from the gateway computer to the rest of the network. Maurice entered a quick IPConfig for the computer and obtained the IP address of the ethernet adapter. He had a hunch the value-added retailer must have configured the correct network ID into this computer before taking his leave. The IP address was 198.100.145.1.

Maurice could tell from the first number in the dotted-decimal address (198) that this was a Class C network. On a Class C network, the first three bytes make up the network ID. "The network ID is 198.100.145.0," he told the nephew. While he was there, he also checked the TCP/IP configuration to ensure that IP forwarding was enabled.

It occurred to Maurice that the network would be capable of supporting only 254 computers with the available host IDs in the Class C address space. But, he concluded, that probably wouldn't matter, because many users did not want their computers anyway so it was unlikely more than 254 users would be accessing the network at any given time. He configured IP addresses for the members of the morale committee:

198.100.145.10	President
198.100.145.3	Vice president
198.100.145.8	Chief of operations
198.100.145.5	Nephew

He then configured computers for all other possible host IDs. He also entered the address of the gateway computer (198.100.145.1) as the default gateway so that messages and requests could be routed beyond the network. For each IP address, he used the standard network mask for a Class C network: 255.255.255.0, denoting 24 network bits, which, he knew, would appear within the common **classless interdomain routing (CIDR)** address scheme as 198.100.145.0/24.

Maurice used the **ping** utility to test the network. For each computer, he typed ping and the address of another computer on the network. For instance, from the computer 198.100.145.155, he entered ping 198.100.145.5 to ensure that the user of the computer would be able to communicate with the nephew. Also, in keeping with good practice, he always pinged the default gateway:

```
ping 198.100.145.1
```

For each ping, he received replies from the destination machine, ensuring that the connection was working.

Maurice was thinking that the network had come far for one day, and he was feeling that this would be an easy and rewarding job, but the last computer he configured couldn't ping the other computers on the network. After a careful search, he noticed that the computer appeared to be part of an entirely different type of physical network. Someone had attempted to connect the obscure and obsolete network adapter with the rest of the network by ramming a 10BASE-2 ethernet cable into the port. When the cable didn't fit, the responsible party had jumped the circuit with a nail and wrapped the whole assembly with so much duct tape that it looked like something they'd used on Apollo 13.

"Tomorrow," Maurice said.

Day 2: Segmenting

When Maurice arrived for work the next day, he brought in something he knew he was going to need: routers. And although he arrived early, many users were already impatient with him. "What's the matter with this network?" they said. "This is really slow!"

Maurice told them that he wasn't finished. The network was working, but the large number of devices competing directly for the transmission medium was slowing things down. Also, some computers that were configured for a different network architecture (such as the computer he'd discovered at the end of the previous day) could not communicate directly with the other computers. Maurice strategically installed some routers so that they would reduce network traffic and integrate the network elements with a differing physical architecture. Of course, he had to find a router that supported the obsolete architecture, but this was not difficult because Maurice had many connections.

Maurice also knew that some subnetting was in order. He decided to divide the final eight bits after the Class C network ID so that he could use 3 bits for a **subnet** number and the other 5 bits for host IDs on the subnetted networks.

To determine a subnet mask, he wrote out an 8-bit binary number (signifying the final octet) with 1s for the first 3 bits (the subnet bits) and 0s for the remaining bits (the host bits):

```
11100000
```

The last octet of the subnet mask was therefore 32 + 64 + 128, or 224, and the full subnet mask was 255.255.255.224.

From this mask, he could easily see that the network + subnet portion of the address was 8 + 8 + 8 + 3 = 27 bits, which led to a CIDR prefix of /27. The 3 bits of the subnet range offered 8 possible bit combinations. The all zeroes subnet (000) and all ones subnet (111) are officially discouraged, although some routers support them anyway. In CIDR notation, the subnets were named for the lowest address in the range, followed by the /27 CIDR prefix. He determined the lowest address by varying the 3 subnet bits of the last octet, as follows:

Bits	Value	Subnet
00100000	32	198.100.145.32/27
01000000	64	198.100.145.64/27
01100000	96	198.100.145.96/27
10000000	128	198.100.145.128/27
10100000	160	198.100.145.160/27
11000000	192	198.100.145.192/27

Maurice added the new subnet mask for his new subnetted network and assigned IP addresses accordingly. He assigned IP addresses such that the 3 subnet bits were the same for all computers on a given **segment**. He also changed default gateway values on many of the computers, because the original gateway was no longer on the subnet. He instead used the IP address of a router port as the default gateway for the computers on the subnet connected to that router port.

Day 3: Dynamic Addresses

The network was now functioning splendidly, and Maurice was gaining a reputation for results. Some even suggested him as a possible candidate for the morale committee. The nephew, however, differed with this view. Maurice was not destined for the morale committee or for any committee, the nephew mentioned, because so far he was not meeting the objective of his employment. The committee clearly stated that the network should have 1,000 computers, and so far Maurice had given them a network of only 256. "How can we expect morale to improve if the directives of the morale committee are ignored?" he added.

By the
Way

Fewer Addresses

The subnetting in Day 2 actually increased the number of unusable address. The network now had fewer than 254 addresses. The actual number of available addresses within a subnet is not 2^n, but $(2^n - 2)$, where n is the number of host ID bits in the address. Maurice did not see a reason for revealing this fact to the nephew.

But how could Maurice bring Internet access to 1,000 computers with fewer than 256 possible host IDs? His first step was to point out to the nephew that, if they did ever manage to get all 1,000 computers working on the network at once, it would quickly overwhelm the capacity of the multihomed Windows NT system that was serving as an Internet gateway. The nephew was, therefore, forced to bring up this deficiency with the morale committee, and they did indeed agree to purchase a state-of-the-art router/gateway device, which they amortized by ingeniously reducing the portion of salad in the office cafeteria while maintaining a constant price.

This new router provided dynamic IP address assignment through **Dynamic Host Configuration Protocol (DHCP)**. The device was also capable of **Network Address Translation (NAT)**, which meant that Maurice was able to set up the network to use a private, nonroutable address space that would allow him to assign well over 1,000 addresses. He configured the DHCP server to serve addresses in the private address range from 10.0.0.0 to 10.255.255.255. For Internet-bound traffic, the router would handle translating the private address into an actual Internet-ready address from the address range supplied previously by the Internet service provider.

Configuring the router as a DHCP server was easy, at least for Maurice, because he read the documentation carefully and wasn't afraid to look for help on the Web. (He did need to make sure the internal routers he installed on Day 2 were configured to pass on the DHCP information.) The hard part was manually configuring each of the 1,000 computers to access the DHCP server and receive an IP address dynamically. To configure the 1,000 computers in an 8-hour day, he had to configure 125 computers per hour, or a little more than 2 per minute. This would have been nearly impossible for anyone but Maurice. He knocked several people down, but he finished in time for the 6:00 p.m. bus.

Day 4: Domain Name Resolution

The next day Maurice realized that his hasty reconfiguration of the network for dynamic address assignment had left some unresolved conflicts. These conflicts would not have occurred at any other company, but at Hypothetical, Inc., they were real and acute.

The president spoke to Maurice privately and informed Maurice that he expected that he, the highest ranking official in the company, would have the computer with the numerically lowest IP address. Maurice had never heard of such a request and could not find reference to it in any of his documentation, but he assured the president that this would not be a problem. He would simply configure the president's computer to use the static IP address 10.0.0.2 and would exclude the president's address from the range of addresses assigned by the DHCP server. Maurice added that he hoped the president understood the importance of not tampering with the configuration of the internal interface of the gateway router, which would have a lower address: 10.0.0.1. (Actually, Maurice could have changed this address to something higher, but he didn't want to.) The president stated that he did not mind if a computer had a lower IP address as long as that computer didn't belong to another employee. He just didn't want any person to have a lower IP address than his address.

The arrangement between Maurice and the president would have posed no impediment to the further development of the network had not other upper-level managers claimed their own places on this sad ladder of vanity. It was easy enough to give the vice president and the chief of operations low IP addresses, but a bevy of middle managers, none higher or lower than the others, began to bicker about whose computer would be 10.0.0.33 and whose would be 10.0.0.34. At last, the management team was forced to adjourn to a tennis retreat where they sorted out their differences and began each match with love.

In the meantime, Maurice implemented a solution he knew they would accept. He set up a **domain name system (DNS)** server so that each computer could be identified with a name rather than an address. Each manager would have a chance to choose the hostname for his or her own computer. The measure of status, then, would not be who had the numerically lowest computer address but who had the wittiest hostname. Some examples of the middle managers' hostnames included the following:

- ▶ Gregor

- ▶ wempy

- ▶ righteous_babe

- ▶ Raskolnikov

The presence of a DNS server also brought the company closer to the long-term goal of full Internet access. The DNS server, through its connection with other DNS servers, gave the company full access to Internet hostnames, such as those used in Internet URLs.

Maurice also took a few minutes to apply for a domain name so that the company would someday be able to sell its hypotheticals through its own web page on the World Wide Web.

Day 5: Firewalls

Despite all the recent networking successes, the morale of the company was still low. Employees were rapidly resigning and departing like moviegoers exiting a bad film. Many of these employees had intimate knowledge of the network, and managers worried that the disgruntled ones might resort to cybervandalism as a form of retribution. The managers asked Maurice to implement a plan by which network resources would be protected, but network users would have the fullest possible access to the local network and also the Internet. Maurice asked what the budget was, and they told him he could take some change from the jar by the coffee machine.

Maurice sold approximately 50 of the 1,000 computers and used the money to buy a commercial **firewall** system that would protect the network from outside attack. (The 50 computers were completely unused and were blocking the hallway to the service entrance. Janitorial personnel had tried to throw them away at least six times.) The firewall provided many security features, but one of the most important was that it allowed Maurice to block off Transfer Control Protocol (TCP) and User Datagram Protocol (UDP) ports to keep outside users from accessing services on the network. Maurice closed off all nonessential ports. He kept TCP port 21 open, which provides access to File Transfer Protocol (FTP), because at Hypothetical, Inc., information is often dispensed in large paper documents for which FTP is an ideal form of delivery. Maurice carefully configured the firewall so that the port 21 FTP access was authorized only for purposes of connecting to a well-protected FTP server computer.

Day 6: Web Services

At last, the network was safe and well organized. The morale committee decided to use this newfound connectivity to spy on their employees to gain some insights on productivity. To their surprise, they determined that no one was actually accomplishing anything. The processing for new orders was way behind because the company had no automated means for recording, logging, and processing orders of new hypotheticals. Visitors were expected to download new hypotheticals by FTP. A notice on the server instructed the customers to send payments to corporate headquarters, where each envelope was carefully opened and inspected by volunteers in the smoking lounge.

Maurice placed a web server in front of the firewall and configured it so that a customer could place an order through a Hypertext Markup Language (HTML) form. In front of the web server, he placed another firewall, creating a **demilitarized zone (DMZ)** for the server and other Internet-ready computers. He configured another web server on the internal network and devised a web service application to process orders and keep track of inventory. A small client application on the desktop of each employee communicated with the server by exchanging Simple Object Access Protocol (SOAP) messages in Extensible Markup Language (XML) format. The outside web server, which was linked to the internal server through a secure connection, passed in orders from the Web. The server was tied to a back end database that tracked customer transactions, and a secure connection to a credit card processing service offered the miracle of e-commerce for website visitors.

Productivity increased rapidly, resulting in more time for coffee breaks, and the company soon discovered it was overstaffed. The three members of the accounting team were almost laid off, but they soon guaranteed their future significance by developing the specialty of inspecting office furniture to ensure that consecutive tables and chairs had consecutive serial numbers.

Maurice was awarded the right to leave work early, but he stayed around to configure a performance-enhancing reverse proxy system for the website.

Day 7: Signatures and VPNs

The new web services infrastructure brought unprecedented success to Hypotheticals, Inc., and the company was suddenly flooded with new orders. The capacity of the local server was soon exceeded, and Maurice made arrangements with an elastic cloud provider to offer additional processing power in peak hours. Because the order processing systems were all automated, however, the staff paid no particular notice to this upturn in fortune and continued to spend most of the business day in meetings planning other meetings. This success, however, did not escape the notice of the company's competitors. One rival in particular was especially concerned. Although this alternative vendor was not known for high quality or efficient service, the company stayed in business by maintaining extremely low overhead (owing to the location of its headquarters in an abandoned 18-wheeler).

Rather than reacting with innovation, the rival responded in the only way they knew—through imitation. This imitation, however, went beyond the simple refinement of technique and crossed swiftly into the murky hollows of trademark infringement. The company started to claim they actually *were* Hypotheticals, Inc., and began to do business as Hypotheticals, Inc. Because transactions occurred remotely, customers had no independent means of ensuring the identity of the parties.

Luckily, Maurice was ready with a solution, which, because the rest of the company was on a coffee break, he was able to implement with minimal disruption. He signed up with a third-party digital certificate authority and established a digital certificate system that would prove to users that they were dealing with the real Hypotheticals. The success of this measure was cause for a rare office party, at which Maurice was recognized for his leadership and offered an extra ration of trail mix. As the gala ended, he was called to a closed-door meeting with the chief of operations. The chief asked Maurice whether federal law prohibited the wagering of large sums of money on sporting events over the Internet. Maurice told him that he wasn't a lawyer and didn't know the specifics of gambling law.

The chief asked whether, on an unrelated note, Maurice knew of a way by which all correspondence over the Internet would be strictly private so that no one could find out what he was saying or with whom he was communicating. Maurice told him the best technique he knew about was virtual private networking. A **virtual private network (VPN)** is a private, encrypted connection over a public line. A VPN provides a connection that is nearly as private as a point-to-point connection.

"I need one of those right away," the chief said, retiring thoughtfully to his inner office.

Summary

This hour examined a TCP/IP network in a hypothetical company. You received an inside view of how and why network administrators implement IP addressing, subnet masking, DNS, DHCP, and other services.

By the Way

Epilogue

In case you're wondering what happened....

Federal agents arrived at company headquarters sometime after the 7 days and arrested the chief of operations. This left an open seat on the morale committee, which the president gratefully offered to Maurice.

Q&A

Q. *Why did Maurice decide to subdivide the network?*

A. Subdividing the network reduced traffic.

Q. *Why did Maurice leave port 21 open on the firewall?*

A. Maurice left port 21 open to provide access to an FTP server. Note that he later reconfigures the network in Day 6 to place a web server within a DMZ outside of the firewall. Although the story doesn't mention it directly, he might have also moved the FTP server in front of the firewall at this time.

Workshop

The following workshop is composed of a series of quiz questions and practical exercises. The quiz questions test your overall understanding of the current material. The practical exercises give you the opportunity to apply the concepts discussed during the current hour and to build on the knowledge acquired in previous hours of study. Take time to complete the quiz questions and exercises before continuing. Refer to Appendix A, "Answers to Quizzes and Exercises," for answers.

Quiz

1. Why did Maurice choose to use 3 bits for the subnet address?

2. Maurice's choice of a 3-bit subnet left 5 bits for host addresses (enough for 30 hosts—32 possible addresses minus the all-0s address and the all-1s address). How many addresses would be available with a 2-bit subnet? How many subnets would be available?

3. Why did Maurice use a DNS server instead of configuring hosts files?

Exercise

Imagine week 2 in the life of this industrious admin. How do you think Maurice would proceed with configuring the following:

▶ Network monitoring

▶ Voice over IP

▶ Kerberos

▶ IPv6

▶ Semantic Web

Key Terms

Review the following list of key terms:

▶ **Classless interdomain routing (CIDR):** A notation for defining the number of network bits in an IP address without requiring a reference to an address class.

▶ **Dynamic Host Configuration Protocol (DHCP):** A protocol that provides dynamic assignment of IP addresses.

▶ **Demilitarized zone (DMZ):** An intermediate space inhabited by Internet servers that falls behind a front firewall and in front of a more restrictive firewall protecting an internal network.

▶ **Domain name system (DNS):** A system for naming resources on TCP/IP networks.

▶ **Firewall:** A device or application that restricts network access to an internal network.

▶ **Network Address Translation (NAT):** A technique that allows the internal network to operate with nonroutable, private IP addresses, and then translates Internet traffic to and from the routable, Internet-ready address space.

▶ **Ping:** A diagnostic utility used to check the connectivity with another host. This tool is so common that it has also become a verb. *To ping* is to use the ping utility to check connectivity of a TCP/IP configuration.

▶ **Segment:** A division of the physical network separated by a router.

▶ **Subnet:** A logical division of the IP address space defined by a TCP/IP network/subnet ID.

▶ **Virtual private network (VPN):** An encrypted private channel through a public network.

APPENDIX A

Answers to Quizzes and Exercises

Hour 1: What Is TCP/IP?

Quiz

1. A network protocol is a set of rules and data formats that enable communication between computers (or other devices) on the network.

2. End-node verification and dynamic routing are two features that contribute to TCP/IP's decentralization.

3. DNS, the Domain Name Service, is responsible for mapping domain names to IP addresses.

4. An RFC, Request For Comment, is a document that describes an Internet standard or a report from one of the working groups that help run the Internet.

5. A port is a logical channel used to route data to the proper networking application.

Hour 2: How TCP/IP Works

Quiz

1. The Data Link layer and the Physical layer.

2. The Internet layer.

3. UDP is simpler and faster but does not have the error checking and flow control that TCP does.

4. The Network Access layer.

5. A layer-specific header is appended to the data before it is passed down to the next layer.

Exercises

1. The functions of the layers of the TCP/IP stack are as follows:

   Network Access layer: Provides an interface to the network hardware.

   Internet layer: Provides logical addressing and routing for datagrams.

   Transport layer: Provides error checking, flow control, and acknowledgment services.

   Application layer: Provides network troubleshooting facilities, file transfer, remote control, and other network-based utilities. Also provides the API that allows application programs to access the network.

2. The IP and Transport layers deal with datagrams.

3. Only a new Network Access layer would have to be written. The rest of the stack would remain the same.

4. *Reliable* means that TCP uses error checking and acknowledgments to ensure that a TCP segment is delivered if at all possible.

Hour 3: The Network Access Layer

Quiz

1. A CRC (cyclic redundancy check) is a checksum that is used to verify that the data in a frame has not been corrupted.

2. A collision occurs when two nodes on an Ethernet start transmitting at the same time. When the nodes detect that this has happened, a collision detection is said to have occurred.

3. An Ethernet physical address is 48 bits.

4. NDIS and ODI provide a standard interface to the network hardware that TCP/IP and other networking stacks can use to access the network hardware in a consistent and uniform way.

5. ARP provides a link between physical addresses and logical IP addresses.

Exercises

1. ARP and RARP relate physical and IP addresses.

2. Ethernet, IEEE 802.11 (Wi-Fi), IEEE 802.16 (WiMax), and dial-in by phone line are four common networking architectures.

3. The MAC layer provides an interface to the network adaptor. The Logical Link Control layer provides error checking for frames and manages links between network nodes on the subnet.

Hour 4: The Internet Layer

Quiz

1. The TTL field is used to count the remaining hops before an IP datagram is dropped. Its purpose is to prevent datagrams from circulating in the network indefinitely.

2. The network ID is 8 bytes and the host ID is 24 bytes.

3. An octet is an 8-bit piece of data. Today it is commonly called a byte.

4. The IP address addresses individual network interfaces on a computer or networking device.

5. ARP is used to map IP addresses into physical addresses. RARP is used to map physical addresses into IP addresses.

Hour 5: Subnetting and CIDR

Quiz

1. The subnet ID bits are borrowed from the host ID.

2. Because subnetting functions have been subsumed under CIDR.

3. Classless refers to the fact that the traditional network address classes (A, B, C, D) are no longer used but are replaced by the CIDR prefix.

4. The host ID field is 6 bits, and so there can be $2^6 - 2 = 62$ hosts.

5. Combining several smaller networks into a single larger network range is called supernetting.

Exercises

1. You get the CIDR address 180.4.0.0/14.

2. The subnet ID borrows 3 bits from the host ID, leaving 5 bits. Therefore, there are $2^5 - 2 = 30$ hosts possible on the subnet.

3. The subnet ID is 3 bits, and so there are $2^3 - 2 = 6$ possible subnets. Some vendors support assignment of the all 0s subnet and the all 1s subnet, which would mean 8 possible subnets.

4. The lowest host address is 195.50.100.1.

5. The highest host address is 195.50.101.254.

Hour 6: The Transport Layer

Quiz

1. TCP port 25 is SMTP, the Simple Mail Transport Protocol.

2. UDP port 53 is domain, the Domain Name Server.

3. TCP is a stream protocol. Data is delivered as a stream of octets with no notion of records, so the question does not make sense.

4. A passive open indicates an application's willingness to accept connections. An active open is a request to connect to another application on the same or remote host.

5. It takes three steps.

Hour 7: The Application Layer

Quiz

1. The ping utility is used to check network connectivity.

2. HTTP, the Hypertext Transfer Protocol.

3. POP3 (the Post Office Protocol, version 3) and IMAP (the Internet Message Access Protocol).

4. DNS, the Domain Name Service.

5. NTP, the Network Time Protocol.

Hour 8: Routing

Quiz

1. Two types of dynamic routing are distance vector and link-state routing.

2. A router needs at least two interfaces: one that connects to the subnetwork and another that connects to the outside networks.

3. BGP, the Border Gateway Protocol.

4. Because several routing table entries can be collapsed into a single entry in the routing table when networks are combined by supernetting.

5. OSPF is an example of link-state routing.

Exercises

1. Three currently used routing protocols are RIPv2, OSPF, and BGP.

2. OSPF can use several parameters to calculate the cost of a route, whereas RIP can use only hop count.

3. Static routing is simple and does not require a router. However, it is very inflexible and becomes unmanageably complex for anything other than a small network because any change in the network must be dealt with by the system administrator.

Hour 9: Getting Connected

Quiz

1. PPP, the Point-to-Point Protocol, is the most common protocol for transmitting IP datagrams over a phone line.

2. Two broadband technologies suitable for home use are cable broadband and digital subscriber line (DSL).

3. Frame Relay, HDLC, ISDN, and ATM are four common WAN technologies.

4. Independent BSS networks are also called ad hoc networks.

5. A hub creates an environment like a traditional Ethernet cable in that it sends all messages to all ports so that every computer sees every message. A switch maintains a table of physical addresses and sends a message only to the intended computer.

Exercises

1. Dial-up connections are much slower than broadband connections such as DSL or cable modem. They tie up a phone line when being used. Because they tie up a phone line, a computer using a dial-up connection is typically disconnected from the network after each use. This makes using the Internet much less convenient.

Hour 10: Name Resolution

Quiz

1. CNAME; it is used to map an alias to the name specified in an A record.

2. DNSSEC uses a DS resource record stored with the parent zone to identify and authenticate the DNSKEY resource record stored with the child zone. Storing the DS record on the parent allows the query to traverse the chain of trust necessary for verifying the authenticity of the query response.

3. You can implement centralized administration by adding an include statement to the LMHosts file. A line that starts with #INCLUDE and provides the location of an LMHosts file located on a server provides a link to the central file.

4. By using the keyword #PRE on the line of the desired entry in an LMHosts file.

Hour 11: TCP/IP Security

Quiz

1. Many proxy servers cache previously visited web pages. This technique, which is known as content caching, allows the proxy server to serve the page locally, which is much faster than having to request the page from a server on the Internet.

2. Many (even most) computer programs contain hidden errors or unsecure code that could potentially allow an intruder to trick the program into granting the intruder access. These errors are continually corrected through updates. If you want your system to remain safe, you need to install an update that fixes the problem before potential intruders develop a way to exploit the vulnerability.

3. SSL operates above the Transport layer, so an application that uses SSL must be able to be aware of the SSL interface. IPsec, on the other hand, operates lower

in the stack. The application does not have to know about IPsec. From the sound of this scenario, it appears that Ellen might be better off trying IPsec.

4. Nothing (we hope). The session ticket is encrypted with the server's long-term key. As long as the intruder does not have access to the server's long-term key, he cannot crack the ticket. An intruder who has somehow discovered the server's long-term key could decrypt the ticket, extract the session key, and then possibly impersonate the server.

Hour 12: Configuration

Quiz

1. A DHCP relay agent.

2. DNS Service Discovery (DNS-SD) uses the PTR record to help assemble a browse list of service instances and then uses the SRV record to obtain the DNS hostname and port number for the service. The TXT record provides additional information about the service.

Hour 13: IPv6: The Next Generation

Quiz

1. A broadcast is read by all hosts on the network segment, even if the information isn't relevant to them. Multicast restricts the recipients to a group of hosts that can include a smaller subset of the hosts on the local network.

2. IPv6 autoconfiguration generates an address based on the unique physical (MAC) address. The host then checks for a duplicate address before assuming the autoconfigured address. These steps reduce the possibility of an address collision.

3. The 6to4 tunneling system is associated with the IPv6 prefix 2002::/16.

4. Teredo is an IPv6 tunneling technique designed to work around NAT devices.

Hour 14: TCP/IP Utilities

Quiz

1. The first thing to try when the network apparently stops working is to ping some remote site.

2. Use arp -a (or on some UNIX systems arp -g) to see the ARP cache.

3. Use netstat -p tcp to get a list of current TCP connections.

4. Use netstat -r to see the routing table.

5. Network Monitor, tcpdump, and wireshark are examples of protocol analyzers.

Hour 15: Monitoring and Remote Access

Quiz

1. The Telnet utility passes all its information, including passwords, in the clear and is thus unsecure. The SSH utility encrypts its data and thus offers a more secure alternative to Telnet.

2. The Berkeley r* utilities employ the concept of trusted access.

3. SNMP, Simple Network Management Protocol, uses a MIB.

4. SNMP provides a view of what is happening on a specific machine but does not show what is happening on the network as a whole.

5. RMON 2 adds the ability to monitor the upper five layers of the stack.

Exercises

1. Three ways of login into a remote machine (in order of security) are ssh, telnet, and rlogin.

2. Information about interfaces can be found starting at iso.org.dod.internet.mgmt.mb.interfaces or, numerically, .1.3.6.1.2.1.2.

3. The RMON Alarm group is at iso.org.dod.internet.mgmt.mb.mon.alarm or, numerically, at .1.3.6.1.2.1.16.3.

4. Disadvantages of SNMP include the following:

   ▶ It cannot see the lower levels.

▶ It requires an operational protocol stack.

▶ It can generate heavy network traffic.

▶ It provides a lot of data, but it is difficult to analyze it.

▶ It does not provide a view of the network.

Hour 16: Classic Services

Quiz

1. The put command is the basic command that uploads a file to the server; mput lets you upload multiple files in a single command line.

2. No. TFTP can only transfer files. You cannot use TFTP to view the remote directory.

3. Samba was originally designed to promote interoperability with Windows systems by acting as an open source server and client for the SMB file service protocol used by Microsoft. CIFS is an open standard version of SMB. Samba supports CIFS, although the term *SMB* is still used extensively throughout the Samba community.

Hour 17: The Internet: A Closer Look

Quiz

1. A true Tier 1 network has peering arrangements that allow it to share traffic with all other Tier 1 networks free of charge. A Tier 2 network might have some peering agreements, but also might purchase access to other networks. These categories are somewhat theoretical because the actual details of the arrangements between commercial providers are not a matter of public record.

2. The scheme specifies a format for reading the URI and typically references a protocol or service.

3. The scheme occupies the space before the familiar colon double slash at the beginning of the string.

4. Popular schemes include http, https, ftp, ldap, file, mailto, and pop.

5. index.html.

Hour 18: HTTP, HTML, and the World Wide Web

Quiz

1. If the server and browser are configured for different session parameters, the negotiation phase lets them agree on the common settings necessary for successful communication.

2. The HTML content falls between the <HTML> </HTML> tags. Within these tags are the <HEAD> section and the <BODY> section. The <HEAD> section contains title, style, and control settings. The <BODY> section contains the content that will appear in the web browser window. The specification calls for a !DOCTYPE statement before the first HTML tag. The !DOCTYPE statement is often omitted.

3. This scenario is typically handled through scripting on the server side. Because the database is on the server side of the network connection, it is more efficient (and more secure) to assemble the completed code on the server.

4. Of course, many things can go wrong with a new system, but in this case, it is likely that your web browser is not configured to recognize and read PDFs. Depending on your browser or operating system, the solution is to install an appropriate browser plug-in or to associate a PDF reader with the PDF file type so that your browser knows what to do with the file.

Hour 19: The New Web

Quiz

1. A CMS works integrally with the web server to manage and publish web content; the CMS is essentially an extension of the web server system. Placing the CMS on a separate computer would create performance problems and could also cause security issues.

2. Every node is capable of acting as both a client and a server.

3. The RDF triple resembles a simple sentence. The parts are the subject, the predicate, and the object.

4. HTML5 integrates many of the capabilities of tools like Flash, such as drawing and video playback, directly into the HTML.

Hour 20: Web Services

Quiz

1. *Schema* is a generic term for the document that describes the structure of the XML data set. Several schema languages exist, but the term *schema* is also used specifically to describe the XSD schema file written in W3C's official XML Schema Language.

2. PUT replaces an entire resource. POST delivers information to the server that is used to update the resource.

3. REST emphasizes simple, complete operations that leave the system in a complete, predictable state. The PUT method is idempotent, which means a command has the same result no matter how many times you execute it. The more open-ended POST method, which might update only part of the record or cause some arbitrary change executed by the server, makes no guarantee of idempotence and is therefore deemphasized within the REST architecture.

4. REST is thought to provide better and more predictable security because it hides all server operations within the server and away from the interface.

Hour 21: Email

Quiz

1. MIME is the Multipurpose Internet Mail Extensions. It is used to encode non-ASCII attachments to email messages.

2. SMTP, the Simple Mail Transport Protocol, is used to send messages.

3. POP3, the Post Office Protocol, or IMAP (the Internet Message Access Protocol) are used to retrieve email messages from the user's mailbox.

4. The largest complaint about webmail is the performance penalty imposed by the bottleneck of the Internet.

5. Webmail is easy to use and configure and is therefore a good choice for non-technical users. Because it uses HTTP, it is able to cross firewalls that may be closed to SMTP, POP3, and IMAP. Finally, it makes it possible to check email from any computer with access to the Internet.

Hour 22: Streaming and Casting

Quiz

1. Buffering allows the application to deliver sound/video to the user at a constant rate, thus ensuring voices and videos seem natural.

2. RTSP (Real Time Streaming Protocol) enables the end user to send commands to the streaming server, much like a remote control.

3. Both SCTP and DCCP are connection oriented.

4. Podcasts are delivered by RSS.

5. SIP is the Session Initiation Protocol. It is used for starting, stopping, and managing a communication session.

Hour 23: Living in the Cloud

Quiz

1. Because they shift the application processing from the client to the server, SaaS tools are ideal for environments where the client is operating with minimal resources.

2. Maybe you signed yourself up for a cloud printing service, which would make your printer available to remote users who have your permission.

3. Although many options are possible (depending on the specific details), this scenario, which requires general processing power on an occasional basis, might work best with an elastic cloud solution.

4. Running a single application in the cloud works well with PaaS tools. Several PaaS tools support Java, including Google App Engine, Microsoft Azure, and Amazon Beanstalk.

Hour 24: Implementing a TCP/IP Network: 7 Days in the Life of a Sys Admin

Quiz

1. The ideal number of subnet bits depends on the number of subnets and the size of the subnets. Committing additional bits to the subnet number leaves fewer bits for the host address. In this case, Maurice made a judgment based on the existing condition of the network. A 3-bit mask allows 30 hosts per subnet.

2. A 2-bit subnet would leave 6 bits for the host address, which would yield 2^6 total host addresses minus the all-0s address and the all-1s address, or 62 addresses. The 2 subnet bits would yield 2^2 or 4 possible subnets if you used the 0s and 1s subnets or only 2 if you avoided the 0s and 1s subnets.

3. Maurice would have had to spend time configuring each hosts file separately or else create a script that would copy the hosts file around the network. Also, the hosts files would have to be updated whenever a change occurred on the network.

Index

W

Z

X

FREE Online Edition

Your purchase of **Sams Teach Yourself TCP/IP in 24 Hours** includes access to a free online edition for 45 days through the Safari Books Online subscription service. Nearly every Sams book is available online through Safari Books Online, along with more than 5,000 other technical books and videos from publishers such as Addison-Wesley Professional, Cisco Press, Exam Cram, IBM Press, O'Reilly, Prentice Hall, and Que.

SAFARI BOOKS ONLINE allows you to search for a specific answer, cut and paste code, download chapters, and stay current with emerging technologies.

Activate your FREE Online Edition at
www.informit.com/safarifree

> **STEP 1:** Enter the coupon code: PJZJQZG.

> **STEP 2:** New Safari users, complete the brief registration form.
> Safari subscribers, just log in.

   Adobe Press Cisco Press Press IBM Press lynda.com Microsoft Press New Riders

 O'REILLY Peachpit Press PRENTICE que   SAMS SAS Publishing Sun microsystems WILEY